SEXUAL DEVELOPMENT AND BEHAVIOR
Selected readings

THE DORSEY SERIES IN ANTHROPOLOGY
AND SOCIOLOGY

EDITOR   ROBIN M. WILLIAMS, JR.   *Cornell University*

ANDERSON   *Sociological Essays and Research: Introductory Readings*
ANDERSON   *Toward a New Sociology: A Critical View*
BARNOUW   *Culture and Personality*   rev. ed.
BARNOUW   *An Introduction to Anthropology*
    Volume I.   *Physical Anthropology and Archaeology*
    Volume II.   *Ethnology*
BELL   *Marriage and Family Interaction*   3d ed.
BELL   *Social Deviance: A Substantive Analysis*
BELL & STUB (eds.)   *The Sociology of Education: A Sourcebook*   rev. ed.
BREER & LOCKE   *Task Experience as a Source of Attitudes*
GAMSON   *Power and Discontent*
GEORGES (ed.)   *Studies on Mythology*
GOODMAN   *The Individual and Culture*
GORDEN   *Interviewing: Strategy, Techniques, and Tactics*
GOTTLIEB & RAMSEY   *The American Adolescent*
HAGEN   *On the Theory of Social Change: How Economic Growth Begins*
HSU (ed.)   *Psychological Anthropology: Approaches to Culture and Personality*
JACOBS   *Pattern in Cultural Anthropology*
JOHNSON   *Crime, Correction, and Society*   rev. ed.
JOHNSON   *Social Problems of Urban Man*
JUHASZ   *Sexual Development and Behavior: Selected Readings*
KNUDTEN   *Crime in a Complex Society: An Introduction to Criminology*
KNUDTEN   *Crime, Criminology, and Contemporary Society*
KOHN   *Class and Conformity: A Study in Values*
LEMASTERS   *Parents in Modern America*
MARIS   *Social Forces in Urban Suicide*
SALISBURY   *Religion in American Culture: A Sociological Interpretation*
SHOSTAK (ed.)   *Sociology in Action: Case Studies in Social Problems and Directed Social Change*
WARRINER   *The Emergence of Society*
WILSON   *Sociology: Rules, Roles, and Relationships*   rev. ed.

Sexual development and behavior

Selected readings

Edited by

ANNE McCREARY JUHASZ

Loyola University of Chicago

1973   THE DORSEY PRESS   *Homewood, Illinois   60430*
Irwin-Dorsey Limited   *Georgetown, Ontario*

First printing, January 1973

ISBN 0-256-01125-7
Library of Congress Catalog Card No. 72-92426

Printed in the United States of America

To Stephen

Preface

There are two basic problems relating to sexual behavior which face every-one. The first is obtaining accurate information about sexual functions and activity. The second and more complicated problem is the choice of a sexual life style which is in harmony with self-concept, value system, ideals, and goals.

I have organized this book with the second problem in mind. The selections which are included serve as a reference for the young adult. With these materials he can work out for himself a conception of sexuality which is satisfying to him in terms of emotional and social development and ethical acceptability. This book should be especially useful for the college student. However, there is no reason why parents, educators, and paramedical professionals would not also find the material informative and helpful.

Understandably, no single volume can cover the subject of sexual development and behavior in all its aspects. Selections included here have been gathered from scientific and scholarly writings in sociology, psychology, history, and medicine. They represent varied points of view and sometimes contradictory opinions. In the introductory section to each part, I have included suggestions on how to use the material. Systematic analysis of some articles, assigned additional readings to supplement others, and open classroom discussion of all of them will facilitate understanding.

The book is divided into four parts. Part I deals with understanding one-self as a sexual being, being comfortable with sexual feelings, and appreciating intimate sexual relationships by learning an appropriate sex role and developing emotional maturity.

Part II is concerned with the influence which socioeconomic, ethnic, and religious backgrounds have upon sexual behavior. In Part III, I am concerned with change in sexual attitudes, values, and behavior. The final part of the book includes information on a wide variety of subjects which center on the theme of uncertainty or conflict.

I wish to acknowledge my indebtedness to Paul Gebhard, David Holland, Ira Reiss, and Robin M. Williams, Jr. Their comments and suggestions helped me to arrive at what is hopefully the most useful combination of materials for my purpose.

In addition, I wish to express appreciation to the authors who have contributed to this volume. If my goal is realized, then these scholars will indeed be rewarded.

Chicago, Illinois   ANNE McCREARY JUHASZ
January 1973

Acknowledgment

A summer fellowship granted by the Research Committee of Loyola University of Chicago enabled the editor to carry out the extensive research entailed in assembling this volume.

Contributors

Joseph Bensman, Ph.D.
Professor of Sociology
City College of New York

Miriam E. Berger, M.S.W.
Psychiatric Social Worker
Group Relations Ongoing Workshops
New York

John B. Bradley, Ph.D.
Director of Special Programs
Aiken County School District
South Carolina

Carlfred B. Broderick, Ph.D.
Professor of Sociology and
‾‾Head of Marriage Counseling
‾‾Training Program
University of Southern California

Daniel G. Brown, Ph.D.
Consultant in Mental Health
U.S. Public Health Service
Atlanta, Georgia

Harold T. Christensen, Ph.D.
Professor of Sociology
Purdue University

Glenn C. Davis, M.D.
Duke University Medical Center

Keith E. Davis, Ph.D.
Chairman and Professor
Department of Psychology
Rutgers University

James Elias, M.A.
Associate Sociologist
Institute for Sex Research
Indiana University

Paul Gebhard, Ph.D.
Director, Institute for Sex Research
Indiana University

Georgie Anne Geyer, B.A.
Foreign Correspondent
Chicago Daily News

Janet Zollinger Giele, Ph.D.
Sociologist and Fellow
Radcliffe Institute
Cambridge, Massachusetts

Christina F. Gregg, Ph.D.
Instructor in Sociology
University of Nebraska

Richard S. Gross, Ph.D.
Grady Memorial Hospital
Atlanta, Georgia

Seymour L. Halleck, M.D.
Professor of Psychiatry
University of Wisconsin Medical
‾‾Center

Anne McCreary Juhasz, Ph.D.
Professor of Foundations
School of Education
Loyola University of Chicago

Gilbert R. Kaats, Ph.D.
Associate Professor
Department of Psychology
U.S.A.F. Academy

Alfred C. Kinsey, Ph.D.
Deceased

Lester A. Kirkendall, Ph.D.
Professor Emeritus of Family Life
Oregon State University

Roger W. Libby, M.A.
Teaching Assistant
Department of Sociology
Washington State University

Birgitta Linnér, J.K.
Family Counselor,
The Municipal Family Guidance
    Clinic
Stockholm, Sweden

Eleanore B. Luckey, Ph.D.
Professor and Head
Department of Child Development
    and Family Relations
University of Connecticut

David B. Lynn, Ph.D.
Professor of Psychology
College of San Mateo, California

David R. Mace
Professor of Family Sociology
Behavioral Sciences Center
The Bowman Gray School of Medicine

Vera C. Mace, M.A.

Anton S. Makarenko
Deceased
(Translated by Elizabeth Moos)

Judd Marmor, M.D.
Director, Division of Psychiatry
Cedars of Sinai Medical Center
    and Clinical Professor of Psychiatry
University of California School of
    Medicine

Clyde E. Martin, Ph.D.
National Institute for Child
    and Human Development

Peter M. Miller, Ph.D.
Director of Alcohol Program
Veterans Administration Hospital
Jackson, Mississippi

Gilbert D. Nass, Ph.D.
Associate Professor
Department of Child Development
    and Family Relations
University of Connecticut

Charles Palson, M.A.
Organizer for the National Caucus
    of Labor Committees

Rebecca Palson
Organizer for the National Caucus
    of Labor Committees

Eric Pfeiffer, M.D.
Associate Professor of Psychiatry
Project Director, Older Americans
    Resources and Services Program
Duke University Medical Center

Wardell B. Pomeroy, Ph.D.
Private Practice
New York

Ira L. Reiss, Ph.D.
Director, Minnesota Family Study
    Center
University of Minnesota

Ruth Roemer, J.D.
Researcher in Health Law
Institute of Government and
    Public Affairs
University of California

Bernard Rosenberg, Ph.D.
Professor of Sociology
City College of New York

Ellen Rothchild, M.D.
Assistant Professor of Child Psychiatry
School of Medicine
Case Western Reserve University

Isadore Rubin, Ph.D.
Deceased

Edward A. Suchman, Ph.D.
Deceased

Adriaan Verwoerdt, M.D.
Associate Professor of Psychiatry
Duke University Medical Center

Gene H. Wood Jr., Ph.D.
Director of Training
Sumter-Clarendon-Kershaw Mental
    Health Center
Sumter, South Carolina

Contents

part I

Development of human sexuality

In this part of the book, the selections deal with basic aspects of human sexual development. In Reading I, Ellen Rothchild traces the sequence of interdependent biologic and psychologic steps from infancy to adolescence. In practical terms, she explains the developmental tasks and the accompanying problems which the individual faces while moving toward optimal emotional growth and acceptance of himself as a sexual human being.

Several statements in this initial article are open for discussion and argument. Rothchild's opinion on the latency period, the normal heterosexual stage, and the adolescent struggle to suppress masturbation can all be criticized by other authorities in the field of sexual development. It is understandable that no firm agreement can be reached, since controlled study of children's sexual behavior is difficult to conduct. Obviously, each expert speaks from his specific vantage point, influenced by his professional training and background, limited by available subjects for observation, and restricted by his own attitudes and values. Sexual activity, similar to other human behavior, is highly individualized, and to a large extent socially determined. For example, one adolescent may struggle to suppress masturbatory activity, while another may be actively involved with no resulting negative feelings. Attitudes regarding normalcy, rightness, and

1

goodness are learned and thus will vary from child to child depending upon the conditioning which has influenced him.

Reading 2, Carlfred B. Broderick's paper, has as its basis three major points set forth in Freud's theory of the development of infantile sexuality. He examines subsequent behavioral research which provides general support for Freud's contentions that sexual energy is present from birth onward, that sexual socialization is essential, and that psychosexual development is a sequential process. He quotes Kinsey's data on adult recollections of early sexual behavior. Students will find it of interest to examine the articles on heterosexual patterns of behavior which appear in the footnotes to Broderick's article.

The two papers which follow, Reading 3 by James Elias and Paul Gebhard, and Reading 4 by David B. Lynn, explore in greater depth the three contentions of Freud. It was not until 1969 that Elias and Gebhard published their report based on interviews with children from age four to fourteen. These data were collected as part of the original Kinsey study and include information on actual sexual behavior. While this study may appear to be "out of date," no similar report of more recent research or experience is available. Until recently, the mention of sexual activity to children was taboo. To date, researchers have dealt mainly with children's questions about sex, their common vocabulary for sexual organs and functions, and their conceptions about where babies originate. Undoubtedly, future studies will investigate the incidence of various patterns of preadolescent sexual behavior. The Elias and Gebhard paper will then serve as a point of reference from which continuity and change can be determined.

David B. Lynn's paper provides elaboration on the influence of the parents in the process of identification. He presents specific hypotheses related to appropriate sex role learning. Much has been written on this aspect of early development. The mother, the father, the adult who is seen as most powerful, have all been suggested as the most influential model in sex role learning. There is very little agreement on this point.

In Reading 5, Daniel G. Brown and David B. Lynn consider the ways in which heredity, maturation, environment, and social learning influence sexual development and behavior in standard and nonstandard ways. One may question the author's reference to Money's idea that imprinting may be one primary determinant of genital-sex object preference, since more conclusive evidence of the generality of imprinting in humans must be gathered in order to verify this assumption. To date, knowledge of imprinting has been based on animal behavior and is not yet an accepted scientific conclusion.

Sexual learning is a continuous process as the individual passes from infancy to old age, and every age and every stage is important. Specific sexual tasks and adjustments face individuals in the marriage and child-rearing stages of life. These are beyond the scope of this book and are traditionally covered in texts on marriage and the family. However, two readings have been included to reflect the growing awareness and concern for the individual as a sexual human being throughout life. Parents and grandparents of college students are not "over the hill" in terms of potential for sexual activity and enjoyment. In fact, evidence presented by researchers at the Center for the Study of Aging and Human Development in Durham, North Carolina, (Reading 6) suggests that attitudes toward human sexuality and patterns of sexual behavior established early in life continue to be strong determinants of interest and activity throughout the total life span.

Isadore Rubin, in the final paper in Part I, emphasizes the inaccuracy of our social stereotype of the "sexless older years." It is evident from this article, that according to American sexual mores, healthy sexual expression has been confined to a very narrow age range. More accurate information, open discussion, and increased understanding of human sexual expression as a normal, healthy, lifelong occurrence should help young people to anticipate continuing, satisfying sexual relationships in future decades of life.

The readings in Part I, then, highlight important phases of sexual development from birth to old age.

1

Emotional aspects of sexual development*

ELLEN ROTHCHILD

Puzzling her parents by her silent daily sorties to the attic, 5 year old Susan acknowledged finally that she was checking to see if her baby had arrived. In her nightly prayers she had asked God for one and suggested that her old crib, stored in the attic, would be a convenient repository. While yearning to achieve parenthood Susan was overlooking some essential maturational steps, biologic and psychologic, still to be undertaken.

Psychologic growth is grounded in somatic growth: Out of a somatic matrix, sensations and perceptions arise in infancy and become organized into pleasure feelings, motivations, and concepts. From such fundamental biologic precursors, how does the average youngster in our society become familiar with his bodily sexuality, develop love feelings for others, and acquire concepts, attitudes, and behaviors embracing his or her identity as male or female, one who will ultimately choose a partner, reproduce, and rear the next generation?

INFANCY AND PRESCHOOL YEARS

Early origins of sexuality

Nobody ever interviewed a baby; the chief clues to the origins of love ties, bodily awareness, and the sense of belonging to a given sex come

---

* Reprinted from *Pediatric Clinics of North America,* Vol. 16, No. 2 (May 1969), by permission of author and publisher.

5

from observation and experimentation. The foundation for future love relationships begins in the affectional ties that develop between infant and caretaker. Body-warmer, soother of tensions, and sharer of pleasure feelings, mother is the baby's first partner in love. The infant whose mother or other caretaker is reasonably devoted and consistent ordinarily develops a sense of trust and confidence in being cared for which must precede all future feelings of caring for others. Maternally deprived youngsters, such as those reared in institutions of the sort described by René Spitz, tend to devolop more tenuous and distorted relationships (Spitz, 1945, 1946).

Maternal care also fosters bodily awareness. "Institutional" babies who have received a minimum of maternal care are reported to show significantly less bodily exploration and genital play than do home-reared infants; though all the motor capacities to suck, reach, grasp, and touch appear at the expected time, the infants engage in little autoerotic and self-exploring play. This finding suggests that the greater degree of sensory stimulation which the home-reared infant experiences through feeding, bathing, cuddling, diapering, and that totality of conduct deriving from ordinary devoted mothering is an important element in his developing an awareness of his body—where it begins and ends, its potential for yielding pleasure (Spitz and Wolf, 1949; Provence and Lipton, 1962).

Discovery of the genitals, in particular, appears to arise within the second half of the first year as accidental touching is followed by deliberate poking and tugging. But pleasure feelings appear at first poorly localized to the area, and thumbsucking generally affords more pleasure. Daily 24 hour home observations of one boy through his first 2 years indicated that, for this child at least, not until the beginning of the second year was there an observable increase in genital sensitivity with more deliberate self-stimulation; nothing convincingly resembling orgasm was observed (Kleeman, 1965, 1966). Recognizing that children appear to enjoy thumbsucking and other forms of sensory stimulation long before the genitals become a primary source of pleasure sensations, Freud conjectured that initial "pregenital" sources of gratification make a continuing though modified contribution to the personality, manifest in adult sexual life in forms such as kissing, tactile eroticism, and arousal by certain odors (Freud, S., 1905).

Long before bodily exploration documents for a child which sex he belongs to, parents and society have been teaching him to behave in accordance with that sex. Once the universal first question "Is it a boy or a girl?" is satisfied, the parents' expectations and encouragement of gender-appropriate behavior, such as more vigorous activity and assertiveness (among boys) and the selection of particular clothes, hair styles, and toys, conveys the message, "You are a boy" (or "a girl"). Repeated over time, such cues foster the growing child's concept of belonging to the given sex and of sex-appropriate behaviors. The role and importance of such early learning in the acquisition of a "gender identity" has been underscored in a study of over 100 hermaphrodites, in whom it was observed that the orientation and role adopted was usually consistent with the sex to which their parents had assigned and reared them regardless of discrepancies in their chromosomal, gonadal, hormonal, internal, and even external genital endowment. After about two years of age, a time when speech development begins to reinforce intellectual concepts, the original sex assignment became more difficult to reverse (Money, Hampson, and Hampson, 1957).

The toddler phase

Events of the toddler phase more sharply define elements of sexuality. Speech development is significant to the sorting out of ideas and feelings. The first words to be learned usually include designations for family members and body parts; the pronouns "he" and "she" appear at about two years. Attitudes previously taught through looks, gestures, and tones of voice become reinforced through words (as in the instance of the mother who taught her son to name his penis "Dirty-Dirty").

Toilet training, usually another educational landmark of the period, lends itself to increasing awareness of genital sensation and structure. The youngster's attention is now specifically directed to sensations arising from adjacent structures, while wiping further stimulates the anal-perineal area. Sitting on the toilet allows additional inspection and exploration of the genitals. Boys learn to hold the penis and to direct the stream. Whether in direct relation to their toilet training or not, a number of girls by two or three years discover their vaginas (Eissler, 1939). Sufficiently verbal youngsters sometimes demonstrate their easy confusion of anal and genital structures.

Jay, aged two years nine months, had for several days suffered from fecal retention, and accepted the toilet only with much coaxing. Once seated he peered between his legs, pointed to his testicles, and told his mother earnestly, "Those are mine; I *need* them." His mother, sensing he was telling her something about his reluctance to use the toilet, assured him that only his bowel movements dropped in the toilet—not his testicles. Appearing relieved, he passed a bowel movement.

The transition from casual genital handling to deliberate masturbation appears a characteristic of the toddler and preschool child (Spitz, 1962), though only by four or five years may the youngster clearly verbalize subjective sensations such as "itchy feelings in my front bottom" or "I rub myself for the fun of it." Few parents feel entirely comfortable observing their child's genital manipulations, owing not only to embarrassment but also to a sometimes sad recognition that the youngster is no longer so dependent on the parent for comfort. Childhood masturbation in this way constitutes a significant step toward independence.

Consequences of sexual differences

The recognition of sexual differences, like that of differences in skin color and other physical variations, commonly appears between age two and three. Bathing with siblings and observing the diapering or toileting of other children commonly precipitates a boy's query as to how girls urinate or a girl's struggle to understand why she has no penis. At an age when physical properties are still poorly understood, when parts of the body such as hair, skin, nails, and feces are found to have an ephemeral existence, children can elaborate their own explanations for sexual differences along similar lines. Girls may assume that they once had a penis but lost it, that if they wait long enough they too will grow one, or that one is hidden somewhere inside. Boys may wonder whether they can lose the penis.

Events tending to undermine the sense of permanent possession of the genitals are best avoided during this period. The surgical removal of body parts such as tonsils may strengthen the notion that the genitals too can be lost; many a grown man, in fact, awakening from anesthesia, feels first for his genitals by way of reassurance. Postponing elective procedures until school age diminishes this psychologic hazard, while psychologic preparation for immediately necessary surgery should take such thoughts into account.

Though infantile theories concerning sexual differences are seldom directly stated, perceptive parents recognize and try to correct them. Other parents may need help in recognizing conceptions and misconceptions, in finding appropriate words with which to clarify. The parent anxious over wording may welcome a book such as that prepared by the Child Study Association of America (1954). Some parents, determined to disavow a Victorian heritage, use their own nudity as a vehicle for demonstrating differences, a practice probably more confusing than illuminating to a young child. To see a much larger, hairy genital clarifies little and with looking often comes the wish to touch, a request understandably embarrassing to most parents. Initial observations are probably better confined to siblings and other children.

Despite explanations that all little boys (or girls) are born and remain thus, the issue is seldom completely settled. Most youngsters normally continue independent investigations for some time, by barging unannounced into bathrooms, attempting to peek up skirts, or "playing doctor." Often there remains a prevailing sense that there exist the haves and the have-nots. A girl, in her recognition of the boy's greater freedom of urination and his owning "something extra" may feel inadequately compensated to learn that instead she has internal organs which will someday enable her, unlike a boy, to have babies. "Someday" is too far off to wait patiently. In her dissatisfaction she may demand the accoutrements of masculinity—the pants and pistols, a demand which some adult women appear never to have given up. Or she may seek to ignore that the penis exists. Three year old Sally, on first seeing her infant brother diapered, stared intently at his genitals and then exclaimed in shocked tones, "But he has no teeth!"

Less commonly recognized is the boy's parallel wish to have babies, to possess this remarkable ability of mother's. Boys of three or four can lovingly feed, scold, and change their doll babies with infinite tenderness.

Where babies come from is a universal question of preschoolers. Though the rule of explaining only what is asked is a good one, some parents neglect to inquire subsequently into a child's understanding of what he has been told. It may be silently inferred, for instance, that a seed is swallowed, or that the baby emerges through the navel or anus. Gastrointestinal theories of this sort sometimes account for refusal to eat certain foods (e.g., those with pits) or for fecal retention.

Relationships

Commonly by three or four the realization of role differences—mothers have babies, fathers do not—invites questions concerning who is related to whom. It is learned that Mother is not only mother to the child but wife to Daddy and, once long ago, baby to her own mother. How it feels to assume these roles is explored in imagination and play; asked what she wants to be when grown, a girl unhesitatingly replies, "A mommy."

Uncertain still in their sense of time, preschoolers often assume they can catch up with and marry their parents. A boy assures his mother he will marry her and make her proud; a girl confidently expects she will keep house and have babies for her father. Not always openly expressed nor easily relinquished, such youthful marriage plans are accompanied by all the ardor and tenderness at a child's command. But there remains the inconvenient complication that the parent already has a spouse. Some attempted solutions to this obstacle are "then Daddy can marry grandma" or "Mommy can go and keep house next door." Jealousy of, and the wish to replace, the parental rival appear in many guises. Proposing that she take her mother's place in bed with Father, a four year old girl then suggested that Mommy could sleep on the floor. Each evening five year old Mark removed his father's toothbrush from the space beside his mother's, threw it on the floor saying, "Get out of there," and replaced it with his own. This early love triangle, named after the myth of Oedipus, is the prototype for future heterosexual relationships and its character will directly influence—for better or worse—the nature of those relationships.

The romantic attachments of the three to five year old ordinarily come to grief on the realization that the child cannot hope to compete adequately with the same-sex parent. The youngster is not big enough nor can he, still dependent, risk losing the good graces of that parent. Parents can help, during this period, by sympathetically but firmly making clear in words and actions that the child cannot replace the rival; marriage must wait until the child is older and can find a partner his own age. Meanwhile the child can strive to become more *like* the parent—as manly as his father, as feminine as her mother—in preparing to take over such a role in the future.

Some of the passionate attachments of these first years are repressed and become relegated to forgotten memories. By the second grade, when girls have become sissies and dumb, a boy may find it unimaginable that he had once proposed taking his mother on a picnic and leaving Daddy at home. This relative amnesia encompasses not only recollections of old feelings but of earlier events and ideas as well. The kindergarten child loses some of his prodigious memory for makes of cars and out-of-state license plates; he may be unable to recall a class visit made to the dairy only a few months before. Certain infantile theories of body functioning, conception, and birth often suffer a similar fate, though, continuing to operate unconsciously, they sometimes underlie later sexual fantasies. This partial burial of old feelings and ideas, generally appearing around the time of entry into school, robs the youngster of some of his former sparkle, wit, and apparent genius, a disappointment to many parents. Yet the temporary, and only partial, setting aside of old family and body interests also makes way for wider interests in the surrounding world which are necessary to the next step in development, school learning.

During the first five years a vast amount of informal sex education is accomplished by parents, siblings, peers, and the child himself. Physical care stimulates body awareness with a gradual localization of erotic sensation to the genitals; love relationships are established; attitudes and expectations as to role and function are transmitted. Because of the young child's emotions, his limited intellectual grasp and ability to verbalize, he is prone to misinterpret matters such as sexual differences or the origins of babies; deliberate sex education during this period consists primarily in modifying disturbing misconceptions rather than delivering a predetermined set of facts. The raw precursors to adult sexuality, which lie in the young child's physical sensuality, love ties, and curiosity, will contribute not only to his ultimate genital sexuality but also to components of the personality which are not so directly sexual—a growing capacity for pleasure of all kinds, bodily mastery, facility in transacting varied and complex social encounters, and a thrust toward intellectual learning.

THE SCHOOL-AGE CHILD

The period extending, roughly, from the time of school entry until puberty can be viewed as a plateau: the rate of biologic growth diminishes as does the degree of sexual interest and excitement. Psychologists call this interval "latency." Characteristically the intensity of old family attachments is diluted in the wider world of friends, teachers, and other adults. Some of the curiosity formerly invested in babies and bottoms is now applied to reading and geography. Excitement over sexual mysteries may shift to absorption in mystery and detective stories, secret clubs, and codes. Bodily control increases: one learns to ride a bike, look cross-eyed, and whistle through the teeth. With a better understanding of time, space, and causality the world is comprehended in more adult terms and the biology of reproduction becomes less fantastic.

But sexuality is not dormant. Only partly channeled into new interests and skills, it is also better concealed from adult eyes. Masturbation becomes more private. Reading permits independent investigations into dictionaries and home medical guides for sexual information. Agemates become research partners in the game of "I'll show you mine if you show me yours." In his autobiographical *Manchild in the Promised Land*, Claude Brown describes the prevalence of "playing house," the juvenile imitation of adults whose intercourse is more readily observed in crowded urban areas. On school playgrounds a traditional lore of scatologic riddles and jokes is passed from one child to the next.

Anatomy and identity

Anatomic differences continue to shape the personality. For the girl the mental representation of her genital anatomy is still vague; she may have difficulty differentiating her external orifices, let alone imagining the boundaries of her unseen "inner genital" (Kestenberg, 1967). However, an evolving awareness of her anatomic interior may find a parallel in her greater disposition to be guided by inner feelings and perceptions, to "tune in" on and empathize with the feelings of others. It has been suggested that the boy's body scheme similarly influences his greater orientation to the objective, external world, his interest in guns, rockets, and other projectiles, in movement and how things work (Erikson, 1951). Play interests, whether biologically or socially determined, further define and anticipate future roles. Boys seldom read about airline hostesses or nurses, or girls about astronauts or baseball heroes, although girls still dissatisfied with their anatomy ask to be included in touch football, talk tough, and eschew skirts. For the preadolescent girl, to be horse-crazy can represent such longing for masculine power, much like the adolescent boy's hotrod or motorcycle, although the horse may also represent the fiercely loved and protected "child"—a more feminine aim.

Relationships

During latency, boys stick with boys and girls with girls. For a boy to perfer girls' activities is to be a sissy; to show an intterest in one's mother is similarly to be disdained—except in moments of pain, sadness, and tender sentimentality. In this sense latency is a period of normal homosexuality; a boy who consistently prefers play with girls alarms us. The taboos on associating with the opposite sex are less strong among girls; if invited, many would welcome inclusion in boys' activities but, being excluded, the girls generally band together in their contempt for the boys' rough and dirty play.

The negation of heterosexual interests during this period is partly an outgrowth of the need to shift romantic interest away from the parents. Other adults such as teachers and scout leaders now fill the void. Daydreams also foster the transition; William Steig's cartoons, *Dreams of Glory*, illustrate the imagined feats of daring and sacrifice that win love and admiration for the child from those beyond the family. Parents, meanwhile, may be viewed as asexual. Many children try to deny that the parents have any sexual life together. Adolescence will bring a resurgence of heterosexual expression, then directed to those within the same generation.

Latency, characterized by the child's relative evenness of emotion and his superior intellectual comprehension and expression, is an optimal time in which to complete enlightenment as to the major facts of reproduction. The youngster's greater comfort with same-sex individuals suggests that these are the best persons to render formal enlightenment. Nevertheless, information and attitudes now come from many sources—from advertising and television, from companions on playgrounds and in the bushes, as well as from teachers and parents. Some parents delay preparing the child for puberty as if they might thus postpone the ferment of adolescence; however, upheaval is likely to be greater in the face of ignorance, and parents should know that the clock cannot be turned back. Some parents, never having experienced such preparation themselves, feel helpless to find the right words and welcome outside help in doing a better job than did their own parents. Wishing to turn the clock ahead, a few parents rush the preadolescent into premature boy-girl relations; such overly excited parents may require all the restraint one can provide—through direct advice, support, and reassurance—until the youngster is old enough to manage for himself.

ADOLESCENCE

"The young are in character prone to desire and ready to carry any desire they may into action. Of bodily desires, it is the sexual to which they are most disposed to give way, and in regard to sexual desire they exercise no self-restraint." The statement was made by Aristotle some 2300 years ago (Welldon, 1886). A contemporary teenager might echo, "Sex is always on my mind these days." A glance or a touch can excite; double meanings and innuendo are read into the most casual remarks. Though Madison Avenue, uneasy parents, and youth themselves have exalted and manipulated teenage sexuality, behavior today may actually differ little from Aristotle's time. Regardless of era, the biologic foundations for adolescent sexuality remain constant. The physical and physiologic changes of puberty demand of each person that he come to terms with a changing body, one with new possibilities for feeling and acting, and that he revise his sense of identity accordingly.

Reactions to physical change

Even when intellectually well prepared, most youngsters experience mixed feelings as a once familiar body changes. That last year's skirt serves as this year's miniskirt may be agreeable, but pimples are not. Breast development may seem "too much, too soon" or "too little, too late," and a capacious sweatshirt can serve the dual purpose of concealing and revealing. Boys pleased with signs of their developing masculinity may also doubt its adequacy and so purchase tight tee shirts, bar bells, and jockstraps. Rapid physical change sometimes fosters feelings of estrangement from the self ("who is the real me?") or from others ("Sometimes I feel I'm the only living being in a sea of faces"). Sexual maturation now forces a final committment to the given sex.

Though menarche and first ejaculations generally represent a maturational landmark, reactions may differ among the sexes. Owing to the unpredictability of spontaneous erections and nocturnal emissions, the pubertal boy commonly feels a lessened sense of bodily control. The girl, if fortunate enough to settle rapidly into regular cycles, now acquires within herself a stable point of orientation at a time when much else is changing rapidly; uncomfortable or messy though her periods may be, their predictable recurrence and readily localized sensation assist her further "tuning in" to internal perceptions (Kestenberg, 1961). Associating his ejaculations more directly to his masturbation, the boy inclines to share the event only with peers, while the girl is more likely to let her family know she has now "become a woman" (Jacobson, 1964). Both sexes are guarded in expressing what these events mean to them in terms of future sexual functioning. Among themselves boys may share a sometimes disturbing peer lore—that to have an erection while swimming nude with other boys signifies that one is a queer, or that too frequent ejaculation will drain away one's potency. Some boys, fearing the latter, masturbate repetitively in a vicious cycle of reassurance that the semen is still there, only to fear that they have indeed ruined themselves and so must masturbate again. Pleasurable fantasies anticipating reproduction are commoner among girls, though seldom directly voiced.

At the time of her menarche Cathy, 13, had little to say about it but much to say about multiple births. She had heard of a Mexican woman who gave birth to octuplets and of another woman who bore quintuplets when she already had five children. This led to reminiscences over caring for her brother when he was born, and then to recalling the birth of puppies to a friend's dog. Cathy speculated on the chances of breeding her own dog which, like herself, was quite small.

Some girls, consciously or not, associate the pain and bleeding with intercourse. The odor, darker color, and involuntary flow may be likened to a dirty excretory function, impelling some girls to hide themselves socially or hide their soiled napkins and underpants in bureau drawers. If a girl is confused about the separate nature of her vagina and urethra, the idea that the two are but one will further support the excretory concept of menstruation. Urethral instrumentation performed on such a girl is likely to be taken as a loss of virginity unless one specifically clarifies what is done; indeed, gynecologic investigations may be sensed as a sexual exposure or attack by intellectually well-informed girls. Elsewhere I have enlarged upon girls' reactions to puberty (Rothchild, 1967).

Sexual excitability

Heightened sexual excitability finds expression in action, feeling, and thought. More quickly aroused, boys are quicker to discharge excitement through masturbation. Girls, more likely to suppress their masturbation, often seem to be in a state of diffuse, less sharply genital, tension which is partially aroused and partially satisfied by daydreaming or by nonspecific body stimulation such as having their hair stroked or back rubbed. In their erotic fantasies, boys are more likely to dwell on specific bodily attributes—breasts, legs, and genitals—while girls incline to imagine romantic situations of surrender. Erotic imagery and action are also diverted into artistic, intellectual, and athletic pursuits.

Nearly all adolescents struggle over suppressing or yielding to their masturbation. In attempting to control sexual fantasies and impulses they try many maneuvers. Some put off homework so late that bedtime exhaustion will overcome temptation; others keep grim account of the numbers of days abstained, much like the dry alcoholic; less consciously determined are deliberate renunciations of the fleshly pleasures, as in stringent dieting, or feeling states of boredom and apathy. Such measures are usually temporary and seldom contain excitement for long. Nevertheless, the attempt should be respected as another in the individual's series of efforts to gain mastery over himself and his world. Most adolescents who ask medical advice about the frequency of their masturbation are best helped by one's sympathetic support of their wish to control rather than one's taking an extreme stand of permissiveness or prohibition.

A premature flight into intercourse is taken by some young people as a more "normal" or "moral" alternative to masturbation. Others may do so to test their desirability. "Love without commitment" was chosen by an epileptic 16 year old who feared that her seizures would drive any worthwhile man away. Teenage girls who are still strongly attached, psychologically, tc their mothers occasionally take flight into pseudoheterosexuality in which being looked after by the boy—"mothered"—is sought in return for the girl's sexual favors. Group pressures, pressures from parents, as well as internal pressures may precipitate early intercourse. Adopted girls, likening themselves to their unwed biologic mothers and driven sometimes by similar thoughts in the adoptive mother, are a more vulnerable group.

Intercourse undertaken largely as an attempted solution to conflicts such as these risks robbing an adolescent of much pleasure in the act and prematurely closing off other possibilities for adaptation. Once the young person has reached a reasonably secure and genuine heterosexual psychologic orientation, the chances are greater that intercourse will then enrich love relationships and widen possibilities for expression without becoming a vehicle for conflict.

Hormones and behavior

It is tempting to invoke the physiology of puberty to explain the heightened sexual excitability, mercurial moods, variability of thought, and impulsivity that characterize psychologic adolescence, but, though nature has provided some provocative experimental groups, clear-cut correlations are difficult to establish. Precocious puberty does not necessarily precipitate behavioral upheaval or manifestations of a heightened libido (Money and Hampson, 1955; Hampson and Money, 1955; Thomas, 1963); obviously physiologic puberty occurring at 2 years meets a different individual from that occurring at 8 or 12 years, and it would seem that sufficient chronologic maturation with its attendant increment of experience, learning, and psychic integration is at least one requisite to psychologic adolescence. Teenagers who lag significantly in pubertal onset, owing, say, to pituitary or gonadal malfunction, do tend to show less of the nuance of feeling or the wide variability of mood and impulse that typify their peers; strive though they may to imitate contemporary dress, slang, customs, and rituals, they achieve only a pseudoadolescent effect (Wallis, 1960; Sabbath, 1961; Rothchild, Owens, and Spector, unpublished observations). Since these youngsters are often considered by others as "different," and because other stigmata such as short stature often accompany the endocrinopathy, the precise psychologic role of the hormonal deficit is hard to determine. There are also postpubertal teenagers who are only chronologically adolescent, youngsters for whom it seems psychologically necessary to behave more like bland, well-behaved latency children (A. Freud, 1958). Evidently the physiology of puberty alone is insufficient to account for the psychologic process of adolescence.

Relationships

Puberty does not automatically confer a heterosexual orientation. Early adolescent boys commonly engage in homosexual activities such as mutual masturbation or group competitions over who can ejaculate farthest. Less often given to directly genital expression, girls are known for their "crushes" on other girls and older women. The homosexual orientation and experimentation of early adolescence is a widespread phenomenon and need not connote future homosexuality. Heterosexual explorations, tentative at first, are often carried out under the guise of group games involving body contact, such as games in which the "penalty" is kissing. The telephone is a favored medium for teasing and flirtation because it neatly avoids body contact. The triangular situation of childhood seems to repeat itself when a willing third person becomes investigator and messenger in the determination of whether girl A and boy B like each other. During this period many youngsters would prefer to talk about a date than go on one.

The first true feelings of being in love commonly find their object in a boy or girl who resembles or else has qualities the extreme opposite of the parent. Generally based on adoration of qualities more imagined than real, first loves are usually doomed to disappointment as the partner is discovered to have feet of clay. While later loves may never be accompanied by the thrill and selfless devotion of the first one, they allow for choices based less on a resemblance to the parent and more on the individual's own genuine merits. Finding a girl identical to the one who married dear old dad is never to relinquish childhood attachments.

The teenager's move to the world of his contemporaries is accompanied by an emotional withdrawal from home and parents. Most parents are familiar with the "wall of silence" at the dinner table, the locked bedroom door, the maddening declarations that "communication" between the generations is quite impossible. Based partly on a need to declare emancipation from dependent babyhood, this removal from parents is also founded in the youngster's sexual maturation; he or she is now physically able to compete with a same-sex parent and must protect against actually doing so. In avoiding too much closeness, many teenagers try to be as unlike the parents as possible through a temporary repudiation of all the decorum, ideals, and beliefs for which the parents stand. Translated into broader terms, no one over 30 is to be trusted. Painful though this is to parents, the adolescent's noisy demand for a separate existence paves the way to his forming an identity of his own and finding a partner in love within his own generation.

By late adolescence (roughly college age), rapid physical growth has ceased and the body has become more familiar and predictable. The adolescent is now more at home with himself and better able to modulate feelings; mercurial moods and impulsivity are on the wane. A variety of roles, values, interests, and activities have been explored and committment to some will have been made. Many an adolescent, by now, feels emotionally ready to assume the role of marriage partner and child-rearer whether or not our culture makes this easy for him.

Applications

Though the close of adolescence does not mean an end to development, one expects the young person to have acquired a sense of comfort in the given gender role, a capacity to enjoy genital sexuality, and to love a member of the opposite sex within his generation. In the process of attaining these ends, adolescents often bring to physicians doubts about their bodily adequacy and uncertainty about the meaning of body experiences or the wisdom of specific behaviors. As a counselor the physician is often hard put to judge what and how much to say, owing partly to the lability of adolescent feeling and behavior. For the adolescent to expose his feelings can be as embarrassing and exciting as to expose his body; confessions are easy to force from him, thus frightening him away, and one must avoid being pushy. Nevertheless an appraisal of where he stands in his psychologic development is often necessary in order to judge how best to meet requests for cosmetic surgery or contraception, to answer queries concerning the effect of marijuana on a given disease state, or the harmfulness of diverse sexual practices; such an appraisal requires sufficient historical information as well as a knowledge of psychologic developmental landmarks. Added to these challenges in management is the importance of "leveling with" the adolescent; the physician who advises solely on the basis of his own moral beliefs risks being ignored as a "phony," and candor in his appraisal of the given adolescent's psychologic growth and individual circumstances is often better received.

As much if not more attention may be required by parents. Some need a restraining hand against snooping into diaries and drawers for evidence of teenage wrongdoing; others needs support in not anxiously yielding to a "new morality." Most deserve one's sympathetic respect in their task of maintaining reasonable standards for the youngster while permitting him sufficient latitude to explore his own potential and limitations.

CONCLUSION

Unlike Athena, reputed to have sprung full-formed from the head of Zeus, we humans attain adult sexuality only through an unfolding sequence of interdependent biologic and psychologic developmental steps. Modifying these steps is the continuing education to sexuality rendered by parents, peers, the world at large, and the child himself. Through the care he receives and his own explorations the infant begins to establish love ties, a gender identity, and familiarity with his body. Concerns about sexual differences and the origins of babies, and the establishment of relationships prototypic for future heterosexuality mark the preschool period; sex information imparted during this time should be aimed more at correcting misconceptions than delivering a prescribed set of facts. The grade school period, when emotional life is relatively stable and comprehension more advanced, is an optimal time for the deliberate teaching of the broader facts of reproduction. The adolescent, in the process of coming to terms with a changing body and new possibilities for feeling and acting, often wants help in understanding this process and in mastering his feelings and impulses. Though the physician may act as provider of sex information, much of his role as educator rests in preventing undue interferences to optimal emotional growth.

REFERENCES

BROWN, C. Manchild in the Promised Land. New York, Macmillan Co., 1965.

CHILD STUDY ASSOCIATION OF AMERICA. What to Tell Your Children About Sex. New York: Pocket Books, 1954.

EISSLER, K. R. On certain problems of female sexual development. Psychoanal. Quart., 8:191, 1939.

ERIKSON, E. H. Sex differences in the play configurations of preadolescents. Amer. J. Orthopsychiat., 21:667, 1951.

FREUD, A. Adolescence. Psychoanal. Study Child, 13:255, 1958.

FREUD, S. Three Essays on the Theory of Sexuality. London: Hogarth Press, 1953, Vol. 7.

HAMPSON, J., and MONEY, J. Idiopathic sexual precocity in the female. Psychosom. Med., 17:16, 1955.

JACOBSON, E. The Self and the Object World. New York: International University Press, 1964.

KESTENBERG, J. S. Menarche. In LORAND, S., and SCHEER, H. I., eds. Adolescents: Psychoanalytic Approach to Problems and Therapy. New York: Hoeber Medical Division, Harper & Row, 1961.

KESTENBERG, J. S. Phases of adolescence with suggestions for a correlation of psychic and hormonal organizations. Part I. Amer. Acad. Child Psychiat., 6:426, 1967.

KLEEMAN, J. A. A boy discovers his penis. Psychoanal. Study Child, 20:239, 1965.

KLEEMAN, J. A. Genital self-discovery during a boy's second year. Psychoanal. Study Child, 21:358, 1966.

MONEY, J., and HAMPSON, J. Idiopathic sexual precocity in the male. Psychosom. Med., 17:1, 1955.

MONEY, J., HAMPSON, J. G., and HAMPSON, J. H. Imprinting and the establishment of gender role. Arch. Neurol. Psychiat., 77:333, 1957.

PROVENCE, S., and LIPTON, R. C. Infants in Institutions. New York: International University Press, 1962.

ROTHCHILD, E. "Anatomy is destiny:" Psychological implications of adolescent physical changes in girls. Pediatrics, *39*:532, 1967.

SABBATH, J. C., MORRIS, T. A., MENZER-BENARON, D., and STURGIS, S. H. Psychiatric observations in adolescent girls lacking ovarian function. Psychosom. Med., *23*:224, 1961.

SPITZ, R. A. Autoerotism re-examined. Psychoanal. Study Child, *17*:283, 1962.

SPITZ, R. A. Hospitalism: An inquiry into the genesis of psychiatric conditions in early childhood. Psychoanal. Study Child, *1*:53, 1945.

SPITZ, R. A. Hospitalism: A follow-up report. Psychoanal. Study Child, *2*:113, 1946.

SPITZ, R. A., and WOLF, K. M. Autoerotism: Some empirical findings and hypotheses on three of its manifestations in the first year of life. Psychoanal. Study Child, *3/4*:85, 1949.

STEIG, W. Dreams of Glory. New York: Alfred A. Knopf, 1953.

THOMAS, R., FOLKART, L., and MODEL, E. The search for a sexual identity in a case of constitutional sexual precocity. Psychoanal. Study Child, *18*:636, 1963.

WALLIS, H. Psychopathologische Studien bei endokrin gestörten Kindern und Jugendlichen, Ztschr. für Kinderheilk., *83*:420, 1960.

WELLDON, J. E. C. The Rhetoric of Aristotle. London: MacMillan, 1886.

2
Sexual behavior among preadolescents*

CARLFRED B. BRODERICK

It is a part of popular belief about the sexual instinct that it is absent in childhood and that it first appears in the period of life known as puberty. This, though a common error, is serious in its consequences and is chiefly due to our ignorance of the fundamental principles of the sexual life.

With this statement in 1905 Freud introduced his essay on Infantile Sexuality (5), and opened the doors to a modern reevaluation of the place of sex in children's development. It is entirely possible that the social historians of the future may view this revolutionary doctrine as the most significant landmark of the sexual renaissance. It challenged both the traditional concept of childhood and the traditional concept of sexuality.

Freud's pivotal portion in the eventual establishment of this point of view did not grow out of his being the first to observe sexuality in children. Others before him, especially medical writers, had challenged the prevailing doctrine of asexual childhood.[1] Freud, however, was the first

* Reprinted from *The Journal of Social Issues*, Vol. 22, No. 2 (April 1966), pp. 6–21, by permission of the author and of The Society for the Psychological Study of Social Issues.
[1] It is not the purpose of the present paper to trace the history of this idea in any great detail. For such treatment see Albert Moll's early (1912) but comprehensive review of the subject (14). For a more recent review giving additional references see William Reevy's article in *The Encyclopedia of Sexual Behavior* (16).

to develop a systematic theory of human development which included infantile sexuality as an integral element. Moreover, because of the attention which his entire method and theory of psychoanalysis attracted, his views could not be ignored.

Freud's basic contentions could be separated into three main points:

1) Libidinal (sexual) energy is not a product of puberty but a basic life force that manifests itself from birth onwards.
2) The process of channelling this libidinal energy is essentially social rather than merely instinctual. That is, appropriate sexual aims (modes of sexual gratification) and sexual objects are learned.
3) The process of psychosexual development typically involves sequential progress through a series of more or less uniform stages.

The remainder of this paper will address itself to the evaluation of these contentions, first looking more closely at Freud's original observations and then assessing the subsequent research bearing on the validity of the assertions. It should be admitted at the beginning, however, that the sixty years which have intervened since Freud's original essay have not produced as much research as the significance of the subject warrants. Cultural sanctions against sexual investigations of any kind are compounded in the case of children. By cultural definition preadolescents are held to be without sexual interest or capacity, and the investigator is liable at least to ridicule for attempting to find what is not there and at worst to persecution for imperiling the morals of children by putting unnatural ideas into their heads. Ironically, public prejudice has been abetted as a deterrent to research by the too-ready acceptance of Freud's theories by many professionals in the field. As the body of the paper will show, both of these impediments are beginning to yield, and it seems likely that we are on the threshold of a great expansion of research on the process of sexual development in children.

THE SEXUAL RESPONSIVENESS OF CHILDREN

One cannot go far in the literature on children's sexual responsiveness without becoming involved in the question of definitions. What are the criteria of sexuality against which the behavior of children can be evaluated? Opinions range from those of Freud, who came to accept all pleasure seeking as libidinal by definition, to those more austere authorities who dismiss all prepubertal behavior as non-sexual by definition.

For the present purpose it seems justified to apply the following standards of judgment: behavior will be judged as sexual 1) if it involves the stimulation of one's own or another's genitals for pleasure, or 2) if it involves a response to genital stimulation by one's self or another which in an adult would unambiguously indicate a high level of sexual excitement.

The psychoanalytic development of a theory of infantile sexuality

Freud himself came to his theory of infantile sexuality only after a long and painful series of theoretical revisions. His first inkling of the role of sex in childhood came when, in the course of analysis, several of his hysteric patients reported traumatic childhood seductions by adults. He was so struck by the frequency of this report that for four years he maintained that childhood seduction was the principal cause of hysteria. Gradually, however, he came to doubt this interpretation. In the first place, the principal offenders in most of these reported cases were the fathers of his clients, some of whom he knew well enough to find this allegation incredible. Secondly, he could see hysteric symptoms in his own brother and several sisters and he found the idea of his own father performing such a series of seductions unbelievable. Thirdly, about this same time he entered into a period of intense self-analysis and discovered incestuous longings for his mother inside himself. These factors gradually led him to the conclusions that he was dealing principally with children's phantasies rather than adults' depravity. As his chief biographer, Ernest Jones, has put it, ". . . irrespective of incest wishes of parents toward their children, and even of occasional acts of this kind, what he had to concern himself with was the general occurrence of incest wishes of children toward their parents, characteristically toward the parent of the opposite sex" (8, Vol. 1, p. 322).

Thus Freud's initial convictions on the subject of infantile sexuality grew out of his discovery of the Oedipus complex in himself and in several of his patients. Once the basic concept of children's capacity for sexual desire was established in his mind, many other things began to fall into place. For example, he had previously noted that an unexpectedly high proportion of phantasized seductions had involved perverted sexual practice; that is, the child's mouth or anus rather than his genitals were involved. Since Freud had come to believe that all dreams and phantasies were based on the principle of wish fulfillment, this pointed to the oral and anal orifices as major source of childhood erotic satisfaction. From there it was a short step to the reinterpretation of the common observation that young children were indeed more concerned with their mouths and anuses than with their genitals. Thus the concept of erogenous zones developed, and the main elements of Freud's theory of preadolescent development began to fall into place.

That theory will be more fully considered in a later section of the paper. For the present purpose it is enough to note that the first systematic investigation of childhood sexuality consisted of the analysis of adult recall and deductions from adult dreams and phantasies.

The limitations of such techniques of investigation are obvious and, of course were immediately and legitimately pointed out by critics of psychoanalytic theory. Freud was unperturbed by their criticism, retaining the greatest faith in his methodology. Others, including some of the British analysts, attempted to meet these criticisms by getting data closer to the source through child analysis, but neither Freud nor his critics had much confidence in this approach (8, Vol. 3, pp. 137, 197). It is probable that the impasse could not have been resolved except for the introduction of an entirely independent set of observations: those of the anthropologists.

The anthropological evidence

If there is a potential for sexual response in children, surely the best place to observe it would be in a sexually permissive society rather than in a sexually restrictive society such as the society in which Freud practiced. The classic example of this approach, Malinowski's "*The Sexual Life of Savages in North Western Melanesia,*" was published in 1929 (12). By 1951 Ford and Beach were able, with the help of the Human Relations Area Files, to find data on 32 societies which were permissive in their attitude toward children's sexuality (4).

What type of childhood behavior was found in these permissive societies? The Ford and Beach data seem to indicate two important facts about the development of sexual behavior in children. First, if it is permitted, most boys and girls will progress from absent minded fingering of the genitals in the very early years to systematic masturbation by the age of six to eight (4, p. 195). (Of course it cannot be ascertained how much of this is self discovery and how much of it is peer—or even adult-initiated behavior originally.) Secondly, where children are permitted to watch adult love making, oral-genital and copulatory attempts will be made very early in childhood. Among some groups such as the Trobrianders of Melanesia, the Chewa of Africa, and the Lepcha of India it is common for girls and boys to be active participants in full sex relations several years before puberty and in some cases as early as six or seven years of age (4, pp. 197–98). In these societies, however, it should be noted that there is active instruction in these matters by older members of the group. In any case these anthropological studies seem to have established beyond question the fact that prepubertal children are capable of learning to respond sexually several years prior to puberty.

The evidence of the surveyors

The conclusions of anthropologists based on observation in permissive primitive societies have been reinforced in recent years by the finding of sex researchers in our own society. These studies have addressed themselves to at least two different questions: first, what is the actual incidence of the various types of prepubertal sexual behavior in our culture? secondly, what is the inate species-potential for sexual response at early ages?

Sexual experience. Unfortunately the findings of various researchers on preadolescent sexual behavior do not present a consistent picture. The two best surveys, those of Ramsey (15) and Kinsey and his coworkers (10, 11) are particularly divergent in their findings. This is true despite the fact that Ramsey was an early associate of Kinsey's at the Institute for Sex Research and used an interview similar to Kinsey's in collecting his data. There were some important differences in their samples, however. Ramsey interviewed 291 boys in a middle sized midwestern city. They were predominantly white, middle class, and Protestant. Kinsey's national sample involved adults primarily including many who were middle aged and older. It seems probable, therefore that the differences may be due primarily to three factors: 1) As Kinsey himself observed with respect to his data on preadolescent masturbation "these are minimum data, derived chiefly from the memories of adults, and adults sometimes forget their childhood experiences" (10, p. 501). 2) Apart from differential recall there may be real generational differences. 3) It may be that Ramsey's data were drawn from a community with a particularly precocious group of young boys. This last explanation is consistent with the present writer's observation from his own data that the incidence of such sociosexual behavior as kissing, for example, varies considerably from community to community and from one region to another.[2]

Figures 1 through 4 compare the findings of the two studies as accurately as possible. In some instances some ingenuity was necessary to get strictly comparable figures. For example, both Kinsey and Ramsey include "exhibition" as a form of heterosexual play (Fig. 3), but Ramsey excludes this category in his tables on homosexual play while Kinsey includes it. Fortunately Kinsey provides separate data on homosexual exhibition which makes it possible to derive accumulative tables that are comparable to Ramsey's and accurate within a couple of percentage points (Fig. 2). In the case of coital play, or attempted intercourse, Kinsey gives no accumulative figures except incidentally for ages 5 and 13. In this case, since other evidence suggests that the curve is quite straight we simply estimated it with a straight line drawn between those two points (Fig. 4).

Figure 1 on masturbatory behavior shows the greatest discrepancy between the two studies. Five percent of Ramsey's boys reported masturbation by age five whereas none of Kinsey's adults remembered such ac-

---

[2] Compare kissing data in Broderick, Carlfred B. and Fowler, Stanley E. "New Patterns of Relationships Between the Sexes Among Preadolescents." *Marriage and Family Living*, 1961, 23, 27–30, based on a middle class white Georgia sample of preadolescents, with the data on various groups of Pennsylvania children reported in Broderick, Carlfred B. "Social Heterosexual Development Among Urban Negroes and Whites." *Journal of Marriage and the Family*, 1965, 27, 200–204 and "Socio-Sexual Development in a Suburban Community." *Journal of Sex Research*, 1966, 2, 1–24.

FIGURE 1. Accumulative incidence of masturbation among preadolescent boys: Ramsey versus Kinsey

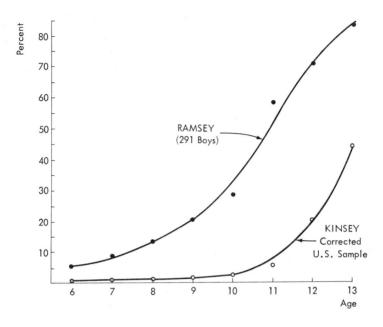

Source: Adapted from Ramsey (15, Table 3) and Kinsey (10, Table 132)

tivities at that age. The discrepancy increased each year until by age 13 85 percent of Ramsey's sample reported this activity compared to only 45 percent of Kinsey's. The problem is further confused by an inconsistency in Kinsey's own report. All of his tables and figures (10, Tables 4, 17, 22, 132; Figures 8, 16, 24, 134, 135) are consistent with the data presented in Figure 1 in this article, but in the text he reports "not more than 10 percent seem to have done so [masturbated] before the age of nine and 13 percent before the age of ten." (10, p. 501). From the tables comparable figures would be 0.3 percent and 2.0 percent. In view of these discrepancies and lacking comparable data from other studies, the student is forced to conclude that the incidence of masturbation among preadolescent boys of various ages is not known with any precision. Probably the two facts that are clear from these data (Fig. 1) are that among boys masturbation does occur before puberty and that it is increasingly likely to occur the closer one approaches puberty.

The data on homosexual play from the two studies show somewhat greater convergence. Homosexual play as it is defined in these studies involves handling the genitals of another boy, primarily, although in a small number of cases it also involved oral or anal contact and occasionally

FIGURE 2. Accumulative incidence of homosexual play among preadolescent boys: Ramsey versus Kinsey

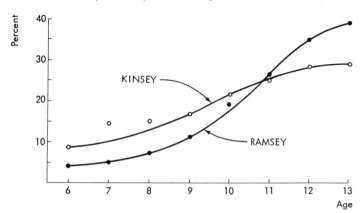

Source: Adapted from Ramsey (15, Table 7) and Kinsey (10, Table 27, 28)

urethral insertions. As mentioned previously homosexual exhibition is not included in the data plotted in Figure 2.

The data on heterosexual play (Fig. 3) and on coital play, that is, attempted intercourse, with or without penetration, (Fig. 4) also show

FIGURE 3. Accumulative incidence of heterosexual play among preadolescent boys: Ramsey versus Kinsey

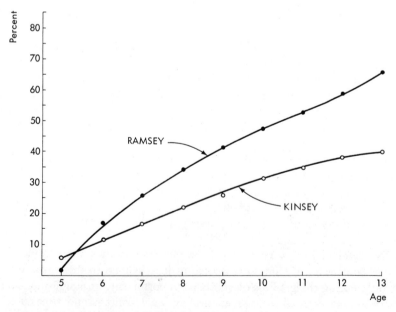

Source: Adapted from Ramsey (15, Table 5) and Kinsey (10, Table 27, 28)

FIGURE 4. Accumulative incidence of coital play among preadolescent boys: Ramsey versus Kinsey

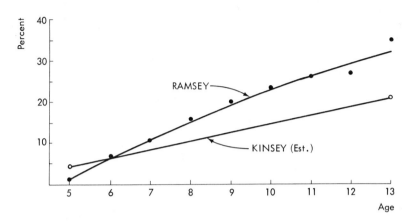

Source: Adapted from Ramsey (15, Table 6) and Kinsey (Table 24, and page 173)

Ramsey's subjects as reporting more activity at earlier ages than did Kinsey's subjects. In contrast to the curves on masturbation, however, there is no evidence of a striking increase in incidence as puberty is approached. In fact, Kinsey's data on *active* incidence for each year (not included here) show that for the boys who later went on to college heterosexual play of all kinds dropped off after about age 10, presumably in response to a redefinition of the meaning of this type of behavior. Among boys who did not later finish high school, however, there was little withdrawal and a high level of continuity with heterosexual behavior in adolescence was reported (10, pp. 162, 174).

Kinsey is the only significant source for information on the sexual behavior of prepubertal girls at each age. Figure 5 indicates the accumulative incidence of masturbation, heterosexual experience (play) and homosexual experience (play). The latter two both include genital exhibition so that strict equivalence with the male data in Figure 2 requires a reduction in the homosexual category of about one-third (11, p. 114).

Kinsey's observations about the heterosexual data are in some ways more informative than the figures themselves. For example, one's interpretation of Figure 5 might be substantially influenced by the information 1) that the *active* (as contrasted to the accumulative) incidence of heterosexual experience decreases every year throughout preadolescence (presumably due to increased awareness of the social significance of sexual behavior by older children), 2) that typically the heterosexual experience reported involved a single or at most two incidents, and 3) that the most common type of experience (40 percent) involved nothing more than genital exposure. It would seem from this that there are very few grounds

FIGURE 5. Accumulative incidence of masturbation and heterosexual and homosexual experience among preadolescent girls

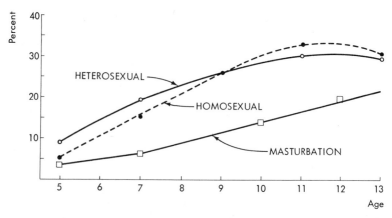

Source: Adapted from Kinsey (11, Table 11, 21)

for predicting adolescent sexual behavior from this type of preadolescent
experience and in fact Kinsey reports little continuity between the two
stages (11, p. 115).

The female volume does not include detailed data on coital play. The
only information which bears on this is an incidental reference to the fact
that about 17 percent of all those with preadolescent heterosexual experience had attempted intercourse.

In the case of homosexual experience the activity curve reached its peak
at about nine years of age and then subsided. As with heterosexual experience at this age, the continuity with adolescent behavior was slight (11,
p. 115).

No information on the *active* incidence of preadolescent masturbation are given by Kinsey, although there is some indication that it may
also be much lower than might be deduced from the cumulative figures
"because of considerable discontinuity" (11, p. 143).

Although the accumulative percentages of Figure 5 mask the difference between the sexes shown by active percentages, it is true that at
each age boys reported more prepubertal sexual activity of every kind
than did girls. It is not clear from these data how much of this difference
is due to biological and how much to social factors.

Innate sexual responsiveness. This brings us to the question of children's innate biological ability to respond to sexual stimulation. This cannot be reasoned from data on sexual experience (even if the data were
univocal) since most children are not exposed to systematic sexual stimulation and so their capacities are never tested. Given the present societal
values concerning the sexual stimulation of children it is clear that this

question can never be answered for any very representative sample of children. Lacking this, one must rely on clinical evidence.

Reliable clinical descriptions of sexual responsiveness in young children can be traced back at least to West's 1895 paper on "Masturbation in Early Childhood" and to Townsend's 1896 report on "Thigh-friction in Children Under One Year." Both are cited in Havelock Ellis (3, Vol. 1, pt. 3, p. 179 and Vol 2, pt. 1, p. 155).

More recently Kinsey supplies us with the reports of a handful of clinically oriented parents who reported systematic observation of their own children's responses to auto-stimulation, or in some cases to parental stimulation. These reports were augmented by the observations of a group of homosexual men who reported their experiences with a fairly large number of young boys (317) whose patterns of sexual responsiveness they followed over a period of years (10, pp. 175–81).

These observations seem to suggest that some boys and girls are capable of orgasm at very young ages indeed. Kinsey reports observations of orgasm-like responses[3] in babies of both sexes at four or five months of age. Of the selected sample on which he has data he reports about one-third of the boys were capable of orgasm within the first year and that this proportion increased steadily until it reached 80 percent just before puberty. The sample of girls is much too small to make any general statements about, but the data were consistent with the more systematic observations of the boys.

In addition to these observational data Kinsey cites a number of male and female adults who retrospectively reported their own prepubertal orgasms. All of this falls far short of establishing the proportion of children capable of this experience at various ages, but it does indicate that the capacity for prepubertal orgasm is present in some children, at least.

Together with the anthropological data, the work of the surveyors has probably laid to rest once and for all the theory that preadolescent children are, by definition, asexual. To this extent Freud's first general contention is supported by auxiliary data.

THE PROCESS OF SEXUAL SOCIALIZATION

Freud conceptualized development toward sexual maturity as a process of differentiation. He viewed the infant as possessed of diffuse libidinal

---

[3] "The orgasm in an infant or other young male is, except for the lack of ejaculation, a striking duplicate of orgasm in an older adult . . . [T]he behavior involves a series of gradual physiologic changes, the development of rhythmic body movements with distinct penis throbs and pelvic thrusts, an obvious change in sensory capacities, a final tension of muscles, especially of the abdomen, hips, and back, a sudden release with convulsions, including rhythmic anal contractions—followed by the disappearance of all symptoms." (10, p. 177). A similar clinical description of orgasm in a female infant can be found in the Kinsey Female volume (11, p. 104).

energy which lacked any attachment to specific objects and which was completely unchannelled in its forms of expression. Psychosexual development occurred as biology and society conspired to focus the libido of this "polymorphous pervert" onto a culturally approved sex object and sex aim or mode of gratification (5).

Freud divided preadolescence into three primary stages. Of the first or pre-Oedipal stage (age 0–3), he had to admit that little was actually known (6, p. 188). It was his surmise, however, that two important developmental sequences took place during this period. First the mother typically became differentiated out of the psychic universe as the first libidinal object of both boys and girls. Second the sexual aim gradually shifted from gratification through the infantile alimentary orifices to gratification through the stimulation of the penis and the clitoris.

The intersection of these two developments in the male was held to lead him more or less inexorably into sexual competition with his father in stage 2 (age 4 to 5), the period of the so-called Oedipus complex. In order to escape the consequences of this competition the boy lapsed into the latency period, stage 3 (ages 6–12), repudiating his mother and with her all other females as sexual objects.

In the case of the girl what happened was less clearly developed, but basically it involved a shift to the father as a more adequate sex object than the mother. Freud expressed doubt that girls experienced either the Oedipus complex or latency with the regularity or intensity that boys did (6, 7).

The final step in this process was the move toward adult genital sexuality which was initiated by puberty. The love object now became an extra-familial member of the opposite sex, and the chief sexual aim became full genital intercourse.

Over the years this model of psychosexual development has been criticized from many sources on both empirical and theoretical grounds. Perhaps the two most systematic attacks have come from the learning theorists and from the anthropologists. The learning theorists believe that the whole theory is unnecessarily complex. To them it seems apparent that sex role learning, like any other type of learning, is simply a process of reinforcing socially approved behavior and punishing undesirable behavior. A substantial body of research on sex role learning has grown up, based on this theoretical position.

Anthropologists have also attacked the idea that each of these stages, and particularly the stage of the Oedipal conflict, is necessary to normal personality development. These objections were based on the observation of societies in which a very different pattern of psychosexual development seemed to occur. See for example Malinowski's classic attack on the universality of the Oedipus complex (13). Several more or less successful attempts have been made to integrate these various points of view and it is beyond the scope of this paper to add another to the list. It may be useful, however, to indicate a few of the cardinal principles of heterosexual development for which there is research support and general theoretical agreement. In addition, the findings from an on-going study of the present writer will be introduced where they throw light on the subject under question.

Early childhood: The period of basic heterosexual orientation

In simplest terms, it is universally agreed that the foundation for later heterosexual attachments is laid in early childhood in the interactions between the child and his parents. There seem to be three primary conditions for normal heterosexual development. First, the parent or parent-surrogate of the same sex must not be so punishing on the one hand or so weak on the other hand as to make it impossible for the child to identify with him. Second, the parent or parent-surrogate of the opposite sex must not be so seductive, or so punishing, or so emotionally erratic as to make it impossible for the child to trust members of the opposite sex. Third, the parents or parent-surrogates must not systematically reject the child's biological sex and attempt to teach him cross-sex role behavior. A number of studies and clinical reports support these generalizations. There is not sufficient space to do an adequate review of the literature here. Kagan's recent summary of the effects of various family patterns on sex role identification does a good job of reviewing the studies based on normal populations (9). The literature on homosexuality is still divided on the question of causes. Increasingly, however, the central significance of the family as a factor in the etiology of homosexuality is being accepted. For a good current review representing this point of view see Bieber (2).

A fourth factor in normal heterosexual development is the necessity of establishing a positive conception of marriage as an eventual goal. Data from a current study of socio-sexual development in children have led the present writer to conclude that the significance of this factor has been underestimated in previous explanations of the mechanisms of heterosexual socialization. Long before most children have any concept of the nature of adult coital sexuality (much less any commitment to it as a sexual aim) they have begun to accept the inevitability and desirability of the heterosexual marital arrangement.

These unpublished data show that five-year-olds have a good idea of the field of eligibles from which they must select an eventual mate (cross-sex peers of the same generation but not of the same family). They are also aware of most of the non-coital content of the marital relationship. But more to the point, the majority of them are already committed to their own eventual marriage. This majority increases at each age throughout childhood. The significance of this positive attitude toward marriage is underscored by the findings that achievement of this attitude seems to be almost a prerequisite to further heterosexual progress during the next stage of development.

Middle childhood: The period of transition

It seems probable that there has been more confusion over the course of heterosexual socialization during the period of middle childhood than during any other period. Freud and the great majority of subsequent writers have referred to this stage as a period of sexual latency. Many have viewed it as a step backward away from heterosexuality into a haven of monosexual attachments and interactions. We have already seen however that both the anthropologists and the surveyors have produced evidence that this is not a sexually stagnant period, and data from the present writer's study indicate that a great deal of significant progress toward eventual full-fledged heterosexuality takes place during these years.[4]

The data were taken from questionnaires administered to all 10- and 11-year-olds attending fifth and sixth grades in ten elementary schools throughout central Pennsylvania. Urban, suburban, and rural schools were included and the full range of social classes was involved. The full report of the analysis is still in manuscript form but the results can be summarized here.

The most significant finding was that progress toward heterosexuality appears to be achieved in a series of steps, with achievement at one level preparing the way for the next. As indicated in the previous section the foundation of subsequent progress seems to be one's attitude toward his own eventual marriage. Next came an emotional attachment to a member of the opposite sex as evidenced by reporting having a special girlfriend (or a boyfriend if it was a girl). The next step was to confess having been in love. After that came an expression of preference for a cross-sex companion rather than a same sex companion when going to a movie. And finally the most advanced step for these preadolescents was actually going out on a date.

Each step, of course, is not an absolute prerequisite to the other, but the nature of the relationships can be indicated by the following sets of comparisons: 74 percent of those who wanted to get married some day reported a boyfriend or girlfriend, but only 34 percent of the others did; 66 percent of those who reported having a girlfriend or boyfriend also reported having been in love, but only 19 percent of the others did so; 43 percent of those who had been in love said they would prefer a cross-sex

---

[4] The fullest development of the relevant data from the present writer's study is a manuscript, Broderick, Carlfred B. "A Scale of Preadolescent Heterosexuality" which will probably appear in print next year. For a list of published reports on this project see footnote 2.

companion at the movies but only 21 percent of the others expressed this preference; and finally 32 percent of those who would prefer a companion of the opposite sex had actually gone out on a date, while only 11 percent of the others had done so.

Each of these differences was significant beyond the .05 level when tested by chi-square and the entire series met the criteria of a Guttman scale.[5]

It may be true that these specific items are not of any great theoretical significance in and of themselves, and that a similar list of different items could be developed which would represent the process of heterosexual socialization equally well. The significant point is that middle childhood is actually a period of great importance in the process of becoming a fully heterosexual adult. It seems logical to assume that the steps typical of this period build upon the experiences of early childhood and in turn determine the course of development during adolescence.

SUMMARY AND DISCUSSION

The sexual behavior of preadolescents first became an area of systematic scientific interest when Freud published his theory of infantile sexuality sixty years ago. Since then the amount of research done has not been very great but such data as there are support at least the major points of Freud's original observations.

There is still a great deal of uncertainty as to the actual incidence of various sexual behaviors among children, but it would seem to be conclusively demonstrated that many children are capable of sexual arousal and even orgasm from a very early age.

Data on the process of sexual socialization are even more scarce than those on sexual behavior. Various aspects of the particular developmental sequence which Freud postulated have been seriously challenged. Nevertheless his main contention, that normal heterosexual development is determined by a child's familial relationships and social experiences rather than by simple biological factors, seems to be borne out by the available data. Before much progress can be made in specifying the precise stages and critical points in development, longitudinal research will have to be designed to plot the process.

Whatever the course of future research in this area, however, enough is already established to make it unlikely that the conceptualization of sex or of childhood will ever revert to its pre-Freudian state. This observation leads us to challenge, in the last analysis, the accuracy of the title of this issue of the *Journal*. Implicit in the phrase "sexual renaissance" is the notion that we are experiencing a rebirth of what was once before. It

---

[5] Ibid.

suggests that this new era of understanding and openness with respect to sex is not really new, but only seems so because it is separated from an earlier edition of itself by an intervening period of great sexual prudery and repression.

It is doubtful whether this point of view is valid for any aspect of sexual behavior but it is certainly an inadequate interpretation of the historical facts about views of childhood sexuality. It is true that in the 13th to 16th centuries records indicate that children were not sheltered from sexual information and stimulation as they have been since the 17th century Reformation, but it is not true that this carefree attitude was evidence of the acceptance of preadolescent sexuality—quite the opposite. As Philippe Ariés has written in his *Centuries of Childhood:*

> . . . gestures and physical contacts were freely and publicly allowed which were forbidden as soon as the child reached the age of puberty, or in other words was practically adult. There were two reasons for this. In the first place the child under the age of puberty was believed to be unaware of or indifferent to sex. Thus gestures and allusions had no meaning for him; they became purely gratuitous and lost their sexual significance. Secondly, the idea did not yet exist that references to sexual matters, even when virtually devoid of dubious meanings, could soil childish innocence, either in fact or in the opinion people had of it: Nobody thought this innocence really existed. (1, p. 106)

The modern view of childhood sexuality is, as far as this author has been able to determine, unique in the history of Western civilization. In contrast to the conceptualizations of any previous century it assumes the capacity of children to experience sexual sensations and emotions and to learn attitudes and behavior patterns with respect to sex. It changes fundamentally the range of questions which society must ask itself concerning the upbringing of children. Formerly one might ask: "At what age should a parent first begin trying to mold the child's ideas about sex?" It is clear that the appropriate question is rather "How shall a parent best deal with the sexual experiences and potentials at each age?" Formerly one might ask "How can a parent protect his child from the intrusion of sexuality until he is old enough to handle it?" Today one might better ask "How can a parent help his child to understand and manage his own sexual nature from infancy onward?" Whatever one's value position, from the most permissive to the most restrictive, the question can never again be "Whether?" or "When?," but rather "How?"

In the matter of attitudes toward the sexual nature of children we are dealing, it seems to me, not with a renaissance, but with a revolution.

REFERENCES

1. Ariés, Philippe. *Centuries of Childhood: A Social History of Family Life.* (Robert Baldick, translator), New York: Albert A. Knopf, 1962.

2. BIEBER, IRVING. "Clinical Aspects of Male Homosexuality." In *Sexual Inversion* (Judd Marmor, Ed.). New York: Basic Books, 1965.

3. ELLIS, HAVELOCK. *Studies in the Psychology of Sex.* New York: Random House, 1942. 2 vol. (Original in 1905).

4. FORD, CELLAN S. and BEACH, FRANK A. *Patterns of Sexual Behavior.* New York: Harper & Brothers, 1951.

5. FREUD, SIGMUND. "Three Contributions to the Theory of Sex." In *The Basic Writings of Sigmund Freud* (A. A. Brill, ed.). New York: The Modern Library, 1938 (Original in 1905).

6. ————. "Some Psychological Consequences of the Anatomical Distinction Between the Sexes." In *Collected Papers* (James Strachey, Ed.). New York: Basic Books, 1959 (Original in 1925), Vol. 5, 186–97.

7. ————. "Female Sexuality." In *Collected Papers* (James Strachey, ed.). New York: Basic Books, 1959 (Original in 1931), Vol. 5, 252–72.

8. JONES, ERNEST. *The Life and Works of Sigmund Freud.* New York: Basic Books, 1953. 3 vol.

9. KAGAN, JEROME. "Acquisition and Significance of Sex Typing and Sex Role." In *Child Development Research: Vol. I.* (Martin L. Hoffman and Lois W. Hoffman, eds.). New York: Russell Sage Foundation, 1964, pp. 137–67.

10. KINSEY, ALFRED C. et al. *Sexual Behavior in the Human Male.* Philadelphia: W. B. Saunders, 1948.

11. ————. *Sexual Behavior in the Human Female.* Philadelphia: W. B. Saunders, 1953.

12. MALINOWSKI, BRONISLAW. *The Sexual Life of Savages in North-Western Melanesia.* New York: Harcourt, Brace, & World, 1929.

13. ————. *Sex & Repression in Savage Society.* New York: The World Publishing Co., 1955 (Original in 1927).

14. MOLL, ALBERT. *The Sexual Life of the Child.* New York: Macmillan, 1923 (Original in 1912).

15. RAMSEY, GLENN V. "The Sexual Development of Boys." *American Journal of Psychology,* 1943, 56, 217–33.

16. REEVY, WILLIAM R. "Child Sexuality." In *The Encyclopedia of Sexual Behavior* (Albert Ellis and Albert Abarbanel, Eds.), New York: Hawthorn Books, 1961, Vol. 1, 258–67.

3
Sexuality and sexual learning in childhood*

JAMES ELIAS and PAUL GEBHARD

The turn of the century saw an awakening interest in sexuality and sexual learning among children. The most significant work of this period was Freud's theory of infantile sexuality, which directed the attention of the world to sexuality in early childhood and its importance for the future adult role. A somewhat neglected work, by Moll (1909), was overshadowed by the Freudian wave; but Moll's observations on the sexual life of the child were the first comprehensive writings done in this field. In an earlier study, Bell (1902) examined childhood sexuality through the study of the activities of children.

RESEARCH SINCE 1917

Numerous studies resulted from this increased interest in childhood sexuality. Among them were Blanton (1917), looking at the behavior of the human infant during the first 30 days of life; Hattendorf (1932), dealing with the questions most frequently asked by preschool children; Isaacs (1933), studying the social development of young children; Dudycha (1933), examining recall of preschool experiences; and Campbell (1939), writing on the social-sexual development of children. Conn (1940a, 1940b, 1947, 1948) has done a series of studies dealing with various phases of sex-

* Reprinted from *Phi Delta Kappan,* Vol. 50, No. 7 (March 1969), pp. 401–5, with the permission of the authors and the publisher.

ual awareness and sexual curiosity in children. Other important studies were made by Halverson (1940), on penile erection in male infants; Conn and Kanner (1947), on children's awareness of physical sex differences; Katcher (1955), on the discrimination of sex differences by young children; and Ramsey (1950), on preadolescent and adolescent boys. Sears, Maccoby, and Levin (1957) present a discussion of labeling and parental sanctioning of sex behavior, and Bandura and Walters (1959) examine parental response to sex information questions.[1]

Current research has tended to move away from direct studies of infant and childhood sexual behavior. Sexuality has its roots in man's biological makeup, and the development of gender role or sex differences has become one of the main focuses of present researchs.[2] Since the molding forces, or socializing agents, are the family and the peer group (among others), sexuality is being pursued as a form of social development. Receiving special emphasis are the development of the male and female role— for example, the part aggression plays in developing and aggressive adult male sexual role and the concomitant emphasis on nonaggressiveness in the development of an adequate female role. Other areas of current research are found in the work of John Money and Joan and John Hampson, on the ontogeny of human sexual behavior.[3]

---

[1] Sigmund Freud, "Three Essays on Sexuality," *Standard Edition of the Complete Psychological Works* (London: Hogarth, 1953), pp. 235–45. Albert Moll, *The Sexual Life of the Child* (New York: Macmillan, 1923 (originally published in German in 1909)); S. Bell, "A Preliminary Study of the Emotion of Love Between the Sexes," *American Journal of Psychology*, 1902, pp. 325–54; M. G. Blanton, "The Behavior of the Human Infant During the First Thirty Days of Life," *Psychological Review*, 1917, pp. 956–83; K. W. Hattendorf, "A Study of the Questions of Young Children Concerning Sex: A Phase of an Experimental Approach to Parent Education," *Journal of Social Psychology*, 1932, pp. 37–65; S. Isaacs, *Social Development of Young Children: A Study of Beginnings* (London: George Routledge and Sons, 1933); G. J. and M. M. Dudycha, "Adolescent Memories of Preschool Experiences," *Pedagogical Seminar and Journal of Genetic Psychology*, 1933, pp. 468–80; E. H. Campbell, "The Social-Sex Development of Children," *Genetic Psychology Monographs*, 1939, p. 4; J. H. Conn, "Children's Awareness of the Origin of Babies," *Journal of Child Psychiatry*, 1948, p. 140–76; "Children's Reactions to the Discovery of Genital Differences," *American Journal of Orthopsychiatry*, 1940a, pp. 747–54; "Sexual Curiosity of Children," *American Journal of Diseases of Children*, 1940b, pp. 1110–19; J. H. Conn and Leo Kanner, "Children's Awareness of Sex Differences," *Journal of Child Psychiatry*, 1947, pp. 3–57; H. M. Halverson, "Genital and Sphincter Behavior of the Male Infant," *Journal of Genetic Psychology*, 1940, pp. 95–136; A. Katcher, "The Discrimination of Sex Differences by Young Children," *Journal of Genetic Psychology*, 1955, pp. 131–43; C. V. Ramsey, *Factors in the Sex Life of 291 Boys* (Madison, N. J.: Published by the author, 1950); R. Sears, E. Maccoby, and H. Levin, *Patterns of Child Rearing* (Evanston, Ill.: Row, Peterson, 1957); A. Bandura and R. Walters, *Adolescent Aggression* (New York: Ronald Press, 1959).

[2] R. Sears, "Development of Gender Role," in Beach (ed.), *Sex and Behavior* (New York: John Wiley and Son, 1965) pp. 133–63; E. Maccoby (ed.), *The Development of Sex Differences* (Stanford, Calif.: Stanford University Press, 1956).

[3] J. Money, J. Hampson, and J. L. Hampson, "Hermaphroditism: Recommendations Concerning Assignment of Sex, Change of Sex, and Psychologic Management,"

THE KINSEY DATA

This discussion utilizes previously unpublished data from the Institute for Sex Research, taken from case histories of prepubescents interviewed by Alfred Kinsey and his co-workers. These histories are somewhat outdated (before 1955), but the information contained in them provides one of the few sources of actual interview information on prepubescent children. Questions were asked regarding sources of sexual knowledge, extent of knowledge, homosexual and heterosexual prepubertal play, and masturbatory activity, all of crucial importance for any educator, counselor, doctor, or other professional who deals with children. Some of the critical problems encountered in preschool counseling find their source in the sexual area. Educators recognize that differences between males and females, ethnic groups, and socioeconomic status groups is essential for an understanding of the attitudinal and behavioral patterns that children exhibit. Adequate sexual adjustment in early childhood is a prime factor in later adult sexual adjustment, as healthy attitudes toward self and sexuality are the foundations of adult adjustment.

Partly through necessity, many school systems are presently moving into education programs with a maximum of speed and often a minimum of preparation regarding the specific needs of the population the particular program is to serve. Sex research can offer some aid to the educational community by providing information about critical factors in the lives of children and how these factors affect later adjustment.

THE SAMPLE

The sample consists of 432 prepubescent white boys and girls ranging in age from four to 14.[4] There are 305 boys and 127 girls in the study, and they are grouped by occupational class (social class) and age.[5] The

		Males		Females	
		N	Mean Age	N	Mean Age
Blue-collar	lower	59	11.2	21	9.5
	upper	79	11.5	17	10.1
White-collar	lower	115	9.9	53	6.9
	upper	37	7.2	35	6.6

Bulletin of Johns Hopkins Hospital, 1955a, pp. 284–300; "An Examination of Some Basic Sexual Concepts: The Evidence of Human Hermaphroditism," *Bulletin of Johns Hopkins Hospital,* 1955b, p. 301–19.

[4] The following table presents the number of boys or girls in each category (N) and the mean age of that category:

[5] The blue-collar—white-collar distinction provides an excellent indication of social level vis à vis the occupational level. The association between occupation and education (used in the original Kinsey publications) is very close. See *Sexual Behavior in the Human Male.* (Philadelphia, Pa.: Saunders, 1948), p. 328.

occupational classifications originally used in the work at the Institute for Sex Research have been combined in order to increase the number of cases and to provide social-class categories. The occupational classifications consist of: 1) unskilled workers who are labeled as lower blue-collar, 2) semi-skilled and skilled workers who comprise the upper blue-collar, 3) lower white-collar workers, and 4) business and professional men, here termed upper white-collar. A mean age is given for the children in each social class to make explicit the unequal age distribution.

The sexual behavior of younger children often lacks the erotic intent attributed to similar adult activities, raising the question, in some cases, of the validity of labeling some childhood activities as sexual. This research does not label childhood behavior as sexual unless it includes one of the following: the self-manipulation of genitalia, the exhibition of genitalia, or the manual or oral exploration of the genitalia of or by other children. Of course, many of these activities could be motivated by mere curiosity concerning a playmate's anatomy.

The term "sex play" as used here includes those heterosexual and homosexual activities involving more than one person which occur before the onset of puberty. Among the males, 52 percent report homosexual prepubertal activity and 34 percent report heterosexual prepubertal activity. These percentages seem accurate when we compare them with the self-reports of adults in the earlier Kinsey volumes. Adult males recalled homosexual experience in their preadolescent period in 48 percent of the cases, just four percent less than is reported by these children in their preadolescence.[6] The adult males also indicated that heterosexual preadolescent activity occurred in approximately 40 percent of the cases, but the reports of the children indicate only about 34 percent of prepubescent males engage in heterosexual experiences.[7] However, many of the children in this study have not reached the average age at which these experiences first occur. The average age among males for homosexual play is 9.2 years and for heterosexual play, 8.8 years.

Among female children, 35 percent report homosexual prepubertal sexual activity and 37 percent report heterosexual prepubertal experiences. The incidence of homosexual activity in the females is much less than that reported by males, but is very close to the percentage recalled by adult females in the 1953 Kinsey volume (33 percent). The adult females recalled heterosexual preadolescent activities in 30 percent of the cases, and the reports of the children show 37 percent with such experience.

One of the noteworthy findings coming from this analysis of the case histories of preadolescents is the surprising agreement between prepubertal report and adult recall. Another important finding is the lack of any

---

[6] A. Kinsey, W. Pomeroy, and C. Martin, *Sexual Behavior in the Human Male* (Philadelphia, Pa.: Saunders, 1948), p. 168.

[7] Ibid., p. 173.

consistent correlation between sociosexual activity and parental occupational class. The percentages do vary, but in no meaningful way.

MASTURBATION

Masturbation is most often described as self-stimulation leading to sexual arousal and usually to climax or orgasm, accompanied (after puberty) by ejaculation on the part of the male. Some writers prefer to believe that prepubertal children do not masturbate but simply fondle their genitals. These present data concerning prepubertal masturbation are not derived from reported "fondling of the genitals" but rather from deliberate activity done for pleasure and often accompanied by pelvic thrusts against an object (e.g., a bed) or manual manipulation. Sometimes a state of relaxation or satisfaction comparable to the postorgasmic state is achieved; in other instances indisputable orgasm occurs.

More males than females masturbate in childhood, as is the case later in adolescence and adulthood. Among prepubescent males, 56 percent report masturbatory activity while only 30 percent of the females do so. In comparison, information received from adults in self-reports indicates preadolescent masturbation in 57 percent of the cases. These actual childhood reports are within one percentage point of the recall data from adults as reported in the earlier works.

Looking at age groupings and social class, one finds that the blue-collar classes contain the highest percentages of boys who have masturbated—60–70 percent. The majority of those in the blue-collar and lower white-collar classes who masturbate are in the 8-10-year age group. The upper white-collar class has the lowest percentage of those who have masturbated (38 percent), with more beginning in the 3-7-year age group than at any subsequent time. The mean age for first masturbation is as follows: Lower blue-collar, 8.6; upper blue-collar, 8.8; lower white-collar, 7.8; and upper white-collar, 6.0. The probable explanation for the lower mean age, lower percentage of those who have masturbated, and lower average age at first masturbation for upper white-collar boys is the fact that their average age at interview is 7.2 years, while the average ages for the boys of other social classes are two to four years older.

Fewer girls tend to masturbate than boys, and only 30 percent of the girls report that they have masturbated. The highest percentage is among the lower blue-collar females (48 percent); the other three classes have lower and quite similar figures (between 25 and 29 percent). The average age of masturbation for girls is lower than that of the boys. By class, it is: lower blue-collar, 7.5; upper blue-collar, 7.4; lower white-collar, 5.7; and upper white-collar, 6.7.

Masturbation has been designated in the past as the prime cause of mental illness, low morals, and stunted growth, among other things. These stigmas are for the most part behind us, but tradition dies slowly and many children are still being told "old wives' tales" concerning the alleged effects of masturbation. This is unfortunate for in early childhood masturbation might influence the child to accept his body as pleasureful rather than reject it as a source of anxiety. Society has progressed to a point where few parents punish their offspring for masturbating, but it is noteworthy that fewer still encourage it.

SEXUAL KNOWLEDGE

In this study, additional measures are taken of current knowledge while controlling for child's age and occupation of father. The occupational level is dichotomized into lower (blue-collar) and upper (white-collar) classes for purposes of analysis. Presence or absence of knowledge about the following topics is examined: intercourse, pregnancy, fertilization, menstruation, venereal disease, abortion, condoms, and female prostitution. In general, the white-collar class surpasses the blue-collar class in all sex knowledge categories. Of special interest to the educator are some of the differences in learning which occur on the part of the children in these two groups. For example, while 96 percent of the blue-collar boys have an understanding of sexual intercourse by ages 13–14, only four percent have any knowledge concerning the "coming together of the sperm and the egg"—fertilization. Twenty-seven percent of the upper white-collar group in the same age range understand the concept of fertilization, and this nearly seven-fold difference is indicative of the language level and sources (hence quality) of information for the two groups. Blue-collar boys learn about intercourse, abortion, condoms, and prostitution earlier than do other males, especially by age 8–10. These words and activities become a part of the sex education of lower-class boys much earlier than of boys whose fathers are employed in higher-status occupations, as a result of most sex information being provided by peers on the street.

This earlier and more extensive knowledge of coitus is reflected in prepubescent heterosexual activity, wherein nearly three times as many blue-collar boys have, or attempt, coitus than do white-collar boys. Interestingly enough, more blue-collar males know of intercourse than know of pregnancy (except in the four-seven-year-old group) and just the reverse is true for the white-collar males. The white-collar male surpasses the blue-collar male in sexual knowledge in later age groupings, perhaps indicating that many of the more formal aspects of his sex education come from his mother, with peers "filling in the gaps" concerning some of the more sensitive areas, such as methods of birth-control and prostitution.

The pattern for girls stands in marked contrast to that for boys. Prepubescent girls, unlike boys, are not inclined to discuss or joke about sexual matters. Also, the girl eavesdropping on conversation by adult females is less apt to hear of such matters than is the boy listening to adult males. Lastly, there is reason to believe that the lower-class mother is more inhibited about, and less capable of imparting sex education to her daughter. Consequently, the lower-class girl generally lags behind her upper-class counterpart in sexual information.

Thus, for example, in age group 8–10, not quite half of the lower-class girls know of coitus, whereas close to three-quarters of the upper-class females have this knowledge. This gap is found even with regard to menstruation, a thing sufficiently removed from overt sexual behavior that one would expect it to escape from taboo. On the contrary, at lower social levels, menstruation is often regarded as dirty and somehow shameful. The result is that among the 8-10-year-olds roughly a quarter of the lower-class and nearly three-quarters of the upper-class girls possess this inevitable knowledge.

On more technical matters the lower-class girls are equally or even more disadvantaged. For example, none of them grasp the concept of fertilization: the idea that pregnancy is the result of the fusion of an egg and a sperm.

Among upper-class girls from age group 8–10 on, the knowledge of pregnancy is universal, whereas many of their lower-class counterparts are unaware of where babies come from. Indeed, in age groups 8–10 and 11–12, more lower-class girls know of coitus than of pregnancy. This situation, so incongruous to an upper-class reader, is explicable. Thanks to their contact, both physical and verbal, with lower-class boys (a substantial number of whom have attempted coitus), more lower-class girls hear of or experience coitus than hear of pregnancy. Note that while a boy may attempt to persuade a girl to have coitus, it is most improbable that he will defeat his aim by informing her of the consequence.

Lastly, the differences in knowledge between upper- and lower-class girls hinge to some considerable extent on literacy and on communication with parents. The upper-class girl, more prone to reading, and in a milieu where books and magazines with sexual content are available to the home, will educate herself or ask her parents to explain what she has read. The upper-class parent, having been told by innumerable magazine articles and books on child-rearing of the desirability of sex education, is far more likely to impart information than is the less knowledgeable and more inhibited lower-class parent. This statement will be substantiated in the following section on sources of sexual knowledge.

SOURCES OF SEXUAL KNOWLEDGE

By looking at the sources of sexual learning for children, one can see the origin of sexual "slang" terms and sexual misinformation frequently unacceptable to the middle-class teacher. Though a large portion of this mislabeled and often incorrect information is the product of children's "pooled ignorance," the problem is only confounded by adult non-communication.

The main source of sex education for most boys is the peer group—friends and classmates. Nevertheless there are important differences, depending on the child's social class (measured here as father's occupation). The peer group is overwhelmingly important as a source of information for all the boys from blue-collar homes: From 75 percent to 88 percent of them report other boys as their major source. The boys of lower white-collar homes seem a transitional group, with 70 percent so reporting, while the boys whose fathers are lower white-collar men find their mothers as important as their peers with respect to information. The boys from upper white-collar homes derive little from their peers, most from their mothers, and a relatively large amount from combined educational efforts by both parents. These figures are in striking contrast to those of the blue-collar boys: only eight percent cite peers as the main source, 48 percent report the mother, and 24 percent both parents. This inverse relationship between parental occupation and the importance of peers as an informational source is one of the major, though anticipated, findings of this study. As the occupational level of the home increases, the child's mother plays a growing role in the sex education of her son, rising to nearly half of the cases for males whose fathers are upper white-collar men. For all occupational levels, the father seems to play a marginal role as a source of sex information for boys, and when he does play a role in his boy's sex education, it is mainly when both parents act as a team. While we can only speculate on the basis of our data, the mother is probably the "prime mover" of the parental educating team. Other sources as major channels of information (e.g., siblings, other relatives, simple observation, etc.) are statistically unimportant, never exceeding four percent.

Some children report that their sources of information are so evenly balanced that they cannot name one as the major source. Boys reporting this situation are more common (20 percent) in homes of lower blue-collar fathers. The percentages tend to decrease progressively as parental occupational status increases, but this trend is unexpectedly reversed by the boys from upper white-collar homes. This reversal is probably not the result of small sample vagary, since the same phenomenon is to be seen among girls. No explanation is presently known.

TEACHER UNIMPORTANT AS SOURCE

It is interesting to note that the teacher is not mentioned by any of the children as the main source of sex education. In fact, throughout the study the contribution of the teacher and the school system of the child's information about sex is too low to be statististically significant. However, with the current proliferation of formal sex education programs in some of our nation's school systems, the role of the teacher and the school has no doubt increased in importance since the time these interviews were conducted, before 1955.

When looking at the main source of sex knowledge for girls, we see similar trends. Peers provide the main source of sex information for 35 percent of the girls whose fathers are lower blue-collar men and for 25 percent of the girls whose fathers are upper blue-collar workers. By contrast, only nine percent and four percent, respectively, of the girls whose fathers are white-collar men report the peer group as their main source of sex education. The mother's importance as a source of sex education increases with increased occupational status, being the major source for 10 percent of the daughters of lower blue-collar workers up to 75 percent of those whose fathers are upper white-collar men.

For girls, fathers provide very little sex education, and then only as a member of a father-mother combination. It is interesting to observe that significantly more girls than boys report no main source of sex education, especially those girls from homes in which the father has a lower-status occupation. For example, 45 percent of the daughters of lower blue-collar workers report no main source of sex education, as compared to 20 percent of the boys whose fathers are at this occupational level. Other possible informational sources, such as siblings and printed material, are inconsequential.

NUDITY

The general level of permissiveness regarding nudity in the home, a sex-related phenomenon, also varies in relation to the occupational level of the family. As a rule, boys are allowed more nudity than girls, except in homes where nudity is a common practice—in which case the girls report a higher incidence of nudity. Differences between occupational groups are great, with 87 percent of the lower blue-collar workers never allowing nudity among their sons, as compared to only 28 percent of upper white-collar men. Again for boys, 40 percent who come from upper white-collar families report nudity as very common, compared to only 3 percent whose fathers are lower blue-collar workers. Among girls, we find the same patterns emerging, with 44 percent of the girls from upper white-collar families reporting nudity as very common, and none of the girls from lower blue-collar families reporting nudity as usual in the home. Thus nudity in the lower-class home is more the exception than the rule for both girls and boys; in the upper-class home almost the reverse is true. This upper-class permissiveness regarding a sex-related behavior, nudity, fits nicely with our finding that upper-class parents communicate more freely on sexual matters with their offspring.

IMPLICATIONS FOR EDUCATION

The main implication of the reported data for those in the field of education is the need for educators to be aware of the differences in information and experience which exist between boys and girls, between different occupational and socioeconomic groups (and though not treated in this article) the differences which may occur between ethnic groups. An apparent problem regarding these differences, still evident in much of our educational system today, is an often inflexible adherence to the "middle-class yardstick."

The sexual experiences and the sexual vocabulary of the heterogeneous student population, especially the pupil who has not come from the same socioeconomic, occupational, or ethnic background as his teacher, create definite problems in expectations, understanding, and communication between teacher and pupil. An adequate knowledge of the sources of sex education, types of experiences, and the vocabulary and attitudes of these students will enable the teacher to gain a wider understanding of some of the problems of pupils regarding sexual matters and to modify his or her teaching accordingly.

Counseling the child in the school system raises some of the same problems encountered by the classroom teacher in an even more intense, personal situation. The counselor should have some idea of differences in preadolescent sexual activities and knowledge, enabling him to aid the child and his parents more intelligently as they deal with questions and problems of sexuality. If the average age for preadolescent homosexual experiences, for instance, is around nine years, this activity should be recognized as possibly a part of normal sexual development rather than as a sexual aberration. There is great danger of confusing activities accompanying normal sexual development with pathological behavior.

It is also apparent from the data presented here that many lower-class children will probably experience problems in learning and adjustment because of the lack of accurate information from informed sources. Neither the teacher nor the parent will completely replace peer-group influence in the process of providing sexual information, especially in the lower class, but the educator has the opportunity to provide programs to meet the needs of children otherwise inadequately prepared to cope with sexuality because of restraints imposed by social-class position. Therefore education should continue to initiate programs which will help fill this void created either by peer misinformation or by similar misunderstanding and reluctance on the part of parents.

4

The process of learning
parental and sex-role
identification*

DAVID B. LYNN

The purpose of this paper is to summarize the writer's theoretical formulation concerning identification, much of which has been published piece-
meal in various journals. Research relevant to new hypotheses is cited,
and references are given to previous publications of this writer in which
the reader can find evidence concerning the earlier hypotheses. Some of
the previously published hypotheses are considerably revised in this paper
and, it is hoped, placed in a more comprehensive and coherent framework.

THEORETICAL FORMULATION

Before developing specific hypotheses, one must briefly define identification as it is used here. *Parental identification* refers to the internalization of personality characteristics of one's own parent and to unconscious
reactions similar to that parent. This is to be contrasted with *sex-role
identification*, which refers to the internalization of the role typical of a
given sex in a particular culture and to the unconscious reactions characteristic of that role. Thus, theoretically, an individual might be thoroughly identified with the role typical of his own sex generally and yet

* From *Journal of Marriage and the Family*, Vol. 28, No. 4 (November 1966), 465–
70. Reprinted by permission of the author and the National Council on Family Relations.

poorly identified with his same-sex parent specifically. This differentiation also allows for the converse circumstances wherein a person is well-identified with his same-sex parent specifically and yet poorly identified with the typical same-sex role generally. In such an instance the parent with whom the individual is well identified is himself poorly identified with the typical sex role. An example might be a girl who is closely identified with her mother, who herself is more strongly identified with the masculine than with the feminine role. Therefore, such a girl, through her identification with her mother, is poorly identified with the feminine role.[1]

Formulation of hypotheses

It is postulated that the initial parental identification of both male and female infants is with the mother. Boys, but not girls, must shift from this initial mother identification and establish masculine identification. Typically in this culture the girl has the same-sex parental model for identification (the mother) with her more hours per day than the boy has his same-sex model (the father) with him. Moreover, even when home, the father does not usually participate in as many intimate activities with the child as does the mother, e.g., preparation for bed, toileting. The time spent with the child and the intimacy and intensity of the contact are thought to be pertinent to the process of learning parental identification.[2] The boy is seldom if ever with the father as he engages in his daily vocational activities, although both boy and girl are often with the mother as she goes through her household activities. Consequently, the father, as a model for the boy, is analogous to a map showing the major outline but lacking most details, whereas the mother, as a model for the girl, might be thought of as a detailed map.

However, despite the shortage of male models, a somewhat stereotyped and conventional masculine role is nonetheless spelled out for the boy, often by his mother and women teachers in the absence of his father and male models. Through the reinforcement of the culture's highly developed system of rewards for typical masculine-role behavior and punishment for signs of femininity, the boy's early learned identification with the mother weakens. Upon this weakened mother identification is welded the later learned identification with a culturally defined, stereotyped masculine role.

(1)* *Consequently, males tend to identify with a culturally defined masculine role, whereas females tend to identify with their mothers.*[3]

---

[1] D. B. Lynn, "Sex-Role and Parental Identification," *Child Development*, 33:3 (1962), pp. 555–64.

[2] B. A. Goodfield, "A Preliminary Paper on the Development of the Time Intensity Compensation Hypothesis in Masculine Identification," paper read at the San Francisco State Psychological Convention, April 1965.

* Specific hypotheses are numbered and in italics.

[3] D. B. Lynn, "A Note on Sex Differences in the Development of Masculine and Feminine Identification," *Psychological Review*, 66:2 (1959), pp. 126–35.

Although one must recognize the contribution of the father in the identification of males and the general cultural influences in the identification of females, it nevertheless seems meaningful, for simplicity in developing this formulation, to refer frequently to *masculine-role identification* in males as distinguished from *mother identification* in females.

Some evidence is accumulating suggesting that (2) *both males and females identify more closely with the mother than with the father*. Evidence is found in support of this hypothesis in a study by Lazowick[4] in which the subjects were 30 college students. These subjects and their mothers and fathers were required to rate concepts, e.g., "myself," "father," "mother," etc. The degree of semantic similarity as rated by the subjects and their parents was determined. The degree of similarity between fathers and their own children was not significantly greater than that found between fathers and children randomly matched. However, children did share a greater semantic similarity with their own mothers than they did when matched at random with other maternal figures. Mothers and daughters did not share a significantly greater semantic similarity than did mothers and sons.

Evidence is also found in support of Hypothesis 2 in a study by Adams and Sarason[5] using anxiety scales with male and female high school students and their mothers and fathers. They found that anxiety scores of both boys and girls were much more related to mothers' than to fathers' anxiety scores.

Support for this hypothesis comes from a study in which Aldous and Kell[6] interviewed 50 middle-class college students and their mothers concerning childrearing values. They found, contrary to their expectation, that a slightly higher proportion of boys than girls shared their mothers' childrearing values.

Partial support for Hypothesis 2 is provided in a study by Gray and Klaus[7] using the Allport-Vernon-Lindzey Study of Values completed by 34 female and 28 male college students and by their parents. They found that the men were not significantly closer to their fathers than to their mothers and also that the men were not significantly closer to their fathers than were the women. However, the women were closer to their mothers than were the men and closer to their mothers than to their fathers.

Note that, in reporting research relevant to Hypothesis 2, only studies of *tested similarity*, not *perceived similarity*, were reviewed. To test this

---

[4] L. M. Lazowick, "On the Nature of Identification," *Journal of Abnormal and Social Psychology*, 51 (1955), pp. 175–83.

[5] E. B. Adams and I. G. Sarason, "Relation Between Anxiety in Children and Their Parents," *Child Development*, 34:1 (1963), pp. 237–46.

[6] J. Aldous and L. Kell, "A Partial Test of Some Theories of Identification," *Marriage and Family Living*, 23:1 (1961), pp. 15–19.

[7] S. W. Gray and R. Klaus, "The Assessment of Parental Identification," *Genetic Psychology Monographs*, 54 (1956), pp. 87–114.

hypothesis, one must measure tested similarity, i.e., measure both the child and the parent on the same variable and compare the similarity between these two measures. This paper is not concerned with perceived similarity, i.e., testing the child on a given variable and then comparing that finding with a measure taken as to how the child thinks his parent would respond. It is this writer's opinion that much confusion has arisen by considering perceived similarity as a measure of parental identification. It seems obvious that, especially for the male, perceived similarity between father and son would usually be closer than tested similarity, in that it is socially desirable for a man to be similar to his father, especially as contrasted to his similarity to his mother. Indeed, Gray and Klaus[8] found the males' perceived similarity with the father to be closer than tested similarity.

It is hypothesized that the closer identification of males with the mother than with the father will be revealed more clearly on some measures than on others. (3) *The closer identification of males with their mothers than with their fathers will be revealed most frequently in personality variables which are not clearly sex-typed.* In other words, males are more likely to be more similar to their mothers than to their fathers in variables in which masculine and feminine role behavior is not especially relevant in the culture.

There has been too little research on tested similarity between males and their parents to presume an adequate test of Hypothesis 3. In order to test it, one would first have to judge personality variables as to how typically masculine or feminine they seem. One could then test to determine whether a higher proportion of males are more similar to their mothers than to their fathers on those variables which are not clearly sex-typed, rather than on those which are judged clearly to be either masculine or feminine. To this writer's knowledge, this has not been done.

It is postulated that the task of achieving these separate kinds of identification (masculine role for males and mother identification for females) requires separate methods of learning for each sex. These separate methods of learning to identify seem to be problem-solving for boys and lesson-learning for girls. Woodworth and Schlosberg differentiate between the task of solving problems and that of learning lessons in the following way:

With a problem to master the learner must explore the situation and find the goal before his task is fully presented. In the case of a lesson, the problem-solving phase is omitted or at least minimized, as we see when the human subject is instructed to memorize this poem or that list of nonsense syllables, to examine these pictures with a view to recognizing them later.[9]

---

[8] Ibid.
[9] R. S. Woodworth and H. Schlosberg, *Experimental Psychology* (New York: Holt 1954), p. 529.

Since the girl is not required to shift from the mother in learning her identification, she is expected mainly to learn the mother-identification lesson as it is presented to her, partly through imitation and through the mother's selective reinforcement of mother-similar behavior. She need not abstract principles defining the feminine role to the extent that the boy must in defining the masculine role. Any bit of behavior on the mother's part may be modeled by the girl in learning the mother-identification lesson.

However, finding the appropriate identification goal does constitute a major problem for the boy in solving the masculine-role identification problem. When the boy discovers that he does not belong in the same sex category as the mother, he must then find the proper sex-role identification goal. Masculine role behavior is defined for him through admonishments, often negatively given, e.g., the mother's and teachers' telling him that he should not be a sissy without precisely indicating what he *should* be. Moreover, these negative admonishments are made in the early grades in the absence of male teachers to serve as models and with the father himself often unavailable as a model. The boy must restructure these admonishments in order to abstract principles defining the masculine role. It is this process of defining the masculine-role goal which is involved in solving the masculine-role identification problem.

One of the basic steps in this formulation can now be taken. (4) *In learning the sex-typical identification, each sex is thereby acquiring separate methods of learning which are subsequently applied to learning tasks generally.*[10]

The little girl acquires a learning method which primarily involves (a) a personal relationship and (b) imitation rather than restructuring the field and abstracting principles. On the other hand, the little boy acquires a different learning method which primarily involves (a) defining the goal, (b) restructuring the field, and (c) abstracting principles. There are a number of findings which are consistent with Hypothesis 4, such as the frequently reported greater problem-solving skill of males and the greater field dependence of females.[11]

The shift of the little boy from mother identification to masculine role identification is assumed to be frequently a crisis. It has been observed that demands for typical sex-role behavior come at an earlier age for boys than for girls. These demands are made at an age when boys are least able to understand them. As was pointed out above, demands for masculine sex-role behavior are often made by women in the absence of readily available male models to demonstrate typical sex-role behavior. Such demands are often presented in the form of punishing, *negative* admonishments, i.e.,

---

[10] D. B. Lynn, "Sex-Role and Parental Identification," p. 561.
[11] Ibid.

telling the boy what not to do rather than what to do and backing up the demands with punishment. These are thought to be very different conditions from those in which the girl learns her mother-identification lesson. Such methods of demanding typical sex-role behavior of boys are very poor methods for inducing learning. (5) *Therefore, males tend to have greater difficulty in achieving same-sex identification than females.*[12] (6) *Furthermore, more males than females fail more or less completely in achieving same-sex identification, but they rather make an opposite-sex identification.*[13]

Negative admonishments given at an age when the child is least able to understand them and supported by punishment are thought to produce anxiety concerning sex-role behavior. In Hartley's words:

> This situation gives us practically a perfect combination for inducing anxiety—the demand that the child do something which is not clearly defined to him, based on reasons he cannot possibly appreciate, and enforced with threats, punishments and anger by those who are close to him.[14]

(7) *Consequently, males are more anxious regarding sex-role identification than females.*[15] It is postulated that punishment often leads to dislike of the activity that led to punishment.[16] Since it is "girl-like" activities that provoked the punishment administered in an effort to induce sex-typical behavior in boys, then, in developing dislike for the activity which led to such punishment, boys should develop hostility toward "girl-like" activities. Also, boys should be expected to generalize and consequently develop hostility toward all females as representatives of this disliked role. There is not thought to be as much pressure on girls as on boys to avoid opposite-sex activities. It is assumed that girls are punished neither so early nor so severely for adopting masculine sex-role behavior.

(8) *Therefore, males tend to hold stronger feelings of hostility toward females than females toward males.*[17] The young boy's same-sex identification is at first not very firm because of the shift from mother to masculine identification. On the other hand, the young girl, because she need make no shift in identification, remains relatively firm in her mother identification. However, the culture, which is male-dominant in orientation, reinforces the boy's developing masculine role identification much more

---

[12] D. B. Lynn, "Divergent Feedback and Sex-Role Identification in Boys and Men," *Merrill-Palmer Quarterly*, 10:1 (1964), pp. 17–23.

[13] D. B. Lynn, "Sex Differences in Identification Development," *Sociometry*, 24:4 (1961), pp. 372–83.

[14] R. E. Hartley, "Sex-Role Pressures and the Socialization of the Male Child," *Psychological Reports*, 5 (1959), p. 458.

[15] D. B. Lynn, "Divergent Feedback and Sex-Role Identification in Boys and Men."

[16] R. E. Hilgard, *Introduction to Psychology* (New York: Harcourt, Brace, and World, 1962).

[17] D. B. Lynn, "Divergent Feedback and Sex-Role Identification in Boys and Men."

thoroughly than it does the girl's developing feminine identification. He is rewarded simply for having been born masculine through countless privileges accorded males but not females. As Brown pointed out:

The superior position and privileged status of the male permeates nearly every aspect, minor and major, of our social life. The gadgets and prizes in boxes of breakfast cereal, for example, commonly have a strong masculine rather than feminine appeal. And the most basic social institutions perpetuate this pattern of masculine aggrandizement. Thus, the Judeo-Christian faiths involve worshipping God, a "Father," rather than a "Mother," and Christ, a "Son," rather than a "Daughter." [18]

(9) *Consequently, with increasing age, males become relatively more firmly identified with the masculine role.*[19]

Since psychological disturbances should, theoretically, be associated with inadequate same-sex identification and since males are postulated to be gaining in masculine identification, the following is predicted: (10) *With increasing age males develop psychological disturbances at a more slowly accelerating rate than females.*[20]

It is postulated that as girls grow older, they become increasingly disenchanted with the feminine role because of the prejudices against their sex and the privileges and prestige offered the male rather than the female. Even the women with whom they come in contact are likely to share the prejudices prevailing in this culture against their own sex.[21] Smith[22] found that with increasing age girls have a progressively better opinion of boys and a progressively poorer opinion of themselves. (11) *Consequently, a larger proportion of females than males show preference for the role of the opposite sex.*[23]

Note that in Hypothesis 11 the term "preference" rather than "identification" was used. It is *not* hypothesized that a larger proportion of females than males *identify* with the opposite sex (Hypothesis 6 predicted the reverse) but rather that they will show *preference* for the role of the opposite sex. *Sex-role preference* refers to the desire to adopt the behavior associated with one sex or the other or the perception of such behavior as preferable or more desirable. *Sex-role preference* should be contrasted

---

[18] D. G. Brown, "Sex-Role Development in a Changing Culture," *Psychological Bulletin,* 55 (1958), p. 235.

[19] D. B. Lynn, "A Note on Sex Differences in the Development of Masculine and Feminine Identification," p. 130.

[20] D. B. Lynn, "Sex Differences in Identification Development," p. 378.

[21] P. M. Kitay, "A Comparison of the Sexes in Their Attitudes and Beliefs About Women: A Study of Prestige Groups," *Sociometry,* 3 (1940), pp. 399–407.

[22] S. Smith, "Age and Sex Differences in Children's Opinion Concerning Sex Differences," *Journal of Genetic Psychology,* 54 (1939), pp. 17–25.

[23] D. B. Lynn, "A Note on Sex Differences in the Development of Masculine and Feminine Identification," p. 130.

with *sex-role identification*, which, as stated previously, refers to the actual incorporation of the role of a given sex and to the unconscious reactions characteristic of that role.

Punishment may suppress behavior without causing its unlearning.[24] Because of the postulated punishment administered to males for adopting opposite-sex role behavior, it is predicted that males will repress atypical sex-role behavior rather than unlearn it. One might predict, then, a discrepancy between the underlying sex-role identification and the overt sex-role behavior of males. For females, on the other hand, no comparable punishment for adopting many aspects of the opposite-sex role is postulated. (12) *Consequently, where a discrepancy exists between sex-role preference and identification, it will tend to be as follows: Males will tend to show same-sex role preference with underlying opposite-sex identification. Females will tend to show opposite-sex role preference with underlying same-sex identification.*[25] Stated in another way, where a discrepancy occurs both males and females will tend to show masculine role preference with underlying feminine identification.

Not only is the masculine role accorded more prestige than the feminine role, but males are more likely than females to be ridiculed or punished for adopting aspects of the opposite-sex role. For a girl to be a tomboy does not involve the censure that results when a boy is a sissy. Girls may wear masculine clothing (shirts and trousers), but boys may not wear feminine clothing (skirts and dresses). Girls may play with toys typically associated with boys (cars, trucks, erector sets, and guns), but boys are discouraged from playing with feminine toys (dolls and tea sets). (13) *Therefore, a higher proportion of females than males adopt aspects of the role of the opposite sex.*[26]

Note that Hypothesis 13 refers to *sex-role adoption* rather than *sex-role identification* or *preference*. *Sex-role adoption* refers to the overt behavior characteristic of a given sex. An example contrasting sex-role adoption with preference and identification is an individual who *adopts* behavior characteristic of his own sex because it is expedient, not because he *prefers* it nor because he is so *identified*.

SUMMARY

The purpose of this paper has been to summarize the writer's theoretical formulation and to place it in a more comprehensive and coherent framework. The following hypotheses were presented and discussed:

---

[24] Hilgard, op. cit.

[25] D. B. Lynn, "Divergent Feedback and Sex-Role Identification in Boys and Men," p. 20.

[26] D. B. Lynn, "A Note on Sex Differences in the Development of Masculine and Feminine Identification," p. 131.

1. Males tend to identify with a culturally defined masculine role, whereas females tend to identify with their mothers.

2. Both males and females identify more closely with the mother than with the father.

3. The closer identification of males with their mothers than with their fathers will be revealed most frequently in personality variables which are not clearly sex-typed.

4. In learning the sex-typical identification, each sex is thereby acquiring separate methods of learning which are subsequently applied to learning tasks generally.

5. Males tend to have greater difficulty in achieving same-sex identification than females.

6. More males than females fail more or less completely in achieving same-sex identification but rather make an opposite-sex identification.

7. Males are more anxious regarding sex-role identification than females.

8. Males tend to hold stronger feelings of hostility toward females than females toward males.

9. With increasing age, males become relatively more firmly identified with the masculine role.

10. With increasing age, males develop psychological disturbances at a more slowly accelerating rate than females.

11. A larger proportion of females than males show preference for the role of the opposite sex.

12. Where a discrepancy exists between sex-role preference and identification, it will tend to be as follows: Males will tend to show same-sex role preference with underlying opposite-sex identification. Females will tend to show opposite-sex role preference with underlying same-sex identification.

13. A higher proportion of females than males adopt aspects of the role of the opposite sex.

5
Human sexual development: An outline of components and concepts*

DANIEL G. BROWN and DAVID B. LYNN

This paper is an attempt to clarify the terminology and to present a conceptual schema relative to human sexuality. The term *sexual* has been used so broadly as to include everything from biological differentiation of male and female, to orgasm, masculine or feminine role behavior, parental behavior, and even the pervasive psychic energy implied in the Freudian usage of the term libido. The boundaries of human sexuality are, in short, unclear. The terms and concepts in this area often lack precise meaning and not infrequently lead to conceptual confusion. Examples of this ambiguity may be seen in the fact that the following terms are used more or less synonymously: male and masculine; female and feminine; hermaphroditism, transvestism, transsexualism, homosexuality, and sexual inversion; and sexual drive, libido, and eroticism.

In recent years there has been an accumulation of research concerned with human sexuality indicating that the notion of an innate, predetermined psychologic sexuality does not correspond with existing evidence.[1]

* From *Journal of Marriage and the Family*, Vol. 28, No. 2 (May 1966), pp. 155–62. Reprinted by permission of the authors and the National Council on Family Relations.

[1] J. Money, "Psychosexual Development in Man," in *The Encyclopedia of Mental Health*, ed. by A. Deutsch (New York: Franklin Watts, 1963), pp. 1678–1709.

Rather, recent investigations suggest that the psychosexual status of the individual is undifferentiated at birth. The individual begins life psychosexually plastic, capable of developing along a variety of lines depending upon the definition of sex roles in his particular culture as well as his unique learning experiences in the first few years of life especially. This psychosexual plasticity has been convincingly demonstrated by research showing that hermaphroditic children, i.e., those with a mixture or inconsistency of male and female components, usually grow up as masculine *or* feminine depending on the sex assigned them and the sex role in which they are reared. Research also suggests, however, that at least as far as sex role identity is concerned, this plasticity does not persist beyond early childhood; once a masculine or feminine sex-role is established, it may be extremely difficult for this basic pattern to be changed or reversed later in life.[2]

The research with hermaphrodites blends well with recent research and theoretical developments concerning sex-role identification, indicating that masculinity or femininity does not emerge as an automatic unfolding, but rather results from familial and other influences as the individual develops.[3]

The following outline is an attempt to provide clarity and a basis for integrating recent findings in the field into a systematic framework. Three major independently varying components of human sexual development and behavior will be differentiated. These are 1) *the biological-constitutional* component, i.e., hereditary, congenital, and maturational factors; 2) *sex-role*, the individual's identification of himself with one sex or the other; and 3) *genital-sex object preference*, the source, aim, and direction of sexual stimulation, desire, activity, and satisfaction. These major components will be reviewed in terms of hypothesized primary determinants, basic terminology, operational definitions, general manifestations, standard developmental outcome or norm, and nonstandard developmental outcome or deviation.

BIOLOGICAL CONSTITUTIONAL COMPONENT

Hypothesized primary determinants

The hypothesized determinants of the biological-constitutional component are hereditary, congenital, and maturational.

---

[2] J. L. Hampson and J. G. Hampson, "The Ontogenesis of Sexual Behavior in Man," in *Sex and Internal Secretions*, ed. by W. C. Young (Baltimore: Williams & Williams, 1961), pp. 1401–32; and J. Money, "Sex Hormones and Other Variables in Human Eroticism," in *Sex and Internal Secretions*, ed. by W. C. Young (Baltimore: Williams & Williams, 1961), pp. 1383–1400.

[3] See, for example, D. G. Brown, "Psychosexual Disturbances: Transvestism and Sex-Role Inversion," *Marriage and Family Living*, 22:3 (August 1960), pp. 218–26; R. E. Hartley, "A Developmental View of Female Sex-Role Definition and Identifica-

Basic terms

The basic terms are male-maleness and female-femaleness. These terms should be used to refer only to the biological aspects of sexuality and should be distinguished from masculine-masculinity and feminine-femininity, which refer to the psychosocial characteristics and behavior patterns typical of one sex in contrast to the other.

Operational definitions

Here the concern is with the relationship between male and female factors in the physiology of the individual, specifically the degree of male and female factors in the following structures and functions: 1) chromosomal composition (XX or XY); 2) gonadal composition (ovarian or testicular tissue); 3) hormonal composition (estrogen-androgen balance); 4) internal accessory structure (vagina, uterus, and fallopian tubes or seminal vesicles and prostate); and 5) external genital (clitoris and labia majora and labia minora or penis and scrotum).

General manifestations

In addition to the overall anatomical and physiological differences in genitalia between the sexes, there are also differences in general physique, body shape, physical dimensions, and other similar manifestations. Even in preschool years there are marked sex differences in body composition in that girls have more fatty tissue, while boys, although only slightly heavier, have more muscle tissue.[4] In adulthood a layer of subcutaneous fat develops, rounding and softening the contours of the face and body of women. The greater growth of the larynx in males results in a deeper voice than that of women. Females develop enlarged breasts, an enlarged bony pelvic basin, and relatively wide hips; whereas males have a widening of shoulders. In addition to differences in pubic hair distribution, males are characterized by a heavy growth of facial and body hair; whereas females develop a light down on the upper lip, forearms, and lower legs.

Standard developmental outcome or norm

The standard outcome in the biological development of the individual is a predominance of anatomical and physiological structures and func-

---

tion," *Merrill-Palmer Quarterly*, 10:1 (January 1964), pp. 3–16; and D. B. Lynn, "Sex-Role and Parental Identification," *Child Development* 33:3 (September 1962), pp. 555–64.

4 S. M. Garn, "Roentgenogrammetric Determinations of Body Composition," *Human Biology*, 29 (1957), pp. 337–53; and S. M. Garn, "Fat, Body Size, and Growth in the Newborn," *Human Biology*, 30 (1958), pp. 256–80.

tions that are the basis of either maleness or femaleness; that is, the chromosomal, gonadal, internal accessory structures, external genitalia, and general manifestations are consistently male or female at maturity.

Nonstandard developmental outcome or deviation

One of the more significant deviations in the biological sexual composition of the individual is that of hermaphroditism. There are other atypical forms of development, such as precocious puberty in which appropriate sex hormones function prematurely. However, hermaphroditism, sometimes referred to as intersexuality, is a biological anomaly of special interest in the behavioral sciences because it provides a basis for studying the interaction of physiological, social, and psychological variables in the sexual development of the individual. Hermaphroditism is a condition in which there is inconsistency in or among one or more of the following factors in the biological composition of the individual: chromosomal, gonadal, hormonal, internal accessory structures, and external genitalia. Examples include an individual showing ambiguity in external genitalia, a person having ovaries and a penis, or one who is chromosomally male but has a vagina and female accessory organs. Androgyny refers to the condition in which a male has female biological traits; gynandry involves a female with male biological traits.

Money, Hampson, and Hampson list the following six varieties of hermaphrodites:[5]

1. Congenital hyperadrenocortical females—externally hermaphroditic; normal internal reproductive organs and sex chromatin pattern. Without cortisone therapy, growth and development is precocious and virilizing.
2. Hermaphrodites with ambiguous or masculinized external genitals— normal functional female internal reproductive structures and ovaries and female sex chromatin pattern. Unlike females with hyperadrenocorticism, this group does not show progressive virilization; secondary feminization at puberty is the rule with reproduction possible.
3. Classical true hermaphroditism—testicular and ovarian tissue both present; enlarged phallus; variable development of the genital ducts; male or female sex chromatin pattern.
4. Cryptorchid hermaphrodites with relatively complete Müllerian differentiation—penis, hypospadic or normal; possible virilizing at puberty; male sex chromatin pattern.
5. Cryptorchid hermaphrodites with relatively incomplete Müllerian dif-

5 J. Money, J. G. Hampson, and J. L. Hampson, "Hermaphroditism: Recommendations Concerning Assignment of Sex, Change of Sex, and Psychological Management," *Bulletin of Johns Hopkins Hospital,* 97 (1955), pp. 284–300.

ferentiation—hypospadic or clitoral phallus; possible virilizing at puberty; male sex chromatin pattern.

6. Simulant females with feminizing inguinal testes and vestigal Müllerian differentiation—blind vaginal pouch; male sex chromatin pattern.

SEX-ROLE COMPONENT

Hypothesized primary determinants

The determinants hypothesized for the sex-role component are environmental conditioning and the social learning experiences of the individual.

Basic terms

Masculine-masculinity and feminine-femininity are the basic terms, in contrast to male-maleness and female-femaleness, which, as previously indicated, refer to the biological composition of the individual.

Operational definitions

Here the concern is with the extent that a person's behavioral patterns and psychological traits are typical of one sex in contrast to the other in a given culture and social environment. In this connection sex-role identification may be distinguished from sex-role preference.[6] Sex-role preference refers to the desire to adopt the behavior associated with one sex or the perception of such behavior as preferable or more desirable. Identification may also be contrasted to sex-role adoption, the latter referring to the actual adoption of behavior characteristic of one sex or the other, not simply the desire to adopt such behavior.[7] The fact that a woman on appropriate occasions wears trousers or short hair does not necessarily mean that she is identified with the masculine role even though she is adopting certain aspects characteristic of that role. Sex-role identification is reserved for reference to the introjection and incorporation of the role of a given sex and to the basic, underlying reactions characteristic of that role.

Thus, a person may identify with the opposite sex but for expediency adopt much of the behavior characteristic of his own sex. In some respects he may prefer the role of his own sex, although there is considerable identification with the opposite-sex role. One would expect such a person, having identified substantially with the opposite sex, to have a number of

---

[6] D. G. Brown, "Sex-Role Preference in Young Children," *Psychological Monographs,* 70:14 (1956), (Whole No. 421).

[7] D. B. Lynn, "A Note on Sex Differences in the Development of Masculine and Feminine Identification," *Psychological Review,* 66:2 (1959), pp. 126–35.

underlying reactions characteristic of the opposite-sex role despite his adopting much of the behavior characteristic of the same-sex role. On the other hand, the woman who on appropriate occasions adopts aspects characteristic of the opposite-sex role, such as wearing trousers or wearing short hair, is certainly not necessarily identified with the masculine role. Thus, sex-role adoption refers to overt behavior characteristic of a given sex, while sex-role identification refers to a more basic, internalized process in which behavioral characteristics of one sex role or the other are incorporated.

General manifestations

Certain attitudes, preferences, social motives, fantasies, dreams, and feelings; gestures, gait, and other expressive movements and postures; general demeanor; communicative qualities such as spontaneous topic of conversation and casual comment, enunciation, word associations, and word choices; some patterns associated with paternal or maternal behavior; and various everyday habits and mannerisms typical of the masculine or feminine role constitute the general manifestations.

Standard developmental outcome or norm

The standard outcome is identification with, preference for, and adoption of the sex role that is consistent with a person's biological constitutional composition, i.e., the acquisition of a masculine role in males and a feminine role in females.

There has been an increasing amount of research and theoretical formulations in recent years concerning sex-role behavior.[8] In general, there is considerable agreement as to the importance of learning in the individual's attaining the role appropriate to his or her sex, i.e., there is a consensus that the individual learns to identify with a given sex role, to prefer one role or the other, and to adopt aspects of one role or the other. Emphasis on the learned aspect of sex or gender role acquisition has been given much support by recent research on hermaphroditism. As previously indicated, individuals of comparable anatomical and physiological deviation

---

[8] See, for example, A. Bandura and A. C. Huston, "Identification as a Process of Incidental Learning," *Journal of Abnormal and Social Psychology*, 63:2 (September 1961), pp. 311–18; U. Bronfenbrenner, "Freudian Theories of Identification and Their Derivatives," *Child Development*, 31:1 (March 1960), pp. 15–40; Brown, "Psychosexual Disturbances: Transvestism and Sex-Role Inversion," op. cit.; Hartley, op. cit.; J. Kagan, "The Concept of Identification," *Psychological Review*, 65 (1958), pp. 296–305; R. R. Sears, "Identification as a Form of Behavior Development," in *The Concept of Development*, ed. by D. B. Harris (Minneapolis: University of Minnesota Press, 1957), pp. 149–61; B. Sutton-Smith, J. M. Roberts, and B. G. Rosenberg, "Sibling Associations and Role Involvement," *Merrill-Palmer Quarterly*, 10:1 (January 1964), pp. 25–38; and R. F. Winch, *Identification and Its Familial Determinants* (Indianapolis: Bobbs-Merrill, 1962).

in composition have been reared successfully as either boys or girls. These studies show that chromosomal sex and gonadal sex can be overridden by learning experiences. That hormonal sex can also be overridden is demonstrated by female hermaphrodites with an androgenital syndrome, but who are raised and living as women. Before the recent advent of cortisone therapy to suppress adrenal androgens, these women were heavily virilized and totally lacking in female secondary sexual characteristics; they sometimes had a very enlarged clitoris, and sometimes a fused, empty scrotal sac. Nevertheless, their assigned sex as women generally dominated their hormonal sex. In reference to the singular importance of sex-role assignment and rearing, Money points out that it is possible for psychosexual differentiation in a person to be contradictory of chromosomal, gonadal, hormonal, or external genital and internal genital sex and to agree instead with assigned sex.[9] The crucial significance of learning in the acquisition of gender role is clearly indicated.

Workers concerned with hermaphroditism have suggested a parallel between the acquisition of sex or gender role in humans and imprinting in lower animals. Thus, there may be a critical period within which the gender role of an individual is established.[10] In a review of the factor of age in psychosexual development in children, Brown suggests that sex-role differentiation is a gradual process beginning between the first and second year of life and becoming definitely established by or during the fifth year.[11] On the basis of hermaphroditic cases of sex reassignment, Money concludes that the critical period for "gender imprinting" is between eighteen months and three years of age, beginning with the onset of mastery of language.[12] He considers the die to be well cast by the age of six with major realignment of gender role and sexual identity rare after that.

Nonstandard developmental outcome or deviation

The nonstandard outcome is the acquisition of a sex role or certain aspects of a sex role not consistent with a person's biological composition.[13] Several examples are discussed below.

---

[9] J. Money, "Developmental Differentiation of Femininity and Masculinity Compared," in *Man and Civilization: The Potential of Women*, ed. by S. M. Farber and R. H. L. Wilson (New York: McGraw-Hill), 1963, p. 56.

[10] See, for example, Brown, "Psychosexual Disturbances: Transvestism and Sex-Role Inversion"; D. G. Brown, "Homosexuality and Family Dynamics," *Bulletin of the Menninger Clinic*, 27:5 (September 1963), pp. 227–32; Hampson and Hampson, "Ontogenesis of Sexual Behavior in Man"; and Money, "Sex Hormones and Other Variables in Human Eroticism."

[11] D. G. Brown, "Sex-Role Development in a Changing Culture," *Psychological Bulletin*, 54 (1958), pp. 232–42.

[12] Money, "Sex Hormones and Other Variables in Human Eroticism."

[13] Actually, the hermaphrodite who has a consistent sex role is, by definition, nonstandard in that his role must be at variance with some aspect of his ambiguous biological composition.

1) *Transvestism* involves the desire for, act of, and emotional satisfactions connected with wearing the apparel of the opposite sex. Apart from their cross-sex dress, transvestites may otherwise establish a heterosexual adjustment. This points up the necessity of clearly distinguishing between transvestism and other concepts, such as homosexuality and sex-role inversion.[14] One factor often found in the life histories of transvestites is that during the first two or three years of life, the child intentionally or otherwise often wears and fondles clothes of the opposite sex and in some instances is praised for his appearance in the clothes of the opposite sex. In childhood some male transvestites have long hair that is curled as a girl's; in the background of still others is a mother who wanted a girl rather than a boy.

2) *Sex-role inversion* is the phenomenon in which a person of one biological sex learns to think, feel, and act like the opposite sex. This involves the acceptance and adoption of the sex role of the other sex. Although transvestism is a component of inversion, it is *not* unique to inverts. Transvestism will almost always be found in cases of inversion since desiring and wearing the clothes of the other sex is one of many aspects of adopting the role of that sex; however, the converse is not true—inversion is *not* necessarily found in transvestites. Thus, a transvestite may be atypical in his sex-role functioning *only* with respect to this lifelong but relatively isolated, compulsive behavioral pattern.

Various incongruous combinations of sex-role behavior may occur in a given person. For instance, a boy may dislike playing with girls, but show an interest in domestic activities, such as cooking, sewing, housekeeping, and using make-up, as well as a liking for mechanical toys, tools, and building materials.[15]

Instances in which a male child has a relatively positive attachment to the father, or at least a relationship which is free of basic rejection or hostility, and at the same time has a mother who allows, encourages, or forces him to wear feminine dress and to develop other feminine patterns are likely to result in some degree of confusion or duality in sex-role development. The person may show some uncertainty as to his sex role, or he may actually develop *two relatively dichotomous selves,* one of which is masculine and one feminine. An individual may describe himself as "ruggedly masculine and aggressive" when dressed in masculine clothes but "passive, gentle and submissive" when attired in feminine clothes. It is evident in such a case that two sex roles coexist in the same personality. A variation of this pattern is seen in the case of a person who reported that he often felt "like two people in one, male and female" and "never completely male

---

[14] D. G. Brown, "Inversion and Homosexuality," *American Journal of Orthopsychiatry,* 28 (1958), 424–29.

[15] Brown, "Psychosexual Disturbances: Transvestism and Sex-Role Inversion."

and never completely female."[16] This individual during his childhood showed a mixture of feminine interests—dolls, cooking, sewing—as well as masculine pursuits—mechanical tasks, tools, playing cowboys. As an adult he alternated between muscle-building exercises and efforts to be "more of a man" and wearing feminine clothing, using cosmetics, and trying to appear more like a woman. Still another person reported that when he was in his feminine phase he tried to approximate the ideal-image of women whom he admired when he was in his masculine role. He attempted to become the kind of woman that his masculine self found most attractive. While in his masculine role his whole personality would change, and he would become thoroughly masculine in interests, dress, and behavior.[17]

It is interesting to note that cases such as those described above bear some resemblance to instances of dual or multiple personality in that there is an alternation between different roles of sex, rather than between roles of "good" and "bad." Part of the time the person is masculine in appearance and behavior; at other times the same person is feminine. Instead of a Dr. Jekyll and Mr. Hyde or an Eve White and Eve Black, there is a "Mr." Doe and a "Miss" Doe. However, there is an important difference between individuals with dual sex roles and those with dual personalities. In contrast to cases of dual personality, in which one of the two selves is amnesic for the other, individuals who develop two sex roles are aware of the existence of both roles. Thus, when such a person is in the feminine role, he will dress, talk, and act like a woman; although he is quite aware of his other self in which he dresses, talks, and acts like a man.

In addition to transvestism, homosexuality should be differentiated from sex-role inversion. While homosexuality typically occurs in individuals who show sex-role inversion, there is considerable evidence that a number of other factors may predispose the individual to the development of homosexuality as well. The homosexual is an individual who desires and/or obtains predominant or exclusive sexual satisfaction with members of his own sex; the invert is one whose thoughts, perceptions, attitudes, fantasies, feelings, preferences, interests, and behavioral tendencies are typical of the opposite sex.[18]

With reference to the determinants of sex-role identification, it might be predicted that a male displaying gender role inversion would have a father who, during the individual's early childhood, had been physically absent most of the time, psychologically ineffective and socially distant,

---

16 B. Karpman, "Dream Life in a Case of Transvestism," *Journal of Nervous and Mental Disease,* 106 (1947), pp. 292–337.

17 C. V. Prince, "Homosexuality, transvestism and transsexualism," *American Journal of Psychotherapy,* 11 (1957), pp. 80–85.

18 D. G. Brown, "The Development of Sex-Role Inversion and Homosexuality," *Journal of Pediatrics,* 50:5 (May 1957), p. 614.

or chronically abusive and cruel to the boy and, in addition, a mother who is "idolized" by the boy, emotionally "smothers" him, or to whom the boy is excessively close and attached. For girls inversion would be expected to develop only in cases in which there is a serious disruption in the mother-daughter relationship and early abnormal attachment to the father that prevents the little girl from identifying with the mother or where the mother herself denies or despises her own femininity and thus exposes the daughter to a distorted feminine model. Another predisposing family pattern, which might function in isolation or in conjunction with those already mentioned, is one in which the parent or parents actually encourage and rear a child of one sex to feel, think, and behave like that of the other.

3) *Transsexualism* involves sex-role inversion and also the desire for surgical sexual transformation, such as the case of George (Christine) Jorgensen. As in most other psychosexual disturbances, transsexualism is primarily associated with men rather than women. For example, following the publicity concerning the "change of sex" case of Jorgensen in Denmark, the endocrinologist who supervised the changeover received three times as many letters from men as from women expressing a desire for medical change of sexual identity.[19] This differential might partially be explained by the fact that the particular operation given the publicity was one involving a change from male to female. Perhaps the apparently greater feasibility of surgical procedures involved in amputating the penis than in constructing male genitalia may also have been a factor. However, it is probable that the suggested predominance of transsexualism among men has more deeply rooted origins than the above explanations. Among the factors which predispose males more readily than females to sex-role inversion may be the fact that, since all infants are attached to the mother or mother-substitute in earliest life, it is the boy, not the girl, who must shift from an initial identification with the feminine model to masculine role identification with the father or father-substitute. In addition, because fathers in this culture are usually away from home much of the time, the girl typically has her model for identification, the mother, with her more often than the boy has his model, the father, with him.

GENITAL-SEX OBJECT PREFERENCE

Hypothesized primary determinants

Environmental conditioning and social learning experiences are hypothesized as the primary determinants for the third component of sexual development, genital-sex object preference.

---

[19] D. G. Brown, "Inversion and Homosexuality."

Basic terms

Genital-sex desire, drive, and gratification are the basic terms. The Freudian term *libido*, although defined variously during the many years of Freud's writing, always encompassed more than genital-sex desire, drive, and gratification.

Operational definitions

Genital-sex object preference is defined as the source of genital-sex arousal, the aim and direction of genital-sex drive, and the nature of the object and situation with which genital gratification or orgasm occur.

General manifestations

This component is manifested in genital sex arousal, excitement, and behavior either directly observable or covertly present at the level of fantasy, dreams, and imagination.

The male orgasm is a relatively simple and easily observable reaction. However, the orgasm in women has been less well understood until the recent highly significant research of Masters and Johnson.[20] These investigators furnish evidence that the muscular spasms of ejaculation in the male have their counterpart in the female. Photographic documentation indicates the tumescence of a cylindrical orgasmic platform immediately inside the vagina and extending along the vaginal barrel for about one-third of its length. The orgasmic platform and adjacent tissues outside the vaginal orifice throb and contract spasmodically during the time orgasm is reported. Meanwhile, the innermost end of the vagina has ballooned out and the cervix has somewhat retracted. The manifestations of orgasm are identical whether stimulation is masturbatory and clitoral or produced by artificial coitus with a hollow, clear-plastic object simulating the phallus.

Although the focus of this section is on genital sexual arousal, extremely intense sexual experience is possible independent of genitopelvic happenings. The paraplegic has no neural connections between the upper and lower parts of the nervous system. Nevertheless, some paraplegic patients describe vivid orgastic experiences in erotic dreams which simulate true

---

[20] W. H. Masters and V. C. Johnson, "The Physiology of the Vaginal Reproductive Function," *Western Journal of Surgery, Obstetrics and Gynecology,* 69 (1961), pp. 105–20; and W. H. Masters and V. C. Johnson, "The Sexual Response Cycle of the Human Female. III. The Clitoris: Anatomic and Clinical Considerations," *Western Journal of Surgery, Obstetrics and Gynecology,* 70 (1962), pp. 248–57. All of the major research and significant findings of Masters and Johnson will be published in a book now in press.

genital orgasm. These "orgastic" dreams, of course, lack erection or ejaculation, because no neural connections exist between the brain and the genital region.[21]

Standard developmental outcome or norm

The standard outcome is heterosexuality. More specifically, the prescribed outcome in our society is monogamous heterosexuality. Heterosexuality has been so taken for granted that until recently it was assumed to be completely biologically determined and any deviation therefrom, the result of some biological defect. The previously mentioned studies, showing that hermaphroditic children with the same anomaly grow up as masculine or feminine in agreement with the assigned sex and acquire the genital-sex object preference appropriate to that sex, make it evident that environmental conditioning and social learning experiences are of crucial importance. In addition, since the male hormone androgen apparently functions as the erotic hormone for women as well as men, an increase in the androgen level may very well increase the erotic drive of a woman yet not result in a shift of her sex object preference nor motivate her to take a masculine role in erotic activity. In other words, a heterosexual woman given androgen may become more strongly erotically motivated, but she does not become homosexual in her desires.

Those investigators who have studied hermaphroditism conclude that genital-sex object choice may be the result of appropriate imprinting at the critical period in the child's development. In this regard Money suggests that a person may engage in a homosexual act when past the critical period without becoming a chronic homosexual. Money reports that, in general, imprinted eroticism appears to be permanent and ineradicable.[22]

Nonstandard developmental outcome or deviation

The following are examples of deviations in the genital component:

1) *Autosexuality* (masturbation) is the genital stimulation and gratification of a person by himself. This sexual outlet is statistically so common, occurring in practically all males and the majority of females, it is considered nonstandard only when it is the exclusive or nearly exclusive erotic preference of an individual. It is also recognized that when masturbation occurs it is often in connection with fantasied heterosexual or homosexual situations.

---

[21] J. Money, "Phantom Orgasm in the Dreams of Paraplegic Men and Women," *Archives of General Psychiatry*, 3 (1960), 373–82.

[22] Money, "Sex Hormones and Other Variables in Human Eroticism."

2. *Homosexuality* refers to the phenomenon in which an individual predominantly or exclusively desires and/or obtains genital sexual stimulation and gratification with a person of the same biological sex.[23] In a previous section of this paper, sex-role or sexual inversion was differentiated from homosexuality. Almost invariably the individual with inverted gender identification desires sexual activity with a person of the same anatomic sex, and when this is the case can be regarded as homosexual. However, there are many homosexuals who are not inverted in their sex or gender role. Homosexuals have in common only their preference for sexual partners of the same biological sex. Often the inverted male homosexual corresponds to what has traditionally been called the passive male homosexual, who takes the role of the opposite sex in homosexual activity. The noninverted homosexual corresponds to the active male homosexual, the one taking the role appropriate to his own biological sex. Similarly, the inverted female homosexual often corresponds to what has been called the active female homosexual, the one taking the masculine role in homosexual activity; and the noninverted female homosexual, the passive female homosexual, often corresponds to the one taking the feminine role in homosexual activity. However, homosexuals sometimes "switch roles" in their sexual activity; the one who is the passive partner on one occasion acts as the active partner on the next occasion. It is very unlikely that they switch sex-role identification in the sense of their basic personality structure, showing role inversion one day and normal role behavior the next, unless there is involved also the dual sex-role phenomenon mentioned previously. Inversion, therefore, should refer to the individual's total personality structure. The invert may be described as a psychosomatic misfit with the physical characteristics of one sex, such as being anatomically male, but the personality characteristic of the other sex, being psychologically feminine.

One would predict that the etiology of homosexuality in cases which are inverted would be quite dissimilar from those which are not inverted. In a previous section the hypothesized determinants of inversion were conditioning experiences. Money considers imprinting an important part in homosexuality, but he does not distinguish between homosexuals who are or are not inverted. "Effectively imprinted at the critical period to respond to homosexual stimuli—a person becomes a chronic homosexual. Effective stimuli may be extremely specific and variable from person to person, which may account for the varieties of homosexual preference."[24] However, Money does not elaborate on the nature of the experiences oc-

---

[23] This concept of homosexuality becomes extremely blurred when dealing with the erotic life of a hermaphroditic individual since his biological sex is ambiguous.

[24] Money, "Sex Hormones and Other Variables in Human Eroticism." p. 1397.

curring between the age of eighteen months and three years—the critical period—which may lead to chronic homosexuality.

3) *Other deviations* include bisexuality, zooerasty, pederasty, exhibitionism, fetishism, sadism, and masochism, all of which involve genital desire, stimulation, and gratification that deviate from the normal heterosexual, interpersonal relationship.

6
Sexual behavior in middle life*

ERIC PFEIFFER, M.D.,
ADRIAAN VERWOERDT, M.D., and
GLENN C. DAVIS

We have previously reported data on sexual behavior in old age (1–5). In these studies, 254 subjects aged 60 to 94 were initially interviewed, and the survivors were interviewed repeatedly at two- to three-year intervals for at least ten years. Cross-sectional as well as longitudinal analyses were carried out.

To date the most important findings have been the following: 1) elderly men in the sample differed markedly from elderly women in reported sexual behavior; 2) the intensity, presence, or absence of sexual interest and activity among elderly women was primarily a reflection of the availability of a socially sanctioned, sexually capable partner; 3) with advancing age, patterns of declining sexual activity and interest were common, but patterns of stable, as well as of increasing, sexual activity also occurred; and 4) when both husband and wife were available for study, a high level of congruence between the reports of the two partners was observed, suggesting that sexual behavior was being reliably reported.

The past studies, however, not only answered some questions but also raised a number of new ones. What were the antecedents of sexual be-

* Reprinted from the *American Journal of Psychiatry*, Vol. 128, No. 10, pages 1262–67, 1972. Copyright 1972, American Psychiatric Association. Reprinted with permission of the authors and publisher.

havior in old age? Did male-female differences in reported sexual behavior exist in middle age as well? At what age was a decline in sexual function noted most commonly, and was this age the same for men and for women? Were there factors in middle age that account for the striking differences between men and women in regard to sexual behavior in old age? The present study was undertaken in an attempt to answer some of these questions.

Like the previous studies on old age, the present one is part of a larger, multidisciplinary, longitudinal project examining some of the determinants of adaptation to middle age. A more detailed description of the over-all project will be published shortly (6). Briefly summarized, however, the study will follow a panel of subjects aged 45 to 69 for a period of six years. Each subject will be studied at two-year intervals for one full day (eight hours) on an ambulatory basis at the Duke University Center for the Study of Aging and Human Development. The scheduled tests, examinations, procedures, and interviews include: demographic data; medical history; physical examination; vision and hearing tests; EKG, EEG, chest X rays, and routine laboratory tests; detailed social history; vigilance tests; and the Psychiatric Symptom Scale.

SUBJECTS

The subjects for this study, as well as for the large project, were 261 white men and 241 white women aged 45 to 69 at the time of selection of the subjects. The initial wave of examinations was carried out approximately one year after selection. Thus each subject had aged approximately one year, and the age range had increased to 46 to 71 years. The average age was 59 for both the men and the women. Our subjects were chosen randomly from the membership lists of the local medical group insurance plan. As such, the subjects were broadly representative of middle-aged persons from the middle and upper socioeconomic levels of the community (6). The sample was stratified into ten age-sex cohorts, as indicated in Table 1. The age of the subjects in this table, as well as throughout this study, is the age at the time of actual interview and examination.

TABLE 1. Age-sex cohorts

Age group	Men	Women
46–50	43	43
51–55	41	41
56–60	61	50
61–65	54	47
66–71	62	60
Total	261	241

Greater numbers of older subjects and of male subjects were included in deference to the higher expected death rates among these subjects over the succeeding six years. It was deemed desirable to still have approximately 40 subjects in each of the age-sex cohorts by the end of the study.

Of the 261 men, 257 were married (98 percent). Two were widowed (1 percent) and two had never married (1 percent). By contrast, 170 of the 241 women were married (71 percent). Forty-four were widowed (18 percent), 13 had never married (five percent), and 14 were separated or divorced (six percent).

METHOD

The data on sexual behavior were gathered as part of a self-administered medical history questionnaire. The questions were similar to those used in the earlier studies. However, this information had previously been gathered during a face-to-face structured interview. This method yielded only incomplete data due to embarrassment about the questions on the part of either the subjects or the interviewers. The data were especially sparse on the current sexual behavior of women who had never married or who were widowed, separated, or divorced. It was hoped that use of the more impersonal paper-and-pencil technique would decrease this embarrassment and thereby increase the yield of data. This was in fact so.

Data were generally far more complete on widowed, separated, and divorced women; however, the 13 women who had never married still provided virtually no data on either current or earlier sexual interest and/ or activity. Responses to questions on sexual behavior were given by 250–256 of the 261 men in the sample and by 219–229 of the 241 women.

The areas of sexual behavior covered in the study were as follows (possible choices are indicated in parentheses).

1. Enjoyment of sexual relations in younger years (none, mild, moderate, strong).
2. Enjoyment of sexual relations at the present time (none, mild, moderate, strong).
3. Sexual feelings in younger years (absent, weak, moderate, strong).
4. Sexual feelings at the present time (absent, weak, moderate, strong).
5. Frequency of sexual relations in younger years (never, once a month, once a week, two to three times a week, more than three times a week).
6. Frequency of sexual relations at the present time (never, once a month, once a week, two to three times a week, more than three times a week).
7. Awareness of any decline in sexual interest or activity (yes, no); if yes, at what age was it first noted (five-year age groupings).
8. If sexual relations have stopped, when were they stopped? (still con-

tinuing, less than a year ago, one to two years ago, two to five years ago, six to ten years ago, 11–20 years ago, more than 20 years ago).

9. Reason for stopping sexual relations (not stopped, death of spouse, illness of self, illness of spouse, self lost interest, spouse lost interest, self no longer able to perform sexually, spouse not able to perform sexually, separated or divorced from spouse).

All the results reported in this paper are cross-sectional only. Thus they do not indicate how *individuals* change over time. They only indicate how *groups* of persons of a given chronological age function in comparison with *groups* of persons of a different age. However, the study is so designed that longitudinal data will eventually become available. Longitudinal as well as cross-sequential analyses, as described by Schaie and Strother (7), can then be carried out.

RESULTS

A great deal of interest centers on the current level of sexual interest and activity of men and women at different ages. The basic data in regard to these two variables are presented in Tables 2 and 3.

Current level of sexual interest

Only six percent of the men in the sample said they no longer had any sexual feelings. On the other hand, strong current sexual interest was indicated by 12 percent. While there is, as table 2 shows, a decline in current interest in each of the age brackets from 45 to 65 years of age, there is actually a small rise in interest in sex in the oldest age category. This

TABLE 2. Current level of sexual interest, in percentages

Group	Number	None	Mild	Moderate	Strong
Men					
46–50	43	0	9	63	28
51–55	41	0	19	71	10
56–60	61	5	26	57	12
61–65	54	11	37	48	4
66–71	62	10	32	48	10
Total	261	6	26	56	12
Women					
46–50	43	7	23	61	9
51–55	41	20	24	51	5
56–60	48	31	25	44	0
61–65	43	51	37	12	0
66–71	54	50	26	22	2
Total	229	33	27	37	3

TABLE 3. Current frequency of sexual intercourse in percentages

Group	Number	None	Once a Month	Once a Week	2–3 Times a Week	More than 3 Times a Week
Men						
46–50	43	0	5	62	26	7
51–55	41	5	29	49	17	0
56–60	61	7	38	44	11	0
61–65	54	20	43	30	7	0
66–71	62	24	48	26	2	0
Total	261	12	34	41	12	1
Women						
46–50	43	14	26	39	21	0
51–55	41	20	41	32	5	2
56–60	48	42	27	25	4	2
61–65	44	61	29	5	5	0
66–71	55	73	16	11	0	0
Total	231	44	27	22	6	1

suggests that individuals who survive into their late 60s and early 70s may constitute an elite group, their weaker brothers having succumbed at an earlier age(2, 8). We have already pointed out previously that decline is not the only pattern in evidence when sexual behavior is followed longitudinally. Steady or even increased performance has been noted(2, 3).

Among the women, a similar pattern of declining interest was shown. However, the percentage of women indicating no sexual interest was higher than that among men in all the age categories; the percentage indicating strong sexual interest was lower than that among men in all the age categories. As with men, the percentage of women indicating moderate or strong sexual interest was higher in the oldest age category than in the next-to-the-oldest category, suggesting again that the oldest group constitutes a group of elite survivors.

Overall, however, the data clearly indicate a pattern of decline in sexual interest from the younger to the older age categories for both men and women ($p < .001$).

Current frequency of sexual intercourse

Only 12 percent of the men in the sample said they no longer had any sexual relations. None in the group aged 46–50 but 24 percent in the group aged 66–71 gave this reply, with a stepwise increase in this percentage with increasing age. In the same direction, the higher frequencies of sexual relations (two to three times a week and more than three times a week) were checked less and less frequently by the older age groups.

Interestingly, sexual activity showed no increase in the oldest age category compared with the next-to-the-oldest category (see Table 3). This widening interest-activity gap, as we have called it, has already been described previously for elderly men(2).

Among the women a similar pattern of declining sexual activity obtained. The frequency of sexual relations was lower for women than for men in all age categories. There was no increase in sexual activity in the oldest age group in comparison with the next-to-the-oldest age group.

For both men and women, the data showed a significant decline in sexual activity with increasing age ($p < .001$).

Awareness of decline in sexual interest and activity

A question concerning the subjects' own awareness of decline in sexual interest and activity was not included in the previous studies. However, this question suggested itself on the basis of the previous studies. It demands of the subjects a longitudinal assessment of their own sexual behavior. One of us (E.P.) has previously pointed out the superiority of such longitudinal assessments over single-point-in-time assessments(8). Thus a "change in health status" question was a more powerful predictor of longevity than a "current health status" question.

The results in regard to an awareness of decline are presented in Table 4. In the youngest age group, 51 percent of the men reported no decline in sexual activity or interest up to that time. But this percentage dwindled in stepwise fashion for each succeeding age group. However, even in the oldest group, 12 percent still averred no decline. The sharpest drop in the proportion reporting no awareness of decline occurred between the group aged 46–50 and that aged 51–55.

Among the women a somewhat lower proportion reported no decline in sexual interest or activity. In the youngest age group this proportion was 42 percent, declining again in a stepwise manner to 4 percent in the oldest age group. As with the men, the sharpest drop in the proportion re-

TABLE 4. Awareness of decline in sexual interest and activity

		Men		Women
Group	Number	No decline (percent)	Number	No decline (percent)
46–50	43	51	43	42
51–55	41	29	41	22
56–60	61	28	48	21
61–65	54	11	43	12
66–71	61	12	54	4
Total	260	25	229	19

porting no awareness of decline occurred between the 46–50 and the 51–55 groups.

Age of cessation of sexual intercourse

Only 36 men but 97 of the women in the sample indicated that they had stopped having sexual relations. They gave a wide scattering of responses as to when they had stopped. This ranged from "within the last year" (eight men and four women) to "more than 20 years ago" (one man and eight women). Not only did a larger proportion of women than of men indicate that they had stopped having sexual relations, but a greater proportion of the women than of the men who had stopped indicated that they had done so more than five years ago (62 out of 97 women, or 64 percent; 12 out of 36 men, or 33 percent). A partial explanation of why more women than men have stopped relations, and why they have done so at an earlier age, becomes apparent when the reasons for stopping are examined for men and women respectively.

Reasons for stopping sexual intercourse

Thirty-five men and 97 women gave reasons why they had ceased to have sexual relations. The results are shown in Table 5. These reasons can be grouped according to whether the subject attributes responsibility for cessation to himself (herself) or to his (her) spouse. These groupings are presented in Table 6. As can be seen, women overwhelmingly attributed responsibility for stopping to their husbands, while men generally attributed the responsibility to themselves ($p < .001$). This study thus confirms our earlier finding that in a marriage it is generally the man who determines whether sexual relations continue or cease(1). While "death of

TABLE 5. Reasons for cessation of sexual relations

	Men		Women	
Reason	Number	Percent	Number	Percent
Death of spouse	0	—	35	36
Separation or divorce from spouse	0	—	12	12
Illness of spouse	5	14	19	20
Loss of interest by spouse	3	9	4	4
Spouse unable to perform sexually	2	6	17	18
Illness of self	6	17	2	2
Loss of interest by self	5	14	4	4
Self unable to perform sexually	14	40	4	4
Total	35		97	

TABLE 6. Responsibility for cessation of sexual relations

	Men		Women	
Responsibility	Number	Percent	Number	Percent
All reasons included				
Attributed to spouse	10	29	87	90
Attributed to self	25	71	10	10
Total	35		97	
Loss of spouse excluded				
Attributed to spouse	10	29	40	80
Attributed to self	25	71	10	20
Total	35		50	

spouse" accounts for the largest number of women who attribute responsibility for cessation to their spouse (35 out of 97), the general finding that men blame themselves and women blame their husbands still holds up even after "death of spouse" and "separation from spouse" are removed from the analysis (p < .001).

SUMMARY

We have previously reported data on sexual behavior in old age. These findings made it clear that the aging processes were not confined to persons beyond age 65; instead many of the changes observed in old age had their antecedents in middle age. The present study was undertaken to examine some of these antecedents.

Data on sexual behavior were gathered on 261 white men and 241 white women aged 45 to 69. The subjects were chosen randomly from the membership lists of the local medical group insurance plan. They were thus broadly representative of the middle and upper socioeconomic strata of the community.

Dramatic differences between men and women of like ages were observed in regard to virtually all indicators of sexual behavior, with the men generally reporting greater interest and activity than the women. While there was an overall pattern of decline in interest and activity with advancing age, it was also clear that sex still continued to play an important role in the lives of the vast majority of the subjects studied. Only six percent of the men and 33 percent of the women said they were no longer interested in sex. Only 12 percent of the men and 44 percent of the women said they no longer had sexual relations. Interestingly, the oldest age group indicated higher levels of sexual involvement than did the next-to-the-oldest age group. This suggests that this oldest group actually constituted a group of elite survivors from whose midst less highly advantaged individuals had already been removed.

By age 50, some 49 percent of the men and 58 percent of the women admitted they had noted some decline in their sexual interest and activity. By age 70, 88 percent of the men and 96 percent of the women admitted an awareness of such a decline. The sharpest increase in the percentage of those admitting awareness of a decline occurred between the 45–50 group and the 51–55 group.

Some 14 percent of the men and 40 percent of the women indicated that they had stopped having sexual relations and offered reasons for having done so. The present study confirmed our previous finding that women overwhelmingly attributed responsibility for cessation of sexual relations to their husbands, while men generally hold themselves responsible for cessation.

REFERENCES

1. PFEIFFER, E., VERWOERDT, A., WANG, H. S. "Sexual behavior in aged men and women, I: observations on 254 community volunteers." *Arch. Gen. Psychiat.* 19:753–58, 1968.

2. PFEIFFER, E., VERWOERDT, A., WANG, H. S. "The natural history of sexual behavior in a biologically advantaged group of aged individuals." *J. Geront.* 24:193–98, 1969.

3. VERWOERDT, A., PFEIFFER, E., WANG, H. S. "Sexual behavior in senescence— changes in sexual activity and interest of aging men and women." *J. Geriat. Psychiat.* 2:163–80, 1969.

4. VERWOERDT, A., PFEIFFER, E., WANG, H. S. "Sexual behavior in senescence." *Geriatrics* 24:137–54, 1969.

5. PFEIFFER, E. "Sexual behavior in old age," in *Behavior and Adaptation in Late Life*, edited by Busse, E. W., Pfeiffer, E. Boston, Little, Brown and Co., 1969, pp. 151–62.

6. PFEIFFER, E., DAVIS, G. C. "The use of leisure time in middle life." *The Gerontologist* 11:187–95, 1971.

7. SCHAIE, K. W., STROTHER, C. R. "A cross-sequential study of age changes in cognitive behavior." *Psychol. Bull.* 70:671–80, 1968.

8. PFEIFFER, E. "Survival in old age: physical, psychological and social correlates of longevity. *J. Amer. Geriat. Soc.* 18:273–85, 1970.

DISCUSSION

Stanley R. Dean, M.D. (Gainesville, Fla.)—The authors are to be congratulated upon this latest in a series of papers first published in 1968. Since that time they have played a leading role in directing attention to the important problem of sexual behavior in advancing years. Most of their findings are generally accepted and need no special comment from me.

However, one point of departure is their rather surprising conclusion that aging women exhibit a greater sexual decline than their male counterparts. That, of course, is subject to argument and it seems to me their excellent paper would have benefited by a more detailed discussion of that disparity in the literature. Especially glaring are omissions of such acknowledged investigators as Kinsey and Masters and Johnson.

For example, Kinsey and his team stated, "It must be emphasized that declines in the incidence and frequency of marital coitus . . . do not provide any evidence that the female ages in her sexual capacity . . . It is [the male's] aging (and loss of capacity) rather than the female's loss of interest or capacity which is reflected in her decline"(1).

Masters and Johnson, in their book *Human Sexual Response*, devoted an entire chapter of 24 pages to "The Aging Female." They concluded, "A significant increase in sexual activity marks the sex drive of . . . middle-aged women. Frequently this is the time for casting about for new sexual partners or for the development of [sexual] variations. . . . There is no time limit drawn by the advancing years to female sexuality."(2).

It is undoubtedly true, as Pfeiffer and his coworkers say, that "frequency of sexual relations was lower for women than for men in all age categories" and "women overwhelmingly attribute responsibility for cessation [of sexual relations] to their husbands, while men generally hold themselves responsible for cessation." But this so-called decline in women is one of circumstance, not potential. It is extrinsic rather than intrinsic, and hence subject to prophylaxis and treatment.

Women, because of their passive role, lack men's opportunity and aggressiveness to pursue their desires. So they resign themselves to denial and lead lives of quiet desperation, though often inwardly rebelling at their frustration.

It is an irony of fate and an anatomico-physiological paradox that a male-dominated society has propagated the custom of a man's marrying a woman younger than himself. Many a woman, after reaching the menopause and being freed of the fear of pregnancy, is more desirous of sex than ever before, but it is precisely at such a propitious time that her husband, who is five or ten years older, may begin to show impotence. Many think there would be much less sexual frustration in later years—and perhaps fewer widows—if the chronological trend were reversed so that women marry younger men to begin with.

A few years ago I interviewed several of a large group of elderly couples who had made headlines by living together without benefit of clergy (3). They had resorted to that expedient because of a quirk in the law that would deprive a widow of her Social Security benefits if she remarried. To my surprise I found that the women were fully as resourceful as the men in setting up those clandestine arrangements. I also found, contrary to expectations, that such couples were relatively stable emotionally and were able to rationalize their guilt sufficiently to maintain excellent ego integrity.

Finally, suggestions for further studies of sexual behavior in advancing years might well include such topics as: 1) comparison of mental status between the sexually fulfilled and unfulfilled, 2) solitary sexual practices, and 3) stimulus-seeking behavior with advancing years.

REFERENCES

1. KINSEY, A. C., POMEROY, W. B., MARTIN, C. E. *Sexual Behavior in the Human Female.* Philadelphia, W. B. Saunders Co., 1953, pp. 353–54.

2. MASTERS, W. H., JOHNSON, V. E. *Human Sexual Response.* Boston, Little, Brown and Co., 1966, pp. 223–47.

3. DEAN, S. R. "Sin and Social Security." *Psychiatric Opinion* 3:40–3, 1966.

7
The "sexless older years"— A socially harmful stereotype*

ISADORE RUBIN

It has been suggested that our culture has programmed marriage only until the child-raising period has been completed.[1] If this is true of marital roles in general, it is especially true of sexual roles in the later years. Society has not given genuine recognition to the validity of sexual activity after the child-bearing years, creating a dangerous stereotype about the "sexless older years" and defining as deviant behavior sex interest and activity which may continue vigorously into these older years. Thus, for example, the opprobrious term "lecher" is never coupled with any age group but the old; the young are "lusty" or "virile."

A SELF-FULFILLING PROPHECY

This stereotype has until recently placed its unchallenged stamp upon our culture. In the late 1950s, undergraduates at Brandeis University were asked to take a test to assess their attitudes toward old people.[2] Those taking the test were requested to complete this sentence: "Sex for most old

---

* Reprinted from *The Annals of the American Academy of Politcial and Social Science* (March 1968), pp. 87–95, with the permission of the American Academy of Political and Social Science.

[1] E. Cumming and W. E. Henry, *Growing Old* (New York: Basic Books, 1961), p. 155.

[2] P. Golde and N. Kogan, "A Sentence Completion Procedure for Assessing Attitudes Toward Old People," *Journal of Gerontology*, Vol. 14 (July 1959), pp. 355–63.

people. . . ." Their answers were quite revealing. Almost all of these young men and women, ranging in age from 17 to 23, considered sex for most old people to be "negligible," "unimportant," or "past." Since sex behavior is not only a function of one's individual attitudes and interactions with a partner, but also a reflection of cultural expectations, the widespread belief about the older person being sexless becomes for many a "self-fulfilling prophecy." Our society stands indicted, says psychiatrist Karl M. Bowman, of grave neglect of the emotional needs of aging persons:

Men and women often refrain from continuing their sexual relations or from seeking remarriage after loss of a spouse, because even they themselves have come to regard sex as a little ridiculous, so much have our social attitudes equated sex with youth. They feel uncertain about their capacities and very self-conscious about their power to please. They shrink from having their pride hurt. They feel lonely, isolated, deprived, unwanted, insecure. Thoughts of euthanasia and suicide bother them. To prevent these feelings, they need to have as active a sex life as possible and to enjoy it without fear.[3]

Most of our attitudes toward sex today still constitute—despite the great changes that have taken place in the openness with which sex is treated publicly—what a famous British jurist has called "a legacy of the ascetic ideal, persisting in the modern world after the ideal itself has deceased."[4] Obviously, the ascetic attitude—essentially a philosophy of sex-denial—would have far-reaching effects upon our attitude toward the sexual activity of those persons in our society who have passed the reproductive years. Even so scientific a writer as Robert S. de Ropp, in his usually excellent *Man against Aging*, betrays the unfortunate effects of our ascetic tradition when he says:

For sexual activity, enjoyable as it may seem in itself, still has as its natural aim the propagation of the species, and this activity belongs to the second not the third act of life's drama.[5]

In addition to our tradition of asceticism, there are many other factors which undoubtedly operate to keep alive a strong resistance to the acceptance of sexuality in older people. These include our general tradition of equating sex, love, and romance solely with youth; the psychological difficulty which children have of accepting the fact of parental intercourse; the tendency to think of aging as a disease rather than a normal process; the focusing of studies upon hospitalized or institutionalized older people rather than upon a more typical sample of persons less beset by health,

---

[3] K. M. Bowman, "The Sex Life of the Aging Individual," in M. F. DeMartino (ed.), *Sexual Behavior and Personality Characteristics* (New York: Citadel, 1963), pp. 372–75.

[4] G. Williams, *The Sanctity of Life and the Criminal Law* (New York: Alfred A. Knopf, 1957), p. 51.

[5] R. S. de Ropp, *Man against Aging* (New York: Grove Press, 1962), p. 252.

emotional, or economic problems; and the unfortunate fact that—by and large—physicians have shared the ignorance and prejudices equally with the rest of society.[6]

It is significant, however, that centuries of derogation and taboo have not been successful in masking completely the basic reality that sex interest and activity do not disappear in the older years. Elaine Cumming and William E. Henry point out that our jokes at the expense of older people have revealed considerable ambivalence in the view that all old people are asexual.[7] The contradictory attitude which people possess about sexuality in the later years is also well illustrated by the history of the famous poem "John Anderson, My Jo," written by Robert Burns almost two centuries ago. In the version known today, the poem is a sentimental tribute to an old couple's calm and resigned old age. The original folk version— too bawdy to find its way into textbooks—was an old wife's grievance about her husband's waning sex interest and ability which makes very clear that she has no intention of tottering down life's hill in a passionless and sexless old age.[8] It is also interesting to note that sexuality in older women was an important part of one of Aristophanes' comedies. In his play *Ecclesiazusae* ("Women in Parliament"), Aristophanes described how the women seized power and established a social utopia.[9] One of their first acts was to place sexual relations on a new basis in order to assure all of them ample satisfaction at all times. They decreed that, if any young man was attracted to a girl, he could not possess her until he had satisfied an old woman first. The old women were authorized to seize any youth who refused and to insist upon their sexual rights also.

THE HARMFUL INFLUENCE OF THE MYTH

A British expert in the study of aging has suggested that the myth of sexlessness in the older years does have some social utility for some older women in our society who may no longer have access to a sexual partner.[10] However, the widespread denial of sexuality in older persons has a harmful influence which goes far beyond its effect upon an individual's sexual life.[11] It makes difficult, and sometimes impossible, correct diagnoses of medical and psychological problems, complicates and distorts interpersonal relations in marriage, disrupts relationships between children and parents thinking of remarriage, perverts the administration of justice to

---

6 H. I. Lief, "Sex Education of Medical Students and Doctors," *Pacific Medicine and Surgery*, Vol. 73 (February 1965), pp. 52–58.

7 Cumming and Henry, *Growing Old*, footnote, p. 21.

8 R. Burns, *The Merry Muses of Caledonia*, ed. J. Barke and S. G. Smith (New York: Putnam, 1964), pp. 147–48.

9 H. Einbinder, *The Myth of the Brittanica* (New York: Grove Press, 1964), p. 94.

10 A. Comfort, Review of *Sexual Life after Sixty*, by Isadore Rubin, *British Medical Journal*, II, March 25, 1967, p. 750.

11 Isadore Rubin, *Sexual Life after Sixty* (New York: Basic Books, 1965), chap. i.

older persons accused of sex offenses, and weakens the whole self-image of the older man or woman.

A corollary of the failure to accept sexuality as a normal aspect of aging has been the tendency to exaggerate the prevalence of psychological deviation in the sexual behavior of older men and to see in most old men potential molesters of young children. Seen through the lenses of prejudice, innocent displays of affection have often loomed ominously as overtures to lascivious fondling or molestation. It is common, too, to think of the exhibitionist as being, typically, a deviation of old age.

Actually, the facts indicate the falsity of both of these stereotypes. As research by Johann W. Mohr and his associates at the Forensic Clinic of the Toronto Psychiatric Hospital showed, "contrary to common assumption the old age group is the relatively smallest one" involved in child-molesting.[12] The major age groups from whose ranks child-molesters come are adolescence, the middle to late thirties, and the late fifties. The peak of acting out of exhibitionism occurs in the mid-twenties; and, in its true form, exhibitionism is rarely seen after the age of forty.

In relatively simple and static societies, everyone knows pretty much where he stands at each stage of life, particularly the older members of the group. "But in complex and fluid social systems," notes Leo W. Simmons, "with rapid change and recurrent confusion over status and role, no one's position is so well fixed—least of all that of the aging."[13] For many aging persons, there is a crisis of identity in the very sensing of themselves as old, particularly in a culture which places so great a premium upon youth. David P. Ausubel notes that, just as in adolescence, the tradition to aging is a period where the individual is in the marginal position of having lost an established and accustomed status without having acquired a new one and hence is a period productive of considerable stress.[14] Under such conditions of role confusion, aging persons tend to adopt the stereotype which society has molded for them, in sex behavior as in other forms of behavior. But they do so only at a very high psychic cost.

For many older people, continued sexual relations are important not so much for the pleasurable release from sexual tension as for the highly important source of psychological reinforcement which they may provide. Lawrence K. Frank has said:

Sex relations can provide a much needed and highly effective resource in the later years of life when so often men face the loss of their customary prestige and self-confidence and begin to feel old, sometimes long before they have begun

---

12 J. W. Mohr, R. E. Turner, and M. B. Jerry, *Pedophilia and Exhibitionism* (Toronto: University of Toronto Press, 1964).

13 L. W. Simmons, "Social Participation of the Aged in Different Cultures," in M. B. Sussman (ed.), *Sourcebook in Marriage and the Family* (2d ed.; Boston: Houghton Mifflin, 1963).

14 D. P. Ausubel, *Theory and Problems of Adolescent Development* (New York: Grune and Stratton, 1954), pp. 53 ff.

to age significantly. The premature cessation of sexual functioning may accelerate physiological and psychological aging since disuse of any function usually leads to concomitant changes in other capacities. After menopause, women may find that continuation of sexual relations provides a much needed psychological reinforcement, a feeling of being needed and of being capable of receiving love and affection and renewing the intimacy they earlier found desirable and reassuring.[15]

THE GROWING BODY OF RESEARCH DATA

Gathering data about the sexual behavior and attitudes of the aging has not been an easy task. To the generalized taboos about sex research have been added the special resistance and taboos that center around sexuality in older persons. For example, when the New England Age Center decided to administer an inventory to its members, they included only nine questions about sex among the 103 items.[16] The nine questions were made deliberately vague, were confined largely to past sexual activities, and were given only to married members. Leaders of the Center felt that if they had asked more direct questions or put them to their unmarried members, these people would not have returned to the Center. In California, a study of the attitudes of a sample of persons over sixty years old in San Francisco during the early 1960s included just one general open-ended question about sexual attitudes, apparently because of the resistance which many of the researchers had about questioning subjects in the area of sex.[17] Psychiatrists reporting on this research before the Gerontological Society noted that the people involved in research in gerontology are being hamstrung by their own attitudes toward sex with regard to the elderly in much the same way in which the rest of society is hamstrung with regard to their attitudes toward the elderly in such matters as jobs, roles, and those things which go into determining where a person fits into the social structure.

Fortunately, although no sample has yet been studied that was sufficiently broad or typical to present us with a body of norms, a sufficient amount of data now exists which leaves no doubt of the reality of sex interests and needs in the latter years. While it is true that there are many men and women who look forward to the ending of sexual relations, particularly those to whom sex has always been a distasteful chore or those

---

[15] L. K. Frank, *The Conduct of Sex* (New York: Morrow, 1961), pp. 177–78. [Reprinted by permission of the publisher.]

[16] E. B. Armstrong, "The Possibility of Sexual Happiness in Old Age," in H. G. Beigel (ed.), *Advances in Sex Research* (New York: Hoeber-Harper, 1963), pp. 131–37.

[17] E. H. Feigenbaum, M. J. Lowenthal and M. L. Trier, "Sexual Attitudes in the Elderly." Unpublished paper given before the Gerontological Society, New York, November 1966.

who "unconsciously welcome the excuse of advancing years to abandon a function that has frightened them since childhood,"[18] sexual activity, interest, and desire are not the exception for couples in their later years. Though the capacity for sexual response does slow down gradually, along with all the other physical capacities, it is usually not until actual senility that there is a marked loss of sexual capacity.

With the research conducted by William H. Masters and Virginia E. Johnson, who observed the anatomy and physiology of sexual response in the laboratory, confirmation has now been obtained that sexual capacity can continue into advanced old age.[19] Among the subjects whose orgasmic cycles were studied by these two investigators were 61 menopausal and postmenopausal women (ranging from 40 to 78) and 39 older men (ranging from 51 to 89). Among the women, Masters and Johnson found that the intensity of physiologic reaction and the rapidity of response to sexual stimulation were both reduced with advancing years. But they emphasized that they found "significant sexual capacity and effective sexual performance" in these older women, concluding:

The aging human female is fully capable of sexual performance at orgasmic response levels, particularly if she is exposed to regularity of effective sexual stimulation. . . . There seem to be no physiologic reasons why the frequency of sexual expression found satisfactory for the younger woman should not be carried over into the postmenopausal years. . . . In short, there is no time limit drawn by the advancing years to female sexuality.

When it came to males, Masters and Johnson found that there was no question but that sexual responsiveness weakens as the male ages, particularly after the age of sixty. They added, however:

There is every reason to believe that maintained regularity of sexual expression coupled with adequate physical well-being and healthy mental orientation to the aging process will combine to provide a sexually stimulative climate within a marriage. This climate will, in turn, improve sexual tension and provide a capacity for sexual performance that frequently may extend to and beyond the 80-year age level.

These general findings have been supported by various types of studies which have been made over the course of the years. These studies include the investigation by Raymond Pearl in 1925 into the frequency of marital intercourse of men who had undergone prostatic surgery, all over the age of 55;[20] Robert L. Dickinson and Lura E. Beam's studies of marriages and

---

18 W. R. Stokes, *Married Love in Today's World* (New York: Citadel, 1962), p. 100.

19 W. H. Masters and V. E. Johnson, *Human Sexual Response* (Boston: Little, Brown, 1966), sec. on "Geriatric Sexual Response," pp. 223–70. [Quotations reprinted by permission.]

20 R. Pearl, *The Biology of Population Growth* (New York: Alfred A. Knopf, 1925), pp. 178–207.

of single women, including a number of older single women and widows;[21] the Kinsey studies of the male and the female;[22] older men studied at out-patient clinics by urologists at the University of California School of Medicine at San Francisco;[23] extended study by Duke University psychiatrists of Negroes and whites living in the Piedmont area of North Carolina;[24] Joseph T. Freeman's study of older men in Philadelphia;[25] a study of patients attached to a geriatric clinic in New York;[26] a survey of veterans applying for pensions;[27] a questionnaire survey by *Sexology* magazine of men over 65 who were listed in *Who's Who in America;*[28] and a study of sex attitudes in the elderly at the Langley Porter Neuropsychiatric Institute in San Francisco.[29]

NO AUTOMATIC CUTOFF DATE

All of these studies indicate the continuation of sex needs, interests, and abilities into the later years despite the gradual weakening that may take place. The Kinsey group, quite contrary to general conceptions of the aging process in sex, found that the rate at which males slow up sexually in the last decades of life does not exceed the rate at which they have been slowing up and dropping out of sexual activity in the previous age groups.[30] For most males, they found no point at which old age suddenly enters the picture. As far as females were concerned, the Kinsey investigators—like Masters and Johnson later—found little evidence of any aging in their capacities for sexual response.[31] "Over the years," they reported, "most fe-

---

[21] R. L. Dickinson and L. E. Beam, *A Thousand Marriages* (Baltimore: Williams & Wilkins, 1931), pp. 278–79, 446; and R. L. Dickinson and L. E. Beam, *The Single Woman* (Baltimore: Williams & Wilkins, 1934), p. 445.

[22] A. C. Kinsey, W. B. Pomeroy, and C. E. Martin, *Sexual Behavior in the Human Male* (Philadelphia: W. B. Saunders, 1948); and A. C. Kinsey, W. B. Pomeroy, C. E. Martin, and P. H. Gebhard, *Sexual Behavior in the Human Female* (Philadelphia: W. B. Saunders, 1953).

[23] A. L. Finkle et al., "Sexual Function in Aging Males: Frequency of Coitus Among Clinic Patients," *Journal of the American Medical Association,* Vol. 170, July 18, 1959, pp. 1391–93.

[24] G. Newman and C. R. Nichols, "Sexual Activities and Attitudes in Older Persons," *Journal of the American Medical Association,* Vol. 173, May 7, 1960, pp. 33–5.

[25] J. T. Freeman, "Sexual Capacities in the Aging Male," *Geriatrics,* Vol. 16 (January 1961), pp. 37–43.

[26] L. Friedfeld, "Geriatrics, Medicine, and Rehabilitation," *Journal of the American Medical Association,* Vol. 175, February 18, 1961, pp. 595–98; and L. Friedfeld et al., "A Geriatric Clinic in a General Hospital," *Journal of the American Geriatrics Society,* Vol. 7 (October 1959), pp. 769–81.

[27] L. M. Bowers, R. R. Cross, Jr., and F. A. Lloyd, "Sexual Function and Urologic Disease in the Elderly Male," *Journal of the American Geriatrics Society,* Vol. 11 (July 1963), pp. 647–52.

[28] I. Rubin, "Sex over Sixty-five," in H. G. Beigel (ed.), *Advances in Sex Research* (New York: Hoeber-Harper, 1963), pp. 138–42.

[29] Feigenbaum et al., "Sexual Attitudes in the Elderly."

[30] Kinsey et al., *Sexual Behavior in the Human Male,* pp. 235–57.

[31] Kinsey et al., *Sexual Behavior in the Human Female,* pp. 353–54.

males become less inhibited and develop an interest in sexual relations which they then maintain until they are in their fifties or even sixties." In contrast to the average wife, the responses of the husband dropped with age. Thus, many of the younger females reported that they did not desire intercourse as often as their husbands. In the later years of marriage, however, many of the wives expressed the desire for coitus more often than their husbands were then desiring it.

The Duke University survey—reported by Gustave Newman and Claude R. Nichols—found that only those persons who were seventy-five or older showed a significantly lower level of sexual activity.[32] This study found that Negro subjects were sexually more active than white subjects; men were more active than women; and persons lower in the social and economic scale were more active than those in the upper-income group. A possible explanation of the greater activity reported by males lies in the fact that men and women of the same age were reporting on different age groups. The wives, on the average, would be reporting on sex activity with a husband who was perhaps four years older.

Despite the fact that masturbation has been usually considered an activity that ends with maturity, for many older persons, this practice apparently continues to serve as a satisfactory form of release from sexual tensions when a partner is, for one reason or another, not available.[33]

Several of the studies suggest a correlation between early sex activity and a continuation into the late years. The Kinsey group found that, at age fifty, all of the males who had been sexually active in early adolescence were still sexually active, with a frequency about 20 percent higher than the frequency of the later-maturing males.[34] They report:

Nearly forty years maximum activity have not yet worn them out physically, physiologically, or psychologically. On the other hand, some of the males (not many) who were late adolescent and who have had five years less of sexual activity, are beginning to drop completely out of the picture; and the rates of this group are definitely lower in these older age periods.

They conclude:

The ready assumption which is made in some of the medical literature that impotence is the product of sexual excess, is not justified by such data as are now available.

Freeman[35] found that the sex urge of persons in advanced years correlated strongly with their comparative sex urge when young, and a similar finding was reported by the Duke University survey.[36]

---

32 Newman and Nichols, "Sexual Activities and Attitudes in Older Persons."
33 Rubin, "Sex over Sixty-five"; and Dickinson and Beam, A Thousand Marriages.
34 Kinsey et al., Sexual Behavior in the Human Male, pp. 319–25.
35 Freeman, op. cit.
36 Newman and Nichols, "Sexual Activities and Attitudes in Older Persons."

Masters and Johnson report the same finding, with additional emphasis upon regularity of sexual expression as the essential factor in maintaining sexual capacity and effective performance for both males and females:[37] When the male is stimulated to high sexual output during his formative years and a similar tenor of activity is established for the 31–40-year range, his middle-aged and involutional years usually are marked by constantly recurring physiologic evidence of maintained sexuality. Certainly it is true for the male geriatric sample that those men currently interested in relatively high levels of sexual expression report similar activity levels from their formative years. It does not appear to matter what manner of sexual expression has been employed, as long as high levels of activity were maintained.

FACTORS RESPONSIBLE FOR DECLINING SEX ACTIVITY

On the basis of present data, it is not possible to sort out the emotional element from the purely physiologic factors in the decline in sexual activity of the older male. Some animal experiments have shown that changes in the external environment can result in changes in sexual drive. When aging rats had the opportunity for sex activity with a number of partners, for example, the number of copulations increased considerably.[38] However, as soon as male rats reached a certain age, they failed to respond to females.[39]

Many men also find that, with a new partner, a new stimulus is given to their virility.[40] However, often these men return to their old level within comparatively short periods of time.[41] Present data lead us to conclude, with the Kinsey investigators:

The decline in sexual activity of the older male is partly, and perhaps primarily, the result of a general decline in physiologic capacity. It is undoubtedly affected also by psychologic fatigue, a loss of interest in repetition of the same sort of experience, an exhaustion of the possibilities for exploring new techniques, new types of contacts, new situations.[42]

Masters and Johnson, on the basis of their clinical work with older males, describe six general groups of factors which they believe to be responsible for much of the loss of sexual responsiveness in the later years:

---

[37] Masters and Johnson, *Human Sexual Response.*

[38] J. Botwinick, "Drives, Expectancies, and Emotions," in J. E. Birren (ed.), *Handbook of Aging and the Individual* (Chicago: University of Chicago Press, 1959), pp. 739–68.

[39] L. F. Jakubczak, Report to the American Psychological Association, August 31, 1962.

[40] J. Bernard, *Remarriage* (New York: Dryden, 1956), p. 188.

[41] Kinsey et al., *Sexual Behavior in the Human Male*, pp. 227–29; and A. W. Spence, "Sexual Adjustment at the Climacteric," *Practitioner*, Vol. 172 (April 1954), pp. 427–30.

[42] Kinsey et al., *Sexual Behavior in the Human Male*, pp. 226–35.

(1) monotony of a repetitious sexual relationship (usually translated into boredom with the partner); (2) preoccupation with career or economic pursuits; (3) mental or physical fatigue; (4) overindulgence in food or drink; (5) physical and mental infirmities of either the individual or his spouse; and (6) fear of performance associated with or resulting from any of the former categories.

The most constant factor in the loss of an aging male's interest is the problem of monotony, described by the Kinsey group as "psychologic fatigue." According to Masters and Johnson, many factors may produce this: failure of the sexual relationship to develop beyond a certain stage; overfamiliarity; lack of sexual interest on the female's part; aging and loss of personal attractiveness of the female.

A major deterrent for many men is preoccupation with the outside world and their careers. Overindulgence in food and drink, particularly the latter, takes a high toll. According to Masters and Johnson, secondary impotence developing in the late forties or early fifties has a higher incidence of direct association with excessive alcohol consumption than with any other single factor.

As each partner ages, the onset of physical or mental infirmities is an ever-increasing factor in reducing sexual capacities. The harmful effect of this is sometimes multiplied by the negative or discouraging attitude of the physician. Once a failure in performance has occurred because of any of the factors, the fear of failure becomes an additional factor in bringing about withdrawal from sexual activity. "Once impotent under any circumstances," remark Masters and Johnson, "many males withdraw voluntarily from any coital activity rather than face the ego-shattering experience of repeated episodes of sexual inadequacy."

The very scanty data concerning the sexual attitudes of older persons suggest a more positive attitude toward sex among men than among women, with women being more "culture-bound" and still showing strong evidences of the effects of the Victorian age in which they acquired their attitudes toward sex.[43] A study of dreams of residents of a home for the aged and infirm, on the other hand, indicates a contrasting difference in emotional tone of the sexual content of the dreams of men and women: "Whereas in men sexual dreams revealed anxiety, failure, and lack of mastery, in women they usually depicted passive, pleasurable gratification of dependent needs."[44]

THE UNMARRIED HAVE SEX NEEDS TOO

It is not only the married who have sexual needs. Aging widows, widowers, and single persons, who make up an increasingly large segment of our

---

43 Feigenbaum et al., op. cit.
44 M. Barad, K. Z. Altshuler, and A. I. Goldfarb, "A Survey of Dreams in Aged Persons," *Archives of General Psychiatry*, Vol. 4 (April 1961), pp. 419–24.

population, face even greater problems in respect to sex than do the married. In the survey by Newman and Nichols, only seven of the 101 single, divorced, or widowed subjects reported any sexual activity with partners.[45] Apparently, the strength of the sexual drive of most elderly persons is usually not great enough to cause them to seek a sexual partner outside of marriage in the face of social disapproval and the difficulties of such an endeavor. Interestingly, however, thousands of older couples were reportedly living "in sin—or what they think is sin" because marriage would mean loss of social security payments.[46]

Dickinson and Beam reported that in their study of widows ranging from sixty to eighty years of age there was evidence of masturbation.[47] They reported that when these women underwent pelvic examinations they showed such marked sexual reactions that they found that "it is desirable to relieve the patient's embarrassment by hurting her, lest she have orgasm." Since many older women are quite troubled by their practice of masturbation, marriage counselors have stressed the importance of helping older persons to accept this practice as a valid outlet when they feel the need for it.[48]

THE GREAT NEED FOR INFORMATION

Persons who have worked with "senior citizens" and "golden age" clubs have reported the great need for knowledge, the confusion, and the eager hunger for information about sex shown by persons in these clubs.[49] The many perplexing problems that they raise indicate the extent to which such information is needed to help people solve broader questions of remarriage and interpersonal relationships during their later years. The growing incidence of disease states in these years—each of which may require a difficult readjustment in sexual and other relationships—makes it essential that older people be provided with this information openly and consistently.[50]

It should be clear, however, that unless our entire culture recognizes the normality of sex expression in the older years, it will be impossible for older persons to express their sexuality freely and without guilt. Physicians are particularly crucial in this respect; unless they are convinced of the psychological importance of sexual functioning in the later years, they can

---

45 Newman and Nichols, "Sexual Activities and Attitudes in Older Persons."
46 New York Times, January 12, 1965.
47 Dickinson and Beam, A Thousand Marriages.
48 L. Dearborn, "Autoerotism," in A. Ellis and A. Abarbanel (eds.), The Encyclopedia of Sexual Behavior (New York: Hawthorn, 1961), pp. 204–15; and L. Hutton, The Single Woman (London: Barrie & Rockcliff, 1960), p. 58.
49 Feigenbaum et al., "Sexual Attitudes in the Elderly."
50 Rubin, Sexual Life after Sixty, chaps. 11–13.

do irreparable harm to their patients' sexuality.[51] Fortunately, at long last, medical schools and medical publications have begun to take steps to correct the glaring lacks in the education of medical students, which have in the past resulted in the creation of a body of medical practitioners who, by and large, shared the general prejudices of our society concerning sexuality in older persons.

---

[51] J. S. Golden, "Management of Sexual Problems by the Physician," *Obstetrics and Gynecology*, Vol. 23 (March 1964), pp. 471–74; and A. L. Finkle and D. V. Prian, "Sexual Potency in Elderly Men before and after Prostatectomy," *Journal of the American Medical Association*, Vol. 196, April 11, 1966, pp. 139–43.

part II

Factors influencing sexual behavior

The second part of the book includes articles dealing with various factors which influence sexual behavior and attitudes, ranging from socioeconomic status to national background. Judd Marmor's general paper, Reading 8, sets the stage for the more specific papers which follow. He views the normalcy of sexual behavior in its cultural framework and emphasizes the fact that evaluation of behavior must necessarily be placed within the context of time, place, and situation.

The influence of cultural background is clearly evident in Reading 9 by Bernard Rosenberg and Joseph Bensman. These researchers describe the patterns of sexual behavior among white Appalachians living in Chicago, blacks in Washington, D.C., and Puerto Ricans in New York. Although all three groups in this study are from the lower socio-economic class, still cultural background is a powerful determinant of general life style and sexual practices. There are distinct differences between the sexual mores of the three ethnic groups as well as between those of the lower class and the American middle class.

The three reports that follow span a twenty-year period beginning with Kinsey's reports on the detailed sexual behavior of more than 12,000 Americans, published in 1948 and 1953. Male and female subjects were from all states and socioeconomic levels. Today, the Kinsey data remain the most complete and reliable information on human sexual behavior. Reading 10 is Kinsey's report on male patterns of behavior. In addition, two tables from Kinsey's 1953 book on female sexual behavior are included to enable the reader to compare the sexual outlets of males and females of various ages.

Paul H. Gebhard, Director of the Institute for Sex Research at Indiana University has noted the following which should be kept in mind by the student when reading the Kinsey material:

The figures and some of the generalizations derived from them no longer apply to life today, particularly to college student life. You must remember that the 1948 "Male" volume was written in 1947 and that our youngest subjects (say, aged 15) at that time would now be nearly forty years old. In brief, our data refer, not to the present college generation, but to their parents and grandparents. Our data on females, while somewhat less dated, suffer from this same condition.

Also, the distinctions between the social levels in terms of sexual behavior and attitudes have increasingly blurred in the decades since we gathered data. Mass media, especially in these more permissive times, have made our society more homogeneous. Hence, our old publications with their sharp class differentiations no longer present the contemporary picture.[1]

The research reported by Ira Reiss in Reading 11 was conducted twenty years after the Kinsey survey. Reiss noted little change in sexual behavior, but considerable change in attitudes toward sexual behavior resulting in a narrowing of the gap between the two. In his article he reports on the sexual relationships of a national sample which included whites and blacks, adults and students. His findings, too, will serve as a reference point from which to evaluate change in the coming decades.

In Reading 12, Eleanore Luckey and Gilbert Nass discuss sexual attitudes and behaviors of male and female college students from the United States, Canada, England, Norway, and Germany. This study was done in collaboration with Vance Packard. More complete data on the American sample can be found in Packard's book, *The Sexual Wilderness*[2] which was based on the larger study. Original tables showing male and female responses by nationality, to questionnaire items, have been omitted from this article.

Most uninformed foreigners view Sweden as a nation in which large numbers of adults are permissive and many young people are promiscuous. Birgitta Linnér, a family counselor from Sweden is an authoritative source

---

1 Letter, May 28, 1971.
2 Vance Packard, *The Sexual Wilderness* (New York: David McKay, 1968).

of information on the sexual scene in that country. Her book, *Sex and Society in Sweden*[3] provides a comprehensive view of Swedish sexual behavior and of the attitudes which influence this behavior. Reading 13 was selected for inclusion here because, in it, Birgitta Linnér explains the official Scandinavian attitude toward specific sexual behaviors and outcomes together with the underlying rationale. Her discussion should help the reader to consider so-called Swedish liberalism and permissiveness within the national framework, in line with the basic goals of that society.

In Russia also, the state has specific goals for society as a whole. These are most frequently stated in terms of the family, the children and the party. Indirectly, however, sexual behavior is included. But even indirect reference to sexual behavior in the Soviet Union is difficult to find either within the country or abroad. In an attempt to provide the reader with the little available information on both stated codes and actual sexual behavior, excerpts from the writings of journalists and American and Soviet educators are presented.

Reading 14 from *The Soviet Family*, written by two well known American family life educators, David and Vera Mace, provides a picture of Soviet marriage in 1963. In Reading 15, statements from Anton S. Makarenko's 1937 radio lectures to parents, and also suggestions from Zverev, a Soviet educator, for a current program on sex education, provide an impression of some of the stated goals, and some of the prevalent attitudes in relation to sexual behavior. Makarenko's philosophy of education which emphasizes character building has had a strong influence on Soviet practice since the 1930s. The recommendations for sex education indicate that, forty years later, this influence is still a powerful one.

However, the reports of newswoman Georgie Anne Geyer[4] and those from *Time* and *Newsweek* suggest that in Russia, changes in sexual behavior similar to those in many other nations are taking place. Evidently a more permissive atmosphere toward sexual behavior is continuing to develop. From this mixed bag of varied reports the student may get some idea, form some concept, carry on some comparison of the values which influence sexual behavior in the U.S.S.R., and those of other nations referred to in this part of the book. It is evident that in most nations society does provide some guidelines for sexual behavior in line with national goals. It is also evident that actual behavior does not always reflect agreement with expected behavior.

---

[3] New York: Harper Colophon Books, 1972.

[4] More comprehensive information appears in Geyer's forthcoming book, *The Young Russians,* to be published by W. W. Norton in 1973.

8

"Normal" and "deviant"
sexual behavior*

JUDD MARMOR

It is difficult to approach the topic of human sexuality with the same kind of dispassionate scientific objectivity that can be applied to functions such as speech, digestion, or locomotion. Sexual behavior is so intimately entwined with moral issues, religious and cultural value systems, and even aesthetic reactions, that those who attempt to deal with it too openmindedly are likely to be charged by their contemporaries with being immoral or amoral, if not illegal. Sigmund Freud's efforts at the turn of the 19th century to bring the "problems of the bedroom" under scientific scrutiny caused both colleagues and friends to turn away from him in embarrassment, and even sixty years later, in the relatively enlightened second half of the 20th century, the meticulous physiological studies of Masters and Johnson stimulated cries of outrage in many quarters and titters of embarrassment in others.

Nevertheless, no discussion of human sexual behavior can be truly objective if one does not attempt to stand outside of the narrow framework of one's own cultural bias to see how the raw data of human sexual biology are shaped by and shape the infinitely varied mosaics of human experience in different places and at different times.

---

* Reprinted from *The Journal of the American Medical Association*, July 12, 1971, Volume 217. Copyright 1971, American Medical Association. Used with permission of author and publisher.

HISTORICAL CONSIDERATIONS

Even a cursory look at the recorded history of human sexuality makes it abundantly clear that patterns of sexual behavior and morality have taken many diverse forms over the centuries. Far from being "natural" and inevitable, our contemporary sexual codes and mores, seen in historical perspective, would appear no less grotesque to people of other eras than theirs appear to us. Our attitudes concerning nudity, virginity, fidelity, love, marriage, and "proper" sexual behavior are meaningful only within the context of our own cultural and religious mores. Thus, in the first millennium of the Christian era, in many parts of what is now Europe, public nudity was no cause for shame (as is still true in some aboriginal settings), virginity was not prized, marriage was usually a temporary arrangement, and extramarital relations were taken for granted. Frank and open sexuality was the rule, and incest was frequent. Women were open aggressors in inviting sexual intercourse. Bastardy was a mark of distinction because it often implied that some important person had slept with one's mother. In early feudal times new brides were usually deflowered by the feudal lord (jus primae noctis). In other early societies all the wedding guests would copulate with the bride. Far from being considered a source of concern to the husband, these practices were considered a way of strengthening the marriage in that the pain of the initial coitus would not be associated with the husband.

It was not until the Medieval Church was able to strengthen and extend its control over the peoples of Europe that guilt about sexuality began to be a cardinal feature of Western life. Even the early Hebraic laws against adultery had nothing to do with fidelity but were primarily concerned with protecting the property rights of another man (the wife being considered property). Married men were free to maintain concubines or, if they preferred, multiple wives; also, there was no ban in the Old Testament on premarital sex. The Medieval Church, however, exalted celibacy and virginity. In its efforts to make license in sexual intercourse as difficult as possible, it sanctioned it only for procreative purposes and ordained laws against abortion—laws that had not existed among the Greeks, Romans, or Jews. At one time it went so far as to make sexual intercourse between married couples illegal on Sundays, Wednesdays, and Fridays, as well as for forty days before Easter and forty days before Christmas, and also from the time of conception to forty days after parturition. (By contrast, Mohammedan law considered it grounds for divorce if intercourse did not take place at least once a week.)

Moreover, when the sexual taboos of the Medieval Church began to be widely enforced by cruel sanctions, a veritable epidemic of sexual pathology ensued—sodomy, flagellation, hysterical "possession" by witches and devils, incubi, succubi, phantom pregnancies, stigmata, and the like. In contrast, it is worth noting that in societies in which access to sexuality was open and guilt-free—the early Greeks, Europe prior to the Middle Ages and most "primitive" societies—the so-called sexual perversions tended not to be present. The homosexuality of the early Greeks, incidentally, was not an exclusive homosexuality, but part of a pattern of bisexuality in which homosexual feelings were considered to be as natural as heterosexual ones.

The ideals of romantic love and marriage for love which are taken for granted today are a relatively late development in Western history and did not make their appearance until the 12th century AD.[1] Clearly, there is nothing about our current sexual attitudes and practices that can be assumed to be either sacrosanct or immutable. They have been subject to much change and evolution in the past, and they will undoubtedly be different in the future.

BIOLOGICAL AND CULTURAL CONSIDERATIONS

Before we can proceed, it is necessary to clarify certain fundamental questions about the nature of human sexuality that have a bearing on the problem of sexual deviation. What is the biological core of human sexuality? Is it exclusively heterosexual, or does it have a bisexual composition? Is man "naturally" polygamous? Is woman naturally monoandrous? Are most "perversions" "unnatural?" What form does natural sexuality take in children?

Zoological and cross-cultural studies in recent years clearly demonstrate that the issue of sexual behavior goes far beyond its reproductive functions. Caspari's definition of the sexual process as "the exchange of nuclear material between cells of mating types or sexes" may have validity for relatively primitive forms of life, but as we ascend the phylogenetic scale this definition becomes manifestly inadequate. Patterns of sexual behavior evolve with the species, and at higher mammalian levels there is an increasing emphasis on various sex-related activities rather than on purely reproductive ones.

Sex in human beings is usually spoken of as being an "instinct." By this we mean that it is a fundamental behavioral pattern dependent on internal biological factors but capable of being triggered by external cues. Either may create a state of disequilibrium experienced as urgency or tension; this tension then leads to behavior that has the effect of restoring the previous state of balance, with an accompanying sense of subjective gratification. It is important to remember, however, that such a reaction takes quite a different form in human beings than it does in lower animals, even though the term instinct is used equally for both. The lower in the scale of evolu-

---

[1] G. R. Taylor, *Sex in History* (New York: Vanguard Press, 1954).

tion an animal is, the more totally developed and less modifiable are such instinctual patterns; but as one moves up the evolutionary scale inherited instinctual patterns tend to become less preformed and more subject to modification by learning. This development reaches its highest point in man, whose instinctual patterns at birth tend to be relatively unfocused biological drives, subject to enormous modifiability by learning and experience. This is a major factor in the extraordinary range of human adaptability.

This essentially unfocused quality of man's sexual drive in infancy is what Hampson and Hampson[2] have referred to as man's inherent "psychosexual neutrality" at birth—a neutrality that "permits the development and perpetuation of diverse patterns of psychosexual orientation and functioning in accordance with the life experiences each individual may encounter and transact." This concept of psychosexual neutrality does not, as some have mistakenly inferred, mean a "driveless" state, but rather an inborn biological drive with no specific inborn object, but with the potential for adapting its gratifactory needs to whatever objects the environment makes available to it. The term "psychosexual multipotentiality" probably expresses this more adequately than psychosexual neutrality.

In human sexual behavior, situational and learning factors are of major importance in arousal and response. In the absence of heterosexual objects, human beings (as well as many lower animals) may ultimately seek gratification in homosexual objects, or if no human object is available, in relations with animals of other species, or even by contact with inanimate objects. Even the physiological route of gratification, whether through the genitals or some other erogenous zone, or via patterns of behavior which seem to have no inherent elements of erogenicity in them at all, are subject to conditioning by specific experiences or associations. Other factors in sexual responsiveness include age, health, fatigue, nutritional state, and recency of drive fulfillment.

Freud believed that the bisexual anlage which can be observed in the human embryo is subsequently reflected in a universal bisexual tendency at a psychological level. The evidences of such psychic bisexuality, in this view, are seen in "latent homosexual" manifestations such as affectionate feelings for members of one's own sex and in patterns of behavior or interest that are usually (in our culture) considered to be characteristic of the opposite sex. Examples of these would be artistic or culinary interests or "passive" attitudes in males, or athletic or scientific interests or "aggressive" attitudes in females.

---

[2] J. L. Hampson, Joan G. Hampson, "The ontogenesis of sexual behavior in man," in W. C. Young (ed): *Sex and Internal Secretions* (Baltimore: Williams & Wilkins, 1961), vol. 2, ed. 3. [Reprinted by permission of the authors and publisher.]

This hypothesis was first challenged in the psychoanalytic literature by Rado[3] who pointed out that "in the final shaping of the normal individual the double embryological origin of the genital system does not result in any physiological duality of reproductive functioning." More than this, we now know that with the exception of the relatively uncommon individuals with sexual chromosome abnormalities, in almost all human beings, biological sex is clearly differentiated at the moment of conception by the XX and XY chromosomal patterns. Nevertheless, the theory of psychic bisexuality is sometimes still defended on the basis that both "male" and "female" sex hormones—androgens and estrogens—can be found in the blood of both sexes. However, although the biological activity of these hormones is essential for the growth and maturation of the primary genital apparatus in both sexes and for the development of secondary sexual characteristics, there is no evidence in humans that these hormones affect the direction of human sexuality or that they determine psychological "masculinity" or "femininity."[4] As Money has put it.

There is no primary genetic or other innate mechanism to preordain the masculinity or femininity of psychosexual differentiation. . . . The analogy is with language. Genetics and innate determinants ordain only that language can develop . . . but not whether the language will be Nahuatl, Arabic, English, or any other.[5]

Psychological and behavioral patterns of masculinity or femininity constitute what is meant by "gender role," and are not necessarily synonymous with an individual's biological sex. As the Hampsons have pointed out:

The psychologic phenomenon which we have termed gender role, or psychosexual orientation, evolves gradually in the course of growing up and cannot be assigned or discarded at will. The components of gender role are neither static nor universal. They change with the times and are an integral part of each culture and subculture. Thus one may expect important differences in what is to be considered typical and appropriate masculine or feminine gender roles as displayed by a native of Thailand and a native of Maryland . . .[2]

Opler, in the same vein, comments that

a Navajo Indian may be a he-man, or gambler, and a philanderer while dressing in bright blouses adorned with jeweled belts, necklaces, and bracelets. French courtiers in the retinues of effete monarchs were equally philanderers, though rouged, powdered, and bedecked with fine lace. The Andaman Islanders like

---

[3] S. Rado, Psychoanalysis of Behavior (New York: Grune & Stratton, 1956), vol. 1.
[4] W. H. Perloff, "Hormones and homosexuality," in J. Marmor (ed): Sexual Inversion: The Multiple Roots of Homosexuality (New York: Basic Books, 1965) pp. 44–69.
[5] J. Money, "Developmental differentiation of femininity and masculinity compared," in S. M. Farber, R. H. L. Wilson (eds): Man and Civilization (New York: McGraw-Hill Book Co., 1963), pp. 56–57.

to have the man sit on his wife's lap in fond greetings, and friends and relatives, of the same or opposite sex, greet one another in the same manner after absences, crying in the affected manner of the mid-Victorian woman. . . . Obviously, the style of social and sexual behavior is something of an amalgam and is culturally influenced.[6]

The fact is that the patterning of human sexual behavior begins at birth. From the moment a child is identified as either boy or girl, it begins to be shaped by multitudinous cues which communicate certain gender role expectations to it over the succeeding years. This results in a "core gender identity" of either male-ness or femaleness, which becomes so profoundly fixed by the age of three, that efforts to reverse this identity after that time are almost always doomed to failure.[2]

Within every society, the process of acculturation that takes place during these critical years begins to condition the child's behavior so as to enable it to conform to the mores of its environment—how and what it should eat, where and when it may urinate and defecate, what and whom it may play with, how it should think and express itself, and how and toward whom it may express its sexual needs. The so-called "polymorphous-perverse" sexual behavior of young children described by Freud in his *Three Contributions to the Theory of Sex* constitutes the normal behavior of children before the acculturation processes of our society have funneled their sexual patterns into "proper channels." From it we can infer what form the "natural sexuality" of man would probably take if no cultural taboos or restrictions at all existed in this sphere. Freud obviously was not unaware of this when he wrote that "it is absolutely impossible not to recognize in the uniform predisposition to all perversions . . . a universal and primitive human tendency."[7]

DEVELOPMENTAL FACTORS

In his libido theory, Freud hypothesized that the sexual instinct followed a phylogenetically predestined evolutionary pathway. In the first year of life, the primary erotogenic focus was the oral zone, in the second and third years, the anal zone, and in the fourth and fifth years, the phallic zone. From the sixth year to puberty, the sexual drive then underwent an involutional process—the "latency period"—during which the "sexual energy" was deflected from sexual goals and "sublimated." With puberty, the sexual drive was again unleashed and now directed toward the ultimate adult goal of full genital gratification.

---

[6] M. K. Opler, "Anthropological and cross-cultural aspects of homosexuality," in J. Marmor (ed): *Sexual Inversion: The Multiple Roots of Homosexuality* (New York: Basic Books, 1965), pp 108–23. From Chapter 6, "Anthropological and Cross-Cultural Aspects of Homosexuality" by Marvin K. Opler in *Sexual inversion: The multiple roots of homosexuality* edited by Judd Marmor, © 1965 by Basic Books Inc., Publishers, New York.

[7] S. Freud, *Three Essays on the Theory of Sexuality.* J. Strachey (trans., 1905), (New York: Basic Books, 1962).

With the shift in psychoanalytic theory from an instinct-psychology to an ego-psychology, the unfolding of human sexuality may be viewed in a somewhat different light. The infant's sexual needs are seen as rather primitive and undifferentiated at birth. Such as they are, they find expression in the exercise of the child's relatively undeveloped ego functions—in sucking, in body movements, and in experiencing cutaneous and kinesthetic sensations. In the course of its adaptive development the child discovers sucking its thumb and handling its genitals as special sources of somatic pleasure, and if not discouraged, will utilize these as accessory sources of gratification. Indeed, infantile masturbation may be regarded as one of the earliest experiences of autonomy in normal development. When the child discovers erogenous zones within himself that he can stimulate to give himself pleasure, he has achieved a significant step in ego mastery. Such masturbation is analogous to the behavioral patterns described by Olds[8] in his experimental rats when they discovered their ability to stimulate a "pleasure area" in their hypothalamus.

This author has never been convinced that the shift to "anal erogenicity" during the second year is either as clear-cut or as inevitable as Freud believed. Where it does seem to occur, it may well be the consequence of the emphasis on bowel training which takes place at this time in our culture, and which often becomes the locus for an emotionally laden transaction between child and mother. Moreover, the struggle at this point is not so much over the issue of the child's wish for anal-zone pleasure per se, as it is over the child's wish to move its bowels whenever and wherever it wishes. Thus the issue is not anality, but the broader one of the pleasure-principle versus the reality-principle—the basic battleground of every acculturation process.

It is probably not accidental also that phallic-zone interest develops when it does. The third year of life corresponds with the shift in cultural emphasis from bowel sphincter training to the development of urinary control. Simultaneously, the developing and intrusive ego of the child at this age begins to perceive, and concern itself with, the shame-ridden issues of the anatomical differences between the sexes, where babies come from, and how much fun it is to play with forbidden genitals. This is the period of the "polymorphous-perverse."

That a latency period should occur in our culture after this kind of behavior should not come as a surprise. Freud believed this period to be "organically determined," but the absence of such a reaction of latency in cultures where there are no prohibitions to the free expression of sexuality in children, clearly indicates that this is not so. Sexual latency, when it occurs, is obviously the result of repression in a culture that strongly indoctrinates the child with the conviction that its "polymorphous and perverse" sexual interests are dirty, shameful, and sinful. Under this pressure

---

[8] J. Olds, "Self stimulation of the brain," *Science* 127:315–24, 1958.

with threats of physical punishment and loss of love (both "castration" threats), many children in our society repress their sexuality until the imperative thrust of puberty brings it to the fore again. It is worth noting, however, that there has been evidence in recent years that increasing numbers of children in their prepubertal years continue to be sexually active and interested. This is a reflection of the more accepting attitudes toward sexuality that have been emerging in our culture in recent decades.

The subsequent vicissitudes of adult sexuality also take many forms. Monogamy as a compulsory pattern of mateship, for example, occurs in only a minority of human societies—only 16% of 185 societies studied by Ford and Beach.[9] (Even in that 16%, less than one-third wholly disapproved of both premarital and extramarital liaisons.) Strict monogamy, however, is not necessarily a mark of advanced civilization—some extremely primitive societies are strongly monogamous.

Patterns of monogamy and polygamy (or polyandry) are usually dependent on economic factors. Even in societies where multiple mateships are permitted, only the well-to-do usually are able to exercise this option, and single mateships, although not required, are the rule.

Rules governing premarital and extramarital relations also vary widely in different cultures. There are numerous societies in which extramarital sex is permitted and expected, and in which there is no censure of adultery. Indeed, among the polyandrous Toda of India, there is no word in their language for adultery, and moral opprobrium is attached to the man who begrudges his wife to another! It is interesting to note also that in societies that have no double standard in sexual matters and in which liaisons are freely permitted, women avail themselves of their opportunities as eagerly as men, a fact that casts serious doubts on the popular assumption that females are, by nature, less sexually assertive than males.

DEFINITION OF SEXUAL DEVIATION

How then can one define sexual deviations? It is clear from our preceding discussion that an adequate definition cannot be based on any assumption of the biological "naturalness" of any particular pattern of sexual behavior in man. What is evaluated as psychologically healthy in one era or culture may not be so in another. The normal sexual behavior of an adolescent girl among the Marquesans or Trobrianders would be considered nymphomanic or delinquent in our society. Homosexual behavior is regarded as deviant in many cultures, including our own, but was not so adjudged in ancient Greece and pre-Meiji Japan, or among the Tanalans

---

[9] C. S. Ford, F. A. Beach, *Patterns of Sexual Behavior* (New York: Harper & Bros., 1952).

of Madagascar, the Siwanis of Africa, the Aranda of Australia, the Keraki of New Guinea, and many others.

It is sometimes argued that this kind of culture-oriented relativistic concept of normalcy is fallacious because it fails to recognize that there is an "optimal" conception of health that transcends all cultural norms. The difficulty with this argument is that the concept of optimal itself is culture-bound. Even granting that within any culture a concept such as personality homeostasis or self-realization has validity, the content of such concepts still vary in different times and places. A definition of psychological health in psychoanalytic terms implies the ability of the "ego" to effectively handle and integrate its relationships with the "id," the "superego," and the outer world. Such a definition could undoubtedly be used cross-culturally. But again, its content will vary in different cultural contexts since the nature of the "normal" superego and of the outer-world are culture-dependent.

COMMENT

It seems to this author, therefore, that there is no way in which the concepts of normal and deviant sexual behavior can be divorced from the value systems of our society; and since such value systems are always in the process of evolution and change, we must be prepared to face the possibility that some patterns currently considered deviant may not always be so regarded. The fact that we now refer to sexual "deviations" rather than to "perversions" already represents an evolutionary change within our culture toward a more objective and scientific approach to these problems, in contrast to the highly moralistic and pejorative approach of the previous generation. Perhaps some day we shall talk simply of "variations" in sexual object choice.

Such a relativistic approach to normalcy should not, however, be mistaken for a nihilistic one. We are all products of our culture, and within the context of our current Western cultural value system there are indeed certain patterns that can be regarded as psychologically optimal and healthy.

Although there is a wide spectrum of variations in human sexual motivation and behavior—most human beings, in the privacy of their bedrooms, in one way or another, and at one time or another, violate the rigid conventional standards of "proper" sexual behavior—there are nevertheless certain more widely deviant patterns of sexual behavior that in all likelihood would be considered abnormal in every society. For example, practices that involve serious injury to one of the participants in the sexual relationship could hardly be considered adaptive in any society since they would ultimately jeopardize its survival.

One way of defining a large category of sexual practices that is considered deviant in our culture is that they involve the habitual and preferential use of nongenital outlets for sexual release. The emphasis in this definition is on the terms "habitual" and "preferential," since extragenital gratification may be a part of normal sexual foreplay, or of variations in sexual experiences between perfectly normal adults. When, however, such variant activity becomes an habitual end in itself, it almost always, in the context of our culture, means some disturbance in personality functioning.

It should be noted that the above definition is a psychiatric not a legal one. Statutes in most of the United States regard any use of nongenital outlets for sexual release as illegal. Kinsey and his coworkers, after their extensive surveys of sexual practices of males and females, concluded that there are probably very few adults who have not technically violated such statutes at one time or another.

Other major forms of sexual behavior that are defined as deviant in our society involve activity that is homosexual, or sexual activity with immature partners of either sex (pedophilia), animals (bestiality), dead people (necrophilia), or inanimate objects (fetishism).

Although sexual deviations are commonly separated in terms of their outstanding clinical manifestations, in actuality they are far from discrete phenomena. There is frequent overlapping among them and it is not uncommon for an individual to present simultaneous evidence of more than one of these manifestations. Thus, a fetishist may also be an exhibitionist and a voyeur; a transvestite may also be involved in sadomasochistic practices; incest and pedophilia may be associated in the same person, and so forth.

The reason for this overlapping rests in the underlying psychodynamics that are common to all sexual deviations in our society. The deviant is in almost all instances an individual who has difficulty in achieving normal or satisfactory sexual relations with a mature partner of the opposite sex. Thus his deviant practices represent alternative ways of attempting to achieve sexual gratification; they are displacement phenomena and in many instances the displacement mechanism may operate in more than one direction. Some deviants exhibit polymorphous-perverse patterns of sexual behavior akin to that of very young children who have not yet been adequately acculturated. In this sense they may be considered to have been "fixated" at an early stage of psychosexual development, or to have "regressed" to this stage.

The choice of deviant pattern, like the choice of symptom in neurosis, is dependent on complex determinants which have to be ferreted out by a painstaking history and psychodynamic evaluation in each individual case. Disturbances in core family relationships, impairment in gender identity development, poor ego development, and specific conditioning experiences are all involved.

Apart from such clearly definable deviant patterns, human sexual relationships are often complicated by unconscious motivations of fear, hate, or guilt, which leave their stamps on the quality of the sexual transactions between partners. In our culture, a key distinguishing factor between what is regarded as healthy or unhealthy sexual behavior is whether such behavior is motivated by feelings of love or whether it becomes a vehicle for the discharge of anxiety, hostility, or guilt. Healthy sexuality seeks erotic pleasure in the context of tenderness and affection; pathologic sexuality is motivated by needs for reassurance or relief from nonsexual sources of tension. Healthy sexuality seeks both to give and receive pleasure; neurotic forms are unbalanced toward excessive giving or taking. Healthy sexuality is discriminating as to partner; neurotic patterns often tend to be nondiscriminating. The periodicity of healthy sexuality is determined primarily by recurrent erotic tensions in the context of affection. Neurotic sexual drives, on the other hand, are triggered less by erotic needs than by nonerotic tensions and are therefore more apt to be compulsive in their patterns of occurrence.

A sharp line of distinction, however, cannot always be drawn between healthy and neurotic sexuality. Since patterns of sexual behavior always reflect personality patterns and problems, and since no one in our complex society is totally exempt from individual idiosyncracies, tensions, and anxieties, these will be manifested in sexual patterns no less than in other areas of interpersonal transactions. No human being is perfect, and nowhere is the humanity of man more transparent than in the varied patterns of his sexual relationships.

9

Sexual patterns in three ethnic subcultures of an American underclass*

BERNARD ROSENBERG and
JOSEPH BENSMAN

No American who wishes to discuss love and sex can avoid the long West-ern tradition from within which we, knowingly or unknowingly, come by all our perspectives. Jerusalem, Athens, Rome, and their several sequelae constitute, or symbolize, that tradition. From it, that is to say, from the Hellenic and Judaeo-Christian past, Western man derives not only certain prescriptions and prohibitions, but a whole framework of ideas, concepts, and theories that are his heavy cultural burden. Diffusion and dilution not-withstanding, the sexual analyst and those he discusses share that burden. To be sure, neither need recognize or acknowledge the connection that binds them together in an inescapable matrix.

We have come to our present sexual pass through devious and tangled paths, still strewn with innumerable laws, parables, images, aftereffects, and reflections. In this brief statement, we can do no more than touch upon

* Reprinted from *Annals of the American Academy of Political and Social Science,*
Vol. 376 (March 1968), pp. 61–75, with the permission of the authors and of the
American Academy of Political and Social Science.

a few highlights which may illuminate part of our rich and varied background.

For example, the poems of Sappho and those of Ovid, like a score of other such sources—including philosophical schools, and religious cults—have in common that they celebrate erotic joy. All of them say to us that love (as in the story of Ruth) and sex (as in the mythopoeic figure of Priapus) should involve deep feeling or great pleasure. This notion is currently fashionable among many otherwise disenchanted, proudly "rational," and highly sophisticated people. At the same time, they are affected by those provisions of the Decalogue, as interpreted by Talmudic and Scholastic commentators, that set severe limits upon love and sexuality while emphasizing the responsibilities inherent in sacramental and indissoluble relationships whose purpose is solely reproductive.

With *eros* and *agape*, Plato spiritualized sex. St. Augustine, and, later on, many of the Schoolmen who introduced Aristotelian modifications, took over these Platonic ideas. In various guises, they became essential to both the Catholic and Protestant world view. The Christian churches also fashioned sexual codes of their own which, even when they were systematically violated, produced discrete and historically specialized sexual behavior. In Europe and America, sexual renunciation, with deep intellectual and religious roots, always seems to have had an obverse side, or to have proceeded in dialectical sequence to eroticism. Thus, to condemn the pleasures of the flesh may itself entail, or simply lead to, precisely those pleasures. The medieval denial of sex was in no way incompatible with chivalry and romantic love as practiced at the courts of Aquitaine and Provence. Here, if anywhere, as Denis de Rougemont has shown, are the beginnings of a romantic conception made universally familiar in our time by way of Hollywood films. Dante and Beatrice, Tristan and Iseult, or Romeo and Juliet are prototypic cases in which sexual desire feeds upon the loved one's permanent inaccessibility.

Seventeenth-century Puritanism and nineteenth-century Victorianism, each in its complex and contradictory manner, left us with a dualistic dogma whose force is not yet fully spent. Mind and body (therefore, love and sex) were pitted against each other. As the underside of Victorian life is subjected to increasing exposure, one beholds not only the sexually etherealized woman of virtue, but her fallen sister, whether given to prostitution or not, who is cynically and mercilessly exploited. As hitherto unpublishable memoirs reach the contemporary reader, he comes to know the moralistic upper-class gentleman who collects pornography, indulges in exotic, probably inverted and polymorphous, perverse sexual tastes while practicing hypocrisy, if not perfecting it to a high art.

Victorianism and the revolt against it are our immediate antecedents. And that revolt is largely ideological. The exaltation of eroticism tends to be academic. Proponents of "sexual freedom" contrast it favorably with artificial and hypocritical Victorian conventions. Beginning with feminism as a political movement, proceeding in the 1920s under banners like companionate or trial marriage, through a strident call for emancipation and liberation, to the present "sexual revolution," learned men have set forth their ideas. Hedonists and rationalists, champions of homosexuality, of a return to infantile gratification with "love's body" and no mere fixation on genital pleasure: here is a peculiar gamut from Bertrand Russell to Albert Ellis, Herbert Marcuse, and Norman O. Brown. None of them, the logician, the psychotherapist, the Hegelian, or the Classical scholar, is primarily interested in the restoration of "natural" sexuality. All of them are passionately interested in proving or disproving theories.

Even Sigmund Freud, who did more than anyone else to free Western thought from the straightjacket of Victorianism, was himself a puritan—in perhaps the best Biblical sense of the term. Furthermore, Freud, in his sexual speculations and investigations, drew heavily upon Greek philosophy, specifically the ideas of *agape, eros,* and *curitas.* Freud's "scientific" attitude toward sex is actually permeated with several of the oldest concepts of antiquity—with which they are perfectly continuous. Insofar as Freudian psychology fuels the sexual revolution, it is directed not at the demolition of Western norms, but only at one narrow version of a complicated social heritage.

Like speech, dress, manners, and a score of other visible stigmata, conduct in the sexual sphere has always been class-bound. To speak of the mores dominant in any period is necessarily to be elliptical. For example, the Victorian double standard was, in its own time, mainly an upper-middle-class phenomenon, rarely affecting higher and lower social strata. Similarly, the revolt against it seems to have liberated segments of the middle class at least from the idea of sexual repression. For some time now, as Theodore Dreiser noted over and over in his early novels, the relatively stable blue-collar working class has best exemplified puritanical prudery and sexual hypocrisy.

All the while, romantic writers, artists, and social scientists have been searching for "genuine" or "natural" sexuality, embodied in an eroticized and newly ennobled savage, uncontaminated by that odious sophistication which reduces the physical expression of love to *le contact de deux épidermes.* Thus occurs the idealization of peasants, "earthmen," primitives, those sexually spontaneous and unalienated humans who—when viewed from a safe distance—look so free and easy in all their ways. Are there such groups of people within the underclass of our own society? Does their alleged culture of poverty so far remove them from Western civilization that research in their midst will reveal what love and sex are really like when they are emancipated from history and intellectuality?

THE THREE ETHNIC SUBCULTURES

These are some of the questions implicit in the material that follows.[1] Three miserably, and more or less equally, impoverished areas in New York, Chicago, and Washington, D.C., were selected for prolonged study. Lander and his associates held poverty constant and introduced ethnicity as the variable. They concentrated on all the inhabitants of one social block (with dwellings that face each other) in each of the three cities. In New York, most of the subjects were Puerto Ricans, in Chicago, Appalachian whites, and in Washington, Negroes. Intensive nondirected "tandem interviews" (with two interviewers and one respondent) yielded the qualitative data about adolescent youth that we cite and sift in our analysis.

All three of these ethnic groups are composed largely of recent migrants, who had come to the urban centers from other parts of the United States (including Puerto Rico), and who had brought with them many of their ways of life, perhaps even accentuated by contrast with their new environment and their new neighbors.

A common culture presupposes that those who belong to it speak the same language. There is such a language for all Americans as there is an overarching culture that unifies urban dwellers and farmers, the young and the old, the privileged and the underprivileged. Subcultural segmentation produces "special languages" within the larger linguistic community, and they are intelligible only to initiates, that is, members of ethnic, occupational, regional, and religious groups. That the broadly conceptualized culture (or subculture) of poverty is somewhat illusory can be demonstrated by the variegated speech patterns characteristic of poor Appalachian whites, Negroes, and Puerto Ricans. Indeed, for each of our populations, it would be possible to assemble a glossary of terms widely used by insiders but meaningless to most outsiders. How luxuriant local variation takes place (in meaning, accent, and value) is the proper subject matter of a highly technical discipline called ethnolinguistics. It is not our intention to turn that discipline loose on data gathered for other purposes. Nevertheless, this much must be said: each group living in its own slum moves towards a certain linguistic homogeneity, bringing ancestral speech ways, borrowing symbols from the larger society, and synthesizing them into distinctive configurations. Peculiarities of speech are a rough index of differential association and cultural isolation. Unique idioms emerge from intense in-group living, and disappear at the opposite pole of full acculturation. In between, we find a complex mixture reflecting uneven

---

[1] This essay stems from a much larger study conceived and directed by Bernard Lander under multiple sponsorship, including the President's Committee on Juvenile Delinquency and Youth Crime, Notre Dame University, and the Lavanburg Corner House Foundation.

exposure to the wider institutional order, which is itself in constant flux. A few illustrations from the heterosexual sphere may be in order.

Chicago

In our sample, the adolescent males among the New York Puerto Ricans and Washington Negroes are unresponsive to questions about dating. The word does not appear in their lexicon, and, as it turns out, this fact points to a substantive different in behavior between these boys and those in Chicago. Every respondent among the Chicago Appalachian whites knows what a date is. One at first defines it as "goin' out with a fox," then adds, "You just go out driving, make some love, catch a crib—and that's all." Here, indeed, are the cadences, the inflections, and the semantics of a special language in which "fox" means girl and "crib" stands for house or apartment, which, in turn, signifies a trysting place that one "catches" along with the "fox." Such expressions may have their origin in the hill country of Kentucky and Alabama, whence they were transplanted to the Midwest and, merged with much else, produced a dynamic amalgam that cannot be duplicated elsewhere.

There are fuzzy edges around every word that is variously defined not only at different levels of the social hierarchy, but within any one level. For those who generalize in the grand manner, dating is understood to be "an American" phenomenon; the more sophisticated family sociologists (who prepare textbooks for college students) see it as a peculiar ritual, a courtship pattern, practiced by middle-class youth in the United States. In our samplings of the underclass, only the poor white teenagers date, and they do so in ways similar to and dissimilar from those of their middle-class counterparts. The telephone, for instance, plays no great part in their activities, as it does among more privileged adolescents, but the automobile is central. Neither matters much with Puerto Ricans and Negroes.

The Chicago boys, who will sometimes commit crimes to get a car, and need it to commit other crimes, and whose vocabulary is rich with the knowledge they have of car parts, may be said to live in a car complex. This circumstance provides them with a degree of physical mobility far greater than that of any other economically deprived group we have studied. In a crisis, occasioned, say, by the impregnation of a girl friend (scarcely a rare occurrence), they can always take to the road, ranging widely over Illinois and adjacent states. The automobile liberates them, up to a point, not only from their constricted neighborhood, but from the metropolis itself. And, given the car, they are able to date girls in a more or less conventional manner. The "portable bedroom" can be used for preliminary sex play most conveniently at drive-in movies, where two or three couples commonly occupy one car. Asked what he usually does on a date, a fifteen-year-old Chicago boy replies, in part:

If your friend's got a girl he's taking to the drive-in, you take her with him. And you take your girl to the show, go out to eat, dance, stuff like that.

On.the average, what does a date cost?

Well, if you go to a show, you won't have to spend but about, at the most, five, maybe six dollars. . . . If you go to the drive-in, you spend a dollar and a half for each one to get in. That's three dollars. Give the kid who's driving the car a buck, split the gas bill, you know, help to pay for some of the gas—and you eat. Oh, it costs you about six dollars.

Bowling and roller-skating are other diversions deemed to be suitable on dates in our Chicago sample. Neither is a popular boy-girl pastime in the other cities—where boys like sports that they play with other boys. Pick-ups are made on the street from a car, in neighborhood movie houses, and in teen-age bars which are frequented with great regularity only by the Appalachians.

All of this sounds a great deal like the textbook account, even to a general preference for double-dating. Yet, the reasons behind that preference give us a clue to something different, and specific to the Chicago group, namely, that a heavy streak of violence is woven into the texture of their heterosexual behavior. Hence: "I like to go out with other couples because it's better when you travel together. When you're alone, there's always other guys trying to start trouble." You date, but you appear alone with a girl at your own peril, as this little vignette makes clear:

I saw her walking down the hall with another boy, and I got pretty jealous. I started saying, "If you like that guy so much, go ahead and go out with him," and he walked up and started smartin' off to me. So I hit him, and then I beat him up. She turned around and slapped me. She called me a brute or something. . . . So that didn't hit me just right, and I said, "Forget it."

If a date culminates in sexual intercourse, it is also useful to have someone else along:

I was going with a girl. She was sixteen. She squealed on me, and they tried to get me on statutory rape. And, oh, she gave 'em a big long story, trying to get me into a lot of trouble. But there was another kid along with me on that date. And she claimed that he held her down and that I held her down. But this boy's stories matched and hers didn't. Otherwise, I would have been sunk.

With dating, there go the lineaments of a rating-dating complex, which does not precisely parallel Willard Waller's famous description of a widespread campus phenomenon, but does imply a measure of respect for the girls one dates, by contrast with the disrespect accorded girls and older women who are nothing but sexual objects. The following example is somewhat extremely but highly indicative:

I consider a girl you go out with and a girl you have intercourse with two different kinds of girls. There's a girl I date. I like to hold hands with her and make out with her, kiss her, but that's as far as I want to go with any girl I take out. If I like the girl, I don't want to mess her up. But then, there is the other girls I just don't care about because they give it to the other guys—which means they don't care too much for theirselves.

The type of boy who makes this provisionally puritanical division between good girls (with lovers who hold back from final consummation) and bad girls who "give it to the other guys," is yet capable of treating "good girls" with even greater harshness. This double standard means that there are separate norms; less is expected of the promiscuous girl, much more of the girl you date who may, after all, become your wife. If so, unquestioning submission to male authority is expected:

> What if you married a girl who talked back to you? What would you do?
> Shut her up.
> How?
> Well, I'd fix her where she wasn't able to talk too much.

The specter of violence is omnipresent. It may issue from association with either type of girl, and although there are always two types, criteria for establishing them vary. (Asked whether he still considers girls decent if they go to bed with him, a Chicago boy answers, "It's a matter of how hard I have to work. If I have to work real hard I think a lot of them. If they give it to me right off I think they're pigs.") Infidelity in a girl friend will ordinarily provoke a physical assault of some sort. What to do if the woman you marry is unfaithful? "Beat the shit out of her" is the semiautomatic response.

Acts of aggression connected with sex are, no doubt, intensified by heavy consumption of alcohol. Sex, liquor, and violence form a *Gestalt* in Chicago not nearly so discernible in New York or Washington. In another context, whiskey and beer act as a catalyst for serious fighting, possibly with recourse to knives and firearms. In the sexual context, alcohol is also believed to be useful as a means of emboldening the boy and rendering the girl more compliant to his advances:

> Do the girls get pretty wild when they've had a few drinks?
> Yes.
> Do most of the guys try to get the girls loaded?
> Yes.
> How often are you successful?
> We're not very successful at getting them loaded. I mean that takes a little money.

Beer is cheaper than whiskey and favored for that reason; a low alcohol content notwithstanding, it is believed to serve the purpose. Girls plied with beer are considered "better," that is, more available, than those who remain unlubricated. They can more easily be "cut"—which is typical and revealing Chicago argot for the sex act.

New York City

In the New York sample, there is no "cutting." The first few interviews with Puerto Rican youth revealed little about sex, a topic concerning which we had not anticipated that there would be unusual reticence. The breakdown in communication turned out to be no more than terminological. Once in possession of key words and phrases, the interviewers encountered no serious resistance to the free discussion of plain and fancy sex. There are taboo topics, notably religion as it shades off into magic, but sex is not one of them. The linguistic breakthrough occurred in this matter when a resident observer advised us to ask about "scheming." We did so, causing faces to light up that had remained blank as long as we struggled vainly to find the right conventional or unconventional sexual expression. "Scheming" was that expression. Equivalent, in a way, to "cutting" which suggests sex-and-sadism, "scheming" has mildly conspiratorial overtones. It stands for kissing, necking, petting, and full sexual consummation, everything from prepubertal exploration to real coitus, which is secret, exploitative, and pleasurable, but seldom brutal. With appropriate language, much information can be elicited, and comic misunderstandings are left behind. (To the question, "Did you ever have a girl sexually?" the young Puerto Rican respondent answers by asking, "Did I ever have a girl *sectionally?*" And some minutes are consumed, to no avail, in disentangling the adverbs. We want to know from another boy whether he goes to bed with girls, whether he sleeps with them, and he takes us literally: "No. I sleep by myself, in my own bed.")

Scheming is initiated at parties, and parties are called sets. They function as substitutes for going out, picking up, and dating. Young people at or around twenty may have apartments of their own which, like any of many vacant apartments on the block, can be used for sets, as they can be and are used for private or collective sexual adventures. At sets, boys and girls meet, play records, dance, drink beer or whiskey more or less moderately, smoke cigarettes and take pot more or less immoderately, and, under dim colored lights, engage in uninhibited foreplay. With twenty or more in attendance, sets seem to be fairly large affairs, and while some are organized during the week by hedonistic truants, there are sure to be others around the clock on weekends. Since the youngsters use stimulants and depressants that are costly, and Saturday is the traditional day for pilfering small objects whose sale produces money with which to buy supplies, the best sets are most likely to occur on Saturday nights. You drink a little, you smoke a lot, you are high, a girl offers to dance with you, and by and by, when the dim lights go out altogether, you fondle her. Presently, you step outside with your girl and scheme in the hallway, at her place if no one is at home, on a roof-top—this one, or another at the nearby housing project. And:

If you got a really good friend, and the girl is willing if she's really bad off or somethin', you know what she will do? *She'll pull the train.*
Pull the train?
Yes, that's what we call it: pulling the train. You take one chance. Then another guy takes a chance. You know.
Usually, how many guys are there?
Two.
Not like ten guys with one girl?
Oh, depends like on what kind of a girl. . . . I been in a situation with about six guys.

"Pulling the train" is by no means an everyday occurrence. Sets are. They may be regarded as a spontaneous expression of youth culture, an informal device contrived by teenagers for their own pleasure, a technique for circumventing official and established organizations, an escape from uplift sponsored by benevolent adults. Sets provide an arena—or constitute a preparation—for scheming, which, in most cases, means private and secret sexual activity. Boys do boast, with a probable admixture of phantasy and exaggeration, about sexual conquests, but they are loath to name names and thus cause "trouble" for themselves or their girl friends. The set in which they begin to participate at about age fifteen is understood to be somewhat illicit. It may become a pot party or sex party (our respondents are ambivalent and divided among themselves about which they like best)—and either one, if publicized, can lead to unpleasant sanctions.

Washington, D. C.

Boy-girl relations in the Washington poor Negro community are neither as car- and show-centered as in the Chicago white group nor as party-centered as in the New York Puerto Rican group. In Washington, the school, despite all its deficiencies, is much more pivotal than we would have supposed. Young people attend school dances now and then, meet classmates formally and informally, and, while ungoverned by any particular protocol, they begin to "go out" with one another. Soon there is sex play, and, in many cases, real sexual involvement. Things tend to begin in school, and there, too, the "facts of life" are transmitted most frequently and most effectively. Only in our Washington Negro sample do high school children use technical (now and then garbled) scientific terms for the sex act and the sex organs. They describe human reproduction as it has been explained to them by their biology teachers:

We had it in school. I know how the sperms come down, when a boy is having sex relations with a girl; they meet the egg, go up through the vagina, stay in the womb and grow month after month. And then after a period of time, the woman have a baby.

We're supposed to do that next half, after we finish with music (find out where babies come from and things like that).

Well, I know the process of starting—I mean, you have to have two unions, I mean a fusion of, uh, male and female, between the two organs. I mean the vulva and the, um, penis. The vulva and the penis. And, um, it takes a union of sperm and meeting with the egg. And after that, I know the situation of— what do you call it?—the embry—yeah, embry—and that's the first stage of the child. . . . And the food which the child receives comes from the navel of the mother. It's connected to the child, I believe mouth-to-navel, something like that. And after a nine month period, the child's supposed to be born.

A boy whose parents told him "all about it" at age twelve, says:

They explained it to me, that it was the entrance of the penis into the woman's vulva. I mean, they used other terms, but that's the terms I would use because, let's say, I'm more up on it now, on this education.

Again:

Well, uh, let's see, when the sperm, I think goes into the vagina, something like that, then, it meets the other sperm I think, and it starts doing something.

However imperfectly they may have absorbed their biology lessons, these teenagers show a degree of sophistication unavailable to their counterparts among the New York Puerto Ricans and in Chicago, where sexual knowledge is more likely to be associated with the street—and its earthly language—than with the classroom. (With the Puerto Ricans, a self-taught, semi-demi-social worker has helpfully taken it upon himself to provide some sex instruction in yet another linguistic style—largely Spanish, partly English argot.) For children to seek or parents to offer information, even when it is urgently needed, seems to be a rare occurrence. (We suspect that parent-youth embarrassment on this score is a class phenomenon. There is reason to believe that the middle-class parent now speaks freely to his children about the facts of life while evading questions about the facts of death.) The young mother of two illegitimate children in Washington tells us that she developed early: "At the age of twelve I was as developed as any girl of fourteen or fifteen. Being young, I never paid too much attention to it, but older people in the community noticed." As she recounts it, men got fresh; some began to follow her home, and she took to making "smart" remarks. Then, after awhile, "I had one man run me home from school." She ran and found sanctuary on a neighbor's porch, and "the man started to come after me till he looked up and spotted a lady and another man on the porch. After that my mother came over, and we told her about it, and the three of them walked around, but they didn't see him." This incident was but the first of several, including one "proposition" from a preacher, about which the mother was informed. She still divulged nothing to her daughter, and the daughter observes, "I just could not bring myself to look up at my mother and ask her what was happening."

The whole story, "the nitty gritty," came from experience with "fellows," who, however, were judged to be stupid, as well as girls on the street and an older sister. From her own account, but never officially, she was a sexual delinquent by age thirteen.

On the other hand, in Washington, a Negro boy may experience sexual initiation under his father's auspices. If there is an older woman who wishes to "come some," that is, who wishes to have a sex partner, the father sometimes encourages his son to cooperate. We have one such case on record:

> She (the older woman) came down to see my sister, and she started liking me. She started paying my way to the movies and all that. So my father told me to go on and do it. So I did. . . . He say, "I know you going to do it when I ain't around." So he gave me a protector, and I go on and do it. . . . He say we were going to do it behind his back anyhow, and that he just wanted to help me along. I ain't never used the protection, though.

Attitude comparisons

Although he tends to confuse protection against venereal disease with protection against pregnancy, the Negro teenager is generally more knowledgeable about this, too, than his Puerto Rican or poor white age mate. He more often recognizes and applies terms like contraceptive, diaphragm, coil, prophylactic, or rubber—for one reason, because he more often knows what they mean. Not that he or his girl friend is much inclined to use any of these objects, for their interposition threatens the individual with loss of his "cool"—an important but amorphous quality which must be maintained at all times. Although among all three ethnic samples, only a minority favor contraception, the Negro youth understand best, and Puerto Rican youth least, just what it is that they habitually decline to use. And, while amorality or *anomie* tends to prevail in sexual matters, it assumes a degree of egocentricity among the poor white boys unequalled elsewhere. In this exchange, we have an extreme but not atypical expression of the Chicago attitude:

> Do you ever use contraceptives?
> Nope.
> How about women? Do they ever use anything?
> Nope.
> Do you ever think about it?
> Nope.
> Are you afraid of what might happen?
> Nope. *They can't touch me. I'm under age.*

Seeing it exclusively from his own standpoint, and then only insofar as his conduct may lead to legal jeopardy, he is not afraid of making girls pregnant. Later on, when he does come of age, in order to avoid possible charges of statutory rape, such a boy will prefer sexual relations with older women. Even then, this respondent insists, he "ain't gonna use anything." Told by the interviewer about diaphragms and how they work, he vehemently protests against their use. They would interfere with his pleasure: "Might get in my way." To be sure, without contraception, it is possible to spawn an illegitimate child, something he at first claims to have done at least once—before second thoughts cause him to cast doubt on the "mother's" veracity. This is his complete verbatim statement on the matter:

She told me we were gonna have a kid. I said "Tough." She said, "Ain't it though?" I said, "What you gonna do about it?" She said, "I ain't gonna do nothin' about it. How about you?" I said nothin'. She said, "That's good." I said goodbye and she said goodbye. And that's the last I saw of her. I mean I *saw* her in school. She's still goin' to school. I don't believe that we had a kid, though. She just said we did.

Risk or no risk, boys are generally hostile to the idea of prophylaxis. One objection is phrased purely in terms of the pleasure principle, most colorfully by a Chicago boy who exlains why he never uses anything like a rubber, "I tried it once. It's like riding a horse with a saddle instead of bareback." Is he afraid of "knocking a girl up?" Answer: "Sure. *I worry about it afterwards.* I guess I'm lucky so far. That's all." The cost factor appears again in Chicago where the poor-white boys are markedly more reluctant than the Negroes and Puerto Ricans in Washington and New York, respectively, to spend money on contraceptive frills. At the climactic moment, their impecuniosity can be frustrating. As a rule, in the white population, girls are no more eager than boys to insure against pregnancy, but once in awhile they are:

Oh, I've used them a couple of times. Like one time, a broad got all worried, and she told us to lay off. . . . We had her pants off and everything. She ask me if I didn't have some rubbers. Uh-uh. "Get off." I had to wait a little longer. I didn't have any money either.

In the Chicago underclass, there is, then, a minimum of anxiety about the consequences of sexual intercourse, a strong disinclination to take any responsibility for what happens. Most boys are poorly informed and unconcerned about measures taken or not taken by their sex partners. "I wouldn't know if they did or not [use anything to prevent pregnancy]. I don't care if they do or not." Does he know what girls might do to protect themselves? "Well, there's with the hot water, like that. Then, there's, they press on their stomachs someplace . . . on some cords, usually when you get done, the girl has to go to the bathroom. She goes in, she presses here and there, and it all comes out. They claim that's one of the best ways." Ignorance of the facts should not be discounted, but knowledge may or may not be correlative with action. Even if a girl asks for restraint, so that she will not have to cope with unwed motherhood, the boy is likely to refuse:

Do many girls ask you to stop before you come?
Most don't. Some do.
They don't want to get pregnant?
That's right.
Do you usually oblige them?
Well, not usually, no.

Biologists like Ashley Montagu have established the existence of adolescent sterility, a period after the onset of puberty during which reproduction presumably cannot take place. Widespread premarital sexual experimentation, not always related to courtship, among "primitive peoples" to whom puritanism is unknown, has been noted for over a century. Adolescent sterility helps anthropologists to account for the smoothness with which such relations occur. In ever larger sectors of our own society, birth control has "sterilized" teen-agers, thereby insuring them against the many complications of illigitimacy. Neither of these mechanisms seems to be significantly operative in any of our cities. Adolescent *fertility* is high, and respondents (males only slightly more so than females) express a very nearly uniform distaste for every kind of contraceptive device. Significant differences are, in the first instance, more attitudinal than behavioral. How much responsibility does a boy who has got his girl with child feel? Some in the Puerto Ricans and Negroes of New York and Washington; virtually none in the whites of Chicago. That unimpeded sexual contact can and does lead to babies is something a transplanted Appalachian white boy is likely to know only too well. For the most part, he "couldn't care less"; the interviewer asks such a boy: "What's stopping you from knocking up girls?" Answer: "Nothin'. I've got four kids, maybe five. Two here in Chicago, two in Wisconsin, and when I left Wisconsin, I heard there was one more." Does he support any of them? "Shit no." After getting a girl pregnant, "I just take off."

Less able to "take off," as careless but more likely to be "trapped," hemmed in on every side, the New York Puerto Rican boy generally finds insemination of his girl friends a worrisome matter. It is seldom a question of direct responsibility to the "victim"—which would presuppose a kind of socialization or internalization of standards evident neither among "good boys" nor among "bad boys." What if the girl has a baby? "Maybe the parents might make him marry her." Coercion under these circumstances into unwanted matrimony is a nightmare in the New York group to the like of which no one in Chicago ever alludes. We pursue the issue one step farther: "Suppose they didn't make you. Would you marry her anyhow?" The response is a derisive, "Nah!" But then we want to know whether he would support the baby, and to this the answer is a subculturally typical *yes.* Even if, in order to do so, he would have to quit school (and this respondent values school)? Yes, even so, although, "that would be pretty bad."

The qualitative difference we wish to point up is more than a matter of nuance. Lloyd Warner and his associates were able to rank people, whom they interviewed in Yankee City, by class-typed responses to interview questions. We, in turn, can situate boys and girls (and could do so "blind," that is, without any accompanying data) in one of three impoverished subcultures, by their responses to a variety of straightforward, nondirective, and projective questions. Thus, a Puerto Rican boy who presents a tougher "front" than the one just quoted above is still unmistakably a Puerto Rican, and not an Appalachian or Negro boy:

Do you try to avoid getting a girl pregnant or don't you care?
I try to avoid it.
Suppose you did, and she found out where you lived?
I'd have to marry the broad.
Would you like that?
No, that's a hell of a mess.

The less insouciant type, a boy, for instance, whose presentation of self is somewhat gentler, simply says of the hypothetical girl he has impregnated: "You've got to marry her," leaving implicit why you have got to.

Since precautions to avert childbirth are unpopular, and pregnancy takes place willy-nilly, abortions should be common. If so, boys in Chicago tend to feel that it is no business of theirs. How different is the attitude that emerges in New York where, to select one of many examples, an advanced adolescent remarks apropos a girl friend who might get pregnant, "If I liked the girl enough I would marry her, or something." Suppose he didn't like her all that much, would he still feel obligated? "Yeah." In what way, we wonder. Would he arrange for an abortion? "No. That would mess her up too much. . . . Cause some ladies, they just do it to get money out of it; they don't really do it to help a person at all." Nonmedical abortionists, charging about eighty dollars a job, are said to abound on the street. Nevertheless, the white boys recoil from availing themselves of these services, obviously not for financial reasons, which are important in Chicago, since the stated alternative, assuming marital or nonmarital responsibility for support, would be so much costlier than disposition of an undesired fetus.

The differential warmth, involvement, and concern for "the other" in sexual affairs, while significant, should not be exaggerated. It is nonetheless present whatever tack we take. The myth of *machismo*, incorporating an alleged need for constant dramatic assertions of masculinity, notwithstanding, our Puerto Rican teenage boys do not preen themselves on their virility. Most of them accept the code which prohibits tattling "to other guys about girls they have schemed with." Some do engage in invidious talk about "street girls" whose well-known promiscuity makes it impossible to take pride in having "scored" with them. Similarly, the reaction to betrayal is a mild one. Violent assault on a girl may occur if she is suspected of having squealed to the police about stealing or fighting—not so about sexual defections. When they occur, New York boys say, "I walk away," "I tell her not to do that again," "I call it quits." The gorge does not rise very high, one's manhood is not called into question, and violence flares up but rarely. Likewise, the readiness to spare a girl friend undue embarrassment—or to share it with her by prematurely shouldering the parental responsibility—is quite exceptional. Commenting on the large number of unmarried girls with babies that boys refuse to support, a respondent explains, "Maybe one guy has her, then another, and then another. She doesn't know who the father is." Then what? "The last guy gets the blame." And getting the blame, more often than not, seems to mean accepting the blame, which, in turn (age permitting), means marriage. In this realm, as elsewhere, *fatalismo* apparently counts for more than *machismo*.

Sexual experience, which begins early and mounts in frequency, if not intensity, should not be equated with sexual sophistication. Indeed, the manifest naïvete is sometimes monumental. So:

> How do you avoid getting girls pregnant? (Long pause) I don't really know.
> Nobody ever told you about that?
> Nobody ever told me.
> Well, how do you keep the girl from having a baby?
> I guess you kill the baby.
> Do you know about killing babies?
> I don't know, but . . .
> Is that what they do around the block?
> If they gonna kill the babies, they gonna kill theirself.
> So you never heard about protection? Like a rubber?
> What did you say? Girdle? Maybe that's the only way. I know a girl lives in
> my neighborhood. She had a baby, but you couldn't tell, and after awhile they
> found out she had a girdle on. But she still had a baby. I don't really know how
> you could stop it. The only way, I suppose, is wearing a girdle.

Another boy reports making a girl pregnant, but there was no baby, "because she took it out." How he does not know or will not say. Yet another, asked what he would do if he got his girl friend pregnant, replies, "There's nothing I could do," and, for lack of options, lets it go at that.

Early marriage ensues, in a spirit best described as resignation. This "solution" becomes all the more irrational whenever boys protest, as they do with great vehemence, that it is the one thing that they wish, above all, to avoid. They speak of no marriage or late marriage, drawing the lesson of delay and circumvention from their own experience in unsatisfactory family relations. And, pointing to others all around them, they declaim against too many people marrying too soon, having too many children. It is on the basis that they diagnose most of their own trouble and most of the ills that others encounter in a slum environment. It all starts, they say, when a young man fathers a child he does not want—whose conception he will do nothing to prevent. Here, indeed, for one part of the underclass is the way of all flesh: Fully aware of the danger, our young man tumbles headlong into it, doing exactly what he had sworn not to do, classically entering a scene he had resolved to sidestep, with some, no doubt, unconscious, propulsion into a trap he professes to abhor.

A finer distinction must be made among Appalachians in Chicago. There, group-affiliated males show a consistent unwillingness to marry, holding out for very long, while, among the unaffiliated, there is a noticeably higher incidence of early marriage. When it takes place, males tend to be several years older than females, even if both are still in their teens. In the majority of cases, delay is secured through reinforcement of a powerful male peer group that seemingly functions much like the one analyzed by William Foote Whyte in *Street Corner Society*. It is the opinion of two long-time resident observers in Chicago that "most of the males find it impossible to maintain regular and satisfying experiences with a girl and quickly withdraw their attention and return to the male peer group." They also indicate that despite a well-nigh-universal claim to early sexual experience, many of the male youths admit to prolonged periods of disengagement both from overt heterosexual activity and coed sociability. Much of the sexual play that does take place involves a group of boys who exploit one or two females, many of them "young run-aways" or disillusioned young wives, viewed as "easy scores" for all. After a week or so of intensified sexuality with one such female, she usually disappears. Then the males resume their involuntary celibacy. Later, they embark once again on the same cycle. All of this is absolutely affectless.

Appalachian girls in Chicago stress early marriage as a female adjustment. They hope for husbands who "won't be unfaithful," "won't drink," "will be nice," and "will work hard." Demographic findings and intimate observation make it clear that, personal preference apart, a girl often marries the first young male adult with whom she has a steady relationship. Our resident observers also tell us that their "noncodified observations yield another interesting pattern of marital relationship in the next older group," which they feel may have a bearing on "the essentially brittle relations of the teenagers." During our study, a number of marriages have been observed to dissolve into a peculiar pattern of realignment, such that: Male A, aged thirty-five, establishes a liaison with Female X, his own age or older; wife of A establishes a liaison with unmarried Male B, aged twenty-five or thirty or with a formerly married male, aged twenty-five to thirty who, in turn, has separated from his younger wife. Consequently, for the second marriage, or for sexual adventures after a first marriage, the male is ordinarily younger than the female. We find, in short, that, parallel to the traditional form (older husband, younger wife), there is a deviant form that leaves separated, divorced, and unfaithful women with younger husbands and lovers. There is a certain distinctiveness in this duality.

CULTURAL VALUES COMPARED

We suspected at the outset of our inquiry that the rhetoric and the activity of impoverished American subcultures would be far removed from traditional Western ideas of love and sex. They are. Middle-class standards, in all their present disarray, carry those ideas (or reactions against them) in a confusing mélange that can only bewilder young people who are their residuary legatees. Not so in the underclass, where, with all its diversity, these ideas appear—if at all—only in mutilated form.

With a mixture of envy and indignation, middle-class people often impute pure sensual pleasure to their social inferiors, who are thought to pursue this objective heedlessly, if not monomaniacally. There is no warrant for this judgment. Puerto Rican youth in New York seem, somewhat more than the other groups, to stress sensual pleasure, but even they are manifestly more interested in *collective* fun, in "the set" itself, than in pure hedonism. All the same, insofar as "scheming" is an act of rebellion against authority, it does not much differ from taking pot or ingesting alcohol. In any class, youthful manifestations of defiance are a tacit acknowledgement of that coercive culture which some choose to resist. On the face of it, a Puerto Rican boy willing to "accept the responsibility" of marriage to, or help for, the girl he has impregnated, responds in accordance with one element of the Western Catholic tradition. For him, heterosexual dalliance imposes an obligation, but only if "the worst should happen," and then only when he is actuated by a sense of fatality rather than by love or duty. Chance has dealt him a heavy blow, rendered him powerless to fight back, left him a plaything of mysterious forces, destroyed his capacity to act as a free agent.

That culturally induced responsibility for one's sex acts cannot be taken for granted is clear enough in the other two groups, whose members refuse to do what the New York Puerto Rican boy feels that he must do. In this milieu, a residue of the declining tradition may still be observed. Not so in the Washington and Chicago samples of Negroes and Appalachian whites.

Given time, any group encapsulated in a constricted ghetto can be severed, not just from the mainstream of a larger culture but from its ancestral subculture as well. The unique circumstances of isolation and contact, impoverishment and opportunity, continuity and rupture with the past, will produce new codes, new standards, new articulations, and new behavior patterns. The Appalachian whites and the Washington Negroes are in most ways slightly less "Westernized" (that is, made into middle-class people) than Puerto Rican youth in New York. All, however, have rural, but by no means identical, origins. And all have moved into hideous urban ghettos where, to varying degrees, they are shut off from the major values of Western society. For people from the Southern hill country or the Southern plantation, lack of contact with outsiders is an old story. Urbanization, even in ghettos, reduces their isolation. The Appalachian white may have been culturally on his own since the pre-Revolutionary settlement of this country. For lower-class Negroes, isolation may have begun with the capture of their ancestors in Africa, and continued through Southern slavery to Northern segregation. The Negro subclass has had practically no exposure to Western sexual ideals, and the Appalachian white's exposure occurred so long ago that its effects are virtually inoperative.

For these submerged peoples, our dominant sexual ideologies have little relevance. Neither emotional and material responsibilities, nor their opposite, pure joy in unrestrained sexuality, is much in evidence. Sexual fulfillment is experienced merely as a physical release—the "friction of two membranes"—in which the female is the necessary but unequal partner. Otherwise, sexual conquest provides a trophy calculated to enhance one's prestige in peer-group competition. Masculinity is affirmed as part of a game whose competitors must incessantly prove themselves before an audience of others engaged in the same pastime. Since it is a competitive game, the boy who plays cannot expect to earn points for scoring over an easy mark, a "pig." Victory consists in overcoming the largest possible number of inaccessible girls. The conversion of females into trophies reduces them to nonpersons. Their personal, sexual, or simply human, needs do not matter. They exist to be tricked, deceived, manipulated—and abandoned. Skill in all these techniques is a sign of stylistic virtuosity. For a boy to abuse his sexual partner in many ingenious ways makes him a big winner. To all this, the lush rhetoric and varied responses elicited from our interviews are ample testimony. Customary allusions to Western concepts of love and sex are "foreign" to people who cannot express them verbally or in terms of their actual conduct. They are historically and personally alienated from the amorous and sexual context that Western idealism, with all its twists and turns, has to offer. That condition, for which no single urban ghetto is a carbon copy, can only deepen as subcultural segregation runs its course.

Investigation of ethnic underclass sexual mores in our own society, while it points to important differences, certainly does not provide us with examples of "natural," spontaneous, unrepressed, and nonneurotic sensual pleasure. Sexual practices are indissolubly linked to nonsexual aspects of lifestyle. For this reason, it would in any case be impossible to transfer the really illusory freedom of slum sex codes to an academic and bureaucratic world. If in that world, "intellectualized," "artificial," and "abstract" standards prevail, they cannot be banished by sexual personalism. No more than primitive or peasant society do subcultures of poverty offer us solutions to our sexual dilemma.

10

Social level and sexual outlet in the human male*

ALFRED C. KINSEY, WARDELL B. POMEROY,
and CLYDE E. MARTIN

PATTERNS OF BEHAVIOR

Within any single social level there are, of course, considerable differences between individuals in their choice of sexual outlets, and in the frequencies with which they engage in each type of activity. The range of individual variation in any level is not particularly different from the range of variation in each other level. Within each group, each individual pattern is more or less duplicated by the patterns of individuals in every one of the other social levels. Nevertheless, the frequencies of each type of variant are so different for different social levels that the means and the medians and the general shapes of the frequency curves for the several groups are perfectly distinct. Translated into everyday thinking, this means that a large proportion of all the individuals in any group follows patterns of sexual behavior which are typical of the group, and which are followed by only a smaller number of the individuals in other groups.

If the mean or median frequencies for each type of sexual activity, at each social level, are brought together in a single chart (Figures 1 and 2),

* Reprinted from *Sexual Behavior in the Human Male*, pp. 374–84, and *Sexual Behavior in the Human Female*, pp. 563–64, by permission of Paul H. Gebhard, Director of the Institute for Sex Research, Inc.

For purposes of comparison, Tables 3 and 4 are reprinted from *Sexual Behavior in the Human Female*.

FIGURE 1. Patterns of sexual behavior at three educational levels, among single males

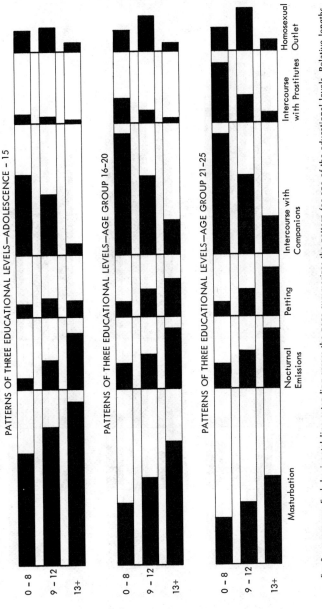

PATTERNS OF THREE EDUCATIONAL LEVELS—ADOLESCENCE - 15

PATTERNS OF THREE EDUCATIONAL LEVELS—AGE GROUP 16-20

PATTERNS OF THREE EDUCATIONAL LEVELS—AGE GROUP 21-25

0 - 8
9 - 12
13+

Masturbation Nocturnal Emissions Petting Intercourse with Companions Intercourse with Prostitutes Homosexual Outlet

For 3 age groups. Each horizontal line extending across the page summarizes the pattern for one of the educational levels. Relative lengths of bars in each outlet show average mean frequencies for the group. The scales vary for different sources of outlet, but there is an approximate indication of the relative importance of each source in the total outlet.

FIGURE 2. Patterns of sexual behavior at three educational levels, among married males

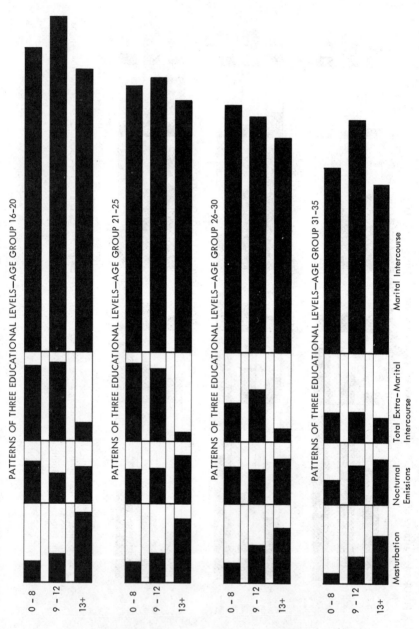

PATTERNS OF THREE EDUCATIONAL LEVELS—AGE GROUP 16–20

PATTERNS OF THREE EDUCATIONAL LEVELS—AGE GROUP 21–25

PATTERNS OF THREE EDUCATIONAL LEVELS—AGE GROUP 26–30

PATTERNS OF THREE EDUCATIONAL LEVELS—AGE GROUP 31–35

Masturbation   Nocturnal Emissions   Total Extra-Marital Intercourse   Marital Intercourse

For 4 age groups. Each horizontal line extending across the page summarizes the pattern for one of the educational levels. Relative lengths of bars in each outlet show average mean frequencies for the group. The scales vary for different sources of outlet, but there is an approximate in-dication of the relative importance of each source in the total outlet.

it becomes possible to see what material differences there are in these patterns of behavior. Each horizontal line, followed across the chart, epitomizes the story for one social level. It is, as it were, a silhouette, a profile representing the essence of the group's attitudes on matters of sex, and the translation of those attitudes into overt sexual activity.

Even a child would comprehend that the creature represented in each of these silhouettes is distinct and unlike the creatures represented in the other silhouettes.

It is, of course, of prime concern to ask why patterns of sexual behavior differ as they do in different social levels. It is of scientific importance to understand how such patterns originate, how they are passed on to each individual, and how they become standards of behavior for such a high proportion of all the individuals in each group. It is of equal importance to understand the social significances of these patterns of sexual behavior. Few of us have been aware that there were such differences in patterns in the various subdivisions of our culture. An understanding of the facts may contribute something toward easing the tensions that arise because individuals and whole segments of the population fail to understand the sexual philosophies and the sexual behavior of groups in which they have not been raised.

We do not yet understand, to the full, the origins of these diverse sexual philosophies; but it will be possible to record what the thinking of each group is in regard to each type of activity.

MASTURBATION

At lower social levels, and particularly among the older generations of the lowest levels, masturbation may be looked down upon as abnormal, a perversion, and an infantile substitute for sociosexual contacts. Although most lower level boys masturbate during their early adolescence, many of them never have more than a few experiences or, at the most, regular masturbation for a short period of months or years, after which they rarely again depend on such self-induced outlets. Among many of these lower level males, masturbation stops abruptly and immediately after the first experiences in heterosexual coitus. The lower level boy who continues to draw any material portion of his sexual outlet from masturbation after his middle teens may be much ashamed of it, and he may become the object of community jokes and of more serious disapproval if his history becomes known. In many instances, these attitudes are bolstered by rationalizations to the effect that masturbation does physical harm; but the objections are in reality based on the idea that masturbation is either abnormal, or else an admission that one is incapable of securing heterosexual intercourse and, therefore, socially inadequate. Among some primitive peoples there is a somewhat similar attitude toward masturbation—an attitude which does not involve moral evaluations as much as it involves amusement at the social incapacity of the individual who has to resort to self-stimulation for his sexual outlet. The better educated portion of the population which so largely depends upon masturbation for its premarital outlet, and which draws a not insignificant portion of its outlet from masturbation after marriage, will be surprised to learn what the less educated segments of the population think of one who masturbates instead of having intercourse.

The upper level more or less allows masturbation as not exactly desirable nor exactly commendable, but not as immoral as a sociosexual contact. Older generations of the upper level were not so ready to accept masturbation. As many males were involved in the older generations, but the frequencies were definitely lower, and there was considerable moral conflict over the rightness or wrongness of the "habit." Upper level males have accepted masturbation more freely within the last two or three decades, and today a high proportion of the teenage boys of the college group frankly and openly admit this form of premarital outlet. During their years in college about 70 percent of these males depend upon masturbation as their chief source of outlet. They derive about 66 percent of their orgasms from this source during their college years.

The upper level's premarital experience leads it to include masturbation as a source of outlet after marriage. The coital adjustments of this group in marriage are frequently poor, particularly because of the low degree of erotic responsiveness which exists among many of the college-bred females. This offers some excuse for masturbation among the married males of the group; but their early acceptance of masturbation in their premarital histories, and their tardy acceptance of heterosexual coitus, are prime determinants in the marital patterns. There are few things in all human sexual behavior which will surprise the poorly educated groups more than this considerable utilization of masturbation by the college-bred male as an outlet after marriage.

PETTING

The social levels are furthest apart in their attitudes on petting and on premarital intercourse. The two items are related, for petting, among males of the college level, is more or less a substitute for actual coitus.

In the upper level code of sexual morality, there is nothing so important as the preservation of the virginity of the female and, to a somewhat lesser degree, the similar preservation of the virginity of the male until the time of marriage. The utilization of premarital petting at this level is fortified by the emphasis which the marriage manuals place upon the importance of precoital techniques in married relations; and the younger generation considers that its experience before marriage may contribute something to the development of satisfactory marital relations. Compared with coitus,

TABLE 1. Sources of sexual outlet for single males, at three educational levels (showing percentage of total outlet derived by each group from each source).

Sources	Adol.– 15	16–20	21–25	26–30	31–35	36–40
	Sources of orgasm: single males *percent of total outlet*					
Educational level 0–8						
Masturbation	52.26	29.15	20.15	20.68	24.24	28.95
Nocturnal emissions	1.82	4.83	5.02	6.26	5.49	5.97
Petting to climax	1.06	1.66	1.23	1.96	0.68	0.05
Intercourse with companions	35.00	50.62	52.84	42.71	23.74	23.08
Intercourse with prostitutes	0.97	6.21	12.55	14.34	18.42	23.35
Homosexual outlet	8.03	6.85	8.06	14.04	27.43	18.60
Animal contacts	0.86	0.68	0.15	0.01		
Total outlet	100.00	100.00	100.00	100.00	100.00	100.00
Number of cases	712	720	361	159	61	47
Total solitary outlets	54.08	33.98	25.17	26.94	29.73	34.92
Total heterosexual outlets	37.03	58.49	66.62	59.01	42.84	46.48
Total homosexual outlet	8.03	6.85	8.06	14.04	27.43	18.60
Educational level 9–12						
Masturbation	59.09	37.17	29.67	27.69	18.48	
Nocturnal emissions	4.44	6.33	8.10	7.48	8.21	
Petting to climax	1.46	2.37	2.77	1.82	1.35	
Intercourse with companions	24.93	39.49	38.02	29.15	42.81	
Intercourse with prostitutes	0.44	2.75	4.66	6.46	10.32	
Homosexual outlet	8.73	10.81	16.31	25.95	18.83	
Animal contacts	0.91	1.08	0.47	0.85		
Total outlet	100.00	100.00	100.00	100.00	100.00	
Number of cases	606	607	263	117	41	
Total solitary outlets	63.53	43.50	37.77	35.17	26.69	
Total heterosexual outlets	26.83	44.61	45.45	38.03	54.48	
Total homosexual outlet	8.73	10.81	16.31	25.95	18.83	
Educational level 13+						
Masturbation	79.61	66.37	53.30	45.88	44.28	
Nocturnal emissions	12.15	15.65	15.67	11.93	10.67	
Petting to climax	1.54	5.26	7.50	5.17	4.98	
Intercourse with companions	2.74	9.13	18.45	24.97	21.52	
Intercourse with prostitutes	0.11	0.80	1.27	3.16	0.65	
Homosexual outlet	3.14	2.43	3.72	8.82	17.90	
Animal contacts	0.71	0.36	0.09	0.07		
Total outlet	100.00	100.00	100.00	100.00	100.00	
Number of cases	2799	2861	1898	487	87	
Total solitary outlets	91.76	82.02	68.97	57.81	54.95	
Total heterosexual outlets	4.39	15.19	27.22	33.30	27.15	
Total homosexual outlet	3.14	2.43	3.72	8.82	17.90	

TABLE 2. Sources of sexual outlet for married males, at three educational levels (showing percentages of total outlet derived by each group from each source).

Sources	Sources of orgasm: married males percent of total outlet						
	16–20	21–25	26–30	31–35	36–40	41–45	46–50
Educational level 0–8							
Masturbation	2.40	2.43	2.44	1.79	1.59	1.41	1.4
Nocturnal emissions	3.08	2.79	3.41	3.03	1.85	2.25	2.6
Intercourse, marital	79.92	81.03	86.15	88.07	88.09	89.96	89.9
Interc., extra-m., comp.	10.91	11.62	6.38	5.51	7.24	4.84	4.7
Interc., extra-m., prost.	0.61	0.80	1.16	1.46	0.93	1.46	1.4
Homosexual outlet	3.08	1.33	0.46	0.14	0.30	0.08	0.0
Total outlet	100.00	100.00	100.00	100.00	100.00	100.00	100.0
Number of cases	158	324	292	186	143	100	70
Total solitary outlets	5.48	5.22	5.85	4.82	3.44	3.66	4.0
Total hetero. outlets	91.44	93.45	93.69	95.04	96.26	96.26	96.0
Total homo. outlet	3.08	1.33	0.46	0.14	0.30	0.08	0.0
Educational level 9–12							
Masturbation	2.75	3.70	5.05	4.04	3.15	1.68	2.8
Nocturnal emissions	2.04	2.85	3.22	3.79	4.48	5.29	2.9
Intercourse, marital	82.19	81.56	81.67	85.18	88.19	89.18	91.0
Interc., extra-m., comp.	9.43	9.35	7.61	4.62	1.76	3.15	3.1
Interc., extra-m., prost.	1.48	1.49	1.49	0.99	1.69	0.70	0.2
Homosexual outlet	2.11	1.05	0.96	1.38	0.73		
Total outlet	100.00	100.00	100.00	100.00	100.00	100.00	100.0
Number of cases	87	164	135	82	58	34	24
Total solitary outlets	4.79	6.55	8.27	7.83	7.63	6.97	5.7
Total hetero. outlets	93.10	92.40	90.77	90.79	91.64	93.03	94.3
Total homo. outlet	2.11	1.05	0.96	1.38	0.73		
Educational level 13+							
Masturbation	8.53	8.79	8.67	9.28	8.26	9.71	9.0
Nocturnal emissions	2.99	4.65	4.69	5.71	6.06	5.87	5.4
Intercourse, marital	85.41	83.94	82.76	78.34	74.41	76.39	68.5
Interc., extra-m., comp.	2.86	1.86	2.72	5.51	9.85	6.07	13.7
Interc., extra-m., prost.	0.05	0.23	0.20	0.41	0.53	0.32	0.4
Homosexual outlet	0.16	0.53	0.96	0.75	0.89	1.64	3.0
Total outlet	100.00	100.00	100.00	100.00	100.00	100.00	100.0
Number of cases	46	440	532	301	189	138	81
Total solitary outlets	11.52	13.44	13.36	14.99	14.32	15.58	14.4
Total hetero. outlets	88.32	86.03	85.68	84.26	84.79	82.78	82.6
Total homo. outlet	0.16	0.53	0.96	0.75	0.89	1.64	3.0

TABLE 3. Percentage of total outlet, by source (in active sample of single females, by educational level).

Source	Adol.–15	16–20	21–25	26–30	31–35	36–40	41–45
		Educational level 9–12					
Masturbation	73	44	36	38	58		
Nocturnal orgasm	1	2	2	2	4		
Petting to orgasm	6	21	23	16	9		
Coitus	14	29	32	32	23		
Homosexual	6	4	7	12	6		
Total outlet	100	100	100	100	100		
Total solitary	74	46	38	40	62		
Total heterosexual	20	50	55	48	32		
Total homosexual	6	4	7	12	6		
Percent with any orgasm	27	51	60	62	65		
Number of cases in total sample	983	976	537	181	65		
		Educational level 13–16					
Masturbation	93	65	48	39	30	32	
Nocturnal orgasm	2	4	3	2	2	2	
Petting to orgasm	3	18	15	9	5	3	
Coitus	1	10	26	40	52	46	
Homosexual	1	3	8	10	11	17	
Total outlet	100	100	100	100	100	100	
Total solitary	95	69	51	41	32	34	
Total heterosexual	4	28	41	49	57	49	
Total homosexual	1	3	8	10	11	17	
Percent with any orgasm	19	46	59	68	69	78	
Number of cases in total sample	3271	3299	1204	313	139	68	
		Educational level 17+					
Masturbation	90	66	47	43	47	40	45
Nocturnal orgasm	3	4	3	3	3	2	2
Petting to orgasm	3	16	20	14	11	6	4
Coitus	2	8	23	27	21	31	42
Homosexual	2	6	7	13	18	21	7
Total outlet	100	100	100	100	100	100	100
Total solitary	93	70	50	46	50	42	47
Total heterosexual	5	24	43	41	32	37	46
Total homosexual	2	6	7	13	18	21	7
Percent with any orgasm	27	48	61	69	75	72	70
Number of cases in total sample	1128	1149	1002	531	309	205	122

"Active sample" refers to those experiencing orgasm from any source.

TABLE 4. Percentage of total outlet, by source (in active sample of married females, by educational level).

Source	16–20	21–25	26–30	31–35	36–40	41–45	46–50
Educational level 9–12							
Masturbation	8	5	5	7	9	9	13
Nocturnal org.	1	1	2	2	3	4	3
Coitus, marital	89	91	90	88	83	73	80
Coitus + Pet., extra-marit.	2	3	3	3	5	14	4
Homosexual	—	—	—	0	—	0	0
Total outlet	100	100	100	100	100	100	100
Total solitary	9	6	7	9	12	13	16
Total hetero.	91	94	93	91	88	87	84
Total homosex.	—	—	—	0	—	0	0
Percent with any orgasm	73	89	91	93	92	93	92
Number of cases in total sample	210	487	489	338	210	117	71
Educational level 13–16							
Masturbation	8	7	7	7	11	7	10
Nocturnal org.	—	—	1	2	1	2	4
Coitus, marital	90	89	84	82	74	82	76
Coitus + Pet., extra-marit.	1	3	7	8	13	9	10
Homosexual	1	1	1	1	1	0	0
Total outlet	100	100	100	100	100	100	100
Total solitary	8	7	8	9	12	9	14
Total hetero.	91	92	91	90	87	91	86
Total homosex.	1	1	1	1	1	0	0
Percent with any orgasm	82	88	92	96	96	92	96
Number of cases in total sample	257	727	670	479	322	181	91
Educational level 17+							
Masturbation	10	7	9	9	10	17	13
Nocturnal org.	4	2	1	1	1	2	1
Coitus, marital	86	90	83	83	79	65	60
Coitus + Pet., extra-marit.	—	1	7	7	10	16	25
Homosexual	—	—	—	—	—	—	1
Total outlet	100	100	100	100	100	100	100
Total solitary	14	9	10	10	11	19	14
Total hetero.	86	91	90	90	89	81	85
Total homosex.	—	—	—	—	—	—	1
Percent with any orgasm	83	89	94	95	96	96	95
Number of cases in total sample	66	368	421	360	268	163	76

"Active sample" refers to those experiencing orgasm from any source.

petting has the advantage of being accessible under conditions where coitus would be impossible; it provides a simpler means of achieving both arousal and orgasm, it makes it possible to experience orgasm while avoiding the possibility of pregnancy, and, above all, it preserves one's "virginity." Whether consciously or unconsciously, petting is chosen by the upper level because intercourse destroys virginity and is, therefore, unacceptable. It is significant to note what different values are attached, at that level, to erotic arousal and orgasm achieved through the union of genitalia, and to erotic arousal and orgasm achieved through physical contact of other portions of the body, or even through genital contact or genital manipulation which does not involve actual copulation. There are many males in the upper level who develop a fine art of achieving orgasm by petting techniques which avoid intercourse. The youth who may have experienced orgasm scores or hundreds of times in petting, and who may have utilized every type of petting technique, including mouth-genital contacts, still has the satisfaction of knowing that he is still a virgin, as his level defines virginity. There are even cases of males who effect genital union; but because they avoid orgasm while in such union they persuade themselves that they are still virgins. The illogic of the situation emphasizes the fact that the basic issue is one of conforming with a code (the avoidance of premarital intercourse, the preservation of one's virginity), which is of paramount importance in the mores of this social level.

The lower educational levels see no sense in this. They have nothing like this strong taboo against premarital intercourse and, on the contrary, accept it as natural and inevitable and a desirable thing. Lower level taboos are more often turned against an avoidance of intercourse, and against any substitution for simple and direct coitus. Petting involves a considerable list of techniques which may be acceptable to the college group, and to some degree to the high school group, but which are quite taboo at lower levels (as discussed above). It is just because petting involves these techniques, and because it substitutes for actual intercourse, that it is considered a perversion by the lower level.

In particular cases, older persons, even at upper levels, have objected to premarital petting; but individual objections do not have the force of long-established mores. Premarital intercourse is condemned by mores which go back hundreds and thousands of years. Such taboos are very different from the criticisms which lone individuals have levied against petting within the last few decades, and for the most part the younger generation has paid little attention to such criticisms.

There is nothing in the behavior of the upper level which is more responsible than petting is for the general opinion that college students are sexually wild. The lower level has many times as much premarital intercourse as the college male has, and it is not the intercourse of the college student which is the source of the lower level's criticism. It is the fact that petting may be engaged in for many hours without arriving at intercourse—it is the fact that intercourse itself is not more often accepted as a premarital outlet by the upper social level.

PREMARITAL INTERCOURSE

With the upper educational level, the question of premarital intercourse is largely one of morals. Some of the younger generation find it modern to insist that they do not avoid premarital intercourse because it is wrong, but because they consider intercourse too precious to have with anyone except the girl that they marry, or because they consider that marriages work out better when there has been no premarital intercourse. To this extent the younger generation is "emancipated"; but the change in the form of its rationalizations has not affected its overt behavior one whit.

A large portion of the 85 percent of the population which never goes to college accepts premarital intercourse as normal and natural. Most of this group would insist that there is no question of right or wrong involved. Even some lower level clergymen, of the group that has never gone beyond grade school or high school, may react as the rest of the community of which they are a part, preaching against profanity, smoking, drinking, gambling, and extramarital intercourse, but considering that no moral issue is involved in premarital intercourse. So nearly universal is premarital intercourse among grade school groups that in two or three lower level communities in which we have worked we have been unable to find a solitary male who had not had sexual relations with girls by the time he was 16 or 17 years of age. In such a community, the occasional boy who has not had intercourse by that age is either physically incapacitated, mentally deficient, homosexual, or ear-marked for moving out of his community and going to college.

Lower level males may have a certain respect for virginity, and this may lead them to insist (in 41 percent of the cases) that they would not marry a girl who had had previous intercourse; but this may be more of a profession than a matter on which they will stand when it comes to the actual choice of a mate. Lower level males are likely to acquire weekly or more than weekly frequencies in intercourse soon after they start in early adolescence, or at least by the middle teens. They are often highly promiscuous in their choice of premarital partners, and there are many who have no interest in having intercourse with the same girl more than once. This strikingly parallels the promiscuity which is found among those homosexual males who are "oncers," as the vernacular term puts it. Some lower level males may have premarital intercourse with several hundred or even a thousand or more different girls before marriage, and here their behavior is most different from the behavior of the college-bred males.

EXTRAMARITAL INTERCOURSE

In lower social levels there is a somewhat bitter acceptance of the idea that the male is basically promiscuous and that he is going to have extramarital intercourse, whether or not his wife or society objects. There is some continuation of the group attitude on premarital intercourse into the realm of extramarital intercourse, at least in the early years of marriage. On the other hand, the upper level male who has been heterosexually restrained for 10 or 15 years before marriage does not freely let down and start extramarital intercourse as soon as he has learned to have coitus with his wife. As a matter of fact, a male who has been so restrained often has difficulty in working out a sexual adjustment with his wife, and it is doubtful whether very many of the upper level males would have any facility in finding extramarital intercourse, even if they were to set out deliberately after it. The lower level's extramarital intercourse does cause trouble, but we do not yet understand all the factors which account for the fact that with advancing age there is a steady decline and finally a near disappearance of extramarital intercourse from lower level marital histories.

The development of extramarital intercourse in the histories of the older males of the upper level is done with a certain deliberation which in some cases may be acceded to and encouraged by the wife.

HOMOSEXUAL CONTACTS

The considerable differences which exist in the incidence and frequencies of the homosexual in the three educational levels would seem to indicate basic differences in attitudes toward such activity; but we are not sure that we yet understand what these differences are.

The fewest objections to the homosexual are found in the very lowest of the social levels, in the best educated groups, and in top society. At the lowest social levels sex, whether it be heterosexual or homosexual, is more or less accepted as inevitable. The children here are the least restrained sexually and usually become involved in both heterosexual and homosexual activities at an early age. Since this is the group in which preadolescent behavior most often carries over into adult behavior, it is not surprising to find a fair number of the males at this level continuing both types of activity through the major portion of their lives. It is notable, however, that there are few individuals in this group who become exclusively homosexual. There are some who definitely condemn the homosexual, but there are many who accept it simply as one more form of sex. Rarely do they interfere with other persons who are involved, even though they themselves may not enter into such activities.

The acceptance of the homosexual in top educational and social levels is the product of a wider understanding of realities, some comprehension of the factors involved, and more concern over the mental qualities and social capacities of an individual than over anything in his sexual history.

The highest incidence of the homosexual, however, are in the group which most often verbalizes its disapproval of such activity. This is in the group that goes into high school but never beyond in its educational career. These are the males who most often condemn the homosexual, most often ridicule and express disgust for such activity, and most often punish other males for their homosexuality. And yet, this is the group which has the largest amount of overt homosexual activity. Their involvement may be due to curiosity, to the fact that one may profit financially by accepting homosexual relations, or to the fact that one may derive a sadistic satisfaction from beating up the partner after orgasm has been achieved in the homosexual activity. In a certain segment of this group the idea is more or less accepted that one may uphold the heterosexual mores while "playing the queers," provided one punishes them after orgasm is achieved in the homosexual relation. As a group these males may strenuously deny that their sexual contacts have anything to do with homosexuality; but the full and complete record indicates that many of them have stronger psychic reactions to other males than they care to admit. When they no longer find themselves being paid for such contacts, many of them begin paying other males for the privilege of sexual relations.

If there are group attitudes in regard to the homosexual, they are not as freely discussed at most social levels. It may be that this explains why community thinking is not so well crystallized on this subject as it is in regard to other forms of sexual activity.

11
How and why America's
sex standards are changing*

IRA L. REISS

The popular notion that America is undergoing a sexual "revolution" is a myth. The belief that our more permissive sexual code is a sign of a general breakdown of morality is also a myth. These two myths have arisen in part because we have so little reliable information about American sexual behavior. The enormous public interest in sex seems to have been matched by moralizing and reticence in scholarly research—a situation that has only recently begun to be corrected.

What *has* been happening recently is that our young people have been assuming more responsibility for their own sexual standards and behavior. The influence of their parents has been progressively declining. The greater independence given to the young has long been evident in other fields— employment, spending, and prestige, to name three. The parallel change in sexual-behavior patterns would have been evident if similar research had been made in this area. One also could have foreseen that those groups least subject to the demands of old orthodoxies, like religion, would emerge as the most sexually permissive of all—men in general, liberals, non-churchgoers, Negroes, the highly educated.

In short, today's more permissive sexual standards represent not revolution but evolution, not anomie but normality.

* Reprinted with the permission of the author and the publisher. Copyright ©
March 1968 by Trans-action, Inc., New Brunswick, New Jersey.

My own research into current sexual behavior was directed primarily to the question, Why are some groups of people more sexually permissive than other groups? My study involved a representative sample of about 1500 people, 21 and older, from all over the country; and about 1200 high-school and college students, 16 to 22 years old, from three different states. On the pages that follow, I will first discuss some of the more important of my findings; then suggest seven general propositions that can be induced from these findings; and, finally, present a comprehensive theory about modern American sexual behavior.

ARE RACE DIFFERENCES ROOTED IN CLASS?

A good many sociologists believe that most of the real differences between Negroes and whites are class differences—that if Negroes and whites from the same class were compared, any apparent differences would vanish. Thus, some critics of the Moynihan Report accused Daniel P. Moynihan of ignoring how much lower-class whites may resemble lower-class Negroes.

But my findings show that there are large variations in the way whites and Negroes *of precisely the same class* view premarital sexual permissiveness. Among the poor, for instance, only 32 percent of white males approve of intercourse before marriage under some circumstances—compared with 70 percent of Negro males. The variation is even more dramatic among lower-class females: 5 percent of whites compared with 33 percent of Negroes. Generally, highschool and college students of all classes were found to be more permissive than those in the adult sample. But even among students there were variations associated with race. (See Table 1.)

TABLE 1. Percent accepting premarital sex.

	Lower-class adults*	Lower-class students**
White men	32% of 202	56% of 96
Negro men	70 of 49	86 of 88
White women	5 of 221	17 of 109
Negro woman	33 of 63	42 of 90

* From national adult sample.
** From five-school student sample.

The difference between Negro and white acceptance of premarital intercourse is not due to any racial superiority or inferiority. All that this finding suggests is that we should be much more subtle in studying Negro-white differences, and not assume that variations in education, income, or occupation are enough to account for all these differences. The history of slavery, the depressing effects of discrimination and low status—all indicate that the Negro's entire cultural base may be different from the white's.

Another response to this finding on sexual attitudes can, of course, be disbelief. Do people really tell the truth about their sex lives? National studies have revealed that they do—women will actually talk more freely about their sex lives than about their husbands' incomes. And various validity checks indicate that they did in this case.

But people are not always consistent: They may not practice what they preach. So I decided to compare people's sexual attitudes with their actual sexual behavior. Table 2 indicates the degree of correspondence between

TABLE 2. Sexual standards and actual behavior.

Current standard	Most extreme current behavior			Number of respondents
	Kissing	Petting	Coitus	
Kissing	64%	32%	4%	25
Petting	15	78	7	139
Coitus	5	31	64	84

attitudes and behavior in a sample of 248 unmarried, white, junior and senior college-students.

Obviously, the students do not *always* act as they believe. But in the great majority of cases belief and action do coincide. For example, 64 percent of those who consider coitus acceptable are actually having coitus; only 7 percent of those who accept nothing beyond petting, and 4 percent of those who accept nothing beyond kissing, are having coitus. So it is fairly safe to conclude that, in this case, attitudes are good clues to behavior.

GUILT IS NO INHIBITOR

What about guilt feelings? Don't they block any transition toward more permissive sexual attitudes and behavior? Here the findings are quite unexpected. *Guilt feelings do not generally inhibit sexual behavior.* Eighty-seven percent of the women and 58 percent of the men said they had eventually come to accept sexual activities that had once made them feel guilty. (Some—largely males—had never felt guilty.) Seventy-eight percent had *never* desisted from any sexual activity that had made them feel guilty. Typically, a person will feel some guilt about his sexual behavior, but will continue his conduct until the guilt diminishes. Then he will move on to more advanced behavior—and new guilt feelings—until over that; and so on. People differed, mainly, in the sexual behavior they were willing to start, and in how quickly they moved on to more advanced forms.

The factor that most decisively motivated women to engage in coitus and to approve of coitus was the belief that they were in love. Of those who accepted coitus, 78 percent said they had been in love—compared with 60 percent of those who accepted only petting, and 40 percent of those who accepted only kissing. (Thus, parents who don't want their children to have sexual experiences but do want them to have "love" experiences are indirectly encouraging what they are trying to prevent.)

How do parents' beliefs influence their children's sexual attitudes and conduct?

Curiously enough, almost two-thirds of the students felt that their sexual standards were at least similar to those of their parents. This was as true for Negro males as for white females—although about 80 percent of the former accept premarital intercourse as against only about 20 percent of the latter. Perhaps these students are deluded, but perhaps they see through the "chastity" facade of their parents to the underlying similarities in attitude. It may be that the parents' views on independence, love, pleasure, responsibility, deferred gratification, conformity, and adventurousness are linked with the sexual attitudes of their children; that a similarity in these values implies a similarity in sexual beliefs. Probably these parental values, like religiousness, help determine which youngsters move quickly and with relatively little guilt through the various stages of sexual behavior. Religiousness, for the group of white students, is a particularly good index: Youngsters who rank high on church attendance rank low on premarital coitus, and are generally conservative.

Despite the fact that 63 to 68 percent of the students felt that their sexual standards were close to their parents' standards, a larger percentage felt that their standards were even closer to those of peers (77 percent) and to those of very close friends (89 percent). Thus, the conflict in views between peers and parents is not so sharp as might be expected. Then too, perhaps parents' values have a greater influence on their children's choice of friends than we usually acknowledge.

THE IMPORTANCE OF RESPONSIBILITY

This brings us to another key question. Are differences in sexual standards between parents and children due to changing cultural standards? Or are they due to their different roles in life—that is, to the difference between being young, and being parents responsible for the young? Were the parents of today that different when they courted?

My findings do show that older people tend to be less permissive about sex—but this difference is not very marked. What is significant is that childless couples—similar to couples with children of courtship age in every other respect, including age—are much more willing to accept premarital intercourse as standard (23 to 13 percent). Furthermore, parents tend to be *less* sexually permissive the *more* responsibility they have for young people. Now, if the primary cause of parent-child divergences in sexual standards is that cultural standards in general have been changing, then older people should, by and large, be strikingly more conservative about sex. They aren't. But since parents are more conservative about sex than nonparents of the same age, it would seem that the primary cause of parent-child divergences over sex is role and responsibility—the parents of today were *not* that different when courting.

Being responsible for others, incidentally, inhibits permissiveness even when the dependents are siblings. The first-born are far less likely to approve of premarital intercourse (39 percent) than are the youngest children (58 percent).

Another intriguing question is, How do parents feel about the sexual activities of their boy children—as opposed to their girl children? The answer depends upon the sex of the parent. The more daughters a white father has, the more strongly he feels about his standards—although his standards are no stricter than average. The more sons he has, the less strongly he feels about his beliefs. White mothers showed the reverse tendency, but much more weakly—the more sons, the stronger the mothers' insistence upon whatever standards they believed in. Perhaps white parents feel this way because of their unfamiliarity with the special sexual problems of a child of the opposite sex—combined with an increasing awareness of these problems.

What explains these differences in attitude between groups—differences between men and women as well as between Negroes and whites? Women are more committed to marriage than men, so girls become more committed to marriage too, and to low-permissive parental values. The economic pressures on Negroes work to break up their families, and weaken commitment to marital values, so Negroes tend to be more permissive. Then too, whites have a greater stake in the orthodox institution of marriage: More white married people than unmarried people reported that they were happy. Among Negroes, the pattern was reversed. But in discussing weak commitments to marriage we are dealing with one of the "older" sources of sexual permissiveness.

The sources of the new American permissiveness are somewhat different. They include access to contraception; ways to combat venereal infection; and—quite as important—an intellectualized philosophy about the desirability of sex accompanying affection. "Respectable," college-educated people have integrated this new philosophy with their generally liberal attitudes about the family, politics, and religion. And this represents a new and more lasting support for sexual permissiveness, since it is based on a positive philosophy rather than hedonism, despair, or desperation.

In my own study, I found that among the more permissive groups were those in which the fathers were professional men. This finding is important: It shows that the upper segments of our society, like the lower, have a highly permissive group in their midst—despite the neat picture described by some people of permissiveness steadily declining as one raises one's gaze toward the upper classes.

PATTERNS OF PERMISSIVENESS

All these findings, though seemingly diverse, actually fall into definite patterns, or clusters of relationships. These patterns can be expressed in seven basic propositions:

1. The *less* sexually permissive a group is, traditionally, the *greater* the likelihood that new social forces will cause its members to become more permissive.

Traditionally high-permissive groups, such as Negro men, were the least likely to have their sexual standards changed by social forces like church attendance, love affairs, and romantic love. Traditionally low-permissive groups, such as white females, showed the greatest sensitivity to these social forces. In addition, the lower social classes are reported to have a tradition of greater sexual permissiveness, so the finding that their permissiveness is less sensitive to certain social forces also fits this proposition.

2. The more liberal the group, the more likely that social forces will help maintain high sexual permissiveness.

There was diverse support for this proposition. Students, upper-class females in liberal settings, and urban dwellers have by and large accepted more permissiveness than those in more conservative settings.

Indeed, liberalism in general seems to be yet another cause of the new permissiveness in America. Thus, a group that was traditionally low-permissive regarding sex (the upper class), but that is liberal in such fields as religion and politics, would be very likely to shift toward greater premarital permissiveness.

3. According to their ties to marital and family institutions, people will differ in their sensitivity to social forces that affect permissiveness.

This proposition emphasizes, mainly, male-female differences in courting. Women have a stronger attachment to and investment in marriage, childbearing, and family ties. This affects their courtship roles. There are fundamental male-female differences in acceptance of permissiveness, therefore, in line with differences in courtship role.

Romantic love led more women than men to become permissive (this finding was particularly true if the woman was a faithful churchgoer). Having a steady date affected women predominantly, and exclusiveness was linked with permissiveness. Early dating, and its link with permissiveness, varied by race, but was far more commonly linked with permissiveness in men than in women. The number of steadies, and the number of times in love, was associated with permissiveness for females, but was curvilinear for males—that is, a man with no steadies, or a number of steadies, tended to be more permissive than a man who had gone steady only once.

Such male-female differences, however, are significant only for whites. Among Negroes, male-female patterns in these areas are quite similar.

4. The higher the overall level of permissiveness in a group, the greater the extent of equalitarianism within abstinence and double-standard sub-groups.

Permissiveness is a measure not only of what a person will accept for himself and his own sex, but of what behavior he is willing to allow the opposite sex. Permissiveness, I found, tends to be associated with sexual equalitarianism in one particular fashion: I found, strangely enough, that a good way to measure the *general* permissiveness of a group is to measure the equalitarianism of two subgroups—the abstinent, and believers in the double-standard. (Nonequalitarianism in abstinence means, usually, petting is acceptable for men, but only kissing for women. Equalitarianism within the double-standard means that intercourse is acceptable for women when in love, for men anytime. The nonequalitarian double-standard considers all unmarried women's coitus wrong.) In a generally high-permissive group (such as men), those adherents who do accept abstinence or the double-standard will be more equalitarian than will their counterparts in low-permissive groups (such as women). The implication is that the ethos of a high-permissive group encourages female sexuality and thereby also encourages equalitarianism throughout the group.

5. The potential for permissiveness derived from parents' values is a key determinant as to how rapidly, how much, and in what direction a person's premarital sexual standards and behavior change.

What distinguishes an individual's sexual behavior is not its starting point—white college-educated females, for instance, almost always start only with kissing—but how far, how fast, and in what direction the individual is willing to go. The fact is that almost all sexual behavior is eventually repeated, and comes to be accepted. And a person's basic values encourage or discourage his willingness to try something new and possibly guilt-producing. Therefore, these basic values—derived, in large part, from parental teaching, direct or implicit—are keys to permissiveness.

Since the young often feel that their sex standards are similar to their parents', we can conclude that, consciously or not, high-permissive parents intellectually and emotionally breed high-permissive children.

6. A youth tends to see permissiveness as a continuous scale with his parents' standards at the low point, his peers' at the high point, and himself between but closer to his peers—and closest to those he considers his most intimate friends.

The findings indicate that those who consider their standards closer to parents' than to peers' are less permissive than the others. The most permissive within one group generally reported the greatest distance from parents, and greatest similarity to peers and friends. This does not contradict the previous proposition, since parents are on the continuum and exert enough influence so that their children don't go all the way to the opposite end. But it does indicate, and the data bear out, that parents are associated with relatively low permissiveness; that the courtship group is associated with relatively high permissiveness; and that the respondents felt closer to the latter. Older, more permissive students were less likely to give "parental guidance" as a reason for their standards.

7. Greater responsibility for other members of the family, and lesser participation in courtship, are both associated with low permissiveness.

The only child, it was found, had the most permissive attitudes. Older children, generally, were less permissive than their younger brothers and sisters. The older children usually have greater responsibility for the young siblings; children without siblings have no such responsibilities at all.

The findings also showed that as the number of children, and their ages, increased, the parents' permissiveness decreased. Here again, apparently, parental responsibility grew, and the decline in permissiveness supports the proposition above.

On the other hand, as a young person gets more and more caught up in courtship, he is progressively freed from parental domination. He has less responsibility for others, and he becomes more permissive. The fact that students are more sexually liberal than many other groups must be due partly to their involvement in courtship, and to their distance from the family.

Thus a generational clash of some sort is almost inevitable. When children reach their late teens or early 20s, they also reach the peak of their permissiveness; their parents, at the same time, reach the nadir of theirs.

These findings show that both the family and courtship institutions are key determinants of whether a person accepts or rejects premarital sexuality. Even when young people have almost full independence in courtship, as they do in our system, they do not copulate at random. They display parental and family values by the association of sex with affection, by choice of partners, by equalitarianism, and so on.

However, parental influence must inevitably, to some extent, conflict with the pressures of courting, and the standards of the courting group. Young people are tempted by close association with attractive members of the opposite sex, usually without having any regular heterosexual outlet. Also, youth is a time for taking risks and having adventures. Therefore, the greater the freedom to react autonomously within the courtship group, the greater the tendency toward liberalized sexual behavior.

This autonomy has always been strong in America. Visitors in the 19th century were amazed at freedom of mate choice here, and the equalitarianism between sexes, at least as compared with Europe. The trend has grown.

Now, families are oriented toward the bearing and rearing of children—and for this, premarital sex is largely irrelevant. It becomes relevant only if it encourages marriages the parents want—but relevant negatively if it encourages births out of wedlock, or the "wrong," or no, marriages. Most societies tolerate intercourse between an engaged couple, for this doesn't seriously threaten the marital institution; and even prostitution gains some acceptance because it does not promote unacceptable marital unions. The conflict between the family and courtship systems depends on the extent to which each perceives the other as threatening its interests. My own findings indicate that this conflict is present, but not always as sharply as the popular press would have us believe.

Courtship pressures tend toward high permissiveness, family pressures toward low permissiveness. It follows that whatever promotes the child's independence from the family promotes high permissiveness. For example, independence is an important element in the liberal position; a liberal setting, therefore, generally encourages sexual as well as other independence.

A COMPREHENSIVE THEORY

To summarize all these findings into one comprehensive theory runs the risk of oversimplifying—if the findings and thought that went into the theory are not kept clearly in mind. With this *caveat*, I think a fair theoretical summary of the meaning of the foregoing material would be: How much premarital sexual permissiveness is considered acceptable in a courtship group varies directly with the independence of that group, and with the general permissiveness in the adult cultural environment.

In other words, when the social and cultural forces working on two groups are approximately the same, the differences in permissiveness are caused by differences in independence. But when independence is equal, differences come from differences in the socio-cultural setting.

There is, therefore, to repeat, no sexual revolution today. Increased premarital sexuality is not usually a result of breakdown of standards, but a particular, and different, type of organized system. To parents, more firmly identified with tradition—that is, with older systems—and with greater responsibilities toward the young, toward the family, and toward marriage, greater premarital sexuality seems deviant. But it is, nevertheless, an integral part of society—their society.

In short, there has been a gradually increasing acceptance of and overtness about sexuality. The basic change is toward greater equalitarianism, greater female acceptance of permissiveness, and more open discussion. In the next decade, we can expect a step-up in the pace of this change.

The greater change, actually, is in sexual attitude, rather than in behavior. If behavior has not altered in the last century as much as we might think, attitudes *have*—and attitudes and behavior seem closer today than for many generations. Judging by my findings, and the statements of my respondents, we can expect them to become closer still, and to proceed in tandem into a period of greater permissiveness, and even greater frankness. I do not, however, foresee extreme change in the years to come—such as full male-female equality. This is not possible unless male and female roles in the family are also equal, and men and women share equal responsibility for child-rearing and family support.

FURTHER READING SUGGESTED BY THE AUTHOR

THE ENCYCLOPEDIA OF SEXUAL BEHAVIOR edited by Albert Ellis and Albert Albarbanel, New York: Hawthorn Books, 1961. The most complete and authoritative source of its kind available. Contains articles by approximately 100 authorities in the field.

JOURNAL OF SOCIAL ISSUES—"The Sexual Renaissance in America"—April 1966. Many of the key figures in this area have contributed to this special journal issue: Robert Bell, Jessie Bernard, Carlfred Broderick, Harold Christensen, Paul Gebhard, Lester Kirkendall, Roger Libby, Lee Rainwater, Ira L. Reiss, Robert Sherwin, and Clark Vincent.

THE SEXUAL BEHAVIOR OF YOUNG PEOPLE by Michael Schofield, Boston: Little, Brown and Co., 1965. A recent, carefully executed study of English teenagers with much fascinating information that can be compared with American studies.

12

A comparision of sexual attitudes and behavior in an international sample*

ELEANORE B. LUCKEY and GILBERT D. NASS

Sexual attitudes and practices of college and university youth have recently been surveyed and reported by numerous investigators. The present study includes data from the United States, Canada, England, Norway, and Germany. It should be stressed at the outset that this research was not designed to pinpoint such facts as how many men and women were having sexual outlets and how many times per week and what kind of outlets these were. The investigation purports rather to be a comparative study that suggests existing sexual attitudes and behaviors and reports similarities and differences which seem to exist between the sampled national populations.

THE SAMPLE

Unmarried, undergraduate university students from five countries were included in the sample. The United States was represented by 21 colleges and universities. These were selected with the aim of geographical distri-

---

* From *Journal of Marriage and the Family*, Vol. 31, No. 2 (May 1969), pp. 364–79. Reprinted by permission of the authors and the National Council on Family Relations.

149

bution that would insure adequate representation of the entire country. Seven were in eastern states: a New England men's college, a private university in New York City, an Ivy League university, a state university in New England, a state college in New England, a private women's college in the northeast, and a private women's college known to have liberal parietal rules. Five were in middlewestern states: a state university, a Catholic university in a metropolitan area, a Protestant university in a non-metropolitan area, a private coed university in a metropolitan area, and one in a non-metropolitan area. Three were in southern states: a state university, a state university in the upper south, and a private university in a metropolitan area. Finally, six were in western states: a state university in the Rocky Mountain area, a state university in the southwest and one in the northwest, a state university in California and a private one there, and a state college in the southwest.

Contained in the American sample were two all-male colleges and two all-female colleges; two were specifically church-related. Public and private, metropolitan and non-metropolitan, secular and non-secular, coeducational and sexually segregated schools were included. The varied sample was chosen to provide data suggestive of a national picture. In each school 100 students were contacted in schools that were coeducational; the population was half male and half female.

A major university was selected from each of the other countries. An equal number of men and women were chosen from each population. From the German University information was solicited from 450 individuals; each of the other foreign populations was 300. The 150 additional subjects in the German sample were included in order to compensate for using a mailed questionnaire rather than one personally handed to the subjects; it was assumed that the response rate would be lower. Choosing one university that is "typical" of any country's student population is difficult if not impossible—this being especially true in England because of the variety of university types. However, in each country the choice of a large university was made because of its diversified population both geographically and demographically.

The number of respondents was gratifying; out of a total of 3,450 solicitations there were 2,230 subjects (64.6 percent) who responded, representing a 66.8 percent return from the United States sample and a 61.6 percent from the foreign universities. The return was considered generally higher than can be expected from a study of this kind and implies an adequate sample from which to generalize. It is interesting that in the North American samples more women responded than men, but in all the European samples the reverse was true. This suggests that European women may be more reluctant to discuss sexual matters than the American and that American men are more reticent than European.

In the United States only third- and fourth-year students were included in the study, but because foreign universities are not structurally comparable with American universities, the subjects were selected according to age; those between 20 and 22 were included. In all samples the ages were *very* similar; the mean for men being 21.1 years and for women, 20.9 years.

PROCEDURE

An inventory composed of 42 questions was designed so that answers could be solicited by checking or circling appropriate responses. In some instances explanatory or further comments were invited. The questionnaire was headed simply "College Checklist" and included questions on social sex roles including career roles for women, attitudes toward marriage especially with regard to sexual behavior, general views on affectional and sexual relationships, affectional and sexual experience of the respondent, and age.

The questionnaire along with a cover letter of explanation was distributed on each of the campuses, except the German, by student distributors who were supervised by a reliable assistant. Confidentiality and anonymity were assured, and stamped, addressed envelopes provided for direct return to the investigators. The German questionnaire which is the only one translated from English to the native language was *mailed* to a random sample of students. In all cases a randomly selected sample was attempted; although in schools where a goodly number of students were known to fit into a special category (for example, students living in their own apartments off campus), a special attempt was made to include some of these subjects.

There were some minor differences in questionnaires in order to keep them appropriate to the population with which they were being used. The German translation modified some of the questions, and therefore the data are not comparable; this will account for lack of German data in some categories.

RESULTS

(1) Sex role differences

Sex roles of the male and female and whether the differences between the sexes should or should not be encouraged give clues to the attitudes youth hold with regard to their own sex and the other, whether "equality" and "sameness" is the current mode or whether sex differentiation is emphasized. Several questions were designed to approach this answer from different angles.

When asked if they thought individuals and society functioned best if male and female roles in life were different though equal, Canadian students provided the strongest approval; Norwegian students were by a considerable margin the least enthusiastic.

Coeducational living arrangements—with men and women occupying separate rooms but in the same dormitories, on the same floors, and in the same wings—were looked on with much more favor in the European schools than in those in Canada and the United States. In all cases men were more disposed to these living arrangements than were women.

At all universities there was little support for separating the sexes in the classroom. Fifteen percent of the males and 10 percent of the females in the United States sample indicated that they believed such separation "would produce a better environment for study." The Canadian and English response was similar, but only five percent of the Norway students held such a belief.

The subjects were asked, "Is a four-year college education generally as essential for the personal fulfillment and life satisfaction of girls as it is for men of comparable intelligence?" As might be expected, there were decidedly more women than men who replied affirmatively. In Norway 91.8 percent of the women and 81 percent of the men replied affirmatively. Only two-thirds of the American men were sure. European men and women were much closer in their agreement than were the North American, and more were sure that there should be equal education. The widest discrepancy between male and female subjects was found in the United States.

Female subjects were asked if they had seriously in mind an occupational career that they would like to pursue most of the next 20 years. Many more of the English and Norwegian women had such careers in mind than those of other countries. Half or fewer of the Canadian, German, and American women planned careers, but more than three-fourths of English and Norwegian. The dilemma posed by career-marriage decisions for women was seen to exist to a considerable degree in all countries. When they were asked if they believed a good many bright girls consciously downgraded their ambitions for a career because of fear that it might hurt their chances of marriage, 71 percent of the Canadian agreed as compared to 57 percent of those in the United States; although about 60 percent of the men in each of the two countries held this position. In all countries except the United States, more women than men believed this to be true. There was a marked difference between opinions of European men, of whom only about a third thought women had to play down their ambitions in contrast with those in North America. Although the percentage of assenting women ranged from 71 to 38, the greatest difference existed between American and Canadian women. There is no ready explanation of this difference, which is inconsistent with practically all the other findings indicating the United States and Canadian populations hold similar views.

Sex role differences were generally emphasized to a greater extent in the North American countries than in the English and Scandinavian sample where men and women expect more equalization and less differentiation. European students, to a greater extent than American students, preferred both mixed-sex dormitory arrangements and classrooms. The European women planned to have careers, saw it as not interfering with marital roles, and recognized need for education. Their men agreed. Americans and Canadians tended more to see the woman's place in the home.

(2) Parental independence

Interesting ambiguities with regard to notions of parental independence were presented by the variation in opinions as to whether or not a strong society would be produced if social arrangements could be made that would enable all young people to be financially independent of their parents by the age of 21 regardless of whether they pursued higher education or not. England and Norway gave this idea the greatest support with about half of them agreeing to it. Germany gave it the least. Men generally favored the idea to a greater extent than women.

A related dimension, that of the parentally financed undergraduate marriage, was supported by two-fifths of the English students, both men and women. About a fourth of the Canadian and United States students supported the position; less than a fifth of Norwegian men did.

The view that young people under 21 desire more guidelines and limits received the greatest support from Canadian and United States students (men 36 percent, women 54 percent). Only about 20 percent of the English supported the position, and in all countries women indicated a greater desire for guidelines than men.

Each national sample provided a different pattern in picking the category of people who should set male-female intimacy guidelines. Among persons who felt there was a need for more clearly defined standards, Canadian and American students most frequently designated "parents" and "adults" should be those to set the standards. English students favored "youthful peers" and "adults," and Norwegian students cited "parents" and "schools." "Churches" were virtually ignored by all males and were not much more frequently cited by the females.

Although no clear-cut or well-defined pattern emerged from these findings, it can be generally concluded that the English and Scandinavian youth favored greater financial and moral independence from the parental generation than the North American. However, the majority of young people in all countries rejected social arrangements which would make them financially independent of parents by age 21. They also rejected parentally financed education-marriage. Decidedly more North American than European students, and women more than men, felt guidelines and limits were needed for sexual standards, and only in England were "youthful peers" favored over adults for determining such standards.

(3) Attitudes toward marriage and sexual behavior

Marriage was given a strong vote of confidence by all the samples, as the majority responded negatively to the question, "Can you visualize a happy, satisfying life for yourself that might not include marriage?" About 20 percent more Canadian and American youth responded "no" than European. Ten percent more of the Norwegian men than women replied negatively; this is the only response where the male percentage was higher than the female. Some of the subjects were not sure; English men more frequently indicated the "uncertain" response (31.6 percent) than any other group. Canadian females (15.7 percent) were less often in doubt than any other group. Twenty-nine percent of the Norwegian females and 26.2 percent of English females responded that they *could* be happy though unmarried, but only about 15 percent of Canadian and American women replied in the affirmative. About a fourth of the male subjects in the United States, Norway, and England believed they could live happily though unmarried. Few Canadian subjects—either men or women—indicated they fancied an unmarried life. Again it is the European samples that have indicated a greater break with the traditional pattern.

The ideal age for marriage was fairly uniform among the universities. Males at all schools indicated about 25 as the model choice. American women most frequently indicated an age between 21 and 23; all other national groups indicated a year or two older. In general, both men and women in all samples indicated a preference for the man to be slightly older than the woman.

The idea that a couple who marry should have their first full sexual experience together, found great support among Canadian and Norwegian females. The least support was by English females. The range of difference was greater between female samples. The greatest congruence between the sexes was found in the United States sample, where about one-half thought this true.

An additional specification that the sexual experience should be "only after marriage" was preferred by all female subjects when compared to male and was marked by subjects of both sexes more frequently in American universities. English men and women, and then Norwegian, marked this qualification least frequently.

In an attempt to appraise attitudes toward the double standard sex code, the question was asked, "Do you think it is reasonable for a male who has experienced coitus elsewhere to expect that the girl he hopes to marry be chaste at the time of marriage?" A "yes" response was interpreted as potential support for the double standard. Virtually no support was given the idea by Norwegian students. American and Canadian females most strongly supported the double standard position with approximately a third of them agreeing; a fifth of the men from these same two countries held this view.

The German questionnaire was modified to read:

One often hears the opinion that it is better for a marriage if the girl is still a virgin before marriage but the man has had sexual experience beforehand. Other people say a man with sexual experience cannot expect to marry a virgin girl. With which opinion do you agree most?

Only 13.2 percent of the men and 18.9 percent of the women supported the double standard position. About a fourth of the women and a fifth of the men believed neither partner should have experience before marriage; two-thirds of the men and slightly more than half of the women believed that both partners should have premarital experience. In all samples subjects rejected the double standard—European students more than North American. Interestingly, in all countries except England, women more frequently than men *supported* the double standard.

Also related to attitudes held toward the double standard was the inquiry, "Would it trouble you to marry a person who had experienced premarital coitus with someone else before becoming seriously involved with you?" The percentage of women answering "No" was highest in the United States and lowest in Canada; the greatest percentage of men was in Norway and the lowest, in Canada. Twice as many women as men in the United States answered "No," and this represented by far the greatest discrepancy between the sexes in any one sample. As was expected, in all cases men indicated more concern than women about the chastity of their marital partner. This suggests that some male students, also primarily American and Canadian, encourage the double standard.

In all the samples both men and women subjects were approximately equally divided between those who held the opinion that an individual might have had numerous sexual affairs before marriage and still bring a deep and enduring commitment to the person he marries and those who either did not think so or were uncertain about it. Certainly it can be said that numerous premarriage sexual partners were not seen as a serious deterrent to the marriage relationship by the majority of students in each of the samples. Sexual activity prior to marriage was viewed negatively by more females than males, and Norwegian women were the most skeptical. Except for the American sample, the difference between countries was not so great as between the two sexes of specific countries. In the United States men and women showed remarkable agreement. It's interesting that in the United States and Canada, where there is considerably less premarital coitus (see Table 3), there are almost as many students who believe numerous sexual affairs would not interfere with marriage as in those countries where there is more premarital coitus. This would indicate that it is not fear that the experience would destroy some quality in the marriage that acts as a deterrent to premarital intercourse.

When asked the following question, "Yes" responses were high in the English and Norwegian samples; low in the American and German:

Regardless of age (after 16) or the stage of formal commitment, do you feel that full intimacy is appropriate if both persons desire it and they have a sense of trust, loyalty, protectiveness, and love?

In general, women subjects consistently were more reluctant to sanction such intimacy. The category receiving the greatest number of responses from all subjects in all countries was "Only if mature."

The following question was answered most frequently by all students in all countries by "Only if married" for ages prior to 18. However, generally marriage is seen as less important as the age of the individual increases. "What kind of relationship should prevail before a male and female should consider coitus as personally and socially reasonable?" Both English men and women, more than any other nationality, indicated that "going steady" and being "casually attracted" between ages 14–17 were appropriate conditions for intercourse; English women checked the response indicating coitus was appropriate *only* in marriage substantially less frequently than did women of any other country in all age categories from 14 to 24 and over.

The widest gap between categories for both men and women, in all age groups, and among all nationalities was between "going steady" and "good friends." In many instances but without a discernible pattern, more male subjects considered it appropriate to have coitus with one to whom he was casually attracted than with a good friend. Women seemed to favor slightly the friend over the casual attraction. These findings undoubtedly reflect the romantic concept that being in love and being physically attracted to a sexual partner is more appropriate than is a basis of friendship.

The English were generally more acceptant than other nationalities of premarital intercourse under a variety of conditions and at younger ages. Females in all samples generally expressed considerably greater support than did the males for consideration of coitus "only if married." Canadian females, the most conservative group, gave no support for coitus outside the married or engaged relationship for ages 14–17, but 27 percent approved when the age was 24 or over. Chronological age, which probably was judged to reflect personal maturity, was held by all subjects as an important factor in determining under what conditions coitus was appropriate.

When questioned about the opinion that a good lovemaking relationship was "almost always consummated by" mutual, simultaneous orgasm, respondents showed no national differences and no differences within the sexes. About half of the men thought it was true, about a third of the women.

By studying the opinions that were expressed toward marriage and sexual behavior, one can generally conclude that although traditional values are held to some extent in all countries, what may be called "liberal views" are also to be found in each of the national samples. European countries are more liberal than those on the North American continent. Men are less invested in marriage and less restricted in sex than women. Marriage is still an overwhelmingly popular way of life, and the age of marriage is ideally the early twenties. Indicative of a swing away from the traditional was the evidence that the double standard of sexual morals is definitely on its way out, and students are not greatly concerned about the first sexual experience being in marriage or being with the partner who eventually becomes the spouse. Even having several sexual partners before marriage was not judged particularly detrimental to the marriage. Age was viewed as a very important factor determining under what conditions coitus was appropriate; the older the individual the more freedom he had.

The English in general were seen to have the least restrictive attitudes toward sexual behavior. Norwegian women, although liberal, tended to be a good deal less liberal than their men. The Canadian sample held somewhat more conservative attitudes than the United States, but in most instances the two samples resembled each other and could be contrasted with the European samples.

(4) Sexual experience and behavior

When women were asked to classify the men whom they had dated in the past year into those they thought (a) would be frightened by real intimacy; (b) those who seemed content with gestures of intimacy such as a farewell embrace; (c) those who were happy enough if their hands were allowed to wander; and (d) those who were disappointed if they couldn't persuade the girl to go all the way, more American and Canadian girls marked b than any other response. English and Norwegian marked d and German marked c (Table 1). The contrast between Canadian and American women when compared to English women is particularly noticeable on response d. The North American women indicated that men were decidedly less demanding than English women reported men to be.

Canadian and United States men give a very congruent picture of their dates during the past year (Table 2). Both indicated most of their dates usually went along for fun up to the point of light petting. English male students most frequently suggested the partner resisted real intimacies unless there had been talk of love. German students most frequently indi-

TABLE 1. Percentage female responses to: "Review in your mind briefly the men you have dated in the past year. How would you classify most of them in regard to interest in intimacy?"

	United States	Canada	England	Germany	Norway
a) I think real intimacy would frighten most of them.	13.8	11.1	13.6	15.7	14.2
b) They seem content with gestures of intimacy such as the farewell embrace.	41.5	44.4	22.2	9.6	26.2
c) If their hands can wander, that seems to keep them happy.	25.0	31.7	18.5	50.6*	28.6
d) They are disappointed if you don't want to go all the way.	16.0	12.8	44.4	24.1	31.0
e) Only dated one.	3.7	0.0	1.3	0.0	0.0
(N)	100% (581)	100% (63)	100% (81)	100% (81)	100% (42)

* German reworded as follows: "Most are satisfied with necking."

TABLE 2. Percentage male responses to: "Review in your mind the girls you have dated this past year. How would you classify most of them in regard to interest in intimacy?"*

	United States	Canada	England	Germany	Norway
They are pretty conservative beyond perhaps a good-night kiss.	22.2	16.7	16.3	45.2	19.7
They will usually go along for fun up to a point of light petting.	46.6	50.6	35.0	8.9	42.1
They resist real intimacies unless there has been talk of love.	43.5	36.4	39.0	22.8	32.9
They seem happy to go as far as I want to go, short of coitus.	27.4	28.6	33.0	31.7	46.1
They seem to want to go all the way if we have a chance.	14.9	24.7	34.1	37.0	40.8
(N)	(609)	(77)	(123)	(101)	(76)

* Multiple responses were suggested in the questionnaire; therefore each figure reports the percent of the total N of each respective sample which agreed with that specific response.

cated their dates were pretty conservative beyond perhaps a goodnight kiss, and Norwegian men most frequently described their dates as "happy to go as far as I want to go, short of coitus."

The description that "They seem to want to go all the way if we have a chance" was marked most frequently by Norwegian students and least frequently by Canadian students. Specific behaviors of dating partners cannot be determined with any reliability by the responses of either women or men subjects or by comparing the two (Tables 1 and 2). The multiple responses of male students are especially difficult to interpret; however the composite picture of dating behavior that does appear from the data is one of conservatism in Canada and the United States, where men and women agree that gestures of affection and light petting are modal. In contrast more European women (especially English and Norwegian) reported that men are disappointed if "you don't want to go all the way," and more European men reported that women want to go all the way! The fact that European students do indeed engage in more sexual activity on dates was confirmed when subjects reported on their own sexual behavior.

Subjects were asked to indicate their participation in a spectrum of sexual behaviors from light embracing and holding hands to coitus (Tables 3 and 4). Among the males, Canadian students generally indicated the highest frequencies of participation in the casual and light petting behavior categories, and the English students the highest in general petting, nude embrace, and coitus. German men consistently reported the lowest rate of involvement in all categories. The pattern of behaviors reported by American and Canadian men was strikingly similar in all categories, with Canadian men consistently reporting somewhat more conservative behavior.

As would be expected, there is a decided drop in the number of subjects who report petting below the waist of the girl and petting below the waist of *both* the man and the girl. Mutual genital petting behavior is reported only slightly more frequently than coitus by men subjects of all countries and by women in European countries; however, 15 percent more American and Canadian girls report mutual genital petting than report coitus. Apparently a crucial point in determining whether most subjects continue to coitus or not is mutual genital petting. This is *less* true for girls in Canada and the United States than for any other group.

The reported coital participation among males in order of frequency was: England highest, followed by Norway, then the United States and Canada, and lowest Germany (Table 3). The pattern indicated by German and Norwegian men is that coitus is more frequent than mutual genital petting. All the other samples reported that for some five to eight percent of the men, genital petting does not continue to coitus.

Men who reported involvement in whipping and spanking together with sexual intimacy were most frequently English. The second highest fre-

TABLE 3. Percent of males reporting experiencing respective sexual behaviors.

Type of Sexual Behavior	United States	Canada	England	Germany	Norway
Light embracing or fond holding of hands	98.6	98.9	93.5	93.8	93.7
Casual goodnight kissing	96.7	97.7	93.5	78.6	86.1
Deep kissing	96.0	97.7	91.9	91.1	96.2
Horizontal embrace with some petting but not undressed	89.9	92.0	85.4	68.8	93.6
Petting of girl's breast area from outside her clothing	89.9	93.2	87.0	80.4	83.5
Petting of girl's breast area without clothes intervening	83.4	92.0	82.8	69.6	83.5
Petting below the waist of the girl under her clothing	81.1	85.2	84.6	70.5	83.5
Petting below the waist of both man and girl, under clothing	62.9	64.8	68.3	52.7	55.1
Nude embrace	65.6	69.3	70.5	50.0	69.6
Coitus	58.2	56.8	74.8	54.5	66.7
One-night affair involving coitus; didn't date person again	29.9	21.6	43.1	17.0	32.9
Whipping or spanking before petting or other intimacy	8.2	5.7	17.1	.9	5.1
Sex on pay-as-you-go basis	4.2	4.5	13.8	9.8	2.5
(N)	(644)	(88)	(123)	(112)	(79)

quency for men was the United States sample which reported less than half the incidence of the English. German men reported the least.

English men reported the greatest patronage of prostitutes; then the German; and lowest were the Norwegian. A little more than four percent of United States and Canadian men reported they had had sex on a pay-as-you-go-basis. It is especially interesting to note that Germany, which had the lowest coital percentage, had the second highest percentage of prostitution, and Norway which has the second highest coital involvement has the lowest prostitution reported. This leads one to conclude that quite a different set of values operate in the two countries, and that Germany

TABLE 4. Percent of females reporting experiencing respective sexual behaviors.

Types of Sexual Behavior	United States	Canada	England	Germany	Norway
Light embracing or fond holding of hands	97.5	96.5	91.9	94.8	89.3
Casual goodnight kissing	96.8	91.8	93.0	74.0	75.0
Deep kissing	96.5	91.8	93.0	90.6	89.3
Horizontal embrace with some petting but not undressed	83.3	81.2	79.1	77.1	75.0
Petting of girl's breast area from outside her clothing	78.3	78.8	82.6	76.0	64.3
Petting of girl's breast area without clothes intervening	67.8	64.7	70.9	66.7	58.9
Petting below the waist of the girl under her clothing	61.2	64.7	70.9	63.5	53.6
Petting below the waist of both man and girl, under clothing	57.8	50.6	61.6	56.3	42.9
Nude embrace	49.6	47.6	64.0	62.1	51.8
Coitus	43.2	35.3	62.8	59.4	53.6
One-night affair involving coitus; didn't date person again	7.2	5.9	33.7	4.2	12.5
Whipping or spanking before petting or other intimacy	4.5	5.9	17.4	1.0	7.1
(N)	(688)	(85)	(86)	(96)	(56)

maintains more of the traditional point of view and condones the double standard to a greater extent.

Women subjects in general reported less participation in all categories of sexual behavior than men did (Table 4). The highest rates for sexual behavior except for light embraces were reported by English women. Canadian, American, and German females showed similar and slightly less participation through the less intimate and the petting behaviors to the nude embrace; in these same categories the Norwegian females consistently reported the least participation. However, with the nude embrace and coitus, the international female pattern changed; a greater proportion of German and Norwegian women reported involvement and a lesser proportion of Canadian and American women. It can be assumed that petting as a prelude to coitus is more frequently the practice with European women, but with American and Canadian women it is either an end in itself or is the cutoff point of sexual activity. The order of coital frequency as indicated by women subjects is: highest, English; then Germany; Norway; and finally the United States and Canada. These data would tend to confirm the male responses which followed the same pattern except for Germany.

A third of the English women reported "one-night stands"; and although more than 20 percent less frequently reported, the Norwegian females ranked second highest. The United States, Canada, and Germany followed in that order. Although the percentages reported by men subjects were considerably higher, the order of frequency was the same.

The one behavior category in which the female subjects reported in both a similar pattern and a similar percentage as the males within their respective sample was that of "whipping and spanking." The generally low percentage may account somewhat for this finding. Both England and Norway, which report a proportionately greater number of students engaged in these sadomasochistic practices, also rank high in coital frequency. The positive correlation of the two factors can be speculated upon, but accounting for the relationship remains for further investigation.

The ages at first petting and first coital experience show that the mean age for males at first petting was lowest (15.6 years) in England and Norway, eight months older in the United States, and a year older for both Canada and Germany. English females began petting earliest at age 15.6; Norwegian females almost a year later; German females at age 17; and finally Canadian and American females still four months later. English students who began petting youngest also had intercourse youngest. German and Norwegian students who were the oldest at first intercourse began petting experiences at approximately the same ages as men in other samples. United States and Canadian men and women report the shortest interval between the age at which they began petting and the age at which it was consummated in intercourse. In all cases men reported first petting at an age younger than women; except for Canadian and English men who reported first coitus at nearly the same age as Canadian and English women, men were also younger at age of first coitus.

It is interesting to note the pattern of delay between first petting and first coitus for each sample. The shortest interval is demonstrated by the Canadian and American girl. This is followed by the American man and the English man and woman. Norwegian and German men and women delay coitus for the longest intervals—all over two years—and Norwegian men wait nearly three years.

Considerable variation exists in the sample in the reported number of coital partners. The greatest promiscuity was reported by English students, with almost three-fourths of the males reporting "several" and "many" partners; and two-thirds of the females reported in these same categories.

About 58 percent of the American male students reported "several" and "many" partners; about half the Norwegian males reported "several" and "many" partners; only a third of the German men reported in those categories. As is to be expected, women students in all samples were less promiscuous. Nearly half of the German, American, and Canadian women reported only "one partner," and congruently, fewer of them indicated "many" and "several." Fewer than a fourth of the Canadian and German women marked these combined categories. About a third of the American women and nearly half of the Norwegian women marked these. Nearly two-thirds of the English women marked one or the other of these categories.

Alcohol was not reported as a major factor in first coital experience by many of the subjects. More English females reported they were under the influence of alcohol when they first had intercourse than any other group in the sample; even so, more than half indicated, "I and my partner had not had anything alcoholic to drink." The English had the highest rate reporting "both under the influence of alcohol"; and the German the lowest except for Norwegian women, none of whom reported the couple had been under the influence of alcohol. More Canadian youth than any other reported *no* involvement with alcohol and first coitus—about three-fourths; 68 percent of the Norwegian men and women reported in that same category and about two-thirds of the American men and women. More English men and women reported alcohol was involved with one or the other or both partners than any other nationality.

Although there are some irregularities and unevenness of pattern, the total picture that one gains from looking at these data is a consistent one presented by the agreement of each sex and by congruent findings in each category of behavior. The English student has more sexual activity, begins younger, has more partners, has more one-night stands, more sado-masochistic experiences, and is more likely to have been influenced by alcohol at the time of the first coital experience.

North American students are less experienced and generally more conservative; the Canadian youth is somewhat less liberal than his counterpart in the United States. The Norwegian student tends to be less the "swinger" than the English. Premarital sexual experience does not start so early and is restricted to fewer partners. Although the picture of German students is not so clear, they generally occupy a place between the liberal English and Norwegian samples and the North American.

SUMMARY AND DISCUSSION

(1) Sex role differences

Some interesting consistencies and inconsistencies are presented by the findings with regard to sex role differences when the various countries are compared. Although in the United States and Canada more students agreed that men and women were indeed different though equal, and fewer than half of the Norwegian students took this position, it was the Norwegian students who in the largest percentage indicated that a four-year college education was generally as essential for women as men. English students tended to agree with the Norwegian; and consistent with this both Norwegian and English female students expressed in greater numbers an intent to follow a career over most of the first 20 years of their out-of-college life.

The Canadian and United States students presented a different picture from the European in that more of them stressed "equality but difference," and fewer of them believed a four-year college education is necessary for women. The North American women tended to be less interested in a career. Canadian men and women more than those of any other country believed women consciously downgraded career ambitions in favor of marriage potential. The European students generally felt this was less true. European schools favored coed living arrangements much more than North American students, but all students favored mixed classes in the classroom.

Making a broad generalization from these statistics, we could say with reliability that the European students—both men and women—indicated a greater acceptance of sexual equality of opportunity, both in the academic world and in the professional. Canadian men and women expressed ideas which to a greater extent indicated that the female's role and her preparation for it was marital rather than professional. They denied, however, that this marital role was not "equal" with the male role.

(2) Parental independence

English students favored independence from parents and early marriage with financial support from parents to a greater extent than students of any other nation and rejected the idea that more definite guidelines and limits for youth were needed. Both American and Canadian students were less inclined to want either earlier independence or subsidized marriage and were more inclined to think adult guidelines would be a good idea. There was virtually no support given to religious agencies as a crucial molder of guidelines or limits for youth in the realm of sexual intimacy.

One might conclude from these responses that English youth felt more competent to start and manage life on their own, given the freedom to do so.

(3) Attitudes toward marriage and sexual behavior

That the majority of youth the world around (or at least in this sample) still believe a satisfying life includes marriage is indicated; however, North

American students were more sure of this than European. It was surprising to the investigators, however, that nearly a quarter of the samples said marriage was *not* necessary. All samples agreed that men should marry ideally at about age 25 and women at about 23.

Except in England, women more than men favored the idea that the man and woman who marry should have their first sexual experience together. Again the more conservative answers were expressed by the North American students, who preferred coital partners to be marriage partners and were more skeptical of promiscuity and its influence in marriage than were the European students.

Women students in general were more conservative (even in liberal countries) than were men. The women, as much as or more than the men, seem to perpetuate the double standard, and it was perpetuated by North American youth more generally than European. Women are willing to accept lack of chastity on the part of the male more readily than the male accepted the lack of chastity of the female; although Norwegian students did not seem to value premarital chastity, they rejected promiscuity and the double standard of behavior. English students seem to operate most nearly on the single sex standard, and that standard was described as liberal. Again, United States and Canadian students were more conservative; they were more caught in the traditional double standard.

The majority of students in all samples agree that "maturity" should be a major criteria on which decision and choice of coital partners should be determined; English students, when compared with students from other countries, indicated that this choice can be made at an earlier age.

(4) Sexual experience and behavior

Reports by both men and women subjects of their sexual behavior was consistent with their attitudes. More European than North American women reported that men wanted to "go farther on dates"; more European than American men said that women were willing to go farther! Canadian and American men and women were more conservative—content with petting and necking.

North American women, contrary to European women, indicated their dates were generally content with a moderate degree of intimacy instead of disappointment if they would not go all the way. European men, contrary to North American men, indicated women dates seemed to want to go all the way when the opportunity was available.

While the investigators tried to construct patterns of sexual behavior from the responses of men and women students indicating their degree of involvement in activities which range from light embracing to coitus, it became obvious that English men and women more freely participate in a gamut of sexual activities including more genital petting, more frequent coitus, more patronage of prostitution, more sadomasochistic practices, more one-night stands. They start both petting and coitus at a younger age, have more sexual partners, and report alcohol has been a factor in initial coital experience. The general ranking of male student coital rates by countries provides the following descending order: England, Norway, United States, Canada, Germany. The order for female student coital rates was: England, Germany, Norway, United States, and Canada.

Canadian and American youth report patterns of behavior very similar to each other and are in general to be considered conservative regarding sexual behavior. German students hold the most conservative attitudes and exhibit the most restricted behavior among the European samples; Norwegian students were more liberal, and the English consistently the most liberal. Females, as one would expect, are more conservative in all countries than are the males. English women, however, hold views and behave very similarly to English men.

It can be generally concluded from looking at this mass of data that both attitudes and behavior of North American students are more conservative than those of the European. On the background of other studies done earlier, it is evident that there is an increasingly liberal attitude toward sex and generally more premarital participation.

The study gives a reliable report on sexual attitudes and behaviors held by university students in the participating countries, but it fails in that it gives little clue to the meaning or motivation associated with these. Meaning can perhaps be projected into the statistics, but so much of interpretation lies in the eye of the interpreter, that these investigators prefer to let the statistics speak for themselves as they can. The cross-cultural aspects of these data have provided a sound basis on which a comparative assessment of general trends in university students' sexual attitudes and behavior can be made. The variations that have been found suggest the need for further study to explicate and inquire into the meaning of the differential findings, as well as to continue the incorporation of research controls through cross-cultural analysis.

REFERENCES: RESEARCH ON PREMARITAL SEXUAL ATTITUDES, STANDARDS, AND BEHAVIOR

CHRISTENSEN, HAROLD T. "Scandinavian and American Sex Norms: Some Comparisons with Sociological Implications," *Journal of Social Issues* (April 1966), 60–75.

COLEMAN, JAMES. "Female Status and Premarital Sexual Codes," *American Journal of Sociology*, 72 (September 1966).

DEDMAN, JEAN. "The Relationship Between Religious Attitude and Attitudes Toward Premarital Sex Relations," *Marriage and Family Living* (May 1959), 171–76.

EHRMAN, WINSTON W. *Premarital Dating Behavior.* New York: Bantam Books, 1959.

FREEMAN, HARROP A., and FREEMAN, RUTH S. "Senior College Women: Their Sexual Standards and Activity," *Journal of National Association of Women Deans and Counselors* (Winter and Spring 1966).

KINSEY, ALFRED et al. *Sexual Behavior in the Human Male.* Wm. Saunders Co., 1948.

———. *Sexual Behavior in the Human Female.* Wm. Saunders Co., 1953.

KIRKENDALL, LESTER A. *Premarital Intercourse and Interpersonal Relationships.* New York: Julian Press, 1961.

MANN, W. E. "Canadian Trends in Premarital Behavior," *The Bulletin for Social Service* (December 1967) whole issue.

REISS, IRA L. *Premarital Sexual Standards in America.* New York: Free Press, 1960.

ROBINSON, IRA, et al. "Changes in Sexual Behavior and Attitudes of Colleges Students," *Family Life Coordinator* (April 1968), 119–24.

ROSS, ROBERT T. "Measures of the Sex Behavior of College Males Compared with Kinsey's Results," *Journal of Abnormal and Social Psychology,* 45 (1950), 753–55.

RUBIN, ISADORE. "Changing College Sex: New Kinsey Report," *Sexology* (June 1968), 780–82.

SCHOFIELD, MICHAEL. *The Sexual Behavior of Young People.* Boston: Little, Brown and Co., 1965.

13

Sexual morality and sexual reality—The Scandinavian approach*

BIRGITTA LINNÉR

I remember how at the meeting of the International Planned Parenthood Association in Stockholm in the summer of 1953 a small group of us sat discussing youth problems. Among us was Abraham Stone, who asked us Scandinavians:

> Why is it that you have so many unwanted pregnancies in the Scandinavian countries when you have all this freedom and sex education in the schools; anyone can buy contraceptives and the doctors cooperate.

It just didn't make sense to him. It was not easy to find the answers to this question. We tried some:

> The sex education in the schools is not good enough, partly because it is a new and difficult subject and partly because some teachers resist it. The contraceptives aren't good enough. Further, at a deeper psychological level some young girls want to be pregnant and therefore avoid protecting themselves. There are always people who are not mature enough to have freedom and responsibility.

---

* From Vol. 36, No. 4, July 1966, pp. 686–93, the *American Journal of Orthopsychiatry*, with permission from Birgitta Linnér. Copyright ©, the American Orthopsychiatric Association, Inc. Reproduced by permission.

Those were some of the answers given. I don't think they were quite satisfactory either to Dr. Stone or to those of us present.

These questions are still pertinent in the Scandinavian countries. Here, I will regard these countries with similar economic and social structure as a unit, although, of course, there are differences among them. Still, what they have in common is more important and, certainly to an American audience, more meaningful.

THE MORAL DEBATE

An article in the New York Times in April, 1964, was a contributing factor, I believe, to my being invited to speak at this annual meeting. I will therefore use this article as a starting point for my speech. I quote the headlines:

Swedes to Scan Teaching on Sex.
Schools and Church Move Toward Views of Young.

A vivid public debate on sexual morality has been going on. The editor of the official church weekly in a TV program, for instance, called for "aligning the Church more closely with reality." He said premarital sexual relations should not be condemned as a sin as long as the couple involved sincerely planned to marry. I quote:

The only possibility the Church has of getting on speaking terms with young people is not to say "no" to what so many do.

The Swedish bishops, however, at a conference in the fall of 1964 declined to accept a change in the attitude of the Lutheran Church:

They said that although "premarital sex relations may be of different moral quality," still "sexual relations do belong to married life exclusively."

Some of the clergy were deeply stirred by the fact that the possibility could even be considered of giving a new look to the moral evaluations of the Church.

At the opposite pole there are radical groups urging that sexual happiness should not be reserved for married life alone, or even for those practicing heterosexual relations. Society should not discriminate against the sexual behavior of any group, as long as the individuals do not hurt each other and children are not involved. This is a way of saying that since sexual behavior is a private matter, up to the conscience of the individual, society should not intervene.

As you see, the positions of the debating groups are quite far apart. Let us remember, however, that each of these extremes in moral approaches has an ethical base to recommend it.

Somewhere between these poles we find the official policy based on the assumption that sexual life certainly has its private sides, but that society has its share in the responsibility for morals. Society's responsibility is not regarded as primarily restrictive in Scandinavia, however. Instead society should try to improve man's possibilities to achieve harmonious sexual relations as part of the whole psychosocial personal life. The middle road is represented by comparatively tolerant trends in legislation and by a general approach stressing frankness, knowledge, education to freedom and responsibility and a mature outlook on sex relations in both men and women. I dare to say that the new morality, which is neither traditional nor licentious, already is established in large groups of the society. The basic fact this new morality has to cope with is the possibility for men and women alike of using sexual life both for procreation and for individual and mutual pleasure—and, of course, also for frustration.

Thus, the Scandinavian countries represent not only *one* established morality requiring a single basic ethical code regarding sex, but also other sex moralities within a multiple value system. In this situation many regard it as the goal of education to train our youth to accept the consequences of their choice of sex ethics. A psychologist from Finland said to me, when we talked about the tensions between ideals and reality:

We have too much of superego morality; we need more of ego morality!

SEX EDUCATION IN THE SCHOOLS

Although some of the Scandinavian countries have had a sex education program for about 20 years, it is assumed that only about 50 to 60 percent of the students get a thorough sex education. Many circumstances contribute to inadequate treatment of the subject, among them the following: the subject is new and difficult; the teachers' training is not good enough; some embarrassed teachers resist the subject; some teachers put off the teaching until the end of the semester, when there is little time left for this subject, which is of such importance to the students.

There is a great deal of interest in improving the whole field of sex education. In Denmark and Sweden Royal Commissions are considering the reforms. Sweden has a handbook for teachers on sex education, also available in English. Iceland has started an interesting program, where the School of Social Work has lectures and films every spring about marriage and family, planned parenthood and sexual ethics.

The radio systems have broadcast sex education to the schools, and TV has had programs for educational purposes for both students and adults.

However, a heated debate has been going on about how much or how little the school should commit itself to the teaching of birth control. Thus we see the different and often irreconcilable attitudes to the moral question of premarital sex relations. In Denmark the debate flared up when a young girl suggested that contraceptives should be supplied by the schools. Many citizens wanted teaching about birth control to be excluded; other groups, liberals and youth organizations, were very strongly opposed to that point of view. In Norway a large group of housewives demanded that sex education should remain the responsibility of the home and the family alone. One hundred and forty medical doctors in Sweden wanted what they labeled "firmer sexual norms" to be taught. On the other hand, a nation-wide organization of students in secondary schools and junior colleges maintained that in this field only facts and not evaluations should be taught the youth.

Some 20 years ago those opposed to sex education and teaching about birth control in particular said it would encourage license, that young people would not want to marry because they could enjoy sex anyhow and that the young generation would not bother to have children. It seems, however, that none of these negative predictions has been confirmed by reality. As yet there is no evidence that family life is being destroyed in the Scandinavian countries. People continue to establish permanent and stable relationships as adults, and they want to provide a home and security for the young. Statistics show that a larger number of young people have married during the last decades than before, that the birth rate has increased and that the divorce rate is quite stable (about one out of six marriages).

To sum up, there are those who have a superstitious belief that a good sex program automatically will solve all problems; others believe such a program encourages looseness and promiscuity. It seems to me that the reality lies somewhere between. There is no doubt that it takes more to build our psychosexual behavioral pattern and our morality than a mere sex program. Nonetheless, and however controversial the subject may be, we have a duty to support the young generation with the knowledge they need so desperately: Sex education should be taught as part of the regular school curriculum.

PREMARITAL SEX RELATIONS AND CONTRACEPTIVES

We know that a very large percentage of young people have premarital sexual relations. Incidentally, this is not quite as recent a phenomenon as it would seem. To a great extent, sexual relations before marriage were accepted in the ancient rural society. Perhaps partly due to this tradition, over 40 percent of all first-born children within wedlock were conceived before marriage. Investigation of Swedish students in 1964 showed that at the age of eighteen no less than 57 percent of the boys and 46 percent of the girls had had premarital sex experience. (I would like to mention, in passing, the excellent cooperation between the Children's Psychiatric Clinic, the City School Board and the Parents' Association.) The behavior of these young people and their moral values seem to be fairly closely related in most cases. One group, however, had a considerably stricter moral code than the rest, but still showed much the same behavior. The wide gap thus found between their philosophy and their behavior pattern worried the investigating doctors as a highly negative factor. They felt it is better for young people to have moral ideas and behavior reasonably close to each other.

The general situation was summed up by a colleague of mine thus:

This young generation does openly what our generation did stealthily and with guilt feelings. Their behavior must surely be much more healthy and emotionally maturing.

Certainly, I am aware of the explosive materials in this view. Still, this point is important to consider if we wish to merge ethics and reality harmoniously.

Needless to say, good contraceptive information and facilities are available with public support. There is an effort to diminish both legal and illegal abortions through improving the facilities for birth control. The need for planned parenthood is on the whole accepted, even if some groups do not like having it taught in the schools. An interview of married women showed that more than 90 percent of them try to apply child-spacing measures. The maternity welfare centers have the obligation of serving all mothers, regardless of marital status. In public places one can see posters bearing messages directed at young people. Such posters, sponsored by the National Association for Sex Education, affiliated with International Planned Parenthood, say:

Both of you are responsible. Can she depend on you? Can you rely on yourself? . . . To be safe is important to both of you.

EARLY MARRIAGES

Generally speaking, early marriages are hardly recommended. It is felt that young people should wait to get married until they are mature enough for a life-long relationship. I do not mean to speak against all early marriages. However, I believe (and so do many others) that marriage should not serve the purpose of merely legitimizing a child or of merely making sexual intercourse legitimate. Thus, parents may say to their son or daughter:

We would prefer that you have no sex relations until you marry. But if you choose to have sex relations, you should use birth control. If you get pregnant nevertheless, you are always welcome here, and we will support you.

The ethical alternatives can be formulated thus.

If, on one hand we assume "sex within marriage" as the only permissible moral, we commit many young people to the possibility of unwanted pregnancies, unwanted marriages with all their complications, illegal abortions and so on. If, on the other hand, we assume that some young people may have intercourse before they meet the person they want to marry, and that this may happen also with our own children, the best thing we can do is to teach them about birth control. It may turn out that they are able to handle their sex life in a much more mature way and less destructively than if they are unable to channel their emotions and sexual urges. Case histories often show that those girls who get into trouble are those who have not received a good sex education and do not know about birth control.

Obviously, whichever alternative one chooses depends on one's own approach to the situation of the youth and the ethical problems involved.

CHILDREN OUT OF WEDLOCK

We do not have illegitimate children in the Scandinavian countries. At one time, the laws referred to an illegitimate child, but that was changed some decades ago as part of a program to improve the status of the unmarried mother and of her child. Our legal provisions reflect a cultural attitude more concerned with the protection of the child than with punishment of the mother.

Every child born out of wedlock is assigned a "child welfare guardian" who is responsible not only for safeguarding the child's rights and interests but also for ensuring that parentage is established and that the father agrees to financial support of the child.

It naturally follows that all family allowances and all maternity care are given without regard to the child's birth status. Unmarried mothers, with minor children, have the right, of course, to live in municipally built dwellings. An unmarried mother with a baby also is considered a family, and in school text books there is reference to one-parent families. Hospitals address unmarried mothers by the title "Mrs."

Thus, the basic attitude of society is to afford support for unmarried mothers, so that they can take care of their children if they so wish. An investigation by the Child Welfare Board of Stockholm showed that among 500 unmarried mothers under the age of 20 the majority wished to keep their children. But there is also a careful procedure for adoption as well as many opportunities for placement of children in foster homes.

Being an unmarried mother does not necessarily prevent a woman from leading a happy, normal life. An indication of this is the current tendency among parents not to force a daughter into marriage because she is expecting a child. Rather, the daughter is encouraged to keep her child, complete her schooling or vocational training, and perhaps at some later date marry a man whom she really loves.

It might be of interest to note that many fewer children are born out of wedlock now than during the nineteenth century. During the last decades, as a matter of fact, the proportion has remained virtually unaltered (about 10 percent of all births).

THE SCANDINAVIAN ABORTION LAWS

The first law legalizing abortion under certain conditions was adopted in Sweden in 1938. (The laws are similar in the other Scandinavian countries.) The main reason behind the reform was the great number of criminal abortions, fatal in a great many cases, which caused considerable alarm among responsible citizens concerned not only with principles of morality but also with the reality of people's lives.

There are five main grounds: (1) medical, (2) social-medical, (3) humanitarian (referring to cases of rape, incest, etc.), (4) eugenic, (5) and therapeutic abortions in cases where there is reason to assume that the child will suffer from severe disease or deformity because of injury during fetal life under an act passed as late as 1963.

Authorization for interruption of pregnancy is in most cases decided by a specially appointed Committee of the National Board of Health after an investigation. Too many women who come from other countries, including the United States, hoping to get a legal abortion are completely unaware of the rather strict rules which I have just mentioned.

There is no general unanimity to be found in this field. The Lutheran State Church, for instance, does accept legal abortions for medical and humanitarian reasons. In a heated debate which has been going on recently, certain groups have maintained that a woman should be allowed to choose whether she wants to give birth to her child or not. They believe, furthermore, that if women were given abortions on demand, criminal abortions eventually would disappear completely. Other groups feel that our present system of compromise on the whole is the best possible. As a matter of fact, the questions are now being debated more violently than ever.

In spite of strongly divergent opinions, it seems that the fundamental principles established in the present laws are generally accepted. In other words, I believe that very few people would, if they had a chance, turn the clock back and make all abortions criminal and thus have women exposed to abortionists again. It is a matter of dispute, however, whether we should go one or more steps further.

WOMAN'S NEW POSITION, AND ITS EFFECT ON SEXUAL MORALITY AND REALITY

The public policy in Scandinavia is to support family life, especially families with small children, while at the same time encouraging the emancipation and personal independence of women. Thus, marriage and family life are regarded as only part of the woman's life.

Ambassador Alva Myrdal, wife of Gunnar Myrdal, gave a speech at an international conference in Stockholm. She noted the nuclear family with few children, the prolongation of the life cycle, the general urbanization and the growing number of women now involved in careers, and concluded:

All these things will further strengthen the necessity for the woman to look upon her own life as an individual destiny.

This means, I believe, that women no longer should be considered as objects, but as subjects. Mature sexuality means that they are not exploited or used. There is a great risk that a woman may be exploited if she does not have a sexual awareness and consciousness. She must be allowed to cope with sexual relationships as with all other responsibilities in her life without overprotective morality.

It may seem difficult to reconcile independence and femininity. However, Scandinavia shows that they are certainly not irreconcilable. I quote a journalist about the Scandinavian women, "Their morals are unique, but they are not immoral." I have asked myself to what extent this sexual freedom (meaning freedom and responsibility between mutually consenting and mature individuals) is publicly approved. Many persons and groups certainly will oppose my way of interpreting the situation. Perhaps I should say once more that the official approval is only indirect: it is shown, for instance, in the concern for the unmarried mother and her child. There is no attempt at humiliation or at castigation. Rather there is a realistic appreciation of the practical problems involved. One sees it in the therapeutic abortion laws, which try to help women avoid illegal abortion and the risks involved.

May I add some questions. As women become more and more economically independent and have professional lives of their own, many ask themselves:

Will this also lead to security in sexual life? How close are sexual life and procreation for the woman? Does her freedom of choice lead to more frustration and to more superficial emotional relations? Finally, will the moral view that sees sex life not as a separate activity, but as an expression of the whole person, disappear? *Or*, will woman's new situation result in a self-evident, harmonious view on the interdependence and mutuality between man and woman?

Let me quote here Dr. Kirsten Auken, sometimes called the Kinsey of Denmark:

We pay a price for the new independence and the new sexuality. How big is the price? We certainly do not know. We do know, however, that we cannot put the clock back again. Nor would we want to.

Traditionally, women have not been allowed to cooperate with men in forming the rules of morality although assuredly they have always been a part of reality! But maybe this is precisely what is occurring in Scandinavia today: a new morality is being advanced by men and women together. May I quote here the words of Erik H. Eriksson in his latest book about a new equal partnership between the sexes:

> The amended Golden Rule suggests that one enhances the uniqueness of the other; it also implies that each to be really unique depends on a mutuality with an equally unique partner.

SOME PERSONAL VIEWS ON THE SITUATION IN THE UNITED STATES

The Scandinavian countries may be regarded as a laboratory provided by history in which certain experiments can be observed. One fact is immediately apparent: the gap between public morality and sexual behavior is less wide than in the United States. What I call public morality is not quite the same thing as it is here. The laws and the various regulations imposed by society play a greater role in the Scandinavian countries in shaping and sometimes in leading public opinion, than they do here. I want to point to the Scandinavian attempts to abolish the concepts of shame as far as unmarried mothers are concerned—certainly a crucial point. Society has taken the lead here in legal and other efforts, and it is supported by public opinion with exceptions, of course. This fact is closely related to another one: premarital sexual relations are accepted to a certain degree. That is, they are accepted indirectly by public policy and with varying degrees of agreement by a large part of the population.

In spite of the state church system in the Scandinavian countries, where most young people go to confirmation class and a majority prefer a church wedding to a civil ceremony, it seems fair to say that there is less influence of the churches on public morality than in the United States.

It should not be forgotten that the influx into the Scandinavian countries of ideas and behavior patterns from America is considerable. But it is not my task here to talk about this interesting phenomenon. Rather, I will conclude by pointing out what I as a Scandinavian feel when looking at the United States. Certainly, a more open and frank debate is to be desired. The cost of not teaching birth control to young people should be realistically weighed against the cost of teaching it. Further, what is the price for a system with teenage marriages, often caused by unwanted pregnancies? A responsible discussion must face questions such as these; regardless of how one evaluates the situation they cannot be concealed. It is amazing how sex books, family life books and human relations columns leave out many quite important matters. They often do not give enough facts, and often they do not discuss conflicting value systems. Let me give you an example: in 13 American books on sex on my bookshelf I did not find a single word about birth control.

Assuredly, there is no simple solution to the American situation to be drawn from the Scandinavian countries. But, I should like for you to import two things: (1) more open, serious discussions and debates about values and reality with both men and women taking part, both young and old, and (2) more sex education in the schools as a part of the broader context of family life education for the younger generation.

REFERENCE

ERIKSSON, ERIK H., 1964. *Insight Responsibility*. New York: W. W. Norton and Co.

14
Getting married Soviet style[*]

DAVID and VERA MACE

The overwhelming majority of Soviet young people marry for love. They start forming friendships later than young Americans do. In Russia marriages don't take place early, because the minimum legal age for marriage is 18. Most boys have to do army service, and marriage under these circumstances is not considered desirable. Students are strongly discouraged from marrying before they graduate. So most Russians marry at a later age than Americans do. When a boy is serious about a girl he invites her home to meet his parents and they can pass judgment. If they begin to think of marriage they go to the girl's parents and ask for their consent.

. . . during the last year at the University a couple might decide to live together while awaiting the results of their finals. Everyone knows that they will marry as soon as their careers are fixed up and they find a room that they can share.

. . . It is forbidden for a Party member to be married with a church ceremony, although in the rural areas, where religious influence remains strong, many of them swallow their scruples to please their family and friends.

Whether or not to have a church wedding may become a matter of serious disagreement between young people planning to marry. In 1950 a member of the Komsomol wrote to *Komsomolskaya Pravda* to ask whether it would be all right for him to go through with the ceremony, purely as a matter of form, in order to make his bride happy. The reply was that he

---

* From *The Soviet Family*, by David and Vera Mace, copyright © 1963 by David and Vera Mace. Reprinted by permission of Doubleday & Company, Inc.

certainly could not, because if he did he would be violating the Komsomol rules. He must convince his intended wife that she should not insist on a church ceremony.[1]

Until recently, this young man would have had no alternative but to drag his bride unwillingly to the ZAGS.[2] But now a better solution to his problem has been found.

. . . . .

Overlooking the river Neva in Leningrad, before the Revolution, Prince Andrei Romanov, cousin of the Tsar, had a palatial home. In 1959 this house was designated by the city administration as the Soviet Union's first Wedding Palace. The idea was to implement the 1944 recommendation and provide for Soviet marriage "a ceremonial procedure"—on the grand scale!

The Wedding Palace was opened for business at the commemoration of the October Revolution in 1959. The real pressure to get this experiment started came, we were told, from the Komsomol members, who were increasingly concerned about the number of young people who were insisting on church weddings.

Georgi Andreivich Medvedev told us that he had been the director of the Palace since it opened, and he seemed to be very proud of his position. We spent several hours there, interviewing members of the staff, chatting with waiting couples, sitting in on wedding ceremonies, joining in congratulations to the newly married. Everyone was enthusiastic about the Wedding Palace and the services it offered.

"The first step," explained Comrade Medvedev, "is for the young man to find a prospective bride. In this matter he is on his own. The Soviet state offers him no assistance. It is entirely a matter," said the director with a twinkle in his eye, "of private enterprise."

"At the ZAGS," he went on, "the couple must give at least three days' notice of their intention to marry. But here, they must notify us usually two or three weeks in advance. Sometimes they have to wait as long as six weeks—although the Palace is open from 9:00 A.M. to 10:00 P.M. every day, and we marry a couple every ten minutes!"

On the wedding day, the bridal party arrives. The girl goes to the "bride's room," where she can put the finishing touches to her appearance. Most brides now wear white, and the bridegrooms are smartly dressed in dark suits with collars and ties.

The bridegroom takes the papers to the office to be checked. The other members of the party, while they wait, can visit the gift shop and buy last-

---

[1] *Komsomolskaya Pravda* (Moscow), March 21, 1950.
[2] The first letters, in Russian, of the State Bureau for the Registration of Acts of Civil Condition (commonly referred to as "ZAGS").

minute wedding presents. Flowers and rings may also be purchased here.

In good time, the bridal party is ushered to the Golden Room, an elaborately decorated anteroom where they may "calm their passions," as one of the attendants expressed it. She meant that they could relax—often they are quite nervous in anticipation of the ceremony.

When all is ready, the large double doors are swung open, and the bridal couple, followed by their party, proceed into the large, ornate Gala Hall where the ceremony takes place. As they move in, music is played through concealed loudspeakers. A new wedding march composed by Sorokin was, we were told, becoming very popular.

The Gala Room is large and long. At the end farthest from the window stands a table with three chairs. Seated in the middle is the director or one of his assistants. On his left is the girl clerk who is responsible for the record. On his right is a people's deputy whose function we shall describe later. Behind them is a bust of Lenin.

The couple stand before the table on a special carpet. The relatives and friends sit or stand round the walls of the room, at a respectful distance. As soon as the music stops, the ceremony begins.

The director addresses the couple. "Have you considered carefully the duties and responsibilities of marriage, and is it your decision to become husband and wife?"

Together, both reply, "Yes."

"And do you understand our Soviet laws about marriage?"

Again they respond together.

The director now invites them to come to the table and sign the marriage register. After this, the clerk produces the ring or rings (two-ring wedding are becoming popular) on a silver plate. In the Soviet Union, the wedding ring is placed by the bridegroom on the third finger of the bride's *right* hand.

Now the people's deputy addresses the couple. He is a city worker, elected from his factory or office to represent the Soviet people. He serves for just half a day, then is replaced by another. He hands the couple the marriage certificate, shakes hands, and says a few simple but sincere words. There is no official formula, but the substance of the speech is this:

"I speak to you officially in the name of our country. From this moment you are husband and wife. From my heart I congratulate you and wish you all good things for the rest of your life together. I hope you will find happiness in one another, and raise a good Soviet family."

The relatives and friends express their agreement in applause, and gather round the happy couple, thrusting flowers into their hands. Everyone kisses everyone else, without distinction of sex, in the warm Russian manner. To the accompaniment of music, the party files out to another room, where toasts are drunk, congratulations offered, and pictures taken.

Soon afterward, the couple and their guests move out to waiting cars, and proceed to the place appointed for the wedding party, which is a very lively affair. We were invited spontaneously to their wedding parties by couples who had never seen us in their lives before. Often they insisted on including us in their wedding photographs.

The couples move steadily through at the rate of ten minutes for each. This is not long, yet there is no feeling of haste. "At the ZAGS," said the director, "they marry four couples in that time!"

As a matter of fact, business at the ZAGS offices (there are twenty of them in Leningrad) is falling off. Everyone wants to be married at the Wedding Palace. We asked one couple in a ZAGS why they had not gone to the Palace.

"We couldn't get a date earlier than six weeks ahead," they said. "We can't wait that long."

They told us at the Wedding Palace that second marriages couldn't ordinarily be celebrated there. "For someone who has been widowed, occasionally we arrange it. But divorced people who are marrying again, no. They must go to the ZAGS." This is typical of the current discouraging attitude toward divorce.

The necessary authorization had been given, we were told, to set up Wedding Palaces all over the Soviet Union. We visited the only other one open at the time, in Kiev, just two days after it went into operation. It happened to be our own wedding anniversary, and they gave us a delightful party. The director in Kiev was a woman, a former high school principal, and a charming lady. The Kiev Palace was not as ornate as the one in Leningrad. But it had introduced a feature which Leningrad lacked— a dazzlingly handsome limousine, upholstered in red velvet, was available with chauffeur to drive the couple home after the ceremony!

15
The changing
sexual scene in the U.S.S.R.

A. Lectures to parents*

ANTON S. MAKARENKO

Always remember that a future citizen is in your charge. If you fail, the grief will not be yours alone. The whole country will suffer. If your factory turned out damaged goods you would be ashamed. Isn't it much more shameful for you to give your country a spoiled or bad human being?

. . . . .

The child must never think that your guidance of the family is only for your own pleasure, but understand that you are meeting your responsibility to society. Even in early years the child must realize that he does not live with his parents on a desert island.

. . . . .

Special methods of sex education are not the decisive factor. By developing honesty, sincerity, straightforwardness, respect for other people, we are at the same time educating the child in sex relations.

---

* Anton S. Makarenko, *Lectures to Parents*, translated by Elizabeth Moos (New York: National Council of American-Soviet Friendship, Inc., 1961). Reprinted with permission.

B.   Zverev on sex education

ANNE McCREARY JUHASZ

Zverev reports that as early as 1919, educators were suggesting that sex education was needed in the schools.

During the 1920s and 1930s biology teaching in the Soviet school devoted considerable attention to the physiological aspects of human sexuality. *Methods of Sex Education*, written by A. I. Lobus in 1927, was used by teachers. However, up until the last few years there has been almost no literature on the topic available to young people. Zverev outlines a desirable program which covers the processes of growth and development throughout the life span of an individual. Emphasis is placed on moral development and the idea that "the development of the human organism is closely dependent upon the life of the collective, on learning, labor, nourishment, physical culture, and sports." He recommends the teaching of the following: (1) Early sexual relations can lead to a weakening of the organism and its early debilitation. (2) It is harmful to induce the emission of semen artificially; this weakens the organism physically and spiritually, distracts from study and work, and causes feelings of depression, dissatisfaction, and weakness. (3) Early marriages lead to premature aging and excessive exhaustion of the organism. (4) Interest in exercise and sports aids in the mastery of sexual feelings. He also recommends that specialists and parents be involved in the program.[1]

C.   The Russian view on childrearing*

GEORGIE ANNE GEYER

The great majority of Russian mothers seem to be sold on the idea that their children are better off in nursery schools than at home with mother or grandmother. During three months in the Soviet Union, every woman I met seemed convinced that children are less egotistical and less spoiled if they are raised with other children. The director of a kindergarten in Volgograd said, "We take the position that, if a mother is working, it is

---

[1] I. D. Zverev, "On the Problem of Sex Education of School Children in Connection with the Study of Human Physiology," *Biologiia v shkole*, No. 3, 1967, pp. 47–52.
  * Reprinted with permission from the *Chicago Daily News*. (July 1968)

best to bring the children to a nursery school. Another reason is that it is better for the child. The parents take too much care of a single child. They spoil it."

Soviet educators and mothers laugh when it is suggested—as is believed in the West—that it harms the infant child to be away from the mother. They say they find this "a little melodramatic."

"It does not harm the child to be away," said a motherly blond who has a school of 145 apparently happy children. "They have a strict routine. At home mother is busy with her own affairs. Children who are here six months are stronger, more steeled."

In sharp contrast to American ideas about a child's best place being in the home, Russian women have enthusiastically embraced the idea of massive state care for their children. Part of the reasoning is their abiding passion for work, and part is the shortage of help in the home.

Before the revolution, 14 percent of the workers in Leningrad were employed in service occupations. Today, it is only one tenth of 1 percent. Despite special contracts through a private servants' union and every possible benefit, the profession exudes little glamor. The Soviet state is spending increasing amounts on personal services—nurseries, clinics, laundries, stores for precooked foods, cleaning establishments and things like the Service of the Dawn, which sends mother substitutes to the home when the child is sick and the mother has to work.

However, the major reason for the takeover of children is that the state believes it can form a certain kind of citizen by getting him early. There was a time, in the early post-Bolshevik years, when permissiveness in education and free love in personal relations reigned. In the early drive for change of every kind, it was believed that the family could be done away with and children completely taken over by the state. Now the pendulum has swung back. Family ties are considered important, but it is also felt that the child grows and develops best under professional care.

At the Pedagogical Institute for Preschool Children in Moscow, research is being conducted on how best to form the child. They stress that the school is "another family" and they believe that abilities are largely created in a child, that they are not primarily inherent. So they create a school that is rich in pictures, colors and rhythm. They say, "If you give me a child with limited potential, I can make him, through a rich environment, a normal human being. If you have one with high potential and do not put him in the best possible environment, he will stay dull forever."

Soviet education is at the opposite end of the spectrum from permissiveness or accidental growth. Children are expected not to form their own subcultures or peer groups with their own values but to be consciously formed to enter the adult society. Moral norms are emphasized—collectiveness, self-sacrifice, comradeship, respect for work.

Professor Urie Bronfenbrenner, a specialist on preschool education, has noted that tests for preschool children in Russia always clearly stress right and wrong, black and white, in contrast to American tests, which are far more complex.

On many levels, the Soviets seem to have dual attitudes toward children. Most modern families do not want many children. Yet, they are obviously devoted to the ones they have. They believe in letting the state care for children and yet they obviously adore them. The children appear to be well-disciplined, well-cared-for, and happy—happier in many cases than the permissively raised American children.

D. The Russian woman: We've got her all wrong*

GEORGIA ANNE GEYER

The Russian woman today is the complete feminist. In three months of travelling across the Soviet Union and talking to Russian women one thing stands out dramatically. They are determined—utterly, wholeheartedly, doggedly determined—to live their own lives, to have their own work and be their own women. And nobody is going to stop them. From the outside it may appear that it is the Soviet state that forces work upon the Soviet women, but from the inside it is clear that the Soviet women are in total agreement.

One day in Volgograd, for instance, I asked a young newspaper editor whether she would ever withdraw from her work. "Oh, no," she said, shaking her head firmly, "no matter how well paid my husband was. Our women can't leave their work, they can't live without work. . . . Our women feel that if they are not at work they are not persons." In referring to the problem of the young wife in the family, she asked, "Should the young married woman take part in community life in the same way as an unmarried one? There is the question of woman's pride when it comes to love. How can she keep her individuality when she is completely in love and forgets herself as a person, when as a person she becomes completely dependent upon the one she loves? We are struggling for a woman who continues working and for a woman who continues to take part in community life."

The determination of Russian women to work—and the fact that this often goes hand in hand with the displeasure of the husbands—is well

---

* Reprinted with permission from the *Chicago Daily News*. (July 1968)

recognized. In Leningrad, in the office of the youth newspaper, the attractive young editor said, "Yes, women have many problems. They are very busy with factory and family life. Some think they do not need education because they are married. But the children are so well-educated, so intelligent, that if she wants her children to respect her, she must find time for education. Now woman has the right to be equal. We teach young women they should be self sufficient."

This is the key to the Soviet woman's passion for employment: It makes her equal. Women make up 58 percent of the national economy; 86 percent of the workers in the National Health Service; 69 percent in education and 38 percent of the scientific workers. Before the Russian revolution, 31 percent of the workers were women. In 1917, the Soviet constitution accorded women equal rights and when labor was needed, women began to work alongside men. In the early years of feminine emancipation, women were forced into manual labor and became known around the world for their husky masculine appearance. Even today, the predominant female on the rocky Black Sea beaches fits this description. However, this is changing. Women are gradually being withdrawn from hard labor. Russians are talking about beauty for beauty's sake and the young feminists are as slim and pretty as any girls in the West.

Russian women probably work harder than any women in the world, often with less recompense and fewer conveniences. A Leningrad survey showed that they have half the leisure time of Russian men and one hour's sleep less a night. They complain that their husbands don't help them enough, that they are tired and harried, that they don't see their children as much as they want. But they do not complain about being unfulfilled or about not having meaning to their lives. They do not have the vacant, tense, unsatisfied look of many Western women. The remarks of Russian women which have been quoted typify the feelings of the majority of Soviet women. There are problems, but the women wouldn't give up their freedom, their work, their equality, for anything in the world.

E.   Sex and the Russian girl*

NEWSWEEK

Beneath a façade of public morality which frowns on any outward display of affection between the sexes, the Soviet Union is fast becoming one of

---

* From *Newsweek*, February 2, 1970. Copyright Newsweek, Inc. 1970, reprinted by permission.

the most sexually uninhibited societies among the industrialized nations of the world. Almost all university dormitories, for example, are coeducational, and liaisons there are as common as they are casual. "Some girls won't sleep with a man at their first meeting," said one student at Moscow University, "but they're in the minority." And although the pill is still rejected by Soviet doctors and intra-uterine devices are used only on an experimental basis, abortion is both legal and free, so that many Russian girls have several before marriage.

F. Russia: Communist Kinseys*

TIME MAGAZINE

The Soviet Union almost never swings, especially as far as sex is concerned. Scoffing at sexy Western-style romance as a symbol of capitalist decadence, the Communists have imposed an almost Victorian prudery upon the country. Prostitution and pornography are outlawed. Soviet films and television usually portray love in terms of hand-holding affection, and foreign sex flicks are forbidden. There are no beauty contests, no pinup girls, no men's magazines. Sex education is almost entirely limited to a single injunction: don't.

Comes the revelation. For the first time since the 1920s, Russia has produced a sociological study on sexual habits and deportment. Entitled "Youth and Marriage," the report was researched by two Leningrad social scientists, A. G. Kharchev and S. I. Golod, who may well become the Communist Kinseys. From their project emerges a plea for a more rational and open treatment of sex in Soviet society.

The two sociologists based their recommendations on a survey of 620 young men and women in Leningrad. Their findings showed that younger Soviet citizens are considerably more relaxed about sex than the older generation. For example, among students 53 percent of the males and 38 percent of the females said that they condoned premarital sex. Attitudes were even more liberal among young graduates who were already earning their own living: 81 percent of the women felt that premarital relations were in order—as long as the girl was in love.

More than half the women reported having had premarital sexual relations before they were 21. Nearly half the men had between 16 and 18. And for the Russians who did not make the statistics? Nearly half of the

---

* From *Time Magazine*, June 29, 1970. Reprinted by permission from TIME, The Weekly News Magazine; © Time Inc.

men said it was purely for "lack of occasion," a reflection of Russia's severe housing shortage, which affords lovers little opportunity to be alone indoors.

Kharchev and Golod called for revamping "socialist morality" from its present double standard of one code for men and another for women to a realistic new code that would grant both sexes equal freedom and responsibility. They singled out for criticism a recent Soviet film in which the man roughs up his fiancée after he discovers that she is not a virgin. It was none of his business, contend Kharchev and Golod. They recommend that "women should have the right to have premarital and extramarital sex life."

Kharchev and Golod hope that Russia can remedy its rampant divorce rate by adjusting the moral code to the realities of human behavior. Since divorce procedures were simplified in 1965 and again in 1968, the yearly number of dissolved marriages has sharply increased; it doubled in 1969, to about 600,000. The two sociologists place much of the blame on Soviet educators, who still refuse to deal candidly with sex information in the schools. "This is a difficult and sophisticated matter," Kharchev and Golod wrote, "which demands, in a number of cases, education and re-education of educators themselves. To put this matter off or to ignore it would be to jeopardize too much because socialism and Communism are first people, and people originate in marriage and family."

part **III**

Changes in attitudes, values, and behavior patterns

Some writers feel that we are in the midst of a sexual revolution while others maintain that, on the contrary, what we observe is merely the steady process of evolution. Undoubtedly, some change is taking place today. However, that is to be expected, since change is a continuous process, one which does not exclude retention of selected aspects from the past and their incorporation into newly emerging patterns of behavior. Juhasz, in her article, has utilized writings from past history to trace the changes which have taken place. She has focused on the aspects of sexual behavior which have remained unchanged or slightly modified when handed down to succeeding generations from early Hebrew times through the nineteenth century. Class discussion of the practices mentioned in this article could continue into the twentieth century, noting change and continuity in attitudes and behaviors, especially in relation to the Women's Liberation Movement. This will help the student to understand the influence of the past upon present behavior and perhaps enable him to determine why specific patterns of behavior were retained by societies throughout the centuries.

The Juhasz article, Reading 16, provides the setting for the other articles in Part Three which deal with some of the changes which have occurred in recent decades, in attitudes and behavior patterns of both students and adults, concerning human sexuality.

Attitudes and values are powerful determinants of all behavior, including sexual realtionships. It is usually less demanding to live in a society which spells out precisely and clearly, the rules and regulations which govern sexual activity. Under these circumstances, the individual has fewer available choices and probably fewer decisions to make. More problems are likely to arise when a society fails to establish or to maintain rigid, uniform guidelines for sexual behavior, thus requiring each individual to set his own standards. There is no doubt that problems arise wherever people exist in societies, regardless of the restrictiveness or permissiveness of the society, and that perhaps a moderate degree of social control is most effective.

In Reading 17, Isadore Rubin points to the fact that in the pluralistic, American society today, there is no single value system regarding sexual morality. This article has been placed in this part of the book because the open discussion and acceptance of choice in sexual values and behavior indicates a change in thinking. Previous generations of Americans agreed that premarital chastity was a value in itself and that any alternative in the matter was immoral. Emphasis has now shifted to the social context of the behavior and many young people decide the appropriateness of their actions in relation to the specific stage of their relationship. At this time in history, sexual expression can be tied to a variety of concepts including love, fun, fulfillment, or marriage.

Rubin analyzes the six most prevalent sex mores and suggests that in view of these competing codes, core values for sex education and behavior should be sought in the core values of a democratic society. He emphasizes the fact that the important task facing the adolescent is the evaluation of the alternative sexual codes and the making of an informed, intelligent choice.

The two readings which follow allow comparison of behavior over a period of time, and point to changing trends and patterns, both in America and abroad. Both provide insight into the attitudes of college students and the values which influence their choice of different sexual behavior. The findings reported here will supplement the material which appeared in readings 12 and 13, Part II.

In Reading 18, Gilbert Kaats and Keith Davis report that engagement is decreasing in importance as a necessary condition for premarital coitus. In their sample, this change has resulted in a premarital coital rate for college women of 41 percent in contrast to the frequently reported figure of 25 percent.

This increasing permissiveness is noted not only in America. A similar trend in attitude was found in a Scandinavian sample. Harold Christensen and Christina Gregg, in Reading 19, present results of a cross-cultural study of sex norms. A comparison of 1958 and 1968 data revealed liberated attitudes toward premarital coitus and a convergence of attitude and behavior for both American and Danish subjects in the study.

It is evident that many young people, making their own decisions about sexual behavior, are placing emphasis upon the quality of the interpersonal relationship. Decisions no longer involve merely abstinence or participation in sexual relationships, but now, in many instances, include serious consideration of the kind of feeling and involvement which the individuals share. One cannot be certain that this is, indeed, a big change in emphasis, especially for the female. Certainly, in the past, it has not been unusual for women, on the verge of sexual intercourse, to question the male, "Do you love me?" In such instances, love has represented the kind of relationship which women attached to the sexual act. It may be that, only now, are researchers beginning to ask the kinds of questions which "get at" interpersonal relationships and feelings.

In Reading 20, Seymour Halleck examines some of the problems the college student experiences in adjusting to this changing sexual scene. As a psychiatrist, his chief concern is with the psychological consequences and the impact upon mental health.

In Reading 21, Lester Kirkendall and Roger Libby discuss the reactions of some adult leaders to this shift in emphasis and in values. In addition, they summarize research associating sex and interpersonal relationships, and point to the need to change research emphasis from concern with avoidance or renunciation of all nonmarital sexual experience to concern for interpersonal relationships as the central issue in the management of sexuality. They present general recommendations related to the important aspects of sexual decision making as they see them.

Miriam Berger, in Reading 22, makes specific suggestions related to one type of living arrangement, "trial marriage." This article fits in here since it deals with a current pattern of living among some young people. It also presents an unusual and constructive adult approach to this type of living arrangement. The author, a marriage counselor, concerned with sound emotional health, recognizes the trend toward trial marriage among college students. She neither condones nor condemns this, but rather, provides historical background and makes suggestions for helping young people benefit from their living-together experience. She feels that if young people analyzed how and why the arrangement succeeded or failed, satisfied or frustrated, they would then be able to develop more satisfactory relationships in the future.

16
Changes through history*

ANNE McCREARY JUHASZ

Attitudes toward sexuality and the customs and rules which govern interpersonal relationships and behavior develop over a period of time. Change
is the essence of life and as civilization and technology develop, other
aspects of life must also change, for to remain static results in either isolation or obliteration. Changes in the mores of a society result when new
needs lead to dissatisfaction and rebellion against old customs. Environment influences both communication and progress. In all parts of the
world people have, at various times, formulated rules of behavior which
met their specific needs. As population increased, new communities developed, and it became evident that there was no single pattern or standard of behavior. Between countries, between rural and urban dwellers
in the same country, and within the same family in a single town, behavior
and attitudes toward sexuality vary. In order to understand the diversities
in sexual and behavioral patterns in Western society today, and the changes
that have created them, we will examine customs as they were in the past.

Rarely is change a complete negation of all that is old, and the adoption of an entirely new system, and in no instance is this more true than
in human sexual behavior. Actually, although there have been vast changes
in other aspects of life throughout the centuries, the present pattern of
sexual customs, actions and attitudes can still be traced back to ancient
history.

* Reprinted from *Adolescents in Society* by Anne McCreary Juhasz and George
Szasz with the permission of the Canadian Publishers, McClelland and Stewart Limited,
© 1969, pp. 32–45.

A look at woman's role and at man's complementary behavior during the past, provides insight into the roots of twentieth century attitudes toward sex. The patterns are so similar that it almost seems that we are on a treadmill, moving round and round in a circle. Man's hope is, however, that the ever-present circle is, in reality, a spiral and that on each revolution we somehow progress upward and outward.

THE EARLY HEBREWS

The earliest influence on attitudes toward sexuality in the Western world can be traced to the Talmud and the Old Testament. For the ancient Hebrews marriage and children were of greatest importance, and the people were commanded "to increase and multiply." Thus propagation of the race was a major goal of society. All men, including priests, had to marry, and the sooner the better. Women, like cattle, were considered possessions, necessary for bearing offspring. Should a wife fail to have children she could be divorced, for it was sinful to remain married but childless, and although monogamy was most common, polygamy was permitted. The groom's relatives chose his bride, and it was usual for the groom to work for the bride's father in payment, as Jacob did for Leah and Rachel.

Thou shalt not covet thy neighbor's house, thou shalt not covet thy neighbor's wife, nor his manservant, nor his ox, nor his ass, nor anything that is thy neighbor's (Ten Commandments, *Exodus, XX:17.*)

When a man hath taken a wife and married her, and it comes to pass that she find no favor in his eyes, because he hath found some uncleanness in her; then let him write her a bill of divorcement, and give it in her hand, and send her out of his house. (*Deuteronomy, XXIV:1.*)

THE ANCIENT GREEKS†

In early Greece and Crete women were dominant. This role changed, however, during the classical period when, under the law, property in Greece could only be handed down through a legal heir. Unmarried men were punished, and male descendents were valued and educated. Thus, it was necessary for a man to make sure that his wife bore only his children. Girls were isolated and protected after marriage, living in separate quarters in their husband's home. Their main function was motherhood, and if a woman failed to produce children she could be packed off to her father, and her dowry returned with her. The husband need only retrieve from her the house keys.

---

† Material for the following was obtained from Hans Licht, *Sexual Life in Ancient Greece* (London: George Routledge and Sons Ltd., 1932).

Thus, not only did the power shift to the male, but in addition, monogamy was established. At this time also, the double standard for men and women emerged, and with it two kinds of prostitution. The ancient belief prevailed that sexual enjoyment was a good thing; that it was every man's right, and that it was essential to his health. This resulted in free indulgence, the subsequent need for prostitutes, and the beginning of what is sometimes called "the oldest profession in the world." Greek women were supposed to be faithful, but men were expected to have lovers or "Hetairai." Today we would class Hetairai as prostitutes. In ancient Greece, they were not only accepted, but they were considered essential. These beautiful, well-educated, intelligent women were expected to accompany men in public life, where wives were forbidden.

The second kind of prostitution began as a means of worshipping the Gods, and the money paid to these "love goddesses" provided the upkeep of the temple. Some girls were given into temple prostitution as gifts, some were taken to supervised brothels as slaves to make money for the state, and some voluntarily sacrificed their virtue to the gods and goddesses. Available evidence indicates that the gods and goddesses were far from chaste. Greek temple decorations would today be considered pornographic, and the drawings on walls would be labelled obscene. Written accounts of life at that time describe orgies which began with excessive drinking, ribald singing and lewd conversation, and proceeded to uninhibited and uncontrolled sexual activity. People believed that gods and goddesses controlled natural phenomena, and that therefore they must worship and appease the angry spirits. Sexual gratification through intermediaries was considered the best method of achieving this.

Not only was female prostitution accepted in ancient civilizations, male prostitution was also present. In addition, homosexuality was a way of life, especially in classical Greece. The body of the adolescent boy was considered just as attractive as that of the female, and older men were expected to have young boys as sexual partners. Both in temples as a part of the worship, and in special residences, provision was made for such meetings. Female homosexuality or lesbianism was also common, in fact the term "lesbian" has its origin in the name of the Greek island of Lesbos, which was the home of many female homosexuals. However, men appreciated female charms also, and Greek literature and art indicate that the female form, especially the bosoms, were of interest.

Several of our wedding customs of today originated in ancient Greece. Marriages were commonly arranged by matchmakers who sought for the man a bride younger than himself and arranged for her dowry. Feasting and toasts to the gods were a part of the ceremony at which the bride wore a scarlet veil and a ring on the third finger of her left hand. After a wedding procession she was carried over the threshold to the bridal chamber.

We marry a woman in order to obtain legitimate children, and to have a faithful warden in the house; we keep concubines for our service and daily care; and Hetairai for the enjoyment of love.[1]

THE ANCIENT ROMANS[††]

There were many similarities between the lives of Greeks and Romans. In ancient Rome, homosexuality was also present, and marriage did not rule out other sexual relations for the male, who could turn either to prostitutes or lovers. Female prostitutes were forced to wear the toga—the traditional male garment. All Roman women were subjected to male authority, first under the father and then under the husband. Unlike her Greek counterpart, however, the Roman woman was honored and respected as wife and mother, and although she was restricted she could leave the house with her husband's permission, and with a male escort for protection. In addition, wives were allowed to share in the social life of their husbands. Divorce was not common, although a husband had the right to divorce his wife for adultery, drinking wine, poisoning her children, or counterfeiting his keys. At certain periods in history, Roman women could even be killed for such misdemeanors. In the latter period of the Roman Empire women obtained more freedom. The Roman bride came to marriage with a dowry, and received from her husband a marriage settlement, or an iron ring which she wore on the fourth finger of her left hand. She wore a special wedding dress and a red veil. Joining of hands by the couple was a part of the marriage ceremony, as it is today. As in Greece, feasting and carrying the bride over the threshold were customary. In general, the Romans demonstrated a high degree of moderation and self control in their interpersonal relations, and had a great deal of respect for the family.

. . . What we call love had hardly any part in these marriages. In addition, the husband and wife were very often betrothed to each other by their parents in early youth, for one motive or another; the reason was usually an economic one. The earliest age at which a man could marry was 15 or 16; a woman could marry when she was 12. Tacitus married a girl of 13 when he was in his middle twenties. If real love developed between husband and wife in these conditions it was generally a fortunate accident rather than the general rule. . . . Tacitus himself says somewhere: "The true Roman married without love and loved without refinement or reverence." Above all, the Romans married to have children to succeed them—that was their free and natural way of regarding sexual matters.[2]

---

[1] Demosthenes, in his oration against Neara.
[††] The material for the following was obtained from Otto Kiefer, *Sexual Life in Ancient Rome* (London: George Routledge & Sons Ltd., 1938), pp. 24–5.
[2] Kiefer, *Sexual Life in Ancient Rome*, pp. 24–25.

Love on the sly delights man; it is equally pleasing to women.
Men are poor at pretense; women can hide their desire.
It's a convention, no more, that men play the part of pursuer.
Women don't run after us; mouse traps don't run after mice.[3]

CHRISTIANITY DURING THE MIDDLE AGES[§]

As the strength of the Roman Empire waned, Christianity became a
powerful force. Man was considered superior, and woman was merely
another possession used for the continuation of the race. From the time of
Adam and Eve woman was considered the second sex, made from man's
rib and the cause of his downfall. In contrast to earlier religions, where
sex played an integral part, sex and sin became synonymous in early
Christianity, for sex was a distraction from the spiritual life which was
the only true Christian life. Paul considered marriage only second to hell-
fire, and virginity was thought to be a truly exalted state. Sexual intercourse, even in marriage, was thought to be unhealthy, unclean and wicked,
and thus all children were born in sin, and all women considered evil and
dangerous. The Church was obsessed with the control of sexuality, but
in time the regulations were changed to allow intercourse for married persons on certain days. Not until the 16th century, by the Council of Trent,
was marriage made one of the seven sacraments, and finally acknowledged
by the Church to be a little less sinful than before. Divorce was forbidden
by the early church and if a marriage was consummated it could never
be terminated.

During the Middle Ages, people began to revolt against the strict rules
of the Church, and a period of laxity resulted. Christian emperors tried
in vain to abolish the ever-increasing prostitution. It was finally accepted
as a necessary evil which served to keep rape and adultery under control. An effort was made to regulate the matter by having the girls register,
and live in designated houses in specific districts. In some instances they
were organized into guilds and dressed in uniforms. Even though they
had steady employment their lot was not a happy one, and often they were
little more than slaves, mistreated and abused by their masters.

An interesting trend in male-female relationships continued to develop
at the same time. Among the aristocracy there developed the concept of
chivalry, inspired by the worship of the Virgin Mary and the idea that love
could be a noble passion when it treated woman as an ideal, placing her

---

[3] Ovid, *The Art of Love* (translated by Rolfe Humphries), (Bloomington: Indiana
University Press, 1957), p. 113.

[§] Material for the following was obtained from the following sources: W. V. Rich-
mond, *An Introduction to Sex Education* (New York: Farrar & Rinehart Inc., 1934); E.
Chesser, *Is Chastity Outmoded?* (Toronto: W. Heineman Ltd., 1960); Ira L. Reiss,
Premarital Sexual Standards in America (Glencoe, Illinois: The Free Press, 1960),
Chapter 2; Fernando Henriques, *Love in Action* (New York; E. P. Dutton & Co. Inc.,
1960). Reprinted by permission of the publisher.

on a pedestal, chaste and untouchable, admired for her soul and character. Thus began the era of romantic love, when a lady's wish was a man's command. Usually the lady was married to someone else, and the man was a bachelor. Sex played no part in this relationship, in fact it was thought that sexual intercourse destroyed love, and love in marriage was inconceivable. However, by the sixteenth century, the pattern changed and woman was not so untouchable. Many a lover found his way to his lady's bed, and love and sex became linked. However, this was by no means always the case, and the gallant knights who granted a lady's every wish and performed deeds of daring for her favor, failed to show similar respect for the peasant girls who were considered fair game. Also, men were not averse to the use of prostitutes, and certainly numerous wars of the times forced many women into this career as a means of supporting themselves.

By the fifteenth century, the rebellion against the Church's attempts to regulate moral behavior had become so open that a reformation movement began. Throughout the fifteenth and sixteenth centuries, increasingly strict rules of conduct were enforced, and the Church punished all who tried to evade them. Thousands of women were burned as witches, and accused of consorting with demons. The chastity belt emphasized the fact that wives were the property of their husbands, and must be (literally) locked up for safe-keeping.

Meanwhile, the Reformation had grown beyond the boundaries of the Catholic Church, and new religious sects were formed which later came to be known as Protestant. One of the first of the new leaders to break with the Church of Rome was Martin Luther. He denounced his vows as a monk, married a nun, and made many revolutionary declarations which included acknowledging the right for all to marry. He also openly recognized not only man's, but woman's, sexual needs, approved of sexual intercourse between married couples twice a week, and announced that sexual frigidity and impotence were grounds for divorce.

By the end of the seventeenth century, the concept of chivalry spread to the middle classes. However, since it was also felt that wives should be faithful, the single girl, and not the married woman, became the object of affection. Parents still chose mates for their children but couples did fall in love and marry, and some even fell in love after marriage. By the eighteenth century, love became the basis for marriage, and love and sexual pleasure were considered an acceptable combination. A swing back to more freedom accompanied this change in attitude, which was also aided by the growing movement for women's rights.

"It is good for them if they abide even as I. But if they cannot contain, let them marry, for it is better to marry than to burn." (*I Corinthians, VII:8–9.*)

No matter how much they (the Church Fathers) legislated, the sex appetite could not be suppressed and marriage came to be tolerated, but for the purpose of procreation only. Woman was more and more degraded; she was called "the organ of the devil," "the gate of hell," "the most dangerous of all wild beasts." She became a soulless creature whose main function was the ensnaring of the souls of men; and it was taught that evil entered the world through her ancestress in the garden of Eden. . . . In 585 the Council of Macon, composed of fifty-nine bishops, decided by a majority of one vote that she had a soul.[4]

The fanciful speculations which had been woven for hundreds of years around the story of Adam and Eve were still accepted as sober history after the Reformation. Through Adam lust had come into the world and everyone had a raging beast lurking within him which was kept at bay with utmost difficulty. As a result of the fall, the human race was oversexed. . . . Sexual feeling was associated with guilt. It was something that happened secretly, in the dark. To be chaste, was to give the impression of being unaware of its existence. For a woman to admit that she experienced pleasure was to confess to unchastity. Prostitutes were for pleasure, wives for procreation, but respectable people did not talk about either function.[5]

THE NINETEENTH CENTURY IN ENGLAND

The nineteenth century was to prove a period of both strict repression and vigorous rebellion as far as both sexual behavior and the rights of women were concerned. The excerpt from E. Chesser (see below) gives a vivid picture of what life was like for society in general and women in particular during the early years of the century.

A veil of silence shadowed the subject of sex from the latter part of the eighteenth century far down into the Victorian era. At least, this was true of the middle classes; and with the rise of industrialism it was they who set the fashion. Chastity had become modesty and a modest woman was so refined that, like a cherub, she appeared to have no body from the neck downwards.

The distortion of sexual attitudes, part of a long heritage, had changed more in its form, perhaps, than its substance. Virginity was seldom directly extolled by name since even to mention it was to border on the indelicate. It was assumed that a woman entered marriage as a virgin because any other state would have been unthinkable in respectable circles. And respectability had become the bourgeois version of sanctity.

The many manuals of advice on correct behaviour provide significant clues to middle-class *mores*. Cosmetics were frowned upon, theatre-going and dancing were widely believed to lead to dissipation. Certain words, such as 'womb,' 'breast,' and 'pregnant,' were taboo; no refined person would refer to bodily parts or functions except in the most roundabout way.

To be pregnant was to be in 'an interesting condition,' or better still '*enceinte*.' The act of giving birth to a child was safely cloaked in the 'decency' of a foreign language. It was polite to speak of an *accouchement*, or if the truth had to be stated in English, a confinement; but it was coarse to say that a woman had been delivered of a child.

---

[4] Richmond, *Introduction to Sex Education*, pp. 127–28.
[5] Chesser, *Is Chastity Outmoded?* p. 36. (Reprinted with permission of the author.)

Women were expected to be fragile, to blush at the slightest provocation, and to swoon if matters went too far. The ideal was adolescent immaturity, both physical and mental. A well-bred girl did not attempt intelligent conversation or show any response to amorous advances other than a tendency to faint with fright if her chaperone were absent. Jeremy Taylor had expressed the right attitude of the unmarried woman when he wrote that she must strive for modesty. The sign of this was 'an ignorance in the distinction of the sexes of their proper instruments.' And Dr. Acton made the much quoted remark that it was a vile aspersion to suggest that a woman was capable of feeling sexual desire.

✿　✿　✿

Yet the pinnacle to which women were raised by all this evasion bore no relation to their status in reality. Behind all the fair words was the ugly fact that in law they were virtually part of their husband's property, chattels with few rights of their own. The myth of masculine superiority was relentlessly maintained.

Before marriage a girl was under the absolute authority of her father or guardian. She was, as often as not, kept in total ignorance of what marriage would mean. A vigilant eye was kept upon the courting couple and the young girl was not permitted to accept a gift without the consent of her future husband.

Even after marriage she had no 'legal personality.' In other words she could not sue or be sued. Her husband, admittedly, was responsible for her debts; on the other hand, any property she might have had passed to him. If she earned money after marriage he could claim it. There was no redress.

She could not make a will without her husband's permission, and any will she made could be revoked by him after her death. Nor was there legal need for him to provide for her in his will. If he died she could not assert control over her children: During his life they were his property and on his death authority passed to the nearest male relative. The mother could be ignored.

If a husband were unfaithful his wife could not apply for a judicial separation (or subsequently, a divorce) on the sole grounds of her husband's adultery. He, though, could end the marriage if she were proved unfaithful.

She had to reside wherever he wished and, if she left him, could be forcibly brought back. It was not until 1891 that a husband lost the right to imprison his wife and compel her to fulfil conjugal duties. He could not only hold her prisoner against her will, he could flog her. Chastity and chastisement were related concerns.[6]

Chesser's description of Victorian attitudes toward sexual activity provides a picture of this aspect of early nineteenth century English life. The ostrich approach to sex and the double standard for sexual behavior set their stamp upon Western culture and had a powerful influence upon the emerging society on the North American continent. Ignorance without bliss characterized this period of history. After the first half century, however, a few courageous women made speeches and campaigned to inform other women of the shabby world outside their refined drawing rooms. Brewer described

---

[6] Ibid., pp. 51–53.

male behavior at this time as "the boozing, whoring, one-standard-for-me, another for my wife, typical Victorian male,"[7] and states that in 1861 in London there were reported to be 80,000 prostitutes with a male population of all ages—1,300,000.

By the late 1800s women were making their mark, and brought a foretaste of the twentieth century. The feminist movement of that time brought vast changes as women entered offices and universities and began pressing for equal rights with men. As male workers moved from home to the factory or office, women became the authority in the home and the most powerful influence on the children. With technology, job requirements changed and women could do more of the tasks previously allotted to men. Laws limiting woman's rights to vote, to own property, and to determine her own destiny, lead to increasing agitation for a single standard for both sexes.

With this goal, sex became a topic for open discussion and the page from the June 1898 issue of *The Adult* indicates the way in which this breakthrough began. The first *Journal of Sex*, mentioned above, was issued in 1897 and caused quite a stir in Britain. Its editor was arrested, threatened with jail and heavily fined for selling copies of Havelock Ellis's *Sexual Inversion*. The journal lasted less than two years, but it was an honest attempt to bring sex out in the open and to air the problems associated with ignorance. Some of the titles indicate the topics which were discussed: "How Can Free Lovers be Happy Though Married?" "The Question of Children"; "Music, Religion and Sex"; "Dress in its Relationship to Sex." Both Emil Zola and George Bernard Shaw were contributors to this magazine which was probably the *Playboy* magazine of the nineteenth century. In addition, people like Miss De Cleyre, with more radical points of view, also wrote for *The Adult*.

. . . I would strongly advise every woman contemplating sexual union of any kind never to live together with the man you love, in the sense of renting a house or rooms and becoming his housekeeper. As to the children, seeing the number of infants who die, the alarm is rather hypocritical, but ignoring this consideration, first of all it should be the business of women to study sex and control parentage—never to have a child unless you want it, and never to want it (selfishly, for the pleasure of having a pretty plaything) unless you, yourself alone are able to provide for it.

Men, on the other hand, may contribute to their children's support, but in virtue of this support being voluntary, they would be put in a position where their opportunity to have anything to say in the management of the children would depend on their good behavior.[8]

---

[7] Leslie Brewer, *The Good News* (London: Putnam, 1962), p. 95.
[8] Miss De Cleyre, *The Adult*, Vol. 1, No. 6, January 1898, pp. 144–45.

THE NINETEENTH CENTURY IN NORTH AMERICA

The first settlers who arrived on the *Mayflower* and landed in the New England States were Puritans, escaping from the upheavals in Europe in an attempt to preserve their own way of life—and this is exactly what they did. The infamous witch hunts of Salem could vie with the most rabid of inquisitions on the European scene. And so the new world began intensive settlement under the "sex is sin" banner.

Accounts of life in New York in 1848, and in Canada in 1835, paint a picture of transplanted Victorianism adapted to pioneer settings. In New York, ladies "sat on a cushion and sewed a fine seam," while in the wilds of Canada, young ladies were expected to help in the fields, but would not dare to join the boys skating on the frozen pond in winter. Certainly, the very nature of rural life offered more frequent occasions for young people to get to know each other than did city life. In both cases, however, the family unit was strong, and a chance to meet unchaperoned was rare. It seems that the practice of bundling (see below) allowed opportunities for a wide range of sexual permissiveness, depending upon the parental attitude, and the inclination of the young people who were involved.

In early America, as in Canada, the challenge of conquering an unknown country demanded the undivided efforts of all family members. There was little time for sexual activity, and little opportunity to put the "double standard" to the test. Women had to be treated as equals, for they acted as equals, bearing their share of the work and substituting for the men when necessary. Survival necessitated quick decisions and immediate action by women at times. And so a new dimension in human relations was added by the pioneer forefathers of this continent: equality of rights, and respect for all members of a family, with the expectation that all would co-operate and work as a team under the leadership of the father, plus an ever-increasing participation by the other. Romantic love was shelved for practical partnership.

Country Life in Canada—1835

It often happened that the old people objected to dancing, and then the company resorted to plays, of which there was a great variety; "Button, Button, Who's Got the Button;" "Measuring Tape;" "Going to Rome;" "Ladies Slipper;" all pretty much of the same character, and much appreciated by the boys, because they afforded a chance to kiss the girls.[9]

"Bundling" in Early New England

At their usual time the old couple retire to bed, leaving the young ones to settle matters as they can; who after having sat up as long as they think proper, get

---

[9] Caniff Haight, *Country Life in Canada Fifty Years Ago* (Toronto: Humber, Rose and Co., 1885), p. 69.

into bed together also, but without pulling off their undergarments in order to prevent scandal. If the parties agree, it is all very well; the banns are published and they are married without delay. If not, they part and probably never see each other again; unless which is an accident which seldom happens, the forsaken fair one prove pregnant and then the man is obliged to marry her under pain of excommunication.

There seem to have been many devices for minimizing temptations between bundlers. One was a low board fitted into slots, dividing the bed into two, but in no way hindering contact of hands or lips. A bolster served a similar purpose. Some prudent mothers tied their daughter's ankles together, or encased the lower parts of their bodies in a tight garment, or made them wear a profusion of petticoats. It was also open to an apprehensive maiden to provide auxiliary defences of her own, either by sewing up her garments at suitable places or laying in an armoury of pins. In real emergencies a scream would always bring immediate aid. But there is no reason to suppose that it was always the girl who was on the defensive.

Sometimes the pair were fussed over, and tucked in, by their parents. The degree of freedom from supervision allowed them may have depended, in some instances, on the eagerness of the parents to see their daughter married. Traditionally, a candle in the girl's window was the signal that the suitor (or indeed any suitor) would be hospitably received. It might be set there by the girl herself, or even by her parents.[10]

Dutch Settlers in New York—1848

. . . a well regulated family always rose with the dawn, dined at eleven, and went to bed at sunset. [At fashionable tea parties] . . . The company commonly assembled at three o'clock and went away about six, unless it was in winter time, when the fashionable hours were a little earlier, that the ladies might get home before dark. . . . At these primitive tea parties the utmost propriety and dignity of deportment prevailed. No flirting or coquetting; no gambling of old ladies nor hoyden chattering and romping of young ones, no self-satisfied struttings of wealthy gentlemen with their brains in their pockets; nor amusing conceits and monkey divertissements of smart young gentlemen with no brains at all. On the contrary, the young ladies seated themselves demurely in their rush-bottomed chairs and knit their own woollen stockings, nor ever opened their lips excepting to say *Yah Mynheer*, or *Ya, ya Vrouw*, to any question which was asked them, behaving in all things like decent, well-educated damsels.[11]

I am quite well aware that a large portion of the religious world is opposed to dancing, nor in this recital of country life as it then existed do I wish to be considered an advocate of this amusement. I joined in the sport then with as much eagerness and delight as one could do. I learned to step off the light fantastic toe as many another Canadian boy has done, on the barn floor, where with

---

[10] E. S. Turner, *A History of Courting* (London: Michael Joseph, 1954), p. 124. Reprinted by permission of the publisher.

[11] Washington Irving's translation of Knickerbocker's *A History of New York* (New York: A. L. Burt, 1848), pp. 103–5.

the door shut, I went gliding up and down, through the middle, balancing to the pitch fork, turning round the old fanning mill, then double-shuffling and closing with a profound bow to the splint broom in the corner. These were the kind of schools in which our accomplishments were learned, and, whether dancing be right or wrong, it is certain the inclination of the young to indulge in it is about as universal as the taint of sin.[12]

By the 1890s, however, the picture was changing rapidly, especially in urban areas. Young people had much more freedom to come and go as they pleased, unchaperoned, and in mixed groups. The female form and ideas of beauty and romance became items of interest with the "Gibson Girl" hourglass figure held up as the ideal. Dorothy Dix made her debut as the advisor of the lovelorn, and the new rhythms of the blues and the tango provided the atmosphere for a more free and relaxed pattern of behavior. According to the editorial in the English journal, *The Adult,* Victorian attitudes were slow to change in America, at least in the press.

Editorial Notes

The *Ladies Home Journal* of Philadelphia has decided to avoid for the future all references in its pages to the subject of ladies' underlinen—"the treatment of the subject in print," says the delicate-minded journal, "calls for minutaie of detail which is extremely and pardonably offensive to refined and sensitive women." This is going a step further than the traditional lady who covered the legs of the piano with frilled calico. Obviously, the *Ladies Home Journal* would regard all reference, even to such covering, as indelicate. Apparently this offensively refined person is in her or (to avoid the use of indelicate pronouns) its proper place as editor of a ladies' fashion paper, many of such journals existing apparently for the sole object of crushing out nature and making women as nearly ugly as anything can make them.[13]

---

[12] Haight, *Country Life in Canada*, pp. 72–73.
[13] *The Adult*, Vol. 2, No. 5, June, 1898, pp. 124–25.

17

Transition in sex values—
Implications for the education
of adolescents*

ISADORE RUBIN

This paper concerns the kind of education which the United States as a pluralistic society can give to adolescents and young adults in its various educational institutions. The concern is *not* with our private set of values either as individuals or parents, but rather with a philosophy of sex education for a democratic society.

THE CONFUSION OF TRANSITION

Family professionals may not agree on the causes of the change, the extent, or the direction, but they do agree that there has been a great transition in sex values in the 20th century. Evelyn Duvall has characterized this transition as "a basic shift from sex denial to sex affirmation throughout our culture."[1]

This transition from sex denial to sex affirmation has not been an easy or smooth one. American culture historically has been rooted in the ideal of asceticism, and only slowly and with a good deal of rear-guard opposi-

* From *Journal of Marriage and the Family*, Vol. 27, No. 2 (May 1965), pp. 185–89. Reprinted by permission of the National Council on Family Relations.

[1] *Sex Ways—In Fact and Faith: Bases for Christian Family Policy*, ed. by E. M. Duvall and S. M. Duvall (New York: Association Press, 1961).

tion is this philosophy being relinquished. Most official attitudes today still constitute what a distinguished British jurist called "a legacy of the ascetic ideal, persisting in the modern world after the ideal has deceased."[2] As a result of the conflict and confusion inherent in the transition of sex values, there exists today an interregnum of sex values which are accepted in theory and in practice by the great majority of Americans.

The confusion is especially great among those who are responsible for the guidance of youth. Last year Teachers' College together with the National Association of Women Deans and Counselors decided to hold a two-week "Work Conference on Current Sex Mores." Esther Lloyd-Jones, Head of the Department of Guidance and Student Personnel Administration at Teachers' College explained why:

"The reason that made me determine to hold that conference was the repeated statement by deans and counselors—as well as by parents—that the kids were certainly confused in the area of sex mores, but that they thought they were just as confused as the kids. They just plain felt they did not know. They were clearly in no position to give valuational leadership."[3]

It is unnecessary to state that this conference—like many others held before it—did not reach agreement on what the sex mores should be.

THE IMPOSSIBILITY OF CONSENSUS

At the present time, there seems no possibility for our pluralistic society as a whole to reach a consensus about many aspects of sex values. We cannot do it today even on so comparatively simple a problem as the moral right of persons who are married to have free access to contraceptive information, or the right of married couples to engage in any kind of sex play that they desire in the privacy of the marriage bedroom, or even the right of individuals to engage in the private act of masturbation. Certainly we cannot expect to do so on so emotionally laden a problem as premarital sex relations.

Even in NCFR, made up of the most sophisticated students of this problem, no consensus has been reached after more than 25 years of debate and dialogue, although, as Jessie Bernard pointed out to NCFR last year, there has been a change. "There was a time," she said, "when those arguing for premarital virginity could be assured of a comfortable margin of support in the group. This is no longer always true. Especially the younger members no longer accept this code."[4]

---

[2] G. Williams, *The Sanctity of Life and the Criminal Law* (New York: Alfred A. Knopf, 1957).

[3] E. Lloyd-Jones, "The New Morality," unpublished paper presented at the New York State Deans and Guidance Counselors Conference, November 3, 1963.

[4] J. Bernard, "Developmental Tasks of the NCFR, 1963–1988," address delivered

This change in NCFR thinking reflects the great debate that is taking place on a national and an international scale. This debate reflects the fact that—whether we like it or not—we do not today possess a code of sex beliefs about which we can agree. Significantly, it is not only those who refuse to look to religion for their answers who seek a new value framework for sex. A growing body of religious leaders recognize that our modern sex morality can no longer consist of laws which give a flat yes-or-no answer to every problem of sex. These leaders concede that there are many moral decisions which persons must make for themselves.[5]

THE MAJOR COMPETING VALUE SYSTEMS

This writer has found it of value to define six major conflicting value systems of sex existing side by side in this transitional period of morality.[6] These value systems extend along a broad continuum ranging from extreme asceticism to a completely permissive anarchy. The major ones are characterized as follows: (1) traditional repressive asceticism; (2) enlightened asceticism; (3) humanistic liberalism; (4) humanistic radicalism; (5) fun morality; and (6) sexual anarchy. To discuss each of these very briefly:

1. Traditional repressive asceticism—which is still embodied in most of our official codes and laws—proscribes any kind of sexual activity outside of the marriage relationship and accepts sex in marriage grudgingly, insisting upon the linkage of sex with procreation.[7] This value system is intolerant of all deviations from restrictive patterns of heterosexual behavior, it places a taboo on public and scientific discussion and study of sex, and it conceives of sex morality solely in absolute terms of "Thou shalt" and "Thou shalt not."
2. Enlightened asceticism—as exemplified in the views of such spokesmen as David Mace[8]—begins with a basic acceptance of the ascetic

at the annual meeting of the National Council on Family Relations, Denver, August 1963, published in *Journal of Marriage and the Family*, 26:1 (February 1964), pp. 29–38.

[5] See, for example, A. T. Robinson, *Christian Morals Today*, Philadelphia: Westminster Press, 1964; and J. M. Krumm, "The Heart and the Mind and the New Morality," unpublished baccalaureate sermon, Columbia University, June 2, 1963.

[6] I. Rubin, *Conflict of Sex Values*, in *Theory and Research*, unpublished paper, Workshop on Changing Sexual Mores, Teachers' College, August 2, 1963.

[7] See A. C. Kinsey et al., *Sexual Behavior in the Human Male*, Philadelphia: W. B. Saunders, 1948: and A. Ellis, *The American Sexual Tragedy* (New York: Grove Press, 1963).

[8] D. A. Mace and R. Guyon, "Chastity and Virginity: The Case For and the Case Against," in *The Encyclopedia of Sexual Behavior*, ed. by A. Ellis and A. Abarbanel (New York: Hawthorn Books, 1961), pp. 247–57; D. A. Mace and W. R. Stokes, "Sex Ethics, Sex Acts and Human Needs—A Dialogue," *Pastoral Psychology*, 12 (October-November 1961), pp. 34–43, 15–22; and W. R. Stokes and D. A. Mace, "Premarital Sexual Behavior," *Marriage and Family Living*, 15 (August 1953), pp. 235–49.

point of view. Mace sees asceticism as a safeguard against the "softness" to which we so easily fall prey in an age when opportunities for self-indulgence are so abundant. He sees youth as the time when invaluable lessons of self-control and discipline must be learned, with sex as one of the supreme areas in which self-mastery may be demonstrated, and he opposes any slackening of the sexual code. However, he takes neither a negative nor a dogmatic attitude toward sex and has been an ardent exponent of the "open forum" in which issues can be stated and weighed.

3. Humanistic liberalism has been best exemplified by the views of Lester Kirkendall.[9] Kirkendall opposes inflexible absolutes and makes his prime concern the concept of interpersonal relationship. He sees the criterion of morality as not the commission or omission of a particular act, but the consequences of the act upon the interrelationships of people, not only the immediate people concerned but broader relationships.

Kirkendall thus is searching for a value system which will help supply internalized controls for the individual in a period when older social and religious controls are collapsing.

4. Humanistic radicalism—exemplified best by the views of Walter Stokes[10]—accepts the humanistic position of Kirkendall and goes further in proposing that society should make it possible for young people to have relatively complex sex freedom. He makes it clear that society must create certain preconditions before this goal may be achieved. He envisions "a cultural engineering project" which may take generations to achieve.

5. Fun morality has as its most consistent spokesman Albert Ellis.[11] Without compromise, he upholds the viewpoint that sex is fun and that the more sex fun a human being has, the better and psychologically sounder he or she is likely to be. He believes that, despite the risk of pregnancy, premarital intercourse should be freely permitted, and at times encouraged, for well-informed and reasonably well-adjusted persons.

6. Sexual anarchy has as its philosopher the late French jurist René Guyon.[12] Guyon attacks chastity, virginity, and monogamy and calls for the suppression of all anti-sexual taboos and the disappearance of the

[9] L. A. Kirkendall, *Premarital Intercourse and Interpersonal Relations* (New York: Julian Press, 1961); L. A. Kirkendall, "A Suggested Approach to the Teaching of Sexual Morality," *Journal of Family Welfare* (Bombay, India), 5 (June 1959), pp. 26–30; and T. Poffenberger et al., "Premarital Sexual Behavior: A Symposium," *Marriage and Family Living*, 24 (August 1962), pp. 254–78.

[10] W. R. Stokes, "Guilt and Conflict in Relation to Sex," *The Encyclopedia of Sexual Behavior*, pp. 466–71; W. R. Stokes, "Sex Education of Children," in *Recent Advances in Sex Research*, ed. by H. G. Beigel (New York: Hoeber-Harper, 1963), pp. 48–60; Mace and Stokes, "Sex Ethics"; and Stokes and Mace, "Premarital Sexual Behavior."

[11] A. Ellis, *If This Be Sexual Heresy* (New York: Lyle Stuart, 1963).

[12] R. Guyon, *The Ethics of Sexual Acts* (New York: Alfred A. Knopf, 1934); and Mace and Guyon, "Chastity and Virginity."

notions of sexual immorality and shame. The only restriction he would apply is the general social principle that no one may injure or do violence to his fellows.

Can educators resolve these competing philosophies of sex? Judging by present disagreements, it is hardly conceivable that a consensus will be possible for a long time to come, even by our best social theorists. In fact, it would be dangerous—on the basis of the fragmentary information we now have—to come to a conclusion too quickly.

EDUCATION VERSUS INDOCTRINATION

What then are the educational implications of the confusion and conflict which exist in this transitional period?

The beginning of wisdom for educators is the recognition of the fact that the old absolutes have gone; that there exists a vacuum of many moral beliefs about sex; and that we cannot ignore the conflicting value systems which are openly contending for the minds not only of adults but particularly of youths.

Our key task—if we are to have a dialogue with youths—is to win and hold their trust. This means that we cannot fob them off with easy, ready-made replies; that we cannot give dishonest answers to their honest questions; that we cannot serve up information tainted with our bias.

If we tell them, for example, that there is only one view concerning the need for sexual chastity, they will quickly learn that there are many views. If we give them false information about any area of sex, they will sooner or later learn that we have lied. If we withhold the available data and merely give them moral preachments, they will nod their heads . . . and seek their answers elsewhere.

Our major educational problem is this: How can we help young people (and ourselves) to find some formula for coping with our dilemmas? How can we help them keep their bearings in a period of rapid and unending change, and help them make intelligent choices among the conflicting value systems?

If we indoctrinate young people with an elaborate set of rigid rules and ready-made formulas, we are only insuring the early obsolescence of these tools. If, on the other hand, we give them the skills and attitudes, the knowledge and understanding that enable them to make their own intelligent choice among competing moral codes, we have given them the only possible equipment to face their future. This type of guidance does not deny that a dilemma exists whenever choices must be made. Each choice commands a price to be paid against the advantages to be gained.[13]

---

[13] C. Kirkpatrick, *The Family: As Process and Institution* (New York: Roland Press, 1954).

There are some adults who would try to hide the obvious from adolescents—that we adults ourselves have no agreement about sex values, that we too are searching. To do this, however, is to forfeit our chance to engage in a dialogue with our youngsters. It is far wiser to admit our own dilemmas and to enlist them frankly in the task of striking a balance in this interim of confusion.

When it comes to sex education, most parents and educators have overlooked a rather simple lesson. The fact of the matter is that we do have a time-tested set of basic principles of democratic guidance that serve us well in many fields, but which are unfortunately laid aside the moment we enter the taboo-laden area of sex.[14]

In teaching politics and government, we do not feel the need to indoctrinate all students into being members of one or another political party. Rather we try to teach them the skills and attitudes which they require to make intelligent choices as adults when faced with a changing world and an array of alternatives.

In science and industry, we do not equip them with a set of tools that will be outmoded in a rapidly evolving technology, but try to equip them with skills which can adjust to a changing field.

Certainly indoctrination of moral values is an ineffective educational procedure in a democratic and pluralistic society where a bewildering array of alternatives and conflicting choices confront the individual—particularly in a period of transition.[15]

A DEMOCRATIC VALUE FRAMEWORK

At this point, the writer hastens to say that he is not advocating that we jettison all the moral values that we have developed over the centuries. He would be very loath to abandon anything that has been tested by time, particularly those institutions that have been found to be almost universal. But there have been virtually no universals in sex values, with only the prohibition of incest coming close to being one.[16] And as the anthropologist Murdock pointed out, as a society we have been deviant—not typical—in our past attitudes toward sex and premarital chastity.[17]

We do have need for a value framework for sex guidance. Value commitments are necessary for any person who forms part of a social group, and no society can survive without a set of core values which the majority of its members really believe in and act upon.[18] However, it is clear that

---

[14] W. H. Kilpatrick, *Philosophy of Education* (New York: Macmillan, 1951).

[15] J. F. Cuber, R. A. Harper, and W. F. Kenkel, *Problems of American Society: Values in Conflict* (New York: Henry Holt, 1956).

[16] M. Edel and A. Edel, *Anthropology and Ethics* (Springfield, Ill.: Charles C Thomas, 1959).

[17] G. P. Murdock, *Social Structure* (New York: Macmillan, 1949).

[18] A. Kardiner, *Sex and Morality* (New York: Bobbs-Merrill, 1954).

most of the values represented in the official sex code have left the core of our culture and entered the arena of competing alternatives. We must then seek our values for sex education in the core values of a democratic society. These values have been defined as (1) faith in the free play of critical intelligence and respect for truth as a definable moral value; (2) respect for the basic worth, equality, and dignity of each individual; (3) the right of self-determination of each human being; and (4) the recognition of the need for cooperative effort for common good.[19]

The acceptance of a scientific point of view in our thinking about sex ethics would be of inestimable importance in the education of youth. Since a great deal of thinking about sex has been based either on religious values, prejudice, or irrational fears, the consistent application of this point of view would be of tremendous significance in bringing about a re-evaluation of our thinking about sex.

It would imply, first of all, that the effect of practices which are not sanctioned in our official codes would be described objectively and scientifically rather than in terms of special pleading for the official code. Reiss has shown that treatment by leading marriage and family texts of the consequences of premarital intercourse "neglects or misinterprets much of the available empirical evidence."[20] Studies by Gebhard et al.[21] (on abortion), Kirkendall[9] (on premarital intercourse), Vincent[22] (on unwed mothers), and other investigators, for example, have shown that behavior contrary to the accepted codes cannot be described solely in terms of negative consequences for individuals engaging in it, even in our present culture.

The application of critical intelligence also implies that moral behavior would be viewed not in terms of obedience to fixed laws, but on the basis of insights from various disciplines "that add to the picture of the world in which man lives and acts, that throw light upon the nature of man and his capacities, social relations, and experiences." It would also mean that adolescent sex activities would be limited for the actual protection of their health and well-being rather than for the protection of adult moral prejudice.[23]

There is no doubt that there is an extremely difficult problem for social control when the individual is allowed a choice in moral behavior. Landis asserts: "In moral codes taboo acts must be condemned regardless of ad-

[19] Kilpatrick, *Philosophy of Education;* and E. Nagel, "Liberalism and Intelligence," Fourth John Dewey Memorial Lecture, Bennington, Vt.: Bennington College, 1957.

[20] I. L. Reiss, "The Treatment of Pre-Marital Coitus in 'Marriage and the Family' Texts," *Social Problems,* 4 (April 1957), pp. 334–38.

[21] P. H. Gebhard et al., *Pregnancy, Birth, and Abortion* (New York: Hoeber-Harper, 1958).

[22] C. E. Vincent, *Unwed Mothers* (Glencoe, Ill.: Free Press, 1961).

[23] R. A. Harper, "Marriage Counseling and Mores: A Critique," *Marriage and Family Living,* 21 (February 1959), pp. 13–9.

vantages gained by certain individuals or groups who violate them. . . .
When acts are no longer forbidden to all, when the individual is authorized to decide whether or not violation will be advantageous, the moral
code vanishes."[24]

This is indeed a dilemma for society. Unfortunately, at the present time
many of the taboos still present in our official codes are no longer accepted
either in precept or in practice by the vast majority of our people. We can
take as an obvious example the proscription against birth control. A great
debate has been opened on many other aspects of our sexual codes. If we
do not equip our adolescents to participate intelligently in this debate, we
do not ensure the protection of our moral codes. What we do ensure is that
youngsters will have no rationale to enable them to make intelligent
decisions.

To advocate autonomy is not necessarily to encourage the flouting of
conventional mores or to encourage libertarian behavior. In the absence
of fixed and rigorously enforced codes, a great deal of adolescent sexual
behavior is determined by the mores of the teenage subculture. The ad-
vocacy of self-determination, therefore, may foster resistance to teenage
pressures rather than to conventional norms.[25]

In short, what the educator must do is not provide ready-made formulas
and prepackaged values, but provide knowledge, insight, and values on
the basis of which the adolescent may choose for himself with some measure of rationality among competing codes of conduct.[26] In a changing
world, we must develop "a frame of mind which can bear the burden of
skepticism and does not panic when many of the habits are doomed to
vanish."[27]

SEX EDUCATION AND SOCIAL POLICY

In our thinking about sex education and the adolescent, we almost always think solely in functional terms of helping the adolescent cope with
his problems and of preparing him for courtship and marriage. We tend
to overlook completely the aspect of social policy—the fact that increasing knowledge of all areas of sex is being required of all individuals as
citizens.

---

[24] P. H. Landis, book review in *Marriage and Family Living*, 24 (February 1962),
pp. 96–7.

[25] D. Riesman, "Permissiveness and Sex Roles," *Marriage and Family Living*, 21
(August 1959), pp. 211–17.

[26] D. P. Ausubel, "Problems of Adolescent Adjustment," *The Bulletin of the National Association of Secondary-School Principals*, 34 (January 1950), pp. 1–84, and
I. Rubin, *A Critical Evaluation of Certain Selected Operational Principles of Sex Education for the Adolescent*, unpublished Ph.D. dissertation, New York University School
of Education, 1962.

[27] K. Mannheim, *Diagnosis of Our Time* (New York: Oxford U. Press, 1944).

Issues dealing with all aspects of sex are more and more entering the arena of national and international debate and decision. On an international scale, problems of birth control, venereal disease, and prostitution have been subject to wide-scale discussion and decision. In legislative and legal arenas, with the concomitant aspects of public discussion, there have been sharp conflicts about public policy concerning censorship, pornography, birth control, abortion, illegitimacy, changes in sex laws, homosexuality, and emergent problems like artificial insemination.

All of these require for their solution an informed citizenry sufficiently open-minded to make required decisions on the basis of rational consideration rather than prejudice and irrationality.

SUMMARY

In summarizing the major tasks of sex guidance of the adolescent, the writer would like to repeat the proposals which he made to the Deans' Workshop on Changing Sexual Mores at Teachers' College last year:

1. Create the "open forum" that Mace has emphasized in the family life field. Do not attempt to hide the obvious from college students—that major value conflicts exist in our society and that no consensus exists among adults. Enlist students to take responsibility for helping resolve the confusion inherent in the transition of values. Re-evaluate texts and curricula so that in this field, as in others, the principles of scientific objectivity will hold.

2. Apply the time-tested and traditionally accepted principles of education in a democracy—give guidance by education rather than indoctrination; deal with all the known facts and results of research; teach critical judgment in dealing with ethical controversy.

3. Adopt as the main goal in regulating adolescent conduct measures that will equip students for intelligent self-determination rather than conformity to procedures which will have no educative effect on their real choices of conduct.

4. Help identify and destroy those outmoded aspects of the ascetic ideal which no longer represent the ideals of the vast majority of American ethical leaders or of the American people, and which no longer contribute either to individual happiness and growth or to family and social welfare.

All of this in no way denies that teachers should have strong ethical convictions of their own, or that they should feel it necessary to conceal these convictions from the adolescents with whom they deal. What they should *not* do is play the role of the apologist for the status quo, devising a "new rationale for an established policy when it has become clear that the old arguments in its favor are no longer adequate."[28]

---

[28] D. Callahan, "Authority and The Theologian," *The Commonweal*, 80 (June 5, 1964), pp. 319–23.

18

The dynamics of sexual
behavior of college students[*]

GILBERT R. KAATS and KEITH E. DAVIS

In marked contrast to pre-1962 data on sexual behavior of college women
was our finding in the spring of 1967 at the University of Colorado of a
reported premarital coital rate of 41 percent—a figure about twice as high
as that which has traditionally been reported at other universities. Of further significance was the fact that the data were gathered in an introduc-
ory psychology course populated largely by 19–20 year old sophomores.
Conversely, the figure for males, 60 percent, was nearly identical with that
which has been reported since the turn of the century. If the findings could
be replicated they may suggest that this university is much more "liberal"
in this area than most or that we are experiencing a marked shift in the
sexual behavior of college women. Let us first consider the evidence for a
more general change in sexual behavior.

For some time now there has been considerable unanimity of opinion
among contemporary analyses of the literature about the percentage of
college women engaging in premarital coitus. Figures vary from 13 to 25
percent (Bell, 1967; Ehrmann, 1959; Freedman, 1965; Kephart, 1966;
Leslie, 1967; Reiss, 1966, 1967, Smigel and Seiden, 1968) and Kinsey's data
(Kinsey *et al.*, 1953) report a figure close to 20 percent for 19–20 year old
college women. Based almost exclusively on data gathered prior to 1962,

[*] From *Journal of Marriage and the Family*, Vol. 32, No. 3 (August 1970), pp.
390–99. Reprinted by permission of the authors and the National Council on Family
Relations.

virtually all of these analyses appear to be in accord with Bell's (1966) conclusion:

On the basis of available evidence, it appears that the greatest changes in premarital coitus for the American female occurred in the period around World War I and during the 1920s. There is no evidence that the rates since that period have undergone any significant change (p. 57).

However, many of the social forces of the past decade would appear to at least have the potential for producing rather sudden behavioral changes —not the least of which is the substantial increase in precoital behavior such as petting (Ehrmann, 1959; Reiss, 1967) and the advent and accessability of birth control pills (Bernard, 1966). Furthermore, there is considerable evidence that sexual attitudes of the college population have steadily changed in a more liberal direction. For example, in discussing the importance of changing trends in sexual attitudes, Reiss (1966) concluded, "The major importance lies in the increasing acceptance of premarital coital behavior rather than increased performance of this behavior" (p. 126). This is particularly true when there is a commitment to marriage (Bell, 1966). Thus, over the past few decades there appears to have been a gap between expressed attitudes and reported behavior. A widely accepted view is that discrepancies between attitudes and behavior are resolved by changing either the attitude or behavior. With regard to sexual attitudes and behavior, the general feeling has been that behavior has been more liberal than expressed attitudes and more people have indulged in intercourse than express attitudes approving of it. If attitudes have been becoming progressively more liberal, it appears highly likely that behavior too, may begin to change in a more liberal direction. Thus, it seems reasonable that marked attitude-behavior discrepancies would contain the potential for sudden change—a potential which has been pointed out by several of the most recent writers. For example, based on current findings at the Institute for Sex Research that females now have earlier experiences with sexuality, Gagnon and Simon (1968) conclude:

If this shift toward earlier experience with sexuality is in fact occurring, then we might entertain thoughts of profound social change waiting in the wings (p. 111).

More to the point, in a recent analysis of a series of articles on the "sexual renaissance" in America, Reiss (1966) concludes:

We may well witness soon an increase in many forms of sexual behavior, since our sexual attitudes seem to have presently caught up with sexual behavior, and the stage is thus set for another upward cycle of increasing sexual behavior and sexual acceptance (p. 127).

But as Smigel and Seiden (1968) pointed out in their recent review, while:

We know that sexual attitudes have changed and that sexual standards appear in a period of transition. . . . We do not know what has happened during the last five years or what is happening now (p. 15).

Some of the more recent studies provide some evidence for a marked change in premarital coital rates of college women. For example, Davis (1970) has reviewed all published and several unpublished studies of college students' sexual behavior in which the data were collected in the 1960s. Although he rejects the notion that we are experiencing a "sexual revolution," Davis points out:

In my examination of the data, I find only two substantial carefully executed studies . . . which showed a nonvirgin rate below 30 percent for college women and most of the studies yield figures in the 40 percent to 55 percent range. . . . Overall, it is clear that there are several schools with rates considerably higher than the classic 25 percent figure, and that *the weight of the data suggests a marked change in the number of college women who experience premarital coitus.* (our italics)

In order to resolve this issue one would, of course, need a national probability sample of college women much like Reiss' (1967) sample of adults. But while we were not in a position at this time to provide such data, we felt that if we could replicate the initial findings we would be in a position to obtain some valuable information on the attitude-background-behavior relationships found among a sample of college students with such a high rate of premarital coitus. If one chooses to conclude that our samples are a portend of the future, such data may offer considerable insight into the nature of future trends in sexual behavior and attitudes.

The waning of the double standard?

Another area where attitudes appear to have undergone considerable change is with respect to the double standard. While the double standard may be defined a number of ways (see Reiss, 1960 for an extensive analysis of the different aspects of the double standard), there seems to be considerable agreement that there has been a steady decrease in the tendency to express different standards for members of one's own sex than for members of the opposite sex. In addition to some earlier indications in the work of Bromley and Britten (1938) and Landis and Landis (1958), more recent research (Bell, 1966; Reiss, 1960, 1967) appears to echo Ehrmann's (1959) belief about the weakening of the double standard:

An important fact about these distributions is that a majority of the males (67 percent) adhered to a single standard, and most of these to a liberal single standard.

But this is not to imply that the double standard is now a thing of the past. Smigel and Seiden (1968), in their work on the decline and fall of the double standard, reach the conclusion that ". . . we are witnessing the decline, but not yet the fall, of the double standard" (p. 17).

In the context of our research sample, the question becomes: Has the double standard "fallen" in a group where more than four out of ten women have had sexual experience? And perhaps an equally important question needs to be raised on the methodological approach to assessment of the double standard. In the research instruments typically employed, the referrents are "males" and "females," "men" and "women." Using this format in our initial study we found no evidence of a double standard among our males—they expressed equally liberal attitudes for "males" and "females." While one might be tempted to conclude that we had found evidence for the decline of the double standard, the question of how much of this equalitarianism could be attributed to the item wording needed to be answered. For example, even though the respondent is encouraged to answer in terms of his personal attitudes, it is quite possible that these generic referents tend to elicit male expressions of equalitarianism which would not be felt if the referents were "your sister" or "your future spouse." In the follow-up study we included these types of items. We hypothesized that, as the female about whom the standard was expressed becomes more meaningful to the respondent, the greater will be the double standard.

Physical attractiveness and sexual behavior

Surprising little is known about the relationship between physical attractiveness and sexual experience, particularly for women. While Bell (1966) suggests that the American girl can be sexually attractive but not sexually active, he cites no data, and there appears to have been little systematic research on the topic. Perhaps one of the major reasons for the lack of research in this area has to do with the methodological difficulties of making physical attractiveness ratings and still insuring the anonymity of respondents. In our follow-up study we devised a method to overcome this difficulty. With respect to our prediction in this area, it is obvious that girls who are above the norm would be more likely to date more frequently and hence be exposed to more opportunities and more pressures from males. But does this greater physical attractiveness make them more self-confident and independent of male pressures or not? On the other hand there is also the possibility that less attractive girls would use sex as a way of obtaining and holding a boy's interest. Although the issue is by no means clear-cut, we hypothesized that the more physically attractive girls have increased opportunities and a higher premarital coital rate. The rationale for the prediction is that more attractive girls will be exposed to more sustained and convincing romantic behavior by suitors, and hence are more likely to have the opportunity to engage in "love-making" with partners who care for them.

Perceived support for premarital intercourse

One way to understand the greater sexual experience of college women is to assume that they have more (and stronger) sources of support for engaging in premarital coitus, particularly among the peer group. To check this possibility, a systematic mapping of the perceived sexual attitudes among individuals and groups who were personally relevant to the students was conducted. Particular attention was paid to various peer groups and to the difference between perceived peer behavior and perceived peer approval of one's own premarital intercourse.

In summary, the research reported here was addressed to four major areas: replication of the initial findings, the degree of male-female sexual equalitarianism, the relationship between physical attractiveness and sexual behavior, and the college student's perceptions of sources of approval or disapproval for premarital coitus.

METHOD

Subjects

All subjects were enrolled in a two-semester introductory psychology course. Completion of both semesters meets the University's Biological Science requirement and, since psychology was at that time the most popular of the three alternative, it contained a fairly representative sample of students at this university. Subjects, males (N = 155) and females (N = 222), for the initial study were drawn from the second half of the course in the spring of 1967 and those in the followup study (males = 84, females = 97) were concurrently enrolled in the second half of the course in the fall of 1967.

Procedure

The initial study was conducted in the laboratory sections of the course and although all subjects did not complete the questionnaire, Kaats and Davis' (1970) data argue against a type of "volunteer" or self-selection bias. In the follow-up study, the experimenters showed up unannounced at a regular class meeting. Males and females were seated in different sections of the auditorium and in alternate seats. A total of 98 percent of subjects completed the questionnaire, and all married or divorced subjects were excluded from the analyses.

Physical attractiveness ratings. To obtain a rating of physical attractiveness, all females brought their completed answer sheets and questionnaires to the front of the auditorium. Two *Es* were stationed in the front of the room and subjects were instructed to turn in their answer sheets, face down, to one *E* and the questionnaire to the other. Each *E* placed the forms in one of six piles corresponding to his rating (on a scale of 1 to 6) of the physical attractiveness of the subject. Questionnaires and answer sheets bore a common number for each subject, and the average of the two E's ratings was used as the subject's physical attractiveness score. The correlation between raters was .79.

Test instrument. The basic instrument was an anonymous 205-item questionnaire which contained, among other items, 24 items from Reiss' (1967) scale of sexual standards for males and females. The standards of permissiveness scales presented in Tables 1 and 2 are derived from 12 items measuring the degree to which three types of sexual behaviors (kissing, petting, and sexual intercourse), are endorsed as acceptable under four types of relationships (not particularly affectionate, strongly affectionate, in love, and engaged). For the "type of activity" scales, acceptance of the activity (petting or sexual intercourse) is computed by summing across all items involving the activity irrespective of the type of relationship. (Items involving kissing failed to discriminate and were not included in the active scales.) Scores for "permissiveness by type of relationship" were computed from the average of the three kinds of activity for the type of relationship indicated. Thus, the "not particularly affectionate" score is the average of three items measuring the acceptance of kissing, petting, and sexual intercourse when the couple is not particularly affectionate toward each other. These items were scored as summative scales, as opposed to Guttman scaling techniques used by Reiss. While part of our decision to use summative scoring was based on pragmatic consideration, we also felt for the assessment of attitudes the summative scaling would yield similar conclusions and avoid some of the criticisms of the use of Guttman techniques. (Scott, 1968).

RESULTS AND DISCUSSION

Replication of initial findings

Comparisons of the standards of permissiveness expressed for men and women by men and women are presented in Table 1. The mean ages in the initial study ($M = 20.4$, $F = 19.9$) were nearly identical to those in the follow-up study ($M = 20.1$, $F = 20.0$), and no significant differences were found with respect to semester in college. In spite of the relatively high premarital coital rate for the women found in the initial sample (41 percent), essentially the same figure (44 percent) was found in the follow-up study. The rates for men also replicated. Striking similarities are seen between the two studies with respect to the expressed attitudes. For neither men nor women were there any significant differences between the initial sample and the follow-up sample on any of the permissiveness standards. Thus, it appears the behavior and attitudes found in the initial study are

TABLE 1. Standards of permissiveness for male and female sexual behavior as expressed by college men and women.[a]

	Standards for men		Standards for women	
	Initial	Follow-up	Initial	Follow-up
College men expressing permissiveness by type of activity:				
Petting	5.19	5.14	5.07	4.97
Sexual intercourse	4.32	4.48	4.21	4.04
Permissiveness by type of relationship:				
Not particularly affectionate	4.45	4.55	4.20	4.06
Strongly affectionate	5.12	5.20	5.01	5.09
In love	5.32	5.39	5.32	5.23
Engaged	5.36	5.37	5.35	5.30
Total standards	5.06	5.13	5.03	4.92
College women expressing permissiveness by type of activity:				
Petting	4.83	4.83	4.45	4.49
Sexual intercourse	3.71	3.75	2.99	2.97
Permissiveness by type of relationship:				
Not particularly affectionate	3.88	3.85	3.20	2.92
Strongly affectionate	4.80	4.75	4.36	4.40
In love	5.15	5.21	4.93	4.36
Engaged	5.21	5.09	5.05	5.11
Total standards	4.77	4.72	4.36	4.40

[a] Based on 1–6 scale where 6 = highly permissive. Items read, "I believe ＿＿＿ is permissible before marriage when the people involved are ＿＿＿."

representative of sophomores and juniors at this University. A subsequent probability sample of the entire campus has confirmed this conclusion.

The double standard

Females. Table 1 provides strong evidence that a double standard exists for our samples of college women in spite of their liberal sexual behavior. When all items, irrespective of the activity or type of relationship, are taken together and viewed as a "total standards" score, all three groups showed significantly ($p = < .02$)[1] more permissiveness for males than for females. Viewing permissiveness by the type of activity involved, the double standard appears to become more pronounced as the activity becomes

---

[1] Unless otherwise indicated, all probability levels in this paper refer to two-tailed tests of significance. When t-tests were used t-values were adjusted for unequal variance when appropriate.

more intimate. When analyzing permissiveness by the meaningfulness of the relationship, differences in male-female standards were most pronounced when there is no affection in the relationship ($p < .01$) and all but disappear for the engaged or those in relationships where love was involved. Thus, even among this relatively liberal female population, the notion of male-standards, must be rejected. It appears that females themselves hold a clearly pronounced double standard.

Males. A comparison of male and female attitudes in Table 1 reveals that males are more permissive on virtually all sexual standards, although these differences become somewhat attenuated as the meaningfulness of the relationship increases. Although not indicated in the tables, all of the differences between male and female subjects were significant at at least the .05 level and the vast majority at the .01 level. It appears, though, that there are only slight suggestions of a double standard among the males. Both samples in Table 1 report slightly higher permissiveness for males than females on the "activity," "relationship," and "total standards" scales, and in no instance do these differences approach significance. Thus, with respect to attitudes toward "females" in general, there is little evidence of a double standard. However, when the analysis is extended to attitudes toward specific females as shown in Table 2, the data strongly supported the existence of a double standard for males and females alike. For both male and female respondents, virginity for the female was considered more important than for the male. Sisters, more than brothers, would be encouraged not to engage in premarital intercourse. And these attitudinal discrepancies toward the male and female are quite pronounced—the differences between the means of items 1–2 and 3–4 are all highly significant ($p < .001$). For males, while 45 percent felt virginity in a prospective mate was an important consideration, only 17 percent of the males felt it was important for them to be virginal. Thus, particularly with respect to males, the data support the hypothesis that as the person about whom the standard is expressed becomes more meaningful to the respondent, the greater is the double standard.

It is also worth noting that there was very little difference in how males and females answer these items. Comparisons of the diagonals of items 1 and 2 (1.80–1.98 and 2.92–3.15) suggest that males wanted to marry a virgin as much as females wanted to be virgins. Conversely, females were as concerned about marrying a male who was a virgin as males were about remaining virginal. Additionally, there also were no significant differences between males and females on either item 3 or 4. It appears that once the standard is for a specific and meaningful female, the male's more liberal attitude all but disappears, and he is as conservative as the female.

The remaining four items in Table 2 also support the existence of a double standard. Respondents would lose more respect for females who engage in premarital intercourse without love than for males and felt that

TABLE 2. Mean scores* for college male and female respondents on items measuring male-female sexual equalitarianism.

Item	Males (N = 110)	Females (N = 162)
1. It is important to me to be a virgin at the time of my marriage.	1.80 ⎫	3.15 ⎫
2. Virginity in a prospective mate is important to me.	2.92 ⎭ †	1.98 ⎭ †
3. If he asked my advice about having sexual intercourse, I would encourage a brother of mine *not* to engage in it before marriage.	2.48 ⎫	2.63 ⎫
4. If she asked my advice about having sexual intercourse, I would encourage a sister of mine *not* to engage in it before marriage.	3.47 ⎭ †	3.65 ⎭ †
5. I would lose respect for a male who engaged in premarital intercourse with a girl he did not love.	2.19 ⎫	2.87 ⎫
6. I would lose respect for a girl who engaged in premarital intercourse with a boy she did not love.	3.11 ⎭ †	3.80 ⎭ †
7. I think having had sexual intercourse is more injurious to a girl's reputation than to a boy's reputation.	4.26 ⎫	4.47 ⎫
8. I have higher standards of sexual morality for females than for males.	3.52 ⎭	3.79 ⎭

* These items were scaled: 1 = strongly disagree, 2 = moderately disagree, 3 = neutral, 4 = moderately agree, 5 = strongly agree.

† $p < .001$. Probability levels based on comparisons between items 1–2, 3–4, 5–6 within each group. Differences between groups on 7 and 8 are not significant.

premarital coitus was more injurious to a girl's reputation than to a boy's. Finally, when asked directly if they had higher standards for females than for males, both males and females tended to agree with this item. The differences between males and females on items 7 and 8 was not significant.

Thus, what initially appeared to be attitudes of sexual equalitarianism among these men turned out to be an artifact due to the insensitivity of the items which employed the generic "male" and "female" referents. With the revised items, it becomes clear that even in this liberal sample a majority of both men and women held a double standard. In this sample where barely more than half of the females were still virgins, 45 percent of the men wanted to marry a virgin. What this may suggest is that, while male attitudes may be changing, they may not be changing as rapidly as the sexual behavior of college women. Consequently, this discrepancy may result in male attitudes which are out of step with changes in the behavior of college women and point to an area which will cause some difficulty and conflict between sexes.

Physical attractiveness

Based on the combined ratings of physical attractiveness rendered by both *Es*, females in the control group were divided into three groups—high, medium, and low. Comparisons were made between the groups on 80 attitudinal, behavioral, and background variables. Virtually no significant differences were found between any of the three groups on the attitudinal measures: male and female permissiveness standards, a 16 item sexual liberalism scale, scales measuring attitudes toward homosexuality, and the values placed on male and female virginity. Nor were any significant differences found on such background items as age, semester in college, family background, birth order, strength of religion, dating status, sorority membership, reasons for abstaining from or indulging in premarital coitus, and frequency of experiencing sexual urges and inhibition of these urges. What appears quite clear then, is that physical attractiveness bears no relationship to attitudinal or background variables that normally serve as strong predictors of premarital coitus. However, for the high group, 56 percent were nonvirgins—a figure significantly higher ($\chi^2 = 5.38$, p $<$ .05) than the "average" group (31 percent) and higher, although not significantly so, than the low group (37 percent). However, although they were more likely to have had premarital intercourse, the physically attractive girls were not more promiscuous. Among the nonvirgins in each group, there were no significant differences with respect to the number of times having had intercourse or the number of persons with whom it occurred. As compared to the low and medium groups, the data in Table 3 showed that girls rated high on physical attractiveness were also more likely to hold a favorable self-picture,[2] rated themselves as physically attractive, had more friends of the opposite sex, believed that more of their friends had had intercourse, dated more frequently, had been in love more often, and had had more noncoital (petting) sexual experience. These differences imply that physically attractive girls are confronted with more opportunities and pressures to indulge in premarital coitus. Thus, the emerging picture is one where the more physically attractive girl is no different from her less attractive peers with respect to her general sexual attitudes or background, but holds a more favorable self-picture, including an awareness that she is more attractive. Her increased popularity, greater frequency of dating, and more noncoital experience would appear to increase greatly her opportunities and pressures for premarital coitus. These data, and the reported higher noncoital experience, appear to support the hy-

---

[2] For a score on the self-description scale, respondents rated each of the following on the degree to which the characteristic described them personally: physically attractive, feminine, self-confident, engaging personality, a good date and a likeable person. Self-ratings were scaled from 1 to 6 (1 = not at all descriptive of me . . . 6 = extremely descriptive of me), and the average of all six ratings was taken as the self-picture score.

TABLE 3. Means for college women (N = 84) on measures of self-description, social and sexual behaviors[a]

Scale and scoring system	Attractiveness (judge's rating)		
	(1) Low	(2) Med	(3) High
Favorable self-description	3.93	4.07	4.50[c, e]
Physically attractive (self rating)	3.71	3.88	4.30[f]
Number of friends-males	2.50	2.96	4.69[c, e]
Number of friends-females	5.29	4.75	5.40
Proportion of friends having had sexual intercourse	1.38	1.70	2.31[c, e]
Dating frequency	4.13	4.11	5.41[c, e]
Number of times in love	1.17	1.32	1.69[b]
Necking experience	3.39	4.44	4.53[b]
Petting experience	2.83	2.79	3.54
Heavy petting experience	1.67	1.75	2.93[b, d]
Number of persons with whom intercourse occurred	1.11	1.67	1.95
Number of times having had intercourse	4.67	3.89	4.22

[a] All probability levels based on t-values adjusted for unequal variances when appropriate.
[b] difference between 1 and 3, $p < .05$
[c] difference between 1 and 3, $p < .01$
[d] difference between 1 and 2, $p < .05$
[e] difference between 2 and 3, $p < .05$
[f] difference between 1 and 3, $p < .05$, one tailed test.

pothesis that girls rated high on physical attractiveness have increased opportunities and higher premarital coital rates.

The final aspect of the research presented here involved assessment of social support for premarital sexual behavior, particularly perceived peer support for sexual behavior.

Support for premarital coitus

Table 4 presents an analysis of expressed acceptance of premarital coitus for the generic categories of "males" and "females" for four levels of involvement in the relationship. The same patterns with respect to male-female differences as mentioned earlier are again evident. However, the double standard is quite pronounced for male and female respondents when the item concerns sexual intercourse in a relationship involving little affection. It appears that for females the percentages accepting sexual intercourse when there is strong affection in the relationship are most closely aligned with the reported percentages of males and females having had

TABLE 4. Mean scores* and percentages agreeing with items assessing acceptance of premarital intercourse under four types of relationships.

Type of relationship	Means and percentage agreeing with item							
	Males (N = 239)				Females (M = 319)			
	Ratings for males		Ratings for females		Ratings for males		Ratings for females	
I believe that full sexual relations are acceptable for the (male) (female) before marriage when (he) (she):	$\overline{X}$	%	$\overline{X}$	%	$\overline{X}$	%	$\overline{X}$	%
is not particularly affectionate toward (his) (her) partner	3.59	55	2.96	37	2.90	37	1.74	14
feels strong affection for (his) (her) partner	4.41	73	4.14	68	3.59	53	2.79	34
is in love	4.80	81	4.63	76	4.29	68	3.76	57
is engaged to be married	4.80	80	4.73	78	4.32	71	3.96	61

* Based on a forced-choice scaling of 1–6 where 1 = strongly disagree and 6 = strongly agree.

sexual intercourse. It is also worth noting that acceptance is virtually the same for the "in love" and "engaged" categories. This appears to confirm the notion that contemporary attitudes are quite liberal when love is involved irrespective of formal commitment to marriage.

Two items in the questionnaire also asked respondents to estimate how many of their friends and acquaintances of the same and opposite sex have engaged in premarital intercourse. The five response categories were: none, one or two, several, most, and all. Both males and females estimated significantly ($p < .001$) higher rates for males than for females. There were no significant differences between the estimates of male and female respondents for the number of males or females that have had intercourse. That is, both sexes agreed on how many male and female friends have had sexual intercourse. The estimate of the number of females having had sexual intercourse was between "one or two" and "several" with only 11 percent answering in the "most" or "all" categories. Estimates of male behavior fell between "several" and "most" with approximately 55 percent responding in the "most" or "all" categories. This generally conservative view of one's peers appears also in the attitudinal perceptions presented in Table 5.

TABLE 5. College student perceptions of attitudes of various reference groups toward sexual intercourse when in love or with a casual date.[a, b]

| | How people below would feel about your having engaged in sexual intercourse with: | | | |
| | Someone you loved | | A casual date | |
Reference group or person	Males	Females	Males	Females
Grandparents	2.23	1.11***	1.54	1.08***
Father	3.44	1.73***	2.38	1.04***
Mother	2.46	1.61***	1.70	1.04***
Sister(s)	3.42	2.76*	2.32	1.28***
Brother(s)	4.71	2.67***	3.70	1.24***
Close personal friends	5.23	3.69***	4.35	1.40***
Sorority sisters or fraternity brothers	5.63	2.87***	5.19	1.21***
Most faculty members of this university	3.72	3.47	3.00	2.34***
My clergyman	2.36	1.91*	1.88	1.23***
The population in general	3.32	2.94*	2.57	2.00**
Most friends of my family	2.67	1.70**	2.12	1.20***

[a] Depending on the item, N varied from Male = 101 to 30; Females = 139 to 47.
[b] 1 = would disapprove very much, 2 = moderately, 3 = slightly, 4 = neutral, 5 = would approve slightly, 6 = moderately, 7 = very much. All t-tests are based upon comparisons between attitude toward males and attitude toward females and are adjusted for unequal variance where appropriate.
* $p < .05$.
** $p < .01$.
*** $p < .001$.

Table 5 presents data on how college students think friends, family and various reference groups would feel about their having had intercourse when in love and with a casual date. For females, even when in love, one sees little indication of perceived approval from any of the groups. Even the two least rejecting groups, close friends and faculty members, were perceived to be on the disapproval side of the continuum—both *less* rejecting than sorority sisters. The data also provided considerable support for Bell's (1966) concept of the "generation conflict" in attitudes between younger and older generations. Grandparents were perceived to be the most rejecting followed in order by parents and brothers and sisters. When intercourse involves a casual date, virtually all groups were perceived to disapprove somewhere between "moderately" and "very much." Even the mean of the least disapproving group, faculty members, fell between "moderate" and "slight" disapproval. Comparisons of the perceptions which males and females hold of the attitudes of these groups revealed sharp differences in perceived disapproval when the person involved was a male or female. Only with the faculty members and when intercourse occurs when in love, were there no differences between the perceptions of what is acceptable for males versus what is acceptable for females. Not only did these students reject the notion of male-female sexual equalitarianism themselves, but they also felt that their close friends, families and other societal groups rejected it as well. Furthermore, the emerging picture for females was one of disapproval for coitus both by close friends and family members. Thus even in a group where 42 percent of the women are not virgins, few of them perceive support for sexual intercourse for women even when the woman is in love.

Males hold the perceptions that fraternity brothers, close friends and brothers would in varying degrees, approve of sexual intercourse when in love. Even with a casual date, fraternity brothers and, to lesser degree, close friends were perceived to approve of sexual intercourse. The same "generation conflict" differences noted for the females were also evident for the males. However, unlike females, fathers were perceived as being significantly ($p < .001$) less disapproving than mothers, and brothers less disapproving ($p < .001$) than sisters. With the exception of fraternity brothers, all groups were significantly more disapproving when intercourse involves a casual date rather than when in love. However, even with the most disapproving group, grandparents, the means for males fall between the "moderate" and "slight" disapproval categories with the majority falling quite close to the neutral category. Hence, for males the perceptions are that sexual intercourse may bring approval from the males' immediate coterie of friends or brothers and, when in love, brings only slight disapproval from most of his reference groups—a strikingly different picture than that facing the college woman who indulges in premarital intercourse.

The preceding also raises questions about how these perceptions differ as a function of having had intercourse. Consequently, comparisons were made between the perceptions of virgins and nonvirgins for each of the reference groups represented in Table 5. Comparisons of virginal versus nonvirginal females revealed that nonvirgins felt significantly *less* disapproval from close friends (4.43–3.17, p < .001), fathers (1.95–1.58, p < .05), brothers (3.18–2.25, p < .01) and clergymen (2.28–1.68 p < .05). No significant differences were noted for any of the other sources of support. In a relative sense, then, the nonvirgin women see more support (or, rather, less disapproval) of their behavior than virgins perceived. But only in the case of close friends was something like approval seen. For males, the only significant differences in the perceptions of virgins and nonvirgins were that nonvirgins perceived less disapproval from fathers (3.72–3.03, p < .05) and clergymen (2.63–1.85, p < .01).

An additional issue of interest here is the correspondence between student perceptions of attitudes significant groups hold as compared to the actual attitudes of such groups. When a topic is taboo for public discussion, one often finds a phenomenon labeled "pluralistic ignorance" by Schank (1932). The relevant comparisons in this case were those between the standards for intercourse when in love (Table 4) and the perceived approval by close personal friends of intercourse when in love (Table 5). For males one finds that 81 percent accepted full sexual relations for a male when he is in love, but only 64 percent of these same males viewed their close personal friends as approving of their "engaging in sexual intercourse with a girl they love." The discrepancy is even more striking in the case of females. Among females, 57 percent of the girls found full sexual intercourse acceptable when the girl was in love with her partner, yet only 28 percent saw their close personal friends as likely to approve of their having engaged in sexual intercourse with a person they loved. It should be noted that, except for fraternity brothers, the "close personal friends" category had a much higher percentage approval rate for both men and women than any other category. Thus, it seems fair to conclude that a state of pluralistic ignorance does exist in which this college population is much more permissive about sexual intercourse when there is a love relationship than they perceive any significant social group would be, including the group of friends and peers.

CONCLUSIONS

1. The replication finding reported in this paper (plus a methodological experiment (Kaats and Davis, 1970) on self-selection biases and a separate probability sample of the campus) clearly establish that the premarital

coital rate for this predominantly sophomore and junior sample of college women fell in the 41–44 percent range. But the premarital coital rate for college men of the same academic class hit at the 60 percent figure that has been commonplace since World War I.

2. In spite of the fact that there was, in this sample, a converging sexual behavior or sexual equalitarianism, a newly devised assessment of the sexual double standard indicated that approximately half of the males held such a standard (one allowing greater sexual freedom for men), particularly when the woman in question was a sister or potential spouse. And this same group of college women who were more liberal in their sexual behavior than their parents apparently were, still adhered to a double standard in their judgments of acceptable sexual behavior.

3. Furthermore, the double standard was quite pronounced in the perceptions college students held of peer, familial, and societal attitudes. Although males viewed family and societal groups as only slightly to moderately disapproving of their having had sexual intercourse when in love or with a casual date, they also felt that close friends, particularly fraternity brothers, would approve of this behavior. College women, on the other hand, held a strikingly different view. They saw virtually all groups, including close friends and sorority sisters, as disapproving of their engaging in intercourse even when they are in love with the person. Furthermore, women perceived that all groups would more strongly disapprove of their sexual behavior than did men.

These results raise a perplexing question: If college students reject the notion of male-female sexual equalitarianism, feel virginity for women is important, and college women feel there is little support even among friends for their having premarital intercourse, what accounts for the significant narrowing of the gap between male and female sexual behavior? It is to this question that we intend to return in a subsequent paper based on additional data.

4. Data on the relationship between sexual behavior and physical attractiveness of women provided evidence for a "meaningful opportunity" interpretation of being physically attractive. Physically attractive women had a higher rate of experience both with petting and intercourse despite the fact that they differed hardly at all from less attractive women in most of the attitudinal and experience items predictive of greater sexual experience. In our view, the more attractive girl is the target of more, more sincere, and more persistent romantic interactions. As such she experiences more opportunities to engage in sexual activity which she can judge to be acceptable. "After all," such girls might say, "It's okay because he loves me." Thus the different rates of coitus for aggregates similar in values but differing in attractiveness follow from the concrete types of experiences likely for these aggregates.

REFERENCES

BELL, R. R. 1966. Premarital Sex in a Changing Society. Englewood Cliffs, N.J.: Prentice-Hall. 1967. Marriage and Family Interaction. Homewood, Ill.: Dorsey Press.

BERNARD, J. 1966. "The fourth revolution." The Journal of Social Issues 22 (April):76–87.

BROMLEY, D. D. and BRITTEN, F. H. 1938. Youth and Sex: A Study of 1300 College Students. New York: Harper & Row.

CHRISTENSEN, H. T. 1966. "Scandinavian and American sex norms: Some comparisons, with sociological implications." The Journal of Social Issues 22 (April):60–75.

DAVIS, K. E. 1970. "Sex on campus: Is there a revolution?" Medical Aspects of Human Sexuality. In press.

EHRMANN, W. W. 1959. Premarital Dating Behavior. New York: Holt, Rinehart & Winston.

FREEDMAN, M. B. 1965. "The sexual behavior of American college women: An empirical study and historical survey." Merrill-Palmer Quarterly of Behavior and Development 11 (January):33–48.

GAGNON, J. H. and SIMON, W. 1968. "Sexual deviance in contemporary America." The Annals of the American Academy of Political and Social Science 376 (March):106–22.

JESSOR, R., GRAVES, T. D., HANSON, R. D. and JESSOR, S. L. 1968. Society, Personality and Deviant Behavior. New York: Holt, Rinehart and Winston.

KAATS, G. R. and DAVIS, K. E. "Effects of volunteer biases in studies of sexual behavior and attitudes." In press, Journal of Sex Research.

KEPHART, W. M. 1966. The Family, Society, and the Individual. (2d ed.) Boston: Houghton Mifflin.

KINSEY, A. D., POMEROY, W. B., MARTIN, C. E. and GEBHARD, P. H. 1953. Sexual Behavior in the Human Female. Philadelphia: W. B. Saunders Company.

KIRKENDALL, L. A. and LIBBY, R. W. 1966. "Interpersonal relationships—crux of the sexual renaissance." The Journal of Social Issues 22 (April):45–59.

LANDIS, J. T. and LANDIS, M. G. 1958. Building a Successful Marriage. (3d ed.) Englewood Cliffs, N.J.: Prentice-Hall.

LESLIE, G. R. 1967. The Family in Social Context. New York: Oxford University Press.

MASLOW, A. H. and SAKODA, J. M. 1952. "Volunteer-error in the Kinsey study." Journal of Abnormal and Social Psychology 47 (April):259–67.

REISS, I. L. 1960. Premarital Sexual Standards in America. Glencoe, Ill. The Free Press. 1964a. "Premarital sexual permissiveness among Negroes and whites." American Sociological Review 29 (October):688–98. 1964b. "The scaling of premarital sexual permissiveness." Journal of Marriage and the Family 26 (January):188–98. 1966. "The sexual renaissance in America:

A summary and analysis." The Journal of Social Issues 22 (April):123–37. 1967. The Social Context of Premarital Permissiveness. New York: Holt, Rinehart & Winston.

SCHANK, R. L. A. 1932. "A study of a community and its groups and institutions conceived as the behavior of individuals." Psychological Monographs 43, Number 2, (Whole Number 195).

SCOTT, W. A. 1968. "Attitude measurement." Pp. 204–73 in G. Lindzey and E. Aronson (eds.), Handbook of Social Psychology, Vol. II. Reading, Mass.: Addison-Wesley.

SIMON, W. and GAGNON, J. 1967. "On psychosexual development." Pp. 733–52 in D. Goslin (ed.), Handbook of Socialization Theory and Research. Chicago: Rand McNally.

SMIGEL, E. O. and SEIDEN, R. "The decline and fall of the double standard." Annals of the American Academy of Political and Social Science 376 (March):6–17.

19
Changing sex norms in America and Scandinavia*

HAROLD T. CHRISTENSEN and
CHRISTINA F. GREGG

It has been popular of late to claim that the so-called *Sexual Revolution* which has been sweeping America during the recent fifties and sixties is little more than a liberalization of attitudes: that there has been no real or significant increase in nonmarital sexual behavior. No one disputes the more or less obvious facts of greater tolerance with respect to the sexual behavior of others or of greater freedom and openness in discussion, in dress and manners, in public entertainment, and throughout the mass media. But when it comes to the question of whether premarital coitus— the practice itself—is undergoing much of an increase, there tends to be either uncertainty or the suggestion that it is not. Part of this may be due to wishful thinking, part to a lack of adequate data, and part to a tendency among scholars to overgeneralize from the data available. At any rate, there is need for new data and for a reexamination of the problem.

Terman (1938:320–3) was one of the first to present solid evidence concerning incidence and trends in premarital coitus. He compared persons born in and subsequent to 1910 with persons born before 1890 and reported increases of premarital coitus for both men and women—though at a more rapid rate for the latter, signifying an intersex convergence.

* From *Journal of Marriage and the Family* (November 1970), pp. 616–27. Reprinted by permission of the authors and the National Council on Family Relations.

Then came Kinsey. Kinsey and associates (1953:298–302) also compared incidence of premarital coitus by decade of birth and reported virtually no trend for males but a very significant increase for females, which likewise pointed to an intersex convergence. Yet even for females there appeared to be little difference in non-virginity among those born during the first, second and third decades of the present century. But non-virginity was more than twice as great for females born in these three decades after the turn of the century as compared with those born before 1900. Since approximately twenty years are required to reach maturity, the suggestion in this finding is that the big change in the liberalization of female sexual behavior took place during the decade following World War I and that the picture has not altered much since that time. It must be noted, however, that these data are not suitable for measuring trends that may have occurred during the 1950s and 1960s.

Nevertheless, Reiss (1969) and certain other scholars (for example, Bell, 1966; Gagnon and Simon, 1970), after drawing upon the Kinsey data, have moved beyond the reach of these findings by claiming that there has been little if any increase in non-virginity over the past twenty years or so. Reiss explains the widespread *belief* concerning an increase as being due largely to the liberalizing of attitudes, which makes people more willing to talk and so increases their awareness and anxiety. In support of his position of no significant trend in premarital coitus since the 1920s, he cites several studies made during the 1950s and 1960s (Ehrmann, 1959; Freedman, 1965; Kirkendall, 1961; Reiss, 1967; Schofield, 1965) which give somewhat similar incidence percentages as those reported earlier by Kinsey. But there is a question of comparability. Although these more recent studies do not show incidence percentages greatly different from Kinsey's, they each tap different populations and employ differing methodologies— so that the no-trend conclusion may be quite spurious. Furthermore, the reported research by Reiss himself deals almost exclusively with attitudes, largely ignoring behavior. It is to his credit though, that he recognized the tenuous nature of the evidence and because of this, states his position somewhat cautiously. He said simply that the common belief that non-virginity has markedly increased of late "is not supported by the research"; and concluded: "Thus, although the evidence is surely not perfect, it does suggest that there has not been any change in the proportion of non-virginity for the past four or five decades equal to that which occurred during the 1920s" (Reiss, 1969:110).

But the message that has come across to the public and even some scholars is that research has established that a virtually static level of premarital coitus has maintained itself since the early post World War I period. This has been the most usual interpretation given recently in the popular press, by radio and television, and in some high school and college textbooks.

Even so, not everyone has believed it. Some, like the authors of this paper, have held mental reservations, though, until recently, have been without appropriate data to test it out. A few years ago Leslie (1967: 387–92) examined this question by classifying chronologically virtually all studies which had reported incidence of premarital coitus, starting with 1915 and ending with 1965. He observed that for both sexes percentages tend to be higher in the more recent studies. Similarly, Packard (1968: 135–204, 491–511, 517–23) took a careful look at the reported findings of over forty studies including one of his own, which elicited student responses from 21 colleges in the United States and five from other countries (Luckey and Nass, 1969). He compared these studies and their findings across time; conceding, of course, the lack of strict comparability due to differing samples and methods. His tentative general conclusion was that ". . . while coital experience of U. S. College males seemed comparable to that of males 15 or 20 years ago, the college females reported a quite significantly higher rate of experience" (Packard, 1968:186).

The very latest information coming to our attention is a report by Bell and Chaskes (1970) wherein the earlier no-evidence-to-support-a-trend position of Bell (1966) is modified with the statement: "The writers believe that change *has* been occurring in the sexual experience of college girls since the mid 1960s" (Bell and Chaskes, 1970:81). These authors report increases in the premarital coitus of coeds between 1958 and 1968: from 10 to 23 percent during the dating relationship, from 15 to 28 percent during the going-steady relationship, and from 31 to 39 percent during the engagement relationship. Since proportionate increase was greatest at the first two dating levels, they conclude that the commitment of engagement has become a less important condition for many coeds participating in premarital coitus. They also report significant reductions at each dating level in the guilt connected with coitus, and point to a suggestion from their data of an increase in promiscuity. Still additional findings— though ones less relevant to our present analysis—were that premarital coitus tends to be associated with non-attendance at church, starting to date at an early age, and dating or going steady with a larger than average number of boys.

The Bell and Chaskes study has an advantage over many of the previous ones in that it taps college students in the same institution with the same measuring instrument at two different points in time, which more clearly enables it to look at *trends*. It nevertheless is limited to females alone on one college campus, and so sees its conclusions as suggestive rather than conclusive of any national change. These authors argue, from what is known about the youth rebellion movement of very recent years, that the increase in the premarital coitus of coeds is a phenomenon of the mid 1960s. It should be noted, however, that there is nothing in their data to establish the change as occurring at that precise point in time as against the early 1960s or even the late 1950s.

Our own research about to be reported has some of the same limitations as certain of the earlier studies (including the small size and non-random character of its samples) but there are added features which we hope will enable us to carry the analysis a little farther. We have involved behavior as well as attitudes, studied males as well as females, compared three separate cultures against each other, and measured identical phenomena in the same manner in the same populations at two different points in time. The focus of this report is to be upon the time dimension, or social change. Nevertheless, by seeing change cross-culturally and in the context of male-female interaction and attitude-behavior interrelatedness, it should be possible to better understand what actually is taking place. There is an interplay among these and possibly other factors. We feel that it is important to try to see the premarital sex phenomenon as a network and to look for interrelationships and then build toward an empirically-based theory to explain it all. Our study is but one start in that direction.

The senior author initiated his cross-cultural research on premarital sex back in 1958, at which time questionnaires were administered to college samples in three separate cultures differing on a restrictive-permissive continuum: highly restrictive Mormon culture in the Intermountain region of western United States; moderately restrictive Midwestern culture in central United States; and highly permissive Danish culture which is a part of Scandinavia (Christensen, 1960; 1966; 1969; Christensen and Carpenter, 1962a; 1962b). The 1958 study involved both record linkage and questionnaire data, but it is only the latter that are of concern in the present writing. He then repeated the study in 1968, using the same questionnaire administered in the same three universities. Every effort was made to achieve comparability across the two years. The unchanged questionnaire was administered in the same way to similar classes in the identical universities. In most instances within both years social science classes were used; the only real change being in Denmark, where large proportions of medical and psychology students were used in 1958 as against an almost exclusively sociology student sample in 1968. The repeat, of course, was chiefly for the purpose of getting at changes which may have occurred during a period of time popularly described as experiencing a sexual revolution. Although the study dealt with all levels of intimacy—necking, petting, and coitus—this report is to be limited to premarital coitus alone. Furthermore, it is limited to only selected aspects of premarital coitus. This is because our analysis of data has just begun, plus the necessity to restrict the length of a journal article.

Respective sample sizes involved in calculations for the statistics now to be reported were: for the Intermountain, 94 males and 74 females in 1958, and 115 and 105 respectively in 1968; for the Midwestern, 213 males and 142 females in 1958, and 245 and 238 respectively in 1968; for the Danish, 149 males and 86 females in 1958, and 134 and 61 respectively in 1968.

SOME MEASURES OF THE LIBERAL ATTITUDE

Three items from the questionnaire have been selected to illustrate comparisons and trends in the attitudinal component. Table 1 has been con-

TABLE 1. Percentages[a] taking liberal positions on sex questions, 1958 and 1968 compared.

	Intermountain		Midwestern		Danish	
Items and years	Males	Females	Males	Females	Males	Females
I. Opposition to Censorship						
1968	61	58	71	59	99	97
1958	42	54	47	51	77	81
Difference	19	4	24	8	22	16
II. Acceptance of Non-virginity						
1968	20	26	25	44	92	92
1958	5	11	18	23	61	74
Difference	15	15	7	21	31	18
III. Approval of Premarital coitus						
1968	38	24	55	38	100	100
1958	23	3	47	17	94	81
Difference	15	21	8	21	6	19

[a] Percentages are based on numbers answering the question. The number of cases leaving a question unanswered varied from 0 to 8 in the various groups.

structed to show percentages of respondents holding liberal or permissive views regarding these matters.

Opposing the censorship of pornography

Presented first are percentages of respondents who indicated agreement with the statement: "It is best not to try to prohibit erotic and obscene literature and pictures by law, but rather to leave people free to follow their own judgments and tastes in such matters." The three comparisons of interest in this analysis are as follows:

(1) As one moves from left to right—from the restrictive Intermountain culture to the permissive Danish culture—percentages taking the liberal stance by agreeing with the statement are seen to increase. This is true for both sexes and with respect to both sample years (with the single exception of the 1958 female comparison between Intermountain and Midwestern).

(2) More females than males opposed the censorship of pornography in 1958, whereas ten years later the reverse was true. Furthermore, this

shift in pattern occurred consistently in each of the three cultures, suggesting that it may be something of a general phenomenon.
(3) The time trend over the decade 1958–68 was consistently in the direction of increasing opposition to this kind of censorship. The trend held for each of the three cultures and for both sexes—although females liberalized on this point in *smaller* degree than did males, which accounts for the shift in the male-female pattern mentioned in the previous paragraph.

Since (as will be shown throughout the remainder of our paper) females generally have liberalized in a proportionately *greater* degree than have males, this contrary finding on censorship requires some attempt at explanation. Our speculation is that females, with their more sheltered life, have been less knowledgeable and realistic regarding pornography and also possibly less attracted by its appeal. This might explain their greater opposition to censorship than males in 1958, not seeing pornography as particularly threatening. But the new openness of recent years undoubtedly has given them greater sophistication in these matters, and they may now better understand the reality of hardcore pornography and its differential appeal to the male; which could explain their lower opposition to censorship than males in 1968.

Accepting the non-virginity of a partner

In the second section of Table 1 are shown percentages of those who indicated *disagreement* with the statement: "I would prefer marrying a virgin or in other words, someone who has not had previous coitus (sexual intercourse)." As with the statement on pornography, permissive attitudes increased for both sexes and in both sample years from lows in the restrictive Intermountain to highs in the permissive Danish; and increased between 1958 and 1968, for both sexes and in each of the three cultures. These trends are shown to be without exception. The male-female comparisons show *females* to be the most *permissive,* in both sample years and in each of the cultures (with the single exception of 1968 Danish respondents, where they were equal).

Since practically every other measure in our questionnaire—as well as virtually all studies now in the literature—show females to be more conservative than males in sexual matters, one must ask "why this exception?" Two possible reasons occur to us: in the first place, the typical female attitude may represent a realistic acceptance that more males do have premarital sex, making her chances of actually marrying a virgin somewhat smaller; and in addition, some females, with a sheltered upbringing and more limited sexual expression, may feel inadequate and hence welcome an experienced male to help show them the way. In this connection, it is interesting to note also that in the Midwestern sample—which may approximately reflect the overall situation for United States—females moved away from insistence on a virginal partner at a much more rapid rate than did males.

Approving coitus among the unmarried

Finally, Table 1 shows percentages of those approving premarital coitus. Respondents were asked: first, to consider an average or typical courtship "in which there is normal love development and mutual responsibility"; next, to assume that this hypothetical relationship progresses at a uniform rate of six months between the first data and the start of going steady, another six months to an engagement, and still another six months to the wedding (or a total courtship of eighteen months); and then to mark on a scale the earliest time they would approve the start of necking, then of petting, and then of coitus. The percentages shown are restricted to coitus and they represent approval at any point prior to the wedding.

This item on approval of premarital coitus is free of the kinds of irregularities mentioned for the previous two. It shows highly consistent results for all three comparisons: a movement toward greater approval from Intermountain to Midwestern to Danish, for both sexes and in both sample years; greater approval given by males than by females (except for a tie among 1968 Danish respondents where both sexes hit the ceiling), for both sample years and each of the three cultures; and a trend toward greater approval over the 1958–68 decade, for both sexes and in each of the three cultures.

In connection with this last point, it is important to note that in each of the cultures females moved toward approval more strongly than did males, which means a trend toward intersex convergence. Females still have more restrictive attitudes than males but the difference is less than formerly.

An additional observation which should not be missed is that, in both sample years, male-female percentages are closer together in Denmark than in the other two cultures. This suggests that norm permissiveness may operate to reduce differences between the sexes seen in cross-cultural comparisons as well as in liberalizing trends over time.

Trend comparison with relevant variables controlled

As a double check on this trend pattern—and to at least partially determine whether it is real or merely the result of differing compositions of the two samples drawn ten years apart—we made a supplementary analysis of matched data. This was done for the Midwestern culture only (the most representative of American society and the most feasible for matched testing because of the larger sizes of its samples) and was further limited to data on premarital coitus (the most central in our present analysis). The matching occurred on four variables: sex of respondent, cumulative number of years in school, frequency of church attendance, and level of courtship development. This had the effect of controlling these variables across the 1958–68 period, while the time trend was being examined. Successful matching was completed for 202 pairs of respondents (127 pairs were male, 75 female).

In Table 2 we show for the Midwestern culture two measures of premarital coital approval for both matched and total samples. The first con-

TABLE 2. Measures of premarital coital approval on matched and total samples, Midwestern culture, 1958 and 1968 compared.

Measures of coital approval	Total sample		Matched sample	
	Males	Females	Males	Females
I. Average score				
1968	8.10	9.02	8.10	9.47
1958	8.58	9.69	8.63	9.67
Difference	−.48	−.67	−.53	−.20
II. Percent approving				
1968	55.4	37.7	55.1	30.7
1958	46.7	17.4	48.0	21.3
Difference	8.7	20.3	7.1	9.4

sists of average (mean) scores computed from the approval timing scale introduced earlier. The scale had ten divisions, with the first representing time of first date and the last representing time of marriage. Scores ranged from 1 to 10 according to markings on the scale, and it is *average* coital scores (means) that are shown here. The lower the score, the farther from marriage is the approved timing of first coitus. It will be observed that, by this measure, both males and females showed up more permissive in 1968 than they did in 1958 and that the trend held for the matched as well as unmatched comparisons.

The second measure is simply percent approving premarital coitus. Unmatched percentages are shown here in juxtaposition to percentages from the matched cases. But again the picture is very clear: matching has not altered the general trend; in the uncontrolled and the controlled analyses the trend was found to be toward greater approval—which is the permissive stance. And this was true for males and females alike, but for the latter the trend was the stronger.

RELATIONSHIP OF BEHAVIOR TO ATTITUDE

Some might argue that most of our generalizations up to this point are obvious, that everyone accepts the fact that attitudes toward premarital coitus have been liberalizing in recent years. The more controversial questions have to do with trends in sexual *behavior* and with how these relate to attitude. Has incidence of premarital coitus remained virtually unchanged since the 1920s, with a decline in guilt brought about by an increasing acceptance of the behavior—which is the position arrived at by Reiss (1962), or has behavior changed with attitudes regarding it?

Incidence of premarital coitus

As a first approach to the behavioral component, we show percentages of respondents claiming the premarital coital experience (Table 3). Our

TABLE 3. Percentage[a] with premarital coital experience, total and matched samples.

| | Sample culture | | | | | |
| | Intermountain | | Midwestern | | Danish | |
Samples and years	Males	Females	Males	Females	Males	Females
I. Total samples						
1968	37	32	50	34	95	97
1958	39	10	51	21	64	60
Difference	−2	22	−1	13	31	37
II. Matched samples						
1968			49	32		
1958			55	25		
Difference			−6	7		

[a] Based upon number answering. The number who failed to answer in any one group varied from 0 to 4.

percentages on incidence of premarital coitus do not, of course, give an accurate picture of total coitus bfore marriage but only of experience up to the time the questionnaire was administered. This fact should not influence our various comparisons, however, since all the data are the same kind and hence comparable. Percentages are given for males and females separately and for the three cultures and both sample years of our study. An added refinement in testing for a time trend is provided for the Midwestern culture by means of matched cases to control for intervening variables, as was done in the case of attitudes.

Before examining the time-trend data, let it be noted that these incidence figures are (1) higher for males than females and (2) higher for the Midwestern than the Intermountain and for the Danish than the Midwestern. These generalizations are consistent for all comparisons (except the one between 1958–68 Danish males and females) and are the same as our earlier ones regarding approval of premarital coitus. Furthermore, there is, as before, the phenomenon of greater male-female similarity in Denmark than the other two cultures, suggesting that norm permissiveness may induce a leveling of gender differences.

Comparisons of 1968 with 1958 produce three additional generalizations. (1) In the two American samples, male incidence of premarital coitus remained approximately the same. Actually the figures show that it decreased slightly, but our conjecture is that this is no more than random variation. (2) On the other hand, female incidence in the two American samples rose sharply, suggesting that, as with coital approval, there is a trend toward intersex convergence. (3) The Danish sample, while showing a slightly higher rise in premarital coitus for females than for males, demonstrated a sharp rise for *both* sexes. This brought incidence figures for that country close to the ceiling. Approximately 95 percent had engaged in premarital coitus; and it will be recalled that 100 percent of both sexes there approved of such activity. It may be, of course, that at least part of the dramatic liberalization shown for Danish respondents is to be explained by the greater weighting of the 1968 Danish sample with sociology students.

The introduction of controls through matched-sample comparisons in the Midwestern culture made no appreciable change in the outcome (Table 3, part II). Although males decreased their behavior more and females increased theirs less in the matched sample as compared with the total sample, the conclusion of greater female than male liberalization and of intersex convergence during the decade seems inescapable.

The approval-experience ratio

It is important to know how approval of and experience in premarital coitus interrelate: to what extent practice corresponds with precept and what are the directions and magnitudes of discrepancies in this regard. The ratios of Table 4 have been calculated by dividing percentages approving premarital coitus (part III of Table 1 and part II of Table 2) by percentages having experienced it (Table 3). A ratio of 1.00 would mean that approval and experience coincide exactly. Ratios lower than this indicate that experience exceeds approval; and higher, that approval ex-

TABLE 4. Comparisons of approval-experience ratios, total and matched samples.

| | Sample cultures | | | | | |
| | Intermountain | | Midwestern | | Danish | |
Samples and years	Males	Females	Males	Females	Males	Females
I. Total samples						
1968	1.05	.73	1.10	1.10	1.06	1.04
1958	.59	.31	.92	.84	1.48	1.35
Difference	.46	.42	.18	.26	−.42	−.31
II. Matched samples						
1968			1.13	.96		
1958			.87	.84		
Difference			.26	.12		

ceeds experience. With the sex drive as strong as it is, one may wonder how the approval-experience ratio could ever be above 1.00: why, if people approve premarital coitus, they don't engage in it. The primary explanation seems to be that the attitude percentages are for approval of coitus occurring *anytime prior to marriage,* and approving respondents may not be close enough to marriage to feel ready for the experience.

The following generalizations seem evident: (1) in 1958, the magnitude of the ratio varies directly with the permissiveness of the culture; which means that restrictive cultures have higher percentages of their offenders who are violating their own standards—though it must be remembered that restrictive cultures have fewer offenders to start with. (2) Except for Midwestern respondents in 1968, females showed up with lower ratios than males, which means that proportionately more of them violate their own standards when they engage in premarital coitus. However, this intersex difference is of large magnitude only within the highly conservative Intermountain culture. (3) The 1958-68 trend was toward a rise in the ratio for both the Intermountain and Midwestern samples, where it previously had been below 1.00, and a lowering of the ratio in Denmark where it previously had been above 1.00. Thus the time trend has been toward a leveling and balancing of the approval-experience ratios, bringing them closer to each other and to the value of 1.00. In 1968, all ratios except for Midwestern males were closer to 1.00 than was true ten years earlier, and Intermountain females represented the only group in the total sample with experience remaining greater than approval (although in the matched sample this was true for Midwestern females also). The evidence suggests that there is less of a gap today between one's values and his behavior; that, regardless of his sex or the culture he is in, a person is more likely now than formerly, to follow his own internalized norms.

Again, the matching procedure has not altered the basic conclusion. With these data, as with the total sample, the trend is seen to be toward a rising ratio. Attitudes have liberalized more rapidly than has behavior, so that the over-all pattern today seems not to be one of violating one's own value system. Some individuals do, of course, but in terms of group averages the evidence is against it.

Evidences of value-behavior discrepancy

In an earlier article (Christensen and Carpenter, 1962b) the senior author has demonstrated from cross-cultural data for 1958 that—even more than the act itself—it is the discrepancy between what one values and what he then does that determines guilt, divorce, and related negative effects. The analysis was based upon both group and individual comparisons between permissiveness scores (measuring attitude) and behavioral percentages (measuring coital experience).

Here we wish to report a slightly different approach applied to the 1958 and 1968 Midwestern samples, first with the total respondents and then with the matched cases. In Table 5 are presented percentages of those

TABLE 5. Percentages with premarital coitus who approved such experience, Midwestern culture, 1958 and 1968 compared.

	Total sample		Matched sample	
	Males	Females	Males	Females
1968	82	78	76	58
1958	65	41	65	37
Difference	17	37	11	21

with premarital experience who answered approvingly of coitus before marriage. These percentages, in other words, are based upon *individual* case-by-case comparisons between coitus and coital approval. They show the proportions of cases in which there was *no discrepancy* of this kind. By subtracting any percentage figure from 100.0, the reader can, if he prefers it that way, determine the corresponding discrepancy magnitude.

It will be observed that the trend between 1958 and 1968 was toward larger approval percentages (or less value-behavior discrepancy). This is true with respect to both sexes and for the matched as well as the total samples. It supports a similar finding based upon grouped data reported in the previous section. In both instances the evidence suggests that attitudes have been catching up with behavior and that proportionally fewer people today violate their own values when they engage in premarital coitus. Nevertheless, some individuals still show this discrepancy—perhaps as many as one-fifth of the males and two-fifths of the females.

It will be observed also that the movement of premarital coital participants toward approving what one does was greater for females than males (consistently shown in both sets of comparisons). Females in 1968 still gave evidence of greater value-behavior discrepancy than did males but the intersex difference in this regard was less than in 1958. And here too, the finding of Table 5 stands in general support of the picture for grouped data shown in Table 4.

Using attitudes to predict behavior

Since the overall evidence is that attitudes have been liberalizing at a greater rate than behavior, which is narrowing the gap between the two, it might be expected that the predictive power of attitudes is increasing. To test this out, we calculated Gammas on the interaction of two variables:

approval of premarital coitus and experience with premarital coitus. The Gammas reported in Table 6 indicate that the expectation was supported:

TABLE 6. Incidence of premarital coitus as related to approval of premarital coitus, Midwestern sample.

Incidence of premarital coitus	Approval of premarital coitus					
	Males			Females		
	Yes	No	Total	Yes	No	Total
			1968			
Yes	98	22	120	63	18	81
No	35	83	118	26	128	154
Total	133	105	238	89	146	235
	Gamma = .83			Gamma = .89		
			1958			
Yes	68	37	105	12	17	29
No	30	73	103	12	95	107
Total	98	110	208	24	112	136
	Gamma = .63			Gamma = .69		

Coital approval was a better predictor of coital behavior for males and females at the end of the decade than at the beginning.

THE COMMITMENT PHENOMENON

Reiss (1969), largely from analyses of his attitudinal data, has concluded that America is moving toward the traditional Scandinavian pattern of "permissiveness with affection." This phrase has been used by Reiss and others to also mean *permissiveness with commitment.* Our own data should permit us to check out this claim at the behavioral level.

Two indices of affection-commitment are presented in Table 7: percentages (of those experienced in premarital coitus) who had confined their overall experience to one partner; and percentages whose first experience was with a steady or fiance(e). It will be noted that the cross-cultural, cross-sex, and time-trend comparisons derived from these two measures are remarkably similar. In both cases (with very minor exceptions that become evident upon close inspection) rather consistent patterns show up: more American than Danish respondents, more female than male respondents, and more 1958 than 1968 respondents confined their total premarital coital experience to one partner and *also* had their first coitus in a commitment relationship. The other side of the coin, so to speak, is that Danes appear to be more promiscuous than Americans, males more promiscuous than females, and 1968 respondents more promiscuous than 1958 respondents. The term "promiscuity" is used here in a non-evaluative sense and merely to designate the opposite of "commitment." Our measures

TABLE 7. Percentage[a] distributions of responses to items showing a commitment in the sexual relationship.

	Sample cultures					
	Intermountain		Midwestern		Danish	
Items and years	Males	Females	Males	Females	Males	Females
I. Experience confined to one partner						
1968	28.6	43.8	39.0	70.0	20.5	25.0
1958	35.1	57.1	33.7	65.5	40.9	42.9
Difference	−6.5	−13.3	5.3	4.5	−20.4	−17.9
II. First experience with a steady or fiance(e)						
1968	53.8	78.1	52.9	86.3	46.3	55.4
1958	47.2	100.0	42.8	75.9	67.8	74.5
Difference	6.6	−21.9	10.1	10.4	−21.5	−19.1

[a] Based upon number answering. The number failing to answer in any one group varied from 0 to 4.

of these two concepts are indirect and imperfect, to be sure, but undoubtedly they tell something.

Not only were the Danish generally more promiscuous than the Americans (1958 Danish males being an exception), but the shift toward greater promiscuity during the decade under study was greater for them. Apparently, Denmark may be moving away from its traditional pattern of premarital sex justified by a commitment relationship, and sexual promiscuity is coming in to take its place. But without further testing, this observation must be regarded as highly speculative, since the two Danish samples lack strict comparability.

It also is worth noting that the Danish male-female differences in response to both of these items tended to be smaller than in either of the other two cultures, another example of the possible leveling effect of norm permissiveness.

Intermountain females also moved dramatically in the direction of greater promiscuity as indicated by these two measures, possibly because, being so near the "floor" at the beginning of the decade, there was opportunity for the general trend toward permissiveness to affect them proportionately more. Intermountain males did not change much by either measure and, with them, direction of change was inconsistent.

In two important respects Midwestern respondents stood out from the rest. In the first place, they tended to show higher proportions in a commitment relationship (1958 males being the most noticeable exception); and in the second place, this was the only culture where both sexes on both measures showed *higher* commitment percentages in 1968 than 1958 (1958 Intermountain males did on the item "first coitus with a steady or fiance"). Could it be that a general trend toward sexual freedom, such as has occurred in recent years, encourages the development of promiscuity in *both* the commitment-oriented permissive society (such as Denmark) and the ascetic-oriented restrictive society (such as the Intermountain Mormon): the same trend but for different reasons—in the first, to escape commitment; in the second, to escape repression? The question needs further research.

At any rate, the time trend in our Midwestern culture seems clear. To the extent that our sample is representative and our measures adequate, the Reiss hypothesis is supported there. Although it must be said that the testing of this important phenomenon has only begun, it probably can be tentatively concluded that at least a major current in premarital sex trends within this country is a movement toward permissiveness with commitment.

While the emerging American pattern seems to be toward the traditional Danish norm of premarital sex justified by commitment, the emerging Danish pattern may be away from both commitment and restriction, toward free and promiscuous sex. Furthermore, in this one respect at least, the converging lines of the two cultures seem now to have passed each other. Today the Danes appear to be less committed and more promiscuous in their premarital sexual contacts than do Midwestern Americans.

NEGATIVE ACCOMPANIMENTS OF COITUS

Considerable interest centers around the question of consequences. Does premarital coitus affect everyone the same, or do the norms of the culture and the values which the individual has incorporated into his personality make any difference? Our working hypothesis has been that values are relevant data; and following this, the consequences of premarital sex acts are to some extent relative to the alignment or misalignment of values and behavior, being most negative where the disjuncture is the greatest. In sociological circles this line of reasoning has been labeled "Theory of Cognitive Dissonance" (Festinger, 1957). Applied to the data of our present study, we would permit greater negative effects in America than Denmark, for females than males, and during 1958 as compared with 1968 since these are the categories showing disproportionately high value-behavior discrepancy.

Table 8 presents data for two negative accompaniments of premarital coitus. The first of these—yielding to force or felt obligation—means simply that there were pressures other than personal desire which were chiefly responsible for the experience. It will be observed that, in general, results turned out as expected: coitus because of pressure is seen to be higher in restrictive than permissive cultures, higher among females than males, and higher in 1958 than in 1968.

One irregularity in the patterns just noted was introduced by an unexpected increase in pressured coitus among Danish males, which also had the effect of reversing the cross-cultural picture for 1968 males. Reasons for this reverse trend for Danish males are not known, but it will be remembered from Table 7 that it also was Danish males who showed the greatest increase in promiscuous coitus. There is at least the possibility that these two phenomena are connected.

TABLE 8. Percentage[a] distributions of responses to items that indicate negative feelings accompanying first premarital coitus.

	Sample cultures					
	Intermountain		Midwestern		Danish	
Items and years	Males	Females	Males	Females	Males	Females
I. First experience either forced or by obligation						
1968	2.4	24.2	2.5	23.1	10.0	18.5
1958	13.5	42.9	9.3	37.9	4.4	35.6
Difference	−11.1	−18.7	−6.8	−14.8	5.8	−17.1
II. First experience followed chiefly by guilt or remorse						
1968	7.1	9.1	6.6	11.1	1.6	0.0
1958	29.7	28.6	12.1	31.0	4.3	2.0
Difference	−22.6	−19.5	−5.5	−19.9	−2.7	−2.0

[a] In I, the percentages are based upon the number answering; the number failing to answer varying from 0 to 6. In II, the total number of cases was used as the base of the percents.

Part II of Table 8 gives percentages of those who specified either guilt or remorse as their predominant feeling the day after first premarital coitus. Here again, the overall patterns were in expected directions: Coitus followed by guilt or remorse is seen to be higher in restrictive than permissive cultures (although Midwestern females exceed the Intermountain), higher for females than males (although not uniformly and with Denmark being a major exception), and consistently higher in 1958 than 1968. Whether the exceptions noted represent anything more than random variation cannot be determined from our non-probability samples. But at least the broad patterns seem clear and the consistency between our two measures builds confidence in the general findings.

Thus, whether measured by a feeling of external pressure at the time or a subsequent feeling of guilt or remorse, the negative accompaniments of premarital coitus appear to be greatest where the sex norms are restrictive (and, significantly, also where value-behavior discrepancy is the greatest)—in the American cultures as compared with the Danish, with females as compared with males, and in 1958 as compared with 1968.

CONCLUSION

The design of our investigation has enabled us to compare premarital sexual attitudes and behavior against each other; and to compare them separately and in combination across a restrictive-permissive continuum of cultures, across the differing worlds of males and females, and across a recent decade in time. Although the primary concern of this paper has been with recent social changes in premarital sex values and practices, the additional involvement of intersex and cross-cultural variables has enabled us to see the phenomena in better perspective and to tease out certain meanings that otherwise may have remained obscure. Furthermore, we have been interested in going beyond mere description, to the discovery of relationships; and then to interconnect these relationships with each other and with relevant concepts and propositions, with theory building as the ultimate goal. To establish needed controls, we have in places made supplementary analyses of Midwestern data including the use of matched sampling techniques. Nevertheless, we regard our study as more exploratory than definitive. We feel that some significant leads have been uncovered but at the same time regard our conclusions as tentative—as plausible for the present, perhaps, but as hypotheses for future research.

We call attention to the strong suggestion from our data that values and norms serve as intervening variables *affecting the effects* of behavior. For the explaining of consequences, it would seem that even perhaps more important than the sexual act itself is the degree to which that act lines up or fails to line up with the standards set. Whether the comparisons have been between males and females, across cultures, or over time, we have demonstrated two parallel and probably interrelated patterns: value-behavior discrepancy is associated with sexual restrictiveness; and certain negative effects of premarital intimacy are associated with sexual restrictiveness. The possibility—we think probability—is that it is primarily value-behavior discrepancy that is causing the difficulty. This facet of our theory has been explored at greater length in earlier writing (Christensen, 1966; 1969).

REFERENCES

BELL, ROBERT R. 1966. Premarital Sex in a Changing Society. Englewood Cliffs, N.J.: Prentice-Hall.

BELL, ROBERT R. and CHASKES, JAY B. 1970. "Premarital sexual experience among coeds, 1958 and 1968." Journal of Marriage and the Family 32 (February): 81–4.

CHRISTENSEN, HAROLD T. 1960. "Cultural relativism and premarital sex norms." American Sociological Review 25 (February): 31–9. 1966. "Scandinavian and American sex norms: Some comparisons, with sociological implications." The Journal of Social Issues 22 (April): 60–75. 1969. "Normative theory derived from cross-cultural family research." Journal of Marriage and the Family 31 (May): 209–22.

CHRISTENSEN, HAROLD T. and CARPENTER, GEORGE R. 1962a. "Timing patterns in the development of sexual intimacy." Marriage and Family Living 24 (February): 30–5. 1962b. "Value-behavior discrepancies regarding premarital coitus in three Western cultures." American Sociological Review 27 (February): 66–74.

EHRMANN, WINSTON W. 1964. "Marital and nonmarital sexual behavior." Pp. 585–622 in Harold T. Christensen (ed.), Handbook of Marriage and the Family. Chicago: Rand McNally. 1959. Premarital Dating Behavior. New York: Holt.

FESTINGER, LEON. 1957. A Theory of Cognitive Dissonance. New York: Harper and Row.

FREEDMAN, MERVIN B. 1965. "The sexual behavior of American college women: An empirical study and an historical survey." Merrill-Palmer Quarterly of Behavior and Development 11 (January): 33–48.

GAGNON, JOHN H. and SIMON, WILLIAM. 1970. "Prospects for change in American sexual patterns." Medical Aspects of Human Sexuality 4 (January): 100–17.

KINSEY, ALFRED C., POMEROY, WARDELL, MARTIN, CLYDE and GEBHARD, PAUL. 1953. Sexual Behavior in the Human Female. Philadelphia: W. B. Saunders Co.

KIRKENDALL, LESTER A. 1961. Premarital Intercourse and Interpersonal Relationships. New York: Julian.

LESLIE, GERALD A. 1967. The Family in Social Context. New York: Oxford University Press.

LUCKEY, ELEANORE B. and NASS, GILBERT D. 1969. "A comparison of sexual attitudes and behavior in an international sample." Journal of Marriage and the Family 31 (May): 364–79.

PACKARD, VANCE. 1968. The Sexual Wilderness: the Contemporary Upheaval in Male-Female Relationships. New York: David McKay Company, Inc.

REISS, IRA L. 1967. The Social Context of Premarital Sexual Permissiveness. New York: Holt, Rinehart & Winston. 1969. "Premarital sexual standards." In Carlfred B. Broderick and Jessie Bernard (eds.), The Individual, Sex, and Society: A Siecus Handbook for Teachers and Counselors. Baltimore: The Johns Hopkins Press.

SCHOFIELD, MICHAEL. 1965. The Sexual Behavior of Young People. Boston: Little, Brown and Co.

TERMAN, LEWIS M. 1938. Psychological Factors in Marital Happiness. New York: McGraw-Hill.

20

Sex and mental health
on the campus*

SEYMOUR L. HALLECK, M.D.

There is general agreement that sexual attitudes and sexual practices in American society are undergoing radical changes. I propose to examine the extent of these changes and to describe their impact upon the mental health of university students. My approach while hopefully not moralistic will not be free of value judgments. Like most psychiatrists I consider mental health to be something more than mere adjustments to the needs of the community. Mental health is defined according to certain values, values such as psychological comfort, intimacy, compassion, social responsibility, and self-knowledge. Once the psychiatrist begins to ask if a given sexual behavior is good or bad for a person's mental health he is no longer in a position to avoid making ethical judgments.

How much change has there been in sexual attitudes and behaviors among university students? Recent surveys suggest that there have been important changes in students' attitudes toward premarital sexual intercourse. These changes are most apparent when student attitudes are compared with those of their parents' generation. In one study when adults were asked if they believed sexual intercourse would be acceptable if a couple were engaged, only 20 percent of adult males and 17 percent of

* Reprinted from *The Journal of The American Medical Association*, May 22, 1967, Vol. 200, pp. 684–90. Copyright 1967, by American Medical Association. Reprinted with permission of the author and publisher.

adult females said yes. In a student group, 52 percent of the males and 66 percent of the females answered the same question affirmatively. In another study, mothers and their coed daughters were asked to respond to the question, "How important do you think it is that a girl be a virgin when she marries?" Of the mothers, 88 percent answered very important; 12 percent, generally important, and 0 percent, not important. Of their daughters, 55 percent answered very important; 34 percent, generally important; and 13 percent, not important.[1] In a preliminary study of sexual attitudes of freshman and sophomore girls at the University of Wisconsin, Dr. Richard Sternbach and I found that only 30 percent felt that premarital intercourse was definitely wrong.

In judging the rightness or wrongness of premarital intercourse, today's student is confronted with alternative value systems which he can either accept or reject. Most students feel free to search for a morality which suits their own needs. They are not necessarily contemptuous nor rebellious toward older generations. Rather they have a live and let live attitude. Students often say, "I wouldn't feel bad if I participated in premarital intercourse, but I wouldn't want my parents to know about it because they would feel my behavior was wrong. What they don't know won't hurt them."

Attitudes toward discussing sex have also changed. In the past two years, members of the University of Wisconsin Department of Psychiatry have had many requests to speak to student groups about sex. We have all noted an amazing openness and frankness on the part of both male and female groups. Seventeen- and 18-year-old girls for example have little shyness in a group setting in asking speakers about such previously taboo subjects as masturbation, orgasm, techniques of intercourse, oral-genital relations, and homosexuality. All students seem to be eager to create a dialogue with older generations as to the pros and cons of premarital intercourse.

Although there is undoubtedly a revolution in attitudes toward sex, accompanied by a refreshing frankness, there is nevertheless little evidence that the actual rate of premarital intercourse has radically changed. It may be true that more and more young people are engaging in heavy petting before marriage. But the physical state of virginity still seems to be the norm. Kinsey, studying volunteers, found that from 1910 to the 1950s there was no appreciable increase in the proportion of girls having intercourse before marriage.[2] More recent depth interview and questionnaire studies of randomly selected populations at major universities suggest that ap-

---

[1] I. Reiss, The Sexual Renaissance: A Survey and Analysis, *J Soc Issues*, 22:123–37 (April) 1966.

[2] A. C. Kinsey, et al., *Sexual Behavior in the Human Female* (Philadelphia: W. B. Saunders Co., 1953).

proximately 4/5 of undergraduate girls have *not* had coital experience.[3,4] At the University of Wisconsin, for example, a 1966 survey of 300 freshman through senior girls indicated that only 22 percent had experienced sexual intercourse.[5]

We might assume that some day the actual behavior of students will more closely approximate their expressed attitudes. Nevertheless, as of this date there is no evidence of a radical increase in premarital intercourse among university students. It may be reassuring in this regard to note that the great majority of students do not condone promiscuity. When they insist that premarital relations are morally justified, they are most frequently referring to intercourse between those who are engaged or deeply in love. Very few girls can envision themselves having relations with more than one partner. Of the 90 girls Dr. Sternbach and I surveyed, only four defended sex as something to be casually enjoyed with several partners. Some behavioral scientists believe that our culture is moving towards the Scandinavian model of sexual behavior which condones premarital sexual relations between people in love.[6] The expressed attitudes and actual behavior of our students reinforce this notion. In other words, it is unlikely that we will become a promiscuous society, but it is quite likely that we are on the way to becoming a nation in which couples who intend to marry begin sexual activity before marriage.

A trend toward sexual permissiveness based on affection and love should not alarm psychiatrists. After all we believe in the values of intimacy and compassion, and the new sexuality seems to be moving in that direction. Unfortunately, the problem is not that simple. If a girl accepts the new attitudes and wishes to have sexual relations with a boy on the basis of mutual affection and love, she must still define the strength of their commitment. Inevitably she must struggle with the question of how close two people can be when not bound to one another by the responsibilities of a marital contract. Any relationship out of wedlock is plagued with certain ambiguities. The girl must struggle with questions such as, "Will the first argument or sign of incompatibility lead to a dissolution of the relationship and a search for a new partner?" If this does happen, will she simply deceive herself into promiscuity under the rationalization that each new relationship is meaningful? Will she "kid herself" into believing that she is in love when in actuality she is only succumbing to social and sexual pressures? It is my belief that these ambiguities have been heightened by

[3] W. Ehrmann, *Premarital Dating Behavior* (New York: Henry Holt & Co., Inc., 1959).

[4] M. B. Freedman, The Sexual Behavior of American College Women, *Merrill Palmer Quart* 11:33–48 (Jan) 1965.

[5] R. E. Grinder, and S. S. Schmidt, Coeds and Contraceptive Information, *J Marriage Family*, 28:471–9 (Nov) 1966.

[6] H. T. Christensen, Scandinavian and American Sex Norms: Some Comparisons With Sociological Implications, *J Social Issues* 22:60–75 (April) 1966.

changes in attitudes toward sex. The stresses associated with choosing or sustaining sexual relationships before marriage have had an especially intense effect upon female students. For some students such stresses have been critical factors in precipitating severe emotional disorders. In this sense a significant number of students are casualties of the sexual revolution.

MENTAL HEALTH AND SEXUAL PERMISSIVENESS

If it is true that rates of sexual intercourse before marriage have not changed appreciably in the general student population, this trend is not apparent in those students who are psychiatric patients. In a recent survey of 24 Madison psychiatrists who were treating University of Wisconsin students, I found that of their 107 unmarried female patients 86 percent had had sexual relationships with at least one person and 72 percent had had relations with more than one person. Permissive sexual activity seems to be highly correlated with mental illness, or at least with a willingness to accept a mental illness role. This data raises some disturbing thoughts. Psychiatrists and other physicians have been in the vanguard of either praising or deploring new trends toward permissive sexuality. Judging from their publications, it appears that psychiatrists have gained the impression that promiscuity is rampant in our youth. However, if we compare the incidence of virginity among nonpatients with that among patients (remember that only 22 percent of the nonpatient students had had sexual intercourse) it appears that psychiatrists err when they generalize from experiences with a somewhat atypical clientele. Patients may be promiscuous, but most of the population is not.

How can we understand the relationship between mental health and permissive sexual behavior? Is it possible that casual sexual behavior can cause girls to be mentally ill? Or does being mentally ill make one more susceptible to free and easy sex? Or does some third factor have a causative influence upon both permissive sexuality and mental illness?

There is certainly a great deal of support for the latter two hypotheses, particularly for the proposition that poor mental health makes one more susceptible to frequent sexual contacts of a promiscuous nature. Martin Loeb has noted that teenagers who trust themselves, who can contribute to others, and who can rely on others tend to have the least number of sexual relationships before marriage.[7] Maslow has described the sexual behavior of very healthy "self-actualized" people and notes that they have fewer premarital sexual contacts than less successful people. Their attitude seems to be, "We don't need sex but we enjoy it when we have it." Maslow points out that self-actualized people enjoy sex more than others

---

[7] M. B. Loeb, *Social Roles and Sexual Identity in Adolescent Males,* Casework Papers, National Association of Social Workers, New York, 1959.

but consider it less essential in their total frame of reference.[8] My own observations of highly disturbed delinquent girls suggests that their promiscuity is determined by primitive neurotic needs and is only one symptom of a pervasive emotional disturbance.[9] These girls seek multiple sexual experiences because they have despaired of finding any other means of obtaining nurturance and affection.

It is also possible that a high concordance of sexual permissiveness and mental illness is related to a third factor such as urban sophistication. Conceivably those who are most willing to accept psychiatric treatment are part of an avant-garde who are also willing to enjoy an unrestrained sexual life. Still another possibility is that a willingness to be a mental patient and a willingness to be a casual sexual partner are related to a general sense of alienation. An increasing number of students have rejected the prevailing norms of their own cultures and have not found substitute moralities with which to identify. Such students may be exceptionally casual about sex, and the painful effects of their identity diffusion may then be likely to bring them to psychiatrists.

Granted that mental illness may lead to promiscuity or that a third factor may be related to both, to what extent is it possible that liberal sexual behavior might be a *cause* of mental illness? Here we must be wary of circular thinking. The lower classes of society are willing to define promiscuity as "badness," but many members of the middle and upper classes automatically define it as "illness." The social conditioning of an upper or middle class girl leads her quickly to accept the patient role once she begins ot think of herself as promiscuous. Sociologists and anthropologists might argue that there is no causative relationship between permissive sexual behavior and mental illness but that society simply equates promiscuity with mental illness as a means of enforcing chastity. They would insist that if permissiveness were the norm, promiscuous girls would not be patients.

The sociological argument is partially correct. I believe, however, that promiscuity can still produce emotional problems and that its causative influence is in practical terms relatively independent of current social definitions of normative behavior. The experiences associated with being promiscuous are in themselves stressful and are not conducive to the development of those personality traits generally considered to be characteristic of the 'healthy' individual. Furthermore, whether society is right or wrong, it does impose social stresses upon the promiscuous girl which are sufficiently painful to drive her to the mental illness role.

I have noted that those students who are patients have a greater tendency towards promiscuity than the average student. It must be acknowl-

---

[8] A. Maslow, *Motivation and Personality* (New York: Harper & Bros., 1954).

[9] S. L. Halleck, *Psychiatry and the Dilemmas of Crime* (New York: Harper & Row, Publishers, Inc., 1967).

edged of course that not every female patient who has had one or several affairs should be considered promiscuous. However, the kinds of stresses such students experience and the manner in which these stresses drive them towards a patient role will be clarified if we consider the case of one highly promiscuous girl.

Joan, an 18-year-old girl, made a psychiatric appointment the morning after she had slept with the tenth different boy in the space of a year. Sensing something self-destructive about her behavior, she made a pledge to seek help after her tenth affair. She had been depressed and unable to study. Her school performance had deteriorated to the point where she was contemplating leaving school. Joan initially had doubts about accepting the role of patient. She defended her sexual behavior, insisting that it was correct and moral. Although she assumed her parents would not approve of her conduct if they knew about it, she derided their values as "phony" and insincere. She maintained that she had experienced orgasm in every sexual encounter and that each new affair was more exciting than the last.

During the first month of treatment, Joan added two more lovers. When the therapist asked what these affairs meant to her, she stated, "It's just fun, like eating a good meal or seeing a good movie. The boys mean nothing to me; they just enjoy me, and I enjoy them." During this time her school performance continued to deteriorate. She smoked marijuana, drank heavily, and increasingly talked about the meaninglessness of life. As she became more depressed, she began to voice thoughts about suicide.

In the 12th hour of therapy, the patient reported that she had recently slept with a boy whom she actually despised. She was agitated and remorseful. At this point she began seriously to review her sexual history. She had had her initial affair one year earlier with a boy she had thought she loved. When he broke up with her, she had three new experiences in rapid succession. In each case Joan tried to convince herself that she was in love with her boyfriend, and in each case her relationship terminated in less than a month. Joan then decided that she would never sleep with another boy unless their relationship was meaningful. The next three relationships however did not last more than a week. Two of the boys did not even bother to call back after the first date. As Joan related the rest of her history she tearfully stated, "The last few months I've just been kidding myself. I try to convince myself that I really love these boys, but really I'm just scared that if I don't sleep with them no one will even ask me out. I begin to hate myself, but I can't stand the loneliness."

Joan was fortunate in having a successful therapy experience. Eventually she was able to feel better, to improve her school work, and to find a boy whom she married. One interesting aspect of her therapy was that after a year of treatment and after she had found a boy who loved her she admitted that she had previously never experienced orgasm during coitus. At this point she wondered how she could ever enjoy sex with anyone but her fiance and admitted to considerable remorse over earlier sexual experiences.

While I was convinced that Joan's personality problems had made her susceptible to promiscuity, it also seemed clear that her promiscuity had contributed to a state of chronic despair. As with so many girls, Joan's initial intention to associate sex only with love was subverted after the first few affairs. Eventually, sex became for her a remedy for loneliness. Her belief that she was finding intimacy and meaningfulness through sex was painfully recognized as a self-deception. It is difficult to see how Joan could have found intimacy or love. Her relationships were simply too transitory. There was no opportunity to get acquainted with her lovers. At the first argument, the first feeling of disgust or the first incompatibility, separation loomed as the most seductive alternative.

Joan's misery was at least in part related to a pervasive sense of guilt about her sexual activities. A sociologist might argue that Joan's guilt was caused by her restrictive upbringing and society's puritanical attitude toward sex. Indeed, Joan accepted this argument and insisted that her guilt was extraneous to her, a foreign body imposed upon her by a malevolent and self-righteous society. I would contend however that such an argument is a simplistic one insofar as it fails to comprehend the manner in which sex is intimately related to interpersonal processes. I do not believe that sex completely free of guilt is possible in modern society. As an interpersonal act, sex is a vehicle for expressing any type of emotional need humans can experience. In addition to being a source of physical pleasure, the sexual act also fulfills dependent needs, status needs, and aggressive needs. Psychoanalysts (particularly Bergler,[10] Brenman,[11] and Reik[12]) have pointed out how the quest for gratification of such needs comes to be associated with feelings of guilt. The girl who uses sex to combat loneliness, to gain status, or to exploit others cannot avoid a certain amount of guilt. Even if she is able to free herself from religious or moralistic scruples, she must deal with those guilt feelings which are associated with the selfish or aggressive uses of sex.

Furthermore, any dishonesty in the sex act, such as pretending to love while not loving, pretending to be someone else, pretending that her partner is someone else, or even pretending to enjoy the act while not enjoying it, can lead a normal person to feel guilty. The partner who constantly feels that she takes more than she gives will also be uneasy. So will the person who uses a moderately deviant fantasy to stimulate her sexual interest. In this day and age we have even invented new guilts, namely guilt for being unattractive or guilt for not having orgasm. It is unlikely that even the marriage contract does much more than attenuate these feelings. It would seem that all of the kinds of guilty feelings I have described are more likely to occur in a promiscuous relationship. To the extent that a girl such as Joan accepts the new sexual attitudes and actively seeks sex

---

[10] E. Bergler, *The Basic Neurosis* (New York: Grune & Stratton, Inc., 1949).

[11] M. Brenman, On Teasing and Being Teased, *Psychoanal Stud Child* 7:264–85, 1952.

[12] T. Reik, *Masochism in Modern Man*, New York: Farrar, Straus & Co., 1941.

without guilt, she deceives herself and runs the additional risk of feeling more guilty simply because she knows she *is* guilty.

Another adverse effect of promiscuity which is apparent in Joan's case is that more sexual freedom for women has not been accompanied by an elevation of their status as women. The double standard is still with us. I have never heard a single phrase from any student, male or female, which suggests that girls were more esteemed as important and worthwhile persons because of their enlightened sexual attitudes. At the same time, I have seen many patients who abandoned career aspirations once they began to be involved with multiple partners. Unfortunately the sexually permissive girl comes to see herself as more of an object and less of an equal partner. At the same time, she is given more responsibility than ever before for prevention of pregnancy and is probably less able than girls of previous generations to count on the help of her boyfriend if she is impregnated. In effect, she is valued by men for her sexual capacities and for these alone. Social conditions may of course change, but the present trends toward sexual permissiveness have not liberated women, they have only strengthened the feminine mystique.

We might also note that a repetitive break with the rules of society pushes the promiscuous girl closer and closer to alienation from society. As her self-esteem declines and as she becomes more accustomed to rule-breaking behavior, she desperately seeks rationalization for her conduct. These are most easily found in attacks upon the entire social code. An overdetermined attack on the beliefs of the older generation moves the promiscuous girl further and further away from her own past. She begins to lose perspective on that part of her own history which identifies her with her society. Such alienation is highly correlated with feelings of powerlessness, with abdication of responsibility and, ultimately, with a willingness to identify oneself as a patient. Some of these problems are closely related to an increasing tendency of our youth to live in the present, to deny fidelity to past values, and to despair of hope in the future. Promiscuous sex contributes to such tendencies by its immediacy. It calls for gratification "now" and denies the possibility of better days ahead. Very few promiscuous girls look forward to a better sexual relationship after marriage. While it is difficult to determine which causes which, promiscuity is usually linked with alienation and seems to encourage withdrawal from social responsibility.

May[13] has defined puritanism as a separation of passion and sexuality. May believes that the old puritans were passionate but not sexual and that many of our students are new puritans in the sense that they are sexual but not passionate. Certainly in the case of Joan and other promiscuous

---

[13] R. May, Antidotes for the New Puritanism, *Saturday Rev*, March 26, 1966, pp. 19–20.

girls, it is difficult to find the kind of passion and commitment that is characteristic of deeply involved people. The new sexuality does seem to be frighteningly sterile. An emphasis on orgasm pervades all age groups in our society. Among university students, the search for the ultimate orgasm has become almost a competitive matter. In Joan's case, it took over a year of therapy before she could admit her relative virginity. In our age, this has become the ultimate confession. I have seen other girls who admitted cheating, stealing, masturbating, and promiscuity with little shame but who wept violently when they confessed that they could not have orgasms.

While promiscuous girls emphasize the importance of orgasm, they are often too immature to actively desire or enjoy sexual intercourse. They are ahead of themselves in the sense that they could enjoy intensive petting, but actual coitus is perceived as alien and frustrating. One of my promiscuous patients stopped taking her birth control pills because of medical problems. Knowing that she could not have intercourse without risking pregnancy she settled for heavy petting on her next date. During an intense petting session she experienced an extremely satisfying orgasm, the first she had ever had outside of masturbation.

The stresses of promiscuity are indeed intense. Not only is the promiscuous girl denied intimacy and plagued with guilt and alienation, but she is often limited in her capacity to feel physical pleasure. Furthermore, she feels obligated to convince herself that she does experience pleasure and is likely to be guilty if she does not. If she feigns orgasm, her guilt is even greater.

THE BORDERLINE GIRL

Let us now leave the problems of the promiscuous girl and consider the girl who believes that intercourse before marriage is morally justified only if it is always associated with love and commitment. What pressures does such a girl wrestle with, and how are these pressures related to her mental health?

In lengthy question and answer sessions following informal talks to female students, I have become convinced that the new sexual attitudes are having a significant influence upon all female students. More girls may not be indulging in premarital intercourse, but more girls feel pressured to do so.

The mass communication media in our country have a tendency to emphasize the most extreme forms of social behavior and to present them as the norm. Our students receive a heavy bombardment of *Playboy* philosophies which argue for the enjoyment of sex for the sake of physical pleasure alone. There are few social forces counteracting these philosophies. Even our religious leaders are modifying their pleas for rigid adherence to premarital chastity. Our youths seem to have accepted a number of questionable beliefs which serve to perpetuate these pressures. For example, many of the girls I have spoken to believe that physical frustration per se is psychologically unhealthy. They are convinced that petting without orgasm will be unhealthy for them and their partners. They continue to believe that there is an erotic health-producing quality to orgasm during intercourse which is not available through masturbation. While this belief is not supported by any current research, it nevertheless continues to exert a powerful influence.

Many girls also fear that denying their sexual charms to boys is a sign of selfishness. In an age where students are deeply concerned with communicating and cutting through one another's defensiveness, the act of intercourse is valued as an easy means to such goals. Not infrequently, the girl who retains chastity is accused of emotional coldness, of not trying to be an open person. Finally, most girls believe that there is more sexual activity taking place than is actually the case. If they do not participate, they see themselves as atypical and strange.

There are other highly varied pressures which produce conflict in the girl who wishes to make a rational decision as to premarital intercourse. Many girls simply feel that they will lose their boyfriends if they do not sleep with them. Others have convinced themselves that technical "know-how" is important for a successful sex life and that experience before marriage will make them better wives. Finally the Vietnam conflict has had a deep impact upon people of draft age. Some girls out of guilt, compassion, or love feel obligated to give themselves to those who could lose their lives. The phrase, "Make love; not war" is a political slogan, but in this day and age, it is also an effective argument for sexual permissiveness. All of these pressures produce conflict in the girl who wavers between chastity or fidelity and greater sexual freedom. Sometimes the conflict is directly related to the development of psychiatric difficulties.

Barbara, an 18-year-old freshman student, came to the clinic because of nervousness, depression, and inability to study. She was unable to sleep, had lost weight, and was becoming increasingly preoccupied with the meaninglessness of life. Barbara had received a Fundamentalist Protestant upbringing with strict sanctions against premarital sex. In spite of this, she had engaged in one prolonged and satisfying affair with her high school sweetheart. She had hoped to marry the boy, but he eventually rejected her.

In the course of her first interview, Barbara revealed that she had been assigned to a dormitory with girls who took a decidedly casual attitude toward sex. Her closest friends, including her roommate, were all promiscuous. She suspected that her friends were emotionally disturbed people, but she liked them and she was deeply impressed by them. As the semester progressed and Barbara learned more about her friends' sexual activities, she began to question her own values. She had always had a strong need for group identifications and a wish to be an "in" person. When her friends chided her as prudish, old-fashioned, and selfish she felt despondent. She was tempted to sleep with boys, but her early upbringing made it impossible to adopt a liberal attitude towards sex without experiencing enormous guilt. Faced with such conflicts, she became increasingly anxious and depressed. By the time she came to the psychiatrist, she was beginning to move toward withdrawal and alienation.[11]

It can be argued that Barbara was an immature girl who would have had difficulties irrespective of the social climate or her fortuitous association with promiscuous dormitory mates. I am not convinced. In a different era, or even in a different dormitory, Barbara's conflict would have been less intense. She had been exposed to a social climate in which the pressures for liberal sexuality were as great as or greater than the pressures for chastity. She was not experienced enough nor had she developed a sufficiently stable identity that she could resolve her conflict by selecting a value system which was congruent with her own sense of self.

Not all girls, of course, are as intensively exposed to subcultures of promiscuity as Barbara. Nevertheless, this subculture does exist on our campuses, and its influence is greater than would be anticipated from the size of its membership. Promiscuous girls are often seen as representing the vanguard of a new and better morality. They are not looked down upon by chaste girls (although interestingly enough, they themselves are quite contemptuous of those who are not promiscuous). Newspapers, periodicals and television describe them as the "new breed," as the "now people," and impressionable youngsters take these images seriously. In such a climate premarital intercourse can be enforced upon a girl in a manner not too dissimilar from that in which chastity was enforced upon girls in an earlier generation. Under such pressures, many girls like Barbara experience intense conflict which cannot be resolved without psychiatric assistance.

THE PROBLEMS OF VIRGINITY

Psychiatric problems associated with efforts to retain virginity until marriage are not too different from those seen in the past. Psychiatrists still see patients whose depression and psychosomatic disorders appear to be directly related to repression of sexual drives. Of course the pressures against virginity are greater today, and a girl may have to develop rigid and highly maladaptive defenses if she wishes to remain chaste. Virginal girls are also tempted to exploit men into committing themselves to a more permanent relationship. This is especially true among those girls who espouse an "everything but" philosophy, who engage in heavy petting but stop at the point of intercourse.

Perhaps a new trend is indicated by a few girls who come to psychiatrists and present virginity as a problem. Such girls accept a moral code which condones premarital intercourse but find that they are unable to go through with the act when partners are available. It does seem in this day and age that girls who remain virgins (unless they have strong backing in religious beliefs) are likely to worry about their normality. The questions I hear in discussion sessions indicate some shame over virginity. It is as though the virginal girl fears that in remaining chaste she fails to prepare herself for the responsibility of love and marriage.

THE PROBLEMS OF BOYS

I have said little about the impact of changes in sexual attitudes upon the mental health of boys. From a moral standpoint there has been little concern about boys. Neither those who advocate liberalism nor those who favor a double standard worry much when boys have abundant opportunities for sex. Yet there are a few aspects of the new sexuality that seem to have an adverse effect upon male students.

One problem is again created by the mass communication media which suggests that sex is everywhere available. There are dozens of sources telling boys that girls are more promiscuous than ever. The boy who chooses to abstain or who has difficulty in finding a partner feels more freakish than ever. When boys do have an opportunity for sex they sometimes take a desperately exploitative attitude toward their partners. Some of the competitive aspects of the new sexuality are manifested in a mechanical striving for perfection. Our clinic sees an increasing number of unmarried men who complain of impotence, premature ejaculation, and inability to have an ejaculation. My impression is that male patients feel under more pressure than ever before to prove themselves through the sex act. Many experience difficulty simply because they are more interested in the statusful than in the tender aspects of lovemaking.

Efforts to prove masculinity through multiple conquests are still common. Those boys who are able to become part of the promiscuous subculture find it convenient to pursue sex as a kind of aggressive game. Many male students are tempted to postpone commitment to one person. Instead they lead the kind of life advocated by the *Playboy* philosophy. In earlier years some of these men might have been seduced into marriage in order to gain sexual gratification. While this old-fashioned resolution was unhealthy for some, it may have been quite healthy for others. Today, a man who fears closeness to or intimacy with a woman has fewer opportunities to resolve his problems. The casualness of his sexual encounters precludes his desiring or becoming entrapped in a relationship which might have eventually resolved his fears of intimacy.

CONCLUSIONS

It is far too early to evaluate the psychological consequences of our sexual revolution. I would, however, like to make a few observations.

First, it seems clear that changes in sexual attitudes and practices do have an influence upon the mental health of some students. The nature of this influence however is too complex to allow for generalizations as to whether a given practice is either good or bad for people. Psychiatrists at one time impugned Victorian sexual attitudes and considered them an important cause of mental illness. They advocated more permissiveness and our society has moved toward more permissiveness. And what has happened? Our patient load has not decreased, yet the majority of our youthful patients are not repressed nor inhibited people. Rather, today's patient is characterized by a high degree of sexual freedom and self-indulgence. The proposition that gratification of sexual needs is highly correlated with mental health seems to be at least questionable.

While I have pointed out the manner in which permissive sexual practices can potentiate mental illness, it would be equally dangerous to conclude that permissive sexual behavior is universally unhealthy. It may be true that our promiscuous patients are unhealthy, but there may be many promiscuous girls who never visit psychiatrists who are quite happy. The psychiatrist simply lacks information about the population as a whole. Until we know much more than we do now, we would be wise to stop generalizing about the relationship of sex to mental health.

At the same time that a psychiatrist must be wary of generalization, once he confronts a patient as an individual he does have some responsibility to help that person decide what is right or wrong. How does he do this? If we were to try to describe an ethical principle by which psychiatrists operate, we would have to include the psychiatrist's commitment to help the patient do what is best for himself, that is, to help the patient lead the most gratifying and most useful life without inflicting pain upon himself or others. Confronted with new sexual attitudes and practices which impose new stresses upon his patients, the psychiatrist finds that he often must interpose himself between a "thou shalt not" and an "anything goes" philosophy. He does this by repeatedly asking his patient, "Are you being honest with yourself? Will this behavior hurt you or those you love? Will it be good for you? Is it really what you want?"

A final consideration is whether psychiatrists or other physicians can help prevent mental illness which is associated with the sexual revolution. Certainly, providing sexual information which is not sensationalized, exaggerated, or contaminated by myth will help many young people make rational decisions about their future conduct. There may also be more specific preventative measures which discourage aimless and unsatisfying promiscuity.

A girl is most vulnerable to promiscuity shortly after she terminates a sexual relationship with her first lover. She has usually elected to give up her virginity because of a commitment to a boy she eventually hopes to marry. When she discovers that their relationship will not be permanent, she experiences a sense of depression over her loss and a sense of freedom from conventional restraints. Both factors militate towards promiscuous sexuality. It would be desirable for every young person who has just terminated an intense sexual relationship to have some opportunity for professional counseling. Perhaps an even more important need is to help our youth understand those conditions which favor and those conditions which interfere with a permanent relationship. If students were more capable of gauging the depth of commitment in their relationships, they would be in a better position to make the initial decisions as to their premarital sexual behavior.

21
Interpersonal relationships—
Crux of the sexual renaissance*

LESTER A. KIRKENDALL and
ROGER W. LIBBY

A debate over whether sexual morality is declining, or whether we are experiencing a sexual revolution, has broken into the open. The controversy, which has been brewing for over a decade, has been mulled by news media, magazines, books and professional conferences. Varying views have been expressed, but one thing is clear—the very foundations upon which sexual morality has rested, and which have governed the exercise of sexual behavior, are being challenged (16). This, of course, is characteristic of a renaissance.

Many influential people are moving away from the view that sexual morality is defined by abstinence from nonmarital intercourse toward one in which morality is expressed through responsible sexual behavior and a sincere regard for the rights of others. While these people do not advocate nonmarital sexual relations, this possibility is clearly seen as more acceptable if entered in a responsible manner, and contained within a relationship characterized by integrity and mutual concern. In other words, the shift is from emphasis upon an act to emphasis upon the quality of interpersonal relationships.

---

* Reprinted from *The Journal of Social Issues*, Vol. 22, No. 2 (April 1966), pp. 45–59, by permission of the authors and of the Society for the Psychological Study of Social Issues. Copyright by the Society for the Psychological Study of Social Issues.

ILLUSTRATIONS OF THE SHIFT

Liberal religious leaders probably provide the most striking illustration of this change. Selections from their writings and pronouncements could be extended considerably beyond the following quotations, but these three are indicative of the changing emphasis.

Douglas Rhymes, Canon Librarian of Southwark Cathedral, writes:

We are told that all sexual experience outside marriage is wrong, but we are given no particular rulings about sexual experience within marriage. Yet a person may just as easily be treated as a means to satisfy desire and be exploited for the gratification of another within marriage as outside it. It is strange that we concern ourselves so much with the morality of premarital and extramarital sex, but seldom raise seriously the question of sexual morality within marriage. . . . (21, p. 25)

John A. T. Robinson, Bishop of Woolwich, in his controversial book asserts:

. . . nothing can of itself always be labeled "wrong." One cannot, for instance, start from the position "sex relations before marriage" or "divorce" are wrong or sinful in themselves. They may be in 99 cases or even 100 cases out of 100, but they are not intrinsically so, for the only intrinsic evil is lack of love (22, p. 118).

Harvey Cox, who is a member of The Divinity School faculty at Harvard University comments:

To refuse to deliver a prepared answer whenever the question of premarital intercourse pops up will have a healthy influence on the continuing conversation that is Christian ethics. . . . It gets us off deadend arguments about virginity and chastity, forces us to think about fidelity to persons. It exposes the . . . subtle exploitation that poisons even the most immaculate Platonic relationships.

By definition premarital refers to people who plan to marry someone some day. Premarital sexual conduct should therefore serve to strengthen the chances of sexual success and fidelity in marriage, and we must face the real question of whether avoidance of intercourse beforehand is always the best preparation (6, p. 215). [Harvey Cox, *The Secular City* rev. ed., Copyright © Harvey Cox, 1965 and 1966.]

What is common to these quotes is readily seen. In each the focus is on what happens to persons within the context of the interpersonal relationship matrix in which they find themselves. Morality does not reside in complete sexual abstinence, nor immorality in having had nonmarital experience. Rather, sex derives its meaning from the extent to which it contributes to or detracts from the quality and meaning of the relationship in which it occurs, and relationships in general.

This changing emphasis is also reflected in marriage manuals—those books purporting to help couples toward an adequate sexual adjustment. One of the earliest to appear in the United States (1926) was *The Ideal Marriage* by Theodore Van de Velde. The physiological aspect predominates in this 320-page book. Thus 310 pages of the 320 are devoted to detailed descriptions of the genital organs and the reproductive system, their hygiene and care. The last 10 pages (one chapter) are devoted to the psychic, emotional, and mental hygiene of the ideal marriage.

To say that the psychological and emotional aspects are completely ignored except for this chapter is not wholly fair, but the book, written by a physician, carries the vivid imprint of the medical profession with its concentration on physiology. At the time of its publication it was a forward-looking book.

The rising concern for interpersonal relationships, however, can be seen in another book written by a physician, Dr. Mary Calderone, in 1960. Dr. Calderone tries to create for her readers a perception of sexuality which is embedded firmly in the total relationship. At one point she comments:

Sex responsiveness comes to those who not only view sex as a sacred and cherished factor in living, but who also retain good perspective about it by being sensitive to the needs of their partners and by taking into account the warmth, graciousness and humor inherent in successful marital sex (5, p. 163).

The historical preoccupation with sex as an act has also been reflected in the character of sex research. Until recently it has concentrated on incidences and frequencies of various forms of sexual behavior. Some of the more pretentious studies broke incidences and frequencies of the total research population into smaller groups, e.g., Kinsey (12, 13). He looked for possible differences in sex behavior in sub-groups distinguished by such factors as religious affiliations, socioeconomic levels, rural or urban residence, adequacy of sex education and similar factors. This analysis, of course, took into account situational factors which could and do influence interpersonal relationships. Strictly speaking, however, the research still remained outside the interpersonal relationships framework.

IMPLICATIONS OF THE SHIFT

If an increasing concern for sex as an interpersonal relationship is the trend of the sexual renaissance, and we think it is, then clearly we must know how sex and sexual functioning are affected by relationships and vice versa. An extensive psychological literature has been developed to explain individual functioning; individual differences, individual growth patterns, individual cognitive development have all been explored. But relatively little is known about *relationships* as such—their components, or what precisely causes them to flourish, or to wither and die. A psychology more concerned with interpersonal relationships is now much needed.

This also suggests the need to develop a field of research devoted to understanding sex and interpersonal relationships.

Finally, as a psychology and a sociology of relationships is developed, and as research findings provide a tested body of content for teaching, parents and educators may find a new stance. They can become less concerned with interdicting sexual expression of any kind, and more concerned with building an understanding of those factors which facilitate or impede the development of interpersonal relationships.

RESEARCH ASSOCIATING SEX AND INTERPERSONAL RELATIONSHIPS

It is only within the last few years that some research has come to focus on interpersonal aspects of sexual adjustment.

That this is a fruitful approach is already evident from the results of some of the recent studies. Such research is still meager in scope and its methods and procedures will undoubtedly be much improved with experience. Much still remains in the realm of speculation and conjecture. But a beginning has been made, and the findings are enlightening and exciting.

One generalization growing out of the studies can be advanced at this point. *A sexual relationship is an interpersonal relationship, and as such is subject to the same principles of interaction as are other relationships.* It too is affected by social, psychological, physiological and cultural forces. The effort, so characteristic of our culture, to pull sex out of the context of ordinary living, obscures this simple but important generalization. Yet research findings constantly remind us of it.

Ehrmann (7) examined the association of premarital sexual behavior and interpersonal relationships. He studied the progression of individuals through increasingly intense stages of intimacy as they moved toward or rejected premarital intercourse. He was interested in understanding the various stages of intimacy behavior in relation to a number of factors. The stages were related to the attitudes with which acquaintances, friends and lovers regarded sexual intimacy, the kinds of controls exercised, and other factors which helped build certain feelings and attitudes in interpersonal relationships.

Two conclusions will illustrate the character of his findings. In discussing the differences in male-female attitudes which are found as affectional ties deepen, Ehrmann writes:

. . . males are more conservative and the females are more liberal in expressed personal codes of sex conduct and in actual behavior with lovers than with nonlovers. In other words, the degree of physical intimacy actually experienced or considered permissible is among males *inversely* related and among females *directly* related to the intensity of familiarity and affection in the male-female relation. . . .

Female sexual expression is primarily and profoundly related to being in love and going steadily. . . . Male sexuality is more indirect and less exclusively associated with romanticism and intimacy relationships (7, p. 269). [From Winston Ehrmann, *Premarital Dating Behavior* (New York: Holt, Rinehart & Winston, Inc.), reprinted by permission.]

Ehrmann, then, has educed evidence that maleness and femaleness and affection influence the character of those interpersonal relationships expressed in sexual behavior.

Similarly, Schofield (24) in a study of 1,873 London boys and girls between the ages of 15 and 19 found that

Girls prefer a more permanent type of relationship in their sexual behaviour. Boys seem to want the opposite; they prefer diversity and so have more casual partners. . . . there is a direct association between the type of relationship a girl has achieved and the degree of intimacy she will permit . . . (24, p. 92).

Kirkendall (15) conducted a study which centered upon understanding the association which he believed to exist between interpersonal relationships and premarital intercourse. He posited three components of an interpersonal relationship—motivation, communication and attitudes toward the assumption of responsibility—and studied the impact of premarital intercourse on them. Two hundred college-level males reported sexual liaisons with 668 females. These liaisons were arrayed along a continuum of affectional involvement. The continuum was divided into six segments or levels which ranged from the prostitute level, where affection was rejected as a part of the relationship, to fiancees—a level involving deep affection.

The relationship components were then studied to determine their changing character as one moved along the continuum. Thus it was found that communication at the prostitute level had a distinct barter characteristic. At the second (pickup) level there was a testing and teasing type of communication. At the deep affectional and the fiancee level there was much more concern for the development of the kind of communication which would result in understanding and insight.

Similarly, the apparent character of the motivation central to the sexual relationship changed from one end of the continuum to the other. As depth of emotional involvement increased, the motivation changed from a self-centered focus to a relationship-centered one. And, increasing emotional involvement resulted in an increasing readiness to assume the responsibilities involved in the sexual relationship.

The study thus provides clear evidence that considering premarital intercourse in blanket terms—as though intercourse with a prostitute could be equated with intercourse with a fiancee—submerged many nuances and shades of meaning. Until these interpersonal differentiations are taken into account, there is little chance of any realistic or meaningful understanding of the character of premarital intercourse.

Burgess and Wallin (4) explored the possibility that premarital intercourse might strengthen the relationship of fiancees who engaged in it. They asked those subjects (eighty-one men and seventy-four women) who reported experience in premarital intercourse if they felt the experience strengthened or weakened their relationship. Some 92.6 percent of the men and 90.6 percent of the women attributed a strengthening effect to intercourse, and 1.2 percent of the men and 5.4 percent of the women considered intercourse to have a weakening effect. The remainder noted no change either way. Burgess and Wallin comment:

. . . This finding could be construed as testimony for the beneficial consequences of premarital relations, but with some reservations. First, couples who refrained from having premarital intercourse were not asked whether not doing so strengthened or weakened their relationship. They might have reported unanimously that their relationship had been strengthened by their restraint.
Such a finding could be interpreted as signifying one of two things: (a) that both groups are rationalizing or (b) that given the characteristics, expectations, and standards of those who have intercourse, the experience strengthens their relationships, and, similarly, that given the standards of the continent couples the cooperative effort of couple members to refrain from sex relations strengthens their union (4, p. 371–72). [From *Engagement and Marriage* by Ernest W. Burgess and P. Wallin. Reprinted by permission of the publisher, J. B. Lippincott Company. Copyright 1953.]

Kirkendall, (15) after an analysis of his data, reinterpreted the findings of Burgess and Wallin. He envisioned a more complex interplay than simply a reciprocating association between sexual experience and the strengthening or weakening of a relationship. He suggested this interpretation:

Some deeply affectionate couples have, through the investment of time and mutual devotion, built a relationship which is significant to them, and in which they have developed a mutual respect. Some of these couples are relatively free from the customary inhibitions about sexual participation. Some couples with this kind of relationship and background can, and do, experience intercourse without damage to their total relationship. The expression "without damage" is used in preference to "strengthening," for it seems that in practically all instances "non-damaging" intercourse occurred in relationships which were already so strong in their own right that intercourse did not have much to offer toward strengthening them (15, p. 199–200). [Reprinted by permission of the publisher, The Julian Press, Inc.]

Kirkendall's study raised a question which the data from his nonrandomly selected population could not answer. What proportion of all premarital intercourse occurs at the various levels of his continuum? Of the 668 sexual associations in his survey, 25 (3.2 percent) involved fiancees and 95 (14.2 percent) couples with deep affection. Associations involving prostitutes, pickups or partners dated only for intercourse accounted for

432 (64.6 percent), and those with dating partners where there was little or no affection numbered 116 (17.4 percent). But would similar proportions be found if a random sampling were used? A study designed to answer this question is needed.

Several studies have linked sexual behavior at the adolescent or young adult level with presumed casual relationships which existed in childhood, particularly those involving some sort of deprivation, usually affectional. This view, of course, will be nothing new to those familiar with psychiatric literature.

An interesting study which demonstrates this linkage is reported by Harold Greenwald (11). Greenwald studied twenty call girls, prostitutes who minister to a well-to-do clientele. He found that ". . . many of the tendencies which lead to the choice of the call girl profession appear early in youth. . . ." (11, p. 182) The childhood backgrounds of the call girls appeared to be lacking in genuine love or tenderness. "The fundamental preventive task, then, becomes strengthening the family as a source of love and growth." (11, p. 182)

Ellis and Sagarin (8), in their study of nymphomania, also suggest that its causation has its roots in inadequate childhood relationships.

In studies made at the San Francisco Psychiatric clinic, Lion (17) and Safir (23) found that promiscuity was related to personality deficiencies, and that these in turn were related to homes characterized by disorganization, weak or broken emotional ties, and lack of loyalties or identification with any person or group.

If a tie of this kind does exist, it would seem logical that changes in the capacity to experience improved personal relationships (arising, for example, through therapy) should result in some change in the sexual pattern. Support for this view comes from Berelson and Steiner (1). In their inventory of scientific findings concerning human behavior, they say that

Changes toward a more positive attitude regarding sexual activity and toward freer, more enjoyable sexual activity than the patient was previously capable of having, are reported as correlates of psychotherapy from several camps (1, p. 290).

Graham (10) obtained information on the frequency and degree of satisfaction in coitus from 65 married men and women before they began psychotherapy. The data from these couples was compared with similar information from 142 married men and women who had been in treatment for varying periods of time. The results indicated, with certain reservations, that psychotherapy did free individuals for "more frequent and more satisfactory coitus experience." (10, p. 95)

Let us explore this logic from another side. If disorganized and aberrant sexual patterns are more frequent in adolescents or young adults who have experienced some form of emotional deprivation in childhood, it seems reasonable to hypothesize that those who had experienced normal emotional satisfactions should display more of what is considered conventional in their sexual practices. Since studies are more commonly done with persons who are recognized as problems, this possibility is not so well documented. There is, however, some evidence to support this view.

Loeb (18) in a study involving junior and senior high school youth, attempted to differentiate between boys and girls who do and do not participate in premarital intercourse. He advanced these conclusions:

First, teenagers who trust themselves and their ability to contribute to others and have learned to rely on others socially and emotionally are least likely to be involved in irresponsible sexual activity.

Second, teen-agers who have learned to be comfortable in their appropriate sex roles (boys who like being boys and wish to be men, and girls who like being girls and wish to be women) are least likely to be involved in activities leading to indiscriminate sexuality (18).

Maslow (19) in his study of self-actualized people makes several comments about the character of sexual functioning and sexual satisfaction in people who are considerably above the average so far as emotional health is concerned. He says:

. . . sex and love can be and most often are very perfectly fused with each other in (emotionally) healthy people . . . (19, p. 241).
. . . self-actualizing men and women tend on the whole not to seek sex for its own sake, or to be satisfied with it alone when it comes . . . (19, p. 242).
. . . sexual pleasures are found in their most intense and ecstatic perfection in self-actualizing people . . . (19, p. 242).

These people do not *need* sensuality; they simply enjoy it when it occurs (19, p. 243).

Maslow feels that the "we don't need it, but we enjoy it when we have it" attitude can be regarded as mature; though the self-actualized person enjoys sex more intensely than the average person, he considers sex less central in his total frame of reference.

Loeb's and Maslow's findings, then, suggest that responsible sexual behavior and satisfying interpersonal relations and personal development are closely related.

MULTIFARIOUS ASSOCIATIONS BETWEEN SEX AND INTERPERSONAL RELATIONSHIPS

The data which have emerged from various studies also make it clear that a tremendous range of factors can influence the quality of relationships which contain sexual expression; that these factors can and do change from time to time in the course of the relationship; and that almost an unlimited range of consequences can result.

Thus, one of the very important factors influencing the meaning of sex in a relationship is the degree of fondness which a couple have for one another. As previously noted, Kirkendall (15) in his study utilized a continuum of affectional involvement. He found that the character of motivation and communication, and the readiness of men to assume responsibility for the consequences of intercourse changed with the degree of emotional involvement. For example, as the length of elapsed time in a dating relationship prior to intercourse increased, there was an increase in the amount of communication devoted to understanding and a decrease in the amount of argumentative-persuasive communication. This finding parallels the findings of Ehrmann (7).

Maturity and developmental level represent still other factors. Broderick (2, 3) has made some interesting studies on the appearance and progressive development of various sexual manifestations with age. In a study of children in a suburban community he found that for many children interest in the opposite sex begins in kindergarten or before. Kissing "which means something special" is found among boys and girls as early as the third and fourth grades. In some communities dating begins for a substantial number of children in the fifth and sixth grades, while "going steady" is common at the junior high school level.

Schofield (24) also found that "those who start dating, kissing and inceptive behavior at an early age are also more likely to have early sexual intercourse." (24, p. 73) In an analysis of family backgrounds he also found that

. . . girls who got on very well with their fathers were far less likely to be sexually experienced. . . .
. . . boys who did not get on well with their mothers were more likely to be sexually experienced. . . .
. . . girls who got on well with their mothers were less likely to be sexually experienced . . . (24, p. 144).

Role concepts, which in turn may be influenced by other factors and conditions, influence the interplay between sexual behavior and interpersonal relationships. This association has already been noted in quoting some of Ehrmann's findings.

The interaction becomes extremely complex as role concepts, sexual standards, cultural changes, sheer biology, and still other factors all become involved in a single situation.

Reiss' work (20), especially his discussion of the interplay between role concepts and the double standard, makes this point most vividly. He shows clearly how adherence to the double standard conditions the individual's concept of his own role and the role of his sexual partners. Thus what the individual may conceive of as freely-willed and consciously-chosen be-havior is actually controlled by concepts deeply rooted in a long-existing cultural pattern.

The complexity is further emphasized as the origins of the double stan-dard are studied. Reiss sees the roots of the double standard as possibly existing in "man's muscular strength, muscular coordination and bone struc-ture. . . ." These "may have made him a better hunter than woman; it may have made him more adept at the use of weapons. Couple this hunt-ing skill with the fact that women would often be incapacitated due to pregnancy and childrearing, and we have the beginning of male monopoly of power." (20, p. 92)

Reiss feels that "The core of the double standard seems to involve the notion of female inferiority." (20, p. 192)

Once the double standard became embedded in the mores, however, cultural concepts reinforced it and helped embed it still more deeply. Now, however, cultural developments have begun to weaken the power of the double standard. The declining importance of the physical strength of the male in the modern economy; the ability to make reproduction a voluntary matter; emphasis on freedom, equality, and rationality—these and other forces have been eroding the power of the double standard, and in the process have been altering the association between sexual behavior and interpersonal relationships.

Shuttleworth (25) made an incisive critique of Kinsey's views on mas-culine-feminine differences in interest in sex as a function and as a physical experience. In the process, he advanced a theoretical position of his own which suggests that much role behavior is inherent in the biological struc-tures of the sexes. He argues that their respective biology disposes male and female to regard their sexual functioning differently. Males, for ex-ample, can experience the erotic pleasures of sex more easily and with less likelihood of negative repercussions than can females. This fact, then, has helped to formulate both male and female sex roles, the attitudes of men and women toward sex and themselves, and to condition their sexual be-havior. If this theoretical view can be established, it definitely has impli-cations for a better understanding of the kind of interpersonal behavior which can be expected to involve the sexes, and how it may develop.

Vincent's (29) study of unwed mothers helped demonstrate that a wide range of outcomes in interpersonal relationships can arise from the cir-cumstances of premarital pregnancy. The attitudes of unwed mothers ranged from those who found the pregnancy a humiliating and terrifying experience to those who found it maturing and satisfying, from those who rejected their child to those who found great satisfaction in having it, from those who rejected and hated the father to those who accepted him fully. When considering the interpersonal reactions of unwed mothers, no stereo-type is possible.

Sexual intercourse in our culture has been invested with so many meanings and such strong emotions have been tied to it that non-participation may have as many consequences for interpersonal relations as participation. Tebor (27) studied 100 virgin college males and found that a large proportion of them felt insecure about their virginity and pressured by their peers to obtain experience. At the same time significant adults—teachers and parents—were quite unaware of what sexual pattern these men were following, and provided them no support in their pattern of chastity.

REQUIREMENTS FOR RESEARCH ON THE RENAISSANCE

The theme of this article has been that a concern for interpersonal relationships as the central issue in the management of sexuality is displacing the traditional emphasis on the avoidance or renunciation of all non-marital sexual experience. Only as a shift of this sort occurs are we in any way justified in speaking of a sexual renaissance.

Some requirements, however, face social scientists who wish to understand this shift. We have four to suggest.

1. *It will be necessary to commit ourselves fully to the study of relationships rather than simply reflecting on them occasionally.* In the area of sex, concern has been over-focused on the physical acts of sex. Thus the senior author, while doing the research for his book, *Premarital Intercourse and Interpersonal Relationships*, became aware that he was giving undue attention to the act of premarital intercourse, even while trying to set it in an interpersonal relationship context. As a consequence, crucial data were ignored. For example, in selecting subjects, if one potential subject had engaged in much caressing and petting, but had renounced the opportunity for intercourse many times, while another possible subject had merely gone through the physical act of copulation a single time, the latter one was defined as a subject for the research and the first was by-passed as though he had engaged in no sexual nor any interpersonal behavior.

With this realization came a decision to do research on decisions made by individuals concerning sexual behavior, regardless of whether they had had intercourse. The result is a recently-completed preliminary study in which 131 non-randomly selected males were interviewed. (14) Of this group 72 (55 percent) had not had intercourse, but apparently only 17 (13 percent) had not been in a situation which required a decision. Eleven of these had made a firm decision against intercourse, quite apart from any decision-requiring situation, thus leaving only six who had never faced the issue of decision-making. In other words, when one thought of sexual decision-making as an aspect of interpersonal relationships, rather than continuing to focus on whether or not an act had occurred, one greatly increased the number who were potential subjects, and vastly increased the range of interpersonal behavior available for study.

We offer one further illustration of the reorientation in thinking necessary as we come to accept a concern for relationships as the central issue. The view which emphasizes the quality of interpersonal relationships as of foremost concern is often labelled as "very permissive" when sex standards and behavior are under discussion. This conclusion is possible when concern is focused solely on whether the commission of a sexual act is or is not acceptable. Certainly the emphasis on interpersonal relationships diverts attention from the act to the consequences. But having moved into this position, one finds himself in a situation which is anything but permissive. Relationships and their outcome seem to be governed by principles which are unvarying and which cannot be repealed. The fiat of parents or the edicts of deans can be softened, but there is no tempering of the consequences of dishonesty, lack of self-discipline, and lack of respect for the rights of others upon interpersonal relationships. If one wishes warm, accepting interpersonal relationships with others he will be defeated by these practices and no one, regardless of his position of authority can change this fact. Proclamations and injunction will be of no avail. There is no permissiveness here!

2. *Conceptual definitions of relationships will have to be developed.* Several social scientists have initiated work on this. For example, Foote and Cottrell (9) have identified six components of interpersonal competence—health, intelligence, sympathy, judgment, creativity and autonomy. Schultz (26) has developed his FIRO test to measure interpersonal behavior around three interpersonal needs—the needs for inclusion, control and affection. As has been noted, Kirkendall (15) centered his study around three components—motivation, communication and readiness to assume responsibility. Communication and motivation have both been frequently recognized aspects of interpersonal relationships.

However, the conceptualization of relationships in a manner which will permit effective research is still at an embryonic level. The numerous (for there are undoubtedly many) components of relationships have still to be determined, and methods and instruments for their measurement must be developed and perfected. Interpersonal relationships as a field of psychological study should be developing concurrently, for only in this way can we gain the needed broadening of our horizons.

3. *Methods and procedures will have to be devised which will enable us to study relationships.* The perceptive reader will have noted that while studies have been cited because, in our estimation, they bore on interpersonal relationships, all of them with the exception of that by Burgess and Wallin (4) obtained their information on interpersonal relationships by using individuals rather than pairs or groups as subjects. This is quite

limiting. Would we not get a different view of premarital intercourse if we could interview both partners to the experience rather than one?

Methods of dealing with couples and groups, and research procedures which can zero in on that subtle, intangible, yet real tie which binds two or more people in an association are needed. Some work has already been done in this direction, but it has not been applied to sex and interpersonal relationships.

4. *The isolation of the most important problems for research is a requirement for progress.* Opinions would naturally differ in regard to what these problems are. We would suggest, however, that since sex relationships *are* interpersonal relationships, the whole field of interpersonal relationships with sex as an integral part needs to be attacked.

Kirkendall (15) has suggestions for further research scattered throughout his book. He suggests such problems as an exploration of the importance of time spent and emotional involvement in a relationship as a factor in determining whether a relationship can sustain intercourse, the factors which produce "loss of respect" when sexual involvement occurs, the meaning of sexual non-involvement for a relationship, factors which impede or facilitate sexual communication, and the relation of knowledge of various kinds of success or failure in sexual relationships.

His study poses many questions which merit answering. How do the emotional involvements of male and female engaged in a sexual relationship differ, and how do they change as the relationship becomes more (or less) intense? How nearly alike, or how diverse, are the perceptions which male and female hold of the total relationship and of its sexual component at various stages in its development? How does the rejection of a proffered sexual relationship by either partner affect the one who extended the offer? And what are the reactions and what produced them in the person receiving it? If there are no sexual overtures, how does this affect relationships?

Which value systems make it most (and least) possible for a couple to communicate about sex? To adjust to tensions which may accompany intercourse or its cessation? Which enable a couple to cope most effectively to the possible traumas of having their relationship become public knowledge, or of pregnancy?

In what diverse ways do premarital sexual experiences affect marital adjustments? What enables some couples who have been premarital sexual partners to separate as friends? Why do others separate with bitterness and hostility? What relation has maturity in other aspects of life to maturity in assessing the meaning of and coping with sexual manifestations of various kinds in the premarital period?

The questions could go on endlessly, yet the isolation of important areas for research remains one of the important tasks before us.

REFERENCES

1. BERELSON, BERNARD and STEINER, GARY A. *Human Behavior.* New York: Harcourt, Brace & World, 1964.

2. BRODERICK, CARLFRED B. *Socio-Sexual Development in a Suburban Community.* University Park: Pennsylvania State University. Unpublished manuscript (mimeographed) 1963.

3. BRODERICK, CARLFRED B. and FOWLER, S. E. "New Patterns of Relationships between the Sexes among Preadolescents." *Marriage and Family Living,* 1961, 23, 27–30.

4. BURGESS, ERNEST W. and WALLIN, PAUL. *Engagement and Marriage.* Philadelphia: J. B. Lippincott, 1953.

5. CALDERONE, MARY. *Release from Sexual Tensions.* New York: Random House, 1960.

6. COX, HARVEY. *The Secular City* (Rev. ed.) New York: Macmillan, 1966.

7. EHRMANN, WINSTON. *Premarital Dating Behavior.* New York: Henry Holt, 1959.

8. ELLIS, ALBERT and SAGARIN, EDWARD. *Nymphomania.* New York: Julian Messner, 1964.

9. FOOTE, NELSON and COTTRELL, LEONARD S., JR. *Identity and Interpersonal Competence.* Chicago: University of Chicago Press, 1955.

10. GRAHAM, STANLEY R. "The Effects of Psychoanalytically Oriented Psychotherapy on Levels of Frequency and Satisfaction in Sexual Activity." *Journal of Clinical Psychology,* 1960, 16, 94–8.

11. GREENWALD, HAROLD. *The Call Girl,* New York: Ballantine Books, 1958.

12. KINSEY, ALFRED C., et al. *Sexual Behavior in the Human Female.* Philadelphia: W. B. Saunders, 1953.

13. KINSEY, ALFRED C., et al. *Sexual Behavior in the Human Male.* Philadelphia: Saunders, 1948.

14. KIRKENDALL, LESTER A. "Characteristics of Sexual Decision-Making." To be published in *The Journal of Sex Research.*

15. KIRKENDALL, LESTER A. *Premarital Intercourse and Interpersonal Relationships.* New York: Julian Press, 1961.

16. KIRKENDALL, LESTER A. and OGG, ELIZABETH. *Sex and Our Society.* New York: Public Affairs Committee, 1964, No. 366.

17. LION, ERNEST G., et al. *An Experiment in the Psychiatric Treatment of Promiscuous Girls.* San Francisco: City and County of San Francisco, Department of Public Health, 1945.

18. LOEB, MARTIN B. "Social Role and Sexual Identity in Adolescent Males," *Casework Papers.* New York: National Association of Social Workers, 1959.

19. MASLOW, ABRAHAM. *Motivation and Personality.* New York: Harpers, 1954.

20. REISS, IRA L. *Premarital Sexual Standards in America.* Glencoe, Ill.: The Free Press, 1960.

21. RHYMES, DOUGLAS. *No New Morality.* Indianapolis: Bobbs-Merrill, 1964, p. 25.

22. ROBINSON, JOHN A. T. *Honest to God.* Philadelphia: Westminster Press, 1963, p. 118.

23. SAFIR, BENNO, M.D. *A Psychiatric Approach to the Treatment of Promiscuity.* New York: American Social Hygiene Association, 1949.

24. SCHOFIELD, MICHAEL. *The Sexual Behavior of Young People.* London: Longmans, Green, 1965.

25. SHUTTLEWORTH, FRANK. "A Biosocial and Developmental Theory of Male and Female Sexuality." *Marriage and Family Living,* 1960, 21, 163–70.

26. SCHUTZ, WILLIAM C. *FIRO: A Three-Dimensional Theory of Interpersonal Behavior.* New York: Rinehart, 1958.

27. TEBOR, IRVING. "Selected Attributes, Interpersonal Relationships and Aspects of Psychosexual Behavior of One Hundred College Freshmen, Virgin Men." Unpublished Ph.D. Thesis, Oregon State College, 1957.

28. VAN DE VELDE, THEODORE H. *Ideal Marriage.* New York: Random House, 1926.

29. VINCENT, CLARK E. *Unmarried Mothers.* New York: Free Press of Glencoe, 1961.

22

Trial marriage:
Harnessing the trend
constructively[*]

MIRIAM E. BERGER

ANTHROPOLOGICAL AND HISTORICAL SURVEY

Trial marriage has been practiced among the Peruvian Indians of Vicos in the Andes for more than four centuries. (Price, 1965; MacLean, 1941) Arranged by the parents in the earlier form, the purpose was to test the girl's work abilities and the couple's general compatibility. In modern Vicos there is a free choice of marriage partners with romantic love playing an important role, but men still seek responsible, hardworking girls who have mastered household skills and can help in the fields. Study of couples who entered a trial marriage for the first time indicated that the average duration of such trials was less than fifteen months and that 83 percent of the relationships were finalized with marriage. There was no stigma if the couple had children, but did not marry. Permanent separations after marriage were rare, occurring in two to three percent of the cases. One of the advantages of these trial marriages noted by Price was the ease of transition from adolescence to adulthood. The couple acquired certain social and sexual advantages of adulthood without assuming full responsibility.

[*] From *The Family Coordinator* (January 1971), pp. 38–43. Reprinted by permission of the author and the National Council on Family Relations.

The Trobrianders had a "bachelor's house" in which courting couples slept together and had exclusive sex prior to marriage. In contrast to Western civilization, before marriage Trobriand couples were not permitted to eat together or share any interests, except sex. (Malinowski, 1929)

In the eighteenth century, Maurice of Saxony, illegitimate son of the Elector Augustus the Strong and Countess Aurora of Konigsmark, sought a solution to the marriage problem. He recommended temporary marriages, contracted for a limited time. If the partners agreed, the contract could be prolonged, but marriage for life was a "betrayal of the self, an unnatural compulsion." (Lewinsohn, 1956)

"Bundling" originated in Europe and was brought to the New World in the eighteenth century. In New England, where it was too cold to sit up late, courting couples were permitted, with parental approval, to get into bed with their clothes on. Some bundling experiences were probably innocent, especially when they included a center-board for the bed (Marriage Museum), but "certainly many got sexually involved and married when conception occurred." (Scott, 1960; Fielding, 1961)

"Trial nights," an old Teutonic custom, (Marriage Museum) is still practiced today in Staphorts, Holland, an insular, inbred town whose customs have for centuries sealed them off from contemporary life. The swain spends three nights a week with his girl friend, with the knowledge of her parents who hope she will prove fertile. Until she becomes pregnant, there can be no marriage. If she is barren, the community regards her with primitive suspicion and contempt. Once she is pregnant, however, the marriage must take place. (Gibney, 1948)

TWENTIETH CENTURY AMERICA

The first American to propose trial marriage as a concept was Judge Ben B. Lindsay (1927). Bertrand Russell who was then teaching in New York, approved of Lindsay's Companionate Marriage, but felt it did not go far enough. Russell favored trial marriage for university students and believed that work and sex were more easily combined "in a quasi-permanent relationship, than in the scramble and excitement of parties and drunken orgies" that were prevalent during the Prohibition Era. Russell felt that if a man and woman chose to live together without having children, it was no one's business but their own. He believed it undesirable for a couple to marry for the purpose of raising a family without first having had sexual experience. (Russell, 1929)

Lindsay and Russell were ostracized, and the concept of trial marriage lay dormant until an evolving sexual morality led anthropologist Margaret Mead to revive it (Mead, 1966). Building on Lindsay's Companionate Marriage, she recommended a two-step marriage: *individual,* in which there would be a simple ceremony, limited economic responsibilities, easy divorce, if desired, and no children; and *parental marriage,* which would be entered into as a second step by couples who were ready to undertake the lifetime obligations of parenthood, would be more difficult to enter into and break off, and would entail mutual continuing responsibility for any children. Her rationale was that sex, now considered a normal need in youth, often drove them into premature and early marriage, frequently leading to unhappiness and divorce. She made the plea that divorce be granted before children are conceived, so that only wanted children of stable marriages are brought into the world. Responses to Dr. Mead's proposal, (Mead, 1968) ranged from disapproval for tampering with tradition (instead of helping couples adjust to traditional marriage) to complaints from students for setting up too much structure. A typical student response was: "Why get married? Why can't we live together, with a full sex life, with no pregnancy, until we're ready to get married and have children?"

Margaret Mead's two-step marriage was elaborated on by Michael Scriven, a philosophy professor, who proposed a three-step plan:

We try to make one institution achieve three aims, which all too often lie in perpendicular dimensions. The aims are sexual satisfaction, social security and sensible spawning. The solution would be to create three types of marriage arranged so that any combination is possible: preliminary, personal and parental marriage. The first would simply be legitimized cohabitation, contractually insulated against escalation into "de facto" commitment. It would be a prerequisite for other kinds and would impose a period of a year's trial relationships before the possibility of conversion to personal marriage. . . . (Scriven, 1967) [Reprinted by permission of the author and Phi Delta Kappa Publications.]

In *The Sexual Wilderness,* Vance Packard (1968) concluded that the first two years of marriage are the most difficult. He recommended a two-year confirmation period, after which the marriage would become final or would be dissolved. Packard felt that this proposal differed from trial marriage because the couple would marry in earnest and with the hope that the marriage would be permanent. He saw trial marriage as highly tentative and little more than unstructured cohabitation. Packard's concept is based on his conviction that the expectation of permanency contributes to success in that it motivates a couple to work hard to adapting, and is, in fact, a strong stabilizing and reinforcing factor.

In "Marriage as a Statutory Five Year Renewable Contract," Virginia Satir, family therapist, said:

Maybe there needs to be something like an apprentice period . . . in which potential partners have a chance to explore deeply and experiment with their relationship, experience the other and find out whether his fantasy matched the reality. Was it really possible through daily living to have a process in which each was able to enhance the growth of the other, while at the same time enhancing his own? What is it like to have to undertake joint ventures and to be with each other every day? It would seem that in this socially approved context, the chances of greater realness and authenticity continuing would be increased, and the relationship would deepen, since it started on a reality base. (1967) [Reprinted by permission of the author.]

Another variation of the renewable contract concept was proposed by Mervyn Cadwallader, a sociology professor, in "Marriage as a Wretched Institution:"

Marriage was not designed to bear the burdens now being asked of it by the urban American middle class. It was an institution that evolved over centuries to meet some very specific needs of a non-industrial society . . . Marriage was not designed as a mechanism for providing friendship, erotic experience, romantic love, personal fulfillment, continuous lay psychotherapy, or recreation. Its purposes . . . have changed radically, yet we cling desperately to the outmoded structures of the past . . . The basic structure of Western marriage is never questioned, alternatives are not proposed or discussed . . . Why not permit a flexible contract, for one or more years, with periodic options to renew? If a couple grew disenchanted with their life together, they would not feel trapped for life . . . They would not have to go through the destructive agonies of divorce, and carry about the stigma of marital failure, like the mark of Cain on their foreheads. Instead of a declaration of war, they could simply let their contracts lapse and while still friendly, be free to continue their romantic quest . . . What of the children in a society that is moving inexorably toward consecutive, plural marriages? . . . If the bitter and poisonous denouement of divorce could be avoided by a frank acceptance of short-term marriages, both adults and children would benefit. Any time spouses treat each other decently, generously, and respectfully, their children will benefit. (Cadwallader, 1966) [Reprinted by permission of the author and publisher. Copyright © 1966, by The Atlantic Monthly Company, Boston, Mass.]

Today many young people have carried the concept of trial marriage a step further, as Bertrand Russell advocated, by living with a roommate of the opposite sex. Sociologist Robert N. Whitehurst coined a word to describe them, "unmalias," a condensation of unmarried liaisons. (1969) Whitehurst mentions some of the problems encountered by students who have an "experimental semester of living together, such as when a male senior must leave the campus for graduate school, job, or military service." (1969)

The Harrad Experiment (Rimmer, 1966) incorporated some of the above mentioned ideas on trial marriage and added some new dimensions. In Rimmer's novel, college students lived with computer-selected roommates of the opposite sex. Unlike the informal arrangements now made by college students on their own, (Karlen, 1969; Life, 1968) the Harrad Experiment was controlled and guided by the Tenhausens, a husband-and-wife team of sociologist and marriage counselor. The novel focused on several couples who married after four years of living together. The students attended various neighboring colleges, but roomed at Harrad during the four years, and were required to take a course in human values at Harrad taught by the Tenhausens and to do required reading in the subjects of marriage, love, sex, contraception, moral values, philosophy, etc. Whenever the students were troubled about their relationships, the Tenhausens were available for consultation. There was also considerable peer support through endless discussions of common problems. Rimmer favored a structured, socially approved form of premarital experimentation that would give the male and female an opportunity to realize themselves fully, without guilt, and to adjust to their new marital roles without legal entanglement, recognizing marriage as the commitment a couple makes to society when they decide to have children. (1969) Accused of trying to undermine America's family structure Rimmer asserted that, on the contrary, he believed a strong family, to be a *sine qua non* of social existence and that his proposals would strengthen and preserve that structure.

In an article in *The Humanist* (1970) Rustum and Della Roy discussed alternatives to traditional marriage in view of the increasing divorce rate:

By one simple swish of tradition, we can incorporate all the recent suggestions for trial marriage . . . and cover them all under the decent rug of the "engagement"—engagements with minor differences—that in today's society, they entitle a couple to live together, but not to have children . . . By no means need this become the universal norm.

NCFR WORKSHOP

A workshop led by the author was conducted at the annual meeting of the National Council on Family Relations in 1969. The participants were primarily college instructors of marriage and family courses, but included a social worker, a clergyman, a sociologist, and a college counselor of students. The following is a summary of the highlights of the workshop:

It was agreed that there ought to be alternative methods of courtship, approved by society, that would serve as a better preparation for marriage than dating. Those opposed to trial marriage as one such alternative felt it was not the same as a real marriage and therefore not a valid preparation for marriage. It was also subject to exploitation and abuse, as was any method of courtship, and was more to the interest of the male than the female, who is likely to be more concerned about security. Opponents also pointed out that it takes a great deal of maturity to make a relationship work, and if a couple are not mature enough to marry, they may not be mature enough to end a relationship when indicated, nor to cope with the attendant rejection, not to mention accidental pregnancy, or a partner who flits from one relationship to another.

Those who favored trial marriage felt it should be morally sanctioned by society as an optional alternative.

CLERICAL ATTITUDES

Although many clergymen disapprove of trial marriage, there have been some notable exceptions. Typical of the negative opinion is that of Dean John Coburn of the Episcopal Theological School, Massachusetts:

How can two people trust one another on a temporary basis? Marriage is a total commitment, and trial marriage is a contradiction in terms. (Eddy, 1968)

On the other hand, a Unitarian minister, Robert M. Eddy (1968), regarding the casual promiscuity and resulting unwanted children as tragic developments of the "new morality," offered the following alternatives:

(1) that parents continue the financial support of their college-attending children who are having companionate marriages

(2) that it be illegal for youngsters under the age of seventeen to conceive; that seventeen to nineteen year olds, after obtaining parental consent, might live together with the privileges and responsibilities of the relationship defined by a contract as detailed or loose as the parents would desire. Such a relationship could be solemnized by a rite similar to the wedding ceremony and could be ended by mutual consent, as long as the couple did not have children. The next type of cohabitation agreement essentially would be identical to the present marriage relationship, but under the new system, would be limited to adults and would be, in effect, a license to raise children. [Reprinted by permission of the publisher and author.]

HARNESSING THE TREND CONSTRUCTIVELY

Whether one's professional or religious beliefs lead to a view of trial marriage as conservative or radical, acceptable or sinful, a valid or non-valid preparation for marriage, there may be a need to recognize that trial marriage and its variations are being practiced by some young people. (Eddy, 1968; Karlen, 1969; Life, 1969; Whitehurst, 1969) As a marriage counselor and emotional health consultant, the author proposes a service that would guide and serve young people who do venture into trial marriage, legal or otherwise, so that they learn from their experiences, rather than stumble blindly from one relationship to another. It is recommended that they assess the experience with a consultant, exploring, individually or in a group, some of the following:

What did I learn about myself from this experience? How did I adjust to living with a peer, as distinguished from living with parents and siblings, or alone? What have the problems of adjustment been? Would I have the same problems with another roommate or spouse? How much did I contribute to these problems and how much was the responsibility of the partner? What neurotic games did we play? What hangups did I bring to the relationship that were reinforced by our interaction? What kind of person do I need to live with, dominant, submissive, detached, involved, affectionate, etc? What was our style of communication, constructive, (Gordon, 1968) silent treatment, hitting below the belt? (Bach, 1968) How effectively do I communicate my needs and feelings? How did our communication problems affect our sexual adjustment? On the assumption that personal happiness is achieved through satisfying closeness to another human being, what problems did I have in achieving and maintaining that closeness?

The author would like to see colleges take the leadership by providing emotional health consultants for the preventive service described above, in addition to the usual counseling services. To encourage college students to avail themselves of the service, its use is recommended as a preventive mental health measure, e.g., at the end of each year when living arrangements are likely to be changed, when students finish the first year in a dormitory, whether single-sex or coed dorm, the second and third years with a roommate of the same sex, and whatever the arrangement is for the fourth year. Once accustomed to using the service and finding the consultant understanding, nonjudgmental, and helpful in developing insight, the student is more likely to use the service to discuss any relationships with the opposite sex. Periodic check-ups would give the consultant a chance to know a student and to provide direction and guidance. When a student is ready to marry his current partner or someone else, his selection of a mate will have greater sophistication and insight, or he may be motivated if he had repeated adjustment problems with successive roommates, to obtain counseling. (Kardiner, 1970) If colleges initiated such a preventive service, it would, in time, become acceptable for noncollegians. In urban centers where many young people live away from their families, the service is available through the facilities of "Check-Up" for Emotional Health; it could also be available in community settings, such as family agencies, premarital counseling services, Y's, community mental health centers, and religious organizations.

RESEARCH INDICATIONS

One critical issue is whether trial marriage is a valid test and preparation for marriage. Some probably know of couples for whom trial marriage culminated in a satisfactory legal marriage. Nevertheless, the following case studies raise questions about the validity of trial marriage as a test:

Sue, age 24, was referred for psychotherapy because of severe anxiety symptoms that had their onset immediately after marriage. She had lived with her husband six months prior to marriage, during which phase she had been relaxed, her real self, and not unduly concerned over the success of the relationship. Exploration revealed that Sue was so anxious for the marriage to succeed that she was repressing all negative feelings, and denying her identity in an effort to fulfill her image of a good wife. Now she was afraid of becoming as aggressive, argumentative, and opinionated as she had been as a teenager.

Ada, age 22, came for psychotherapy because of severe obsessional symptoms. Since her marriage two years earlier, she had been frigid. She had lived with her husband weekends for one year prior to marriage, during which phase she had experienced orgasm. The source of conflict revealed in the exploration was that after marriage she felt her husband was too demanding sexually, that he valued her only for sex, which made it demeaning to her, and that she found it difficult to limit him. She had transferred her excessive need to have her parent's approval to having her husband's approval, resolving the conflict by denying her resentment and thereby becoming frigid and obsessional.

Sue's and Ada's trial marriages were not deliberate tests; both had drifted into their living-together experiences. Perhaps, when the trial marriage is deliberate, similar anxieties would occur before, rather than after the permanent marriage. Was it just that trial marriage was not a valid test for these women with neurotic personalities? It is only the troubled who come to the attention of the professional. Study of the marriages of a large sample of couples who first had trial marriages might provide more reliable information upon which to base a conclusion. In planning the research design, it would be necessary: (1) to distinguish between deliberate trials and unstructured cohabitation that happened to result in permanency; and (2) to explore whether motivation to adapt (Parkard, 1968; Lederer and Jackson, 1968) differed during the trial and in permanency.

REFERENCES

BACH, GEORGE and WYDEN, PETER. *Intimate Enemy.* New York: W. Morrow and Company, 1968.

CADWALLADER, MERVYN. "Marriage as a Wretched Institution," *Atlantic Monthly,* 1966, 218 (5), 62–6.

EDDY, ROBERT M. "Should We Change Our Sex Laws?" *The Register-Leader,* March 1966, Detroit, Michigan.

EDDY, ROBERT M. "Why We Must Allow Sexual Freedom for Teens," *Pageant,* September, 1968, 118–29.

FIELDING, WM. J. *Strange Customs of Courtship and Marriage,* London: Souvenir Press, 1961.

GIBNEY, FRANK. "The Strange Ways of Staphorst," *Life,* September 27, 1948, 2–8.

GORDON, THOMAS. *Parent Effectiveness Training.* 110 South Euclid Avenue, Pasadena, California.

KARDINER, SHELDON H. "Convergent Internal Security Systems—A Rationale for Marital Therapy," *Family Process,* 1970, 9(1), 83–91.

KARLEN, ARNO. "The Unmarried Marrieds on Campus," *New York Times Magazine,* January 26, 1969, 29–30.

LEDERER, WM. J. and JACKSON, DON D. *The Mirages of Marriage.* New York: W. W. Norton and Company, 1968, Ch. 21–3.

LINDSEY, BEN B. "The Companionate Marriage," *Redbook,* October 1926; March 1927.

LEWINSOHN, RICHARD. *The History of Sexual Customs,* New York: Harper Brothers, 1958. Original edition in German, 1956, translated by Alexander Mayce.

MACLEAN, R. "Trial Marriage Among the Peruvian Aborigines," *Mexican Sociology,* 1941, 1, 25–33, in Spanish.

MALINOWSKI, BRONISLAW. *The Sexual Life of Savages.* London: Geo. Routledge and Sons, 1929.

MARRIAGE MUSEUM, formerly located at 1991 Broadway, New York, N. Y.

MEAD, MARGARET. "Marriage in Two Steps." *Redbook,* 1966, 127, 48–9.

MEAD, MARGARET. "A Continuing Dialogue on Marriage," *Redbook,* 1968, 130, 44.

PACKARD, VANCE. *The Sexual Wilderness.* New York: David McKay Company, 1968, 466–68.

PRICE, RICHARD. "Trial Marriage in the Andes," *Ethnology,* 1965, 4, 310–22.

RIMMER, ROBERT H. *The Harrad Experiment.* Los Angeles: Sherbourne Press; 1966.

RIMMER, ROBERT H. *The Harrad Letters.* New York: New American Library, Signet Book No. 4037.

RUSTUM, ROY and RUSTUM, DELLA. "Is Monogomy Outdated?" *The Humanist,* 1970, 30 (2), 24.

RUSSELL, BERTRAND. *Marriage and Morals.* New York: Liveright Publishing Company, 1929.

SATIR, VIRGINIA. "Marriage as a Statutory Five Year Renewable Contract." Paper presented at the American Psychological Association 75th Annual Convention, Washington, D.C., September 1, 1967. Copy available from author, P.O. Box 15248, San Francisco, Calif. 94115.

SCOTT, GEORGE RYLEY. *Marriage—An Inquiry Relating to all Races and Nations from Antiquity to Present Day.* New York: Key Publishing Company, 1960.

SCRIVEN, MICHAEL. "Putting the Sex Back into Sex Education," *Phi Delta* 1968, 49 (9), based on a paper given at a Notre Dame University Conference on "The Role of Women," Fall, 1967.

WHITEHURST, ROBERT. "The Unmalias on Campus," presented at NCFR Annual Meeting, 1969. Copy available from author, University of Windsor, Windsor, Ontario, Canada.

WHITEHURST, ROBERT. "The Double Standard and Male Dominance in Non-Marital Living Arrangements: A Preliminary Statement," paper presented at the American Orthopsychiatric Association Meeting, New York, 1969. Copy available from author, University of Windsor, Windsor, Ontario, Canada.

part IV

Possible future trends

All of the articles in this part of the book deal with the increasing search for freedom of action, dissatisfaction with the traditional way of life, and the attempt to reach goals which may or may not be those of present society. The outcomes are not easily predictable. The ways of life which are described may fall into disuse, the problems which are outlined may cease to be problems. In some cases, reported attitudes, behaviors, and legal actions may point the way for future change and acceptance of diverse patterns of sexual behavior. In other instances, they may become only past history, phases through which specific sub-groups in society have passed. Whatever the outcomes, it appears that a variety of solutions is being sought for the problems encountered by diverse groups.

Most researchers would agree that the interpersonal goals of youth—jobs, homes, and families—are unchanged. However, attaining these goals is not so simple. Specific definitions of these three goals and the means used to reach them are complicated and varied, depending upon the underlying value system or ethic of the individual. This may be completely alien to adults and misunderstood by them.

In the introductory article, Reading 23, Edward A. Suchman relates the "hang-loose" ethic to the spirit of drug abuse. This ethic is characterized by repudiation and questioning of the "Establishment" and by irreverence, and could be expected to influence sexual behavior also. Some recent research supports the hypothesis that drug use is related to sexual be-

289

havior. On one college campus, Goode[1] found that drug users were significantly more likely to engage in sexual intercourse, to engage in it earlier in life, and to engage in it regularly and with a greater variety of partners than non-drug users. He hypothesizes that drug use and sexual behavior are both components of a particular college subculture which is characterized by liberal political views, isolation from agents of social change, dissatisfaction with and alienation from traditional academic life.

Suchman's article opens many questions for discussion on the future trends and implications of both the "hang-loose" ethic and drug use and abuse. One might predict that both the ethic and the use of drugs will survive and persist to some extent, but not necessarily in conjunction. It may be that, for the college student of today, drugs will become what alcohol is for the adult. If so, the factors which influence drug usage could be expected to be many and varied.

In the introduction to this part of the book, it was stated that individuals still have as basic goals, jobs, homes, and families. For some individuals, the family may consist of two persons of the same sex, and this group composition represents one segment of the American society, whether or not one chooses to recognize it as such. The statement has been made that "there is no such thing as a happy, well-adjusted homosexual." In Reading 24, Peter M. Miller and his colleagues present a review of research on homosexuality, covering the years from 1960 to 1966. Their review indicates that this statement can be questioned. In an era when there is more open admission of homosexual preference among adults than ever before, information about this specific sub-group is greatly needed if it is to be understood and accepted.

The next two articles, one on abortion (Reading 25) and the other on venereal disease (Reading 26) are relevant because of the increasing incidence of both, and because of the necessity for decision making; in the first instance (abortion), in terms of attitudes, values, and perhaps behavior; in the second case (venereal disease), whether to seek help and give assistance in locating contacts, or to neglect the problem.

Ruth Roemer's article presents the legal perspective on the controversial issue of abortion. Her excellent overview of the international scene in relation to abortion laws indicates the direction in which we can expect to move in the future. Her presentation of the varied circumstances under which abortion is considered legal, provides a framework for discussion.

Already the implications of the more liberal abortion laws for those involved are under study. To date, reports indicate that adverse psychological effects are suffered primarily by those who have psychological problems previous to the abortion. At this time, no cause and effect relation-

[1] Erich Goode, "Drug Use and Sexual Activity on a College Campus," *American Journal of Psychiatry*, 128:10 (April 1972), 92–95.

ship can be posited. An additional aspect currently under study is the effect upon the unwanted child if abortion is denied the mother who requests it. Professionals in family health services hope that the increasing reliability, availability, and acceptance of methods of contraception will, as Roemer has suggested, provide one answer to the abortion question.[2]

Reading 26 deals with a nagging problem, venereal disease,[3] which continues to flare up time after time. The problem is currently one of both control and prevention. There are experts who anticipate that an upswing in the incidence of venereal disease will accompany the wide-spread use of birth control techniques and the growing sexual permissiveness. Whatever the epidemiology of the disease, we can be sure that it is closely related to sexual activity, and thus will always be of concern until such time as medical science can discover the infallible preventative, for man will not easily be deprived of sexual activity. In this report, prevention and control are emphasized, because the stigma attached to venereal diseases has for long resulted in lack of communication about contacts, thus hindering identification and control. Of course, for the young person, an additional factor in his failure to identify sexual contacts has to do with the accompanying implications of permissiveness and promiscuity, which likewise are condemned by society.

To some observers it appears that only the rebellious youth subcultures and a few psychologically disturbed adults are bucking tradition and changing their life styles. However, this is not an accurate picture. The rapidly changing technological society has forced most individuals, both male and female, married and single to adapt and to formulate patterns of living which differ, somewhat, from those of previous generations. Perhaps this statement is more applicable to women than to men. For example, evidence is mounting to indicate that the traditional life style for women of all ages is rapidly changing. The Women's Bureau of the U.S. Department of Labor highlights the changing pattern of women's lives as follows: "Today, the life expectancy of a baby girl is 74 years. In 1920, it was 55 years. Today, there are 78 girls graduating from high school for every 100 girls 17 years old in the population. In 1920, there were two. Today, 43 percent of all women are in the labor force. In 1920, only 23 percent were workers. Today, the average woman is married and 39 years old. In 1920,

---

[2] Neither contraception nor illegitimacy has been included in this book, since information on the former is readily available from Planned Parenthood organizations, and while the unmarried parent can be a social problem, this is not necessarily so. Moreover, much of the research on illegitimacy applies to non-college student subjects, and in addition, was conducted before the liberalization of attitudes toward contraception and abortion. One might logically anticipate a decrease in the problem of illegitimacy among college students.

[3] Free films and informational materials can be obtained from the U.S. Department of Health, Education, and Welfare, Venereal Disease Branch, Atlanta, Georgia.

she was single and 28."[4] They predict that by 1980 there will be about 36 million women in the labor force.

Accompanying the influx of women into the labor force has been the demand for equality of opportunity and pay. This demand for equality for members of both sexes has spread from the office to the home (with increased expectations that the male will share in household responsibilities) and inevitably to the bedroom, where both the male and the female feel obligated to give and take comparable and equal sexual experience and satisfaction.

Alice S. Rossi points out that the most significant changes in family structure in the past 50 years have been the shift from the city to the suburbs and the decrease in the proportion of the individual woman's lifespan spent in bearing and raising children.[5] Two other developments have caused even stable, settled, middle-class individuals to question their life styles. The first is the publication of various materials on human sexual response which emphasize both variety and innovation in sexual activity and the normalcy of sexual pleasure and gratification. The second influence has been the development of the Human Potentialities Movement with Growth Centers similar to the Esalen Institute, which offers ongoing group experiences, weekend marathons, and seminars designed to help individuals to become sensitive, open and self-actualized.

All these changes have resulted in an increasing number of dissatisfied individuals, bored with marriage and the marriage partner, desirous of change and more excitement. For an increasing number, divorce is the solution. Others are not sufficiently dissatisfied with the relationship to go through the bothersome proceedings involved in divorce. Some suspect that probably another mate would not prove more satisfactory overall than the present one. Some are actually quite comfortable in the present marriage except for a lingering suspicion that something is missing in the sexual relationship. For these individuals, other solutions of a temporary nature are sought.

One of these solutions, "Swinging," bears some resemblance to old-fashioned wife-swapping. Swinging is a type of non-permanent, group-oriented, extra-marital relationship which is purported to enhance the marriage rather than to detract from it. One slogan exemplifying this value is, "The couple that swings together, clings together!"

In Reading 27, Charles and Rebecca Palson give an account of their observations on this activity and suggest some interesting possible relationships between this phenomenon and the state of the national economy.

---

[4] Women's Bureau, U.S. Department of Labor, *Changing Patterns of Women's Lives* (Washington 1970).

[5] Alice S. Rossi, "Family Development in a Changing World," *American Journal of Psychiatry*, 128:9 (March 1972), 47–56.

In the final article, Janet Giele anticipates some ways in which traditional family roles will change with the movement toward equality in women's status in sexual relationships.

Where, then, do we stand in the 1970s? Which are the influences that will shape our sexual behavior? What are the possibilities, the problems, the potential?

In a changing world, there are no certain, sure answers. However, social scientists are not without hope for a happy sexual future, whether this be within the traditional framework of marriage and the family as we presently know it, or in some modified form. For the thoughtful and concerned reader, selections in this part of the book provide a basis for discussion, and perhaps also for decision or action.

23
The "hang-loose" ethic and the spirit of drug use*

EDWARD A. SUCHMAN

Studies of college students made about fifteen years ago found that generation of youth to be "politically disinterested, apathetic, and conservative" (1, p. 199; 2). To an increasing degree, the college student of the current generation is striving to overcome this image of passive conformity and conservatism in order to evolve a new and more meaningful role for himself, both on campus and in the larger community. Reflecting the many social, political, and economic forces that have widened the generational gap between young people and those "over thirty," this youth movement is seeking to develop new values and behavior patterns, often in defiance and opposition to those of the established order.

Central to this new world of youth is a whole new range of recreational and psychedelic drugs. Studies of college students in the last generation found alcohol to be the major campus "vice" and alarming reports were published about the "drinking problem of college students" (3). No mention was made of other drugs. In this respect, the students, displayed one more sign of their conformity—drinking was also the favorite social pastime, and problem, of their parents. Almost as if rejection of the establishment also demanded the development of a different form of "high," the new generation of college students is increasingly turning to other drugs

* Note: Reprinted with permission of The American Sociological Association from *Journal of Health and Social Behavior*, 9(2):146–55, 1968.

for the relaxation and "kicks" their parents found in alcohol. As described by Simmons and Winograd (4, p. 86). "The drug scene is the central plaza of happening America . . . it is here, in the drug scene that generational change in America most vividly thrust itself forward. . . ." And perhaps forgetting their own bouts with the law in the days of prohibition and repressing the serious threat of alcoholism as a major health problem today (5, 6), adults have been almost unanimous in their condemnation of the new and strange intoxicant. As one "over thirty" judge recently opined, alcohol is the socially approved drug of choice for the well-adjusted, responsible, hard-working member of society seeking sociability and pleasant relaxation, while the use of marijuana represents the neurotic and antisocial behavior of the juvenile delinquent.

Unfortunately, there is little empirical data about what is taking place in the colleges today. The present study represents an initial attempt to ascertain basic facts about the use of drugs by one college population and to examine those factors, both causes and consequences, associated with the use of drugs. The major assumption is that drug use on the campuses today is largely limited to the occasional smoking of marijuana cigarettes and represents a social form of recreation far removed in nature from the traditional problem of narcotics addiction and, for that matter, alcoholism (7). Furthermore, the set of hypotheses to be tested is that the use of marijuana will be highly associated with other expressions of a new breed of youth characterized by a "hang-loose" ethic. As described by Simmons and Winograd (4, p. 12). "One of the fundamental characteristics of the hang-loose ethic is that it is irreverent. It repudiates, or at least questions, such cornerstones of conventional society as Christianity, 'my country right or wrong,' the sanctity of marriage and premarital chastity, civil disobedience, the accumulation of wealth, the right and even competence of parents, the schools, and the government to head and make decisions for everyone—in sum, the Establishment."

METHOD OF PROCEDURE

This study was conducted in November 1967, at a West Coast university. A representative sample of 600 students out of a student body of 12,200 was selected at random from the registration lists of undergraduate and graduate students. A questionnaire dealing with drug use and various aspects of college life, educational and political values, and current social issues was prepared on the basis of detailed interviews of students, especially so-called "hippies," and observation of student activities, especially so-called "happenings." Interviews and observation were carried out by 125 students enrolled in a course on social research methods.

The questionnaire was administered in two parts of almost equal length. The first part was a personal interview, while the second, which sought information on more sensitive topics, such as sex, drug use and the draft, was filled out by the respondent and placed with the first part in a sealed envelope without identification. The questionnaires were thus kept anonymous to increase the probability of truthful answers. The completion rate of interviews was 81 percent. The remaining 19 percent were not interviewed largely because the assigned respondent could not be reached during the week allotted to field work, rather than the refusal to be interviewed (less than 5 percent). A comparison of the sample obtained with available demographic characteristics for the entire population shows no characteristic with a difference beyond what might be expected by chance.

Conceptual and operational model

Our dependent variable is frequency of drug use as reported by the respondent. Our major independent variable is degree of adherence to the "hang-loose" ethic as determined by a series of questions designed to tap (1) behavioral patterns, (2) attitudes and values, and (3) self-image and personality. The behavioral patterns refer to such acts as taking part in "happenings" and mass protests, and reading underground newspapers. We view such behaviors as indicative of a rejection of traditional society on the part of the student and subject to disapproval by the representatives of that society. The attitudes and values studied are drawn from the educational area (i.e. worthwhileness of college education, student power), the political area (i.e. Vietnam war, the draft), and the social area (i.e. "hippies," the law, sex and life goals). Finally, we study the student's self-image in such respects as conformity, cynicism, anti-establishment and rebellion in an effort to index his own portrait of himself vis-a-vis the established order.

In all three aspects of behavior, attitudes, and self-image, our major hypothesis is that the more the student embraces the "hang-loose" ethic (as opposed to the so-called "Protestant ethic") the more frequently will he make use of drugs.

FINDINGS

Prevalence of drug use

The following proportions of students reported taking some drugs (Question: "How frequently do you take drugs (marijuana, LSD, etc.)?":

About every day	2.0
Once or twice a week	6.6
Once or twice a month	6.6
Less than once a month	6.0
Do not use drugs	78.8
Total	100.0% (N = 497)

Of the drugs used, marijuana was listed by *all* students taking drugs, with occasional use of LSD mentioned by 18 percent of those taking drugs (2.2 percent of the entire population). A wide variety of other drugs (i.e. "speed," Methedrine,® peyote) also was listed, none by more than 10 percent. There can be little question concerning marijuana's being the recreational drug of choice among this college population, one of five admitting its use, despite its illegality. The word "drugs" as used in this report may therefore be equated largely with marijuana.

This figure of 21.1 percent is quite similar to the results of surveys at UCLA (33 percent) (Santa Barbara News-Press, 1967), Harvard (25 percent), Yale (20 percent), and Princeton (15 percent) (8), although a Gallup Poll of 426 college campuses reports only about 6 percent as having smoked marijuana (9). While this "numbers game" is largely unproductive in the absence of any reliable and valid data, it does seem apparent that marijuana use on the campus is high enough to warrant serious attention.

Most of the students using drugs began in college, 40 percent in their freshman year, although 22 percent had smoked marijuana before coming to college. Almost all began to use drugs through the personal influence of a friend who was already smoking marijuana (10). Drug use usually took place at night as a social activity with other people in the student's or a friend's room.

Overwhelmingly, the reaction of the students smoking marijuana is positive. Four out of five report that they have never gotten sick, although one out of four does mention having experienced a bad "trip." Less than 10 percent want to stop or have ever tried to stop, although 20 percent report being "somewhat" worried.

There is no evidence in these findings to support the claims that smoking marijuana is a predecessor to the use of other, more than dangerous drugs. Marijuana users may occasionally "cross over" to try other drugs, but this is more of a search for new experiences than "progressive degeneration."

Alcohol and marijuana

In addition to the question about their own use of drugs, the students were asked, "How frequently do most of the students you know do the following: smoke marijuana, take LSD, drink alcoholic beverages?" They were also asked in relation to these three recreational drugs, "How strongly do you approve or disapprove doing each of the following?" and "How much pressure do you feel to engage in any of the following?" A comparison of their responses to these three aspects of use, attitude, and pressure for marijuana, LSD, and alcohol is given in Table 1.

TABLE 1. Comparison of drugs according to use, attitudes, and pressures.

| | Alcoholic | Type drug | |
Questions	beverages	Marijuana	LSD
Use*			
Frequently	47.2	14.1	1.2
Occasionally	36.9	24.5	8.8
Seldom	10.0	18.9	16.9
Never	2.4	30.7	53.8
Don't know	3.5	11.8	19.3
Attitude†			
Strongly approve	11.4	5.6	1.2
Approve	59.2	29.5	3.6
Undecided	22.2	31.5	20.9
Disapprove	5.2	20.1	25.7
Strongly disapprove	2.0	13.3	48.6
Pressure††			
A great deal	12.9	3.0	2.8
Some, but not much	38.2	16.5	2.0
Very little	47.0	78.1	92.6
No answer	1.9	2.4	2.6
Total percent	100.0	100.0	100.0
Total cases	497	497	497

* Question: "How frequently do most of the students you know do the following;"
† Question: "How strongly do you approve or disapprove of students doing each of the following;"
†† Question: "How much pressure do you feel to engage in any of the following."

First, we note the higher perception of marijuana use as compared to actual use. While 4 out of 5 students (78.8 percent) report that they do not use marijuana themselves, only 1 out of 3 (30.7 percent) estimates that most of the students they know do not smoke marijuana. Almost 2 out of 5 (38.6 percent) report that most of the students they know smoke marijuana frequently or occasionally.

Second, we see that alcohol continues by far to be most frequently used, with an overwhelming majority of students (84.1 percent) reporting that most of the students they know drink alcohol frequently or occasionally, as compared to 38.9 percent for marijuana and 10.0 percent for LSD.

Third, we note that approval parallels use, with most of the students (70.6 percent) approving alcohol, some approving marijuana (35.4 percent), and few approving LSD (4.8 percent). The ratio of approval to disapproval is 10:1 in favor for alcohol, 1:1 for marijuana and 1:20 against LSD. It would appear that the campus is split on the use of marijuana, but overwhelmingly in favor of alcohol and against LSD.

Fourth, the pressure to use each of these drugs also parallels attitudes and practices. Most students report pressure to drink alcoholic beverages

(51.1 percent), but only 19.5 percent report feeling any pressure to smoke marijuana, with 4.9 percent feeling some pressure to use LSD. These findings underscore the highly personal and voluntary nature of marijuana or LSD use. If anything, students are being more highly pressured toward possible alcoholism than drug addiction. The major recreational drug on the college campuses is still alcohol.

The relationship between pressure toward use of drugs and the actual frequency of use is quite high. An individual who reports feeling pressure to smoke marijuana is twice as likely to be a frequent user of marijuana (at least once a week) than one who reports little or no pressure (15.7 percent vs. 7.2 percent). A similar relationship exists between pressure to use LSD and actual use (16.6 percent vs. 8.5 percent). This finding is supported by the much more frequent use of marijuana among those students who report that most of the students they know also smoke marijuana. As many as 68.6 percent of those students who report that most of the students they know smoke marijuana frequently do so themselves, as compared to only 0.7 percent among those whose friends do not smoke marijuana.

A significant reversal between alcohol and drug use occurs in these data. The more the individual knows other students who drink alcohol, and the more pressure he feels to drink himself, the *less* likely is he to use marijuana. This finding would indicate that marijuana is more of a substitute for alcohol than a supplement. For many students it would appear that the use of marijuana represents a preference over alcohol as a source of "high."

The relationship of attitudes toward use and actual use is, not unexpectedly, extremely high. Approval is much more likely to mean use (45.7 percent), with only a small minority (0.6 percent) disapproving of smoking marijuana at the same time that they do it. This finding once again attests to the voluntary nature of this act. It is also interesting to note that half of the students who approve of smoking marijuana still do not do so themselves. Most of the students (66.6 percent) do not feel that "anyone smoking marijuana is foolish" although only a minority agree that "the use of psychedelic drugs should be a matter of conscience and not legal restriction" (34.7 percent) and that "the university should not cooperate with legal authorities in the enforcement of drug use laws" (23.2 percent). In all cases, those students having positive attitudes towards marijuana, either in the wisdom of its use or in its freedom from legal restrictions, are much more likely to be users of marijuana.

Demographic comparisons

The use of drugs varies significantly by sex, social class, marital status, and religion. No differences were found by age, year in college, birthplace or current marital status of parents. Males are almost three times as likely as females to be using drugs (e.g., smoking marijuana) at least once a week (13.9 percent vs. 4.6 percent), upper income groups twice as likely as lower income groups (14.1 percent vs. 7.3 percent), single students four times as likely as married students (8.9 percent vs. 2.1 percent) (but engaged students show greatest use—10.7 percent), and Atheists and "other religious affiliations" reporting much more use (25.0 percent) than Protestants (4.9 percent), Catholics (4.8 percent), and Jews (4.0 percent). Similar differences occur in the category "less than once a week."

Social class differences are much more pronounced among the females than male students. Among coeds, the proportion smoking marijuana at least once a week rises rapidly from 1.5 percent among those who come from families with annual incomes under $12,000 to 13.1 percent from families with incomes of $20,000 or more. No statistically significant social class differences are found among the male students. In general, our analysis by demographic characteristics would support the findings of others that marijuana smoking is not, like the use of narcotics, linked to a lower income subculture.

The "hang-loose" ethic: Behavioral correlates

Our primary hypothesis has been that drug use is only one aspect of the more general "happening" scene and reflects a broad range of other "anti-establishment" behaviors. Support for this hypothesis comes from our finding that drug use varies considerably according to such activities as participating in "happenings" (34.3 percent drug users among those who participate frequently vs. 17.0 percent among those who do so rarely), reading "underground" newspapers (42.0 percent users among frequent readers vs. 3.7 percent among nonreaders), and participating in mass protests (45.9 percent among those who have done so more than twice vs. 15.2 percent for nonparticipators). It appears from these results that drug use in the form of smoking marijuana is highly associated with "nonconformist" behavior.

If we look at the student's cumulative grade as an index of his academic behavior, we see that drug use is more likely to occur among the poorer than the better students. Among those with an average grade of 3.0 or higher, only 15.3 percent report the use of drugs as compared to 31.0 percent among those with an average of 2.5 or less. This difference in grade probably represents one more manifestation of the rejection of the "hard work-success" ethic of conventional society.

The "hang-loose" ethic: Attitudinal correlates

Similar differences in frequency of drug use are found in relation to a wide range of educational, political, and social attitudes and values indicative of a rejection of the established order. Drug use is more likely to be reported by those students who are relatively antagonistic to the educational system and who are dissatisfied with the education they are receiving. For example, among those students who disagree with the statement, "American colleges today should place more emphasis on teaching American ideals and values," more than seven times as many are frequent smokers of marijuana than among those who agree (13.8 percent vs. 1.8 percent). Similarly, whereas 30.2 percent of those students who "often" feel that what they are learning is a waste of time smoke marijuana, only 12.9 percent of those who don't feel this way do so. However drug use does not mean "apathy" toward academic life—more smokers of marijuana are to be found among those students who believe that students should have a more active role in making decisions about student life than among those who do not (28.4 percent vs. 11.1 percent).

On the political scene, drug use is much more likely to occur if the student is opposed to the Vietnam war (37.5 percent among those favoring immediate military withdrawal vs. 3.0 percent among those supporting President Johnson's policy). Drug users are also more frequent among those who believe that "human lives are too important to be sacrificed for any form of government" (32.4 percent vs. 12.6 percent). Opposition to the draft is another political view associated with drug use. Among those who are opposed to military service, 35.2 percent use drugs as compared to 15.0 percent among those who are not opposed, and, in fact, for those male students whose decision to attend college was affected by the possibility of being drafted, 41.7 percent are drug users as compared to 25.2 percent among those for whom this was not a consideration.

Social attitudes also reflect this "hang-loose" ethic on the part of drug users. Drug users are more likely to be found among those who feel it is all right to get around the law if you don't actually break it (34.6 percent vs. 13.8 percent) and who feel that the "hippie" way of life represents a desire for serious change as opposed to an unproductive expression of nonconformism (26.6 percent vs. 10.5 percent). The student who reports that he expects to get the most satisfaction out of life by means of his leisure time recreational activities is a much more frequent user of marijuana than the student who values participation in civic affairs or family relations (45.2 percent vs. 12.5 percent and 17.0 percent). An indication of possible family conflict among drug users is given by the higher proportion of drug users among those students who feel that their parents don't respect their opinions (29.2 percent vs. 15.3 percent).

One finding in regard to social attitudes appears contrary to many claims made about drug use. A series of four questions designed to index "alienation" (i.e., "These days a person does not really know whom he can count on"; "If you don't watch yourself, people will take advantage of you.") showed no statistically significant relationships to smoking marijuana, despite the claim of Halleck (8) that "Smoking marijuana has become almost an emblem of alienation." Given the large number of significant differences found, this lack of any association between drug use and alienation is impressive. The "hang-loose" ethic, while it may represent antagonism to the conventional world, does not appear to create apathy and withdrawal. Subscribers to this ethic are not so much "anomic" in regard to society in general as critical of the existing "Establishment" in specific.

The "hang-loose" ethic: Personality correlates

The more the student's self-image tends to be rebellious, cynical, anti-establishment, "hippie," and apathetic, the more likely is he to smoke marijuana. Conversely, the more his self-image tends to be conformist, well-behaved, moral, and "square," the less likely is he to make use of marijuana. The greatest differences are to be found between those students who regard themselves as "hippies" (39 percent difference in favor of use) or well-behaved (37 percent difference against use). The smallest differences occur in relation to apathy (8 percent difference in favor of use) and cynicism (10 percent difference in favor of use).

These contrasts in self-image between users and nonusers are congruent with the previous findings in relation to behavioral and attitudinal correlates. Such attitudes as disrespect for the law and skepticism about the worthwhileness of college, coupled with such behaviors as participating in mass protests and "happenings," match the self-portrait of the marijuana smoker as anti-establishment, cynical, and rebellious. If we view these traits as indicative of an underlying value system, we can quite readily see the contrast in "Protestant" vs. "hang-loose" ethic between marijuana smokers and nonsmokers. These self-characterizations do lend face validity to the general public stereotyping of the marijuana smoker as "deviant" and the marijuana's own stereotyping of those who do not use marijuana as "square."

Demographic controls

Each of the major differences in behavior, attitudes, and personality between users and nonusers of marijuana was examined separately by sex, income, and religious group. Since, for example, males are more likely than females to smoke marijuana and also to subscribe to the "hang-loose" ethic, the possibility exists that both ethic and drug use are reflections of sex and are not really associated in and of themselves.

Analysis of the demographic control tables shows that this, by and large, is not the case. In almost every instance, the differences in marijuana use occur independently for both the demographic control and the behavioral, attitudinal, and personality correlates of the "hang-loose" ethic. In other words, the "hang-loose" ethic continues to be related to marijuana smoking regardless of the subgroup of the student population being studied.

This is illustrated in Table 2, which presents the relationship between several different indices of the "hang-loose" ethic and marijuana use sepa-

TABLE 2. Relationship between "hang-loose" ethic and marijuana use, according to sex.

"Hang-loose" ethic	(Percent smoking marijuana)	
	Male	Female
Behavioral		
Participate in mass protests		
No	9.9(141)	3.8(212)
Once or twice	12.5 (48)	5.9 (51)
More than twice	40.0 (25)	16.7 (12)
Attend a "happening"		
Rarely	8.6(116)	2.4(168)
Occasionally	15.5 (58)	3.7 (82)
Frequently	33.3 (33)	20.8 (24)
Attitudinal		
"It is all right to get around the law, if you don't actually break it."		
Disagree	18.2 (99)	11.3(168)
Undecided	34.0 (47)	19.0 (63)
Agree	40.3 (62)	26.7 (45)
"How strongly do you approve or disapprove of students having premarital sexual intercourse?"		
Disapprove	0.0 (18)	1.2 (81)
Undecided	26.8 (56)	11.1 (90)
Approve	33.8(136)	33.3(102)
Personality		
"Anti-establishment"		
Not at all well	18.0(111)	12.1(182)
A little	32.4 (34)	13.2 (38)
Undecided and well	46.9 (64)	32.7 (55)
"Well-behaved"		
Very well	15.6 (32)	4.6 (65)
Fairly well	21.4(131)	17.8(185)
Undecided and not well	56.2 (48)	27.6 (29)

rately for males and females. First, we note that males are more likely than females both to subscribe to the "hang-loose" ethic and to smoke marijuana. Second, we see that for males and females separately, the more the student adheres to the "hang-loose" ethic, either in his or her behavior, attitudes, or personality, the more likely he or she is to smoke marijuana. Thus, we conclude that both sex and ethic contribute independently to marijuana use. This same conclusion appears in general for other demographic variables and for other indices of the "hang-loose" ethic.

We can also see from Table 2, in general, that the relationship between the "hang-loose" ethic and marijuana use is somewhat higher among the males. Also, the differences due to sex are much smaller than those due to variations in behavior, attitudes, or personality. It would thus appear that one's ethic is a more important determinant of marijuana use than one's sex. For example, in all cases, those females who subscribe to the "hang-loose" ethic are much more likely to use marijuana than those males who do not.

Attitude toward use and frequency of use by other students

In the same way that we have analyzed the student's use of marijuana according to various correlates of the "hang-loose" ethic, we can also examine his attitudes toward such use and his reports about how many of the students he knows also smoke marijuana. (Since so few students report feeling any pressure to smoke marijuana, this aspect is omitted from the following analysis.) We present the results of this analysis in a summary fashion in Table 3. With only one exception—the relationship of family income to attitudes to marijuana use—all of the variables listed are significantly related (chi square $p < .05$) to attitudes to use and frequency of use by other students in the same direction as the student's own use of marijuana. That is, the behavioral, attitudinal, and personality correlates of the "hang-loose" ethic also relate to one's attitude toward smoking marijuana and the frequency of marijuana use among the students one knows. These three aspects of attitudes toward use, use by one's friends, and use by oneself, then, all become part of the general picture of marijuana use as such use reflects adherence to the "hang-loose" ethic.

The relative size of the associations (keeping in mind the variations from question to question of the number of answer categories) can be determined in an approximate way from the size of Cramer's V, a coefficient of association (11, p. 230). Self-image tends to be more highly related than either attitudes or behavior. Sex attitudes are, in general, more highly related than either political or educational values. Very high associations are to be found among attitudes and behaviors in regard to smoking marijuana, taking LSD, having sexual intercourse, and drinking alcoholic beverages, in about that order.

In summary, this table of associations underscores the interrelationships between attitudes and use, and between the various correlates of the "hang-loose" ethic and such attitudes and use. It is quite clear that the more one's behaviors, attitudes, and personality conform to the "hang-loose" ethic, the more likely one will be to approve of smoking marijuana and the more likely is it that one will associate with other students who smoke marijuana.

Finally, in Table 4, we show the mutual effects of attitude toward

TABLE 3. Relationship between attitude to use of marijuana, frequency of use by other students and selected characteristics.

Student characteristics*	Attitude to use of marijuana†	Frequency of use by other students††
Demographic		
Sex	.14§	.19
Income	n.s.	.14
Behavior patterns		
Attend "happening"	.17	.30
Read "underground" newspaper	.30	.26
Participate in mass protest	.16	.20
Self-image		
"Hippie"	.28	.30
Anti-establishment	.23	.19
Well-behaved	.23	.22
Educational values		
College a waste of time	.16	.16
Students active in student affairs	.14	.13
Political values		
Vietnam a mistake	.19	.20
Human lives not to be sacrificed in war	.12	.12
Conscientious objection a loophole	.19	17
Social values		
Approval of premarital sex, if consent	.32	.28
Approval of abortion	.22	.20
Approval of birth control	.22	.17
Approval of law-breaking	.15	.14
Frequency of other student behaviors		
Drink alcoholic beverages	.15	.19
Smoke marijuana	.42	—
Take LSD	.29	.41
Have sexual intercourse	.30	.37
Attitude to student behaviors		
Drink alcoholic beverages	.25	.14
Smoke marijuana	—	.42
Takes LSD	.33	.30
Have sexual intercourse	.42	.31

* See previous text for question wording used to determine student characteristics.

† Question: "How strongly do you approve or disapprove of students smoking marijuana?" (Strongly Approve, Approve, Undecided, Disapprove, Strongly Disapprove.)

†† Question: "How frequently do most of the students you know smoke marijuana?" (Frequently, Occasionally, Seldom, Never, Don't Know.)

§ Coefficients of association as determined by Cramer's V.

smoking marijuana and several aspects of the "hang-loose" ethic upon the use of marijuana. By and large, similar differences are found for all other aspects of the "hang-loose" ethic. As hypothesized, these two variables are independently related to drug use with the most frequent use occurring

TABLE 4. Relationship between "hang-loose" ethic, attitude toward marijuana use and use of marijuana.

	(Percent smoking marijuana) Attitude to use of marijuana	
"Hang-loose" ethic	Favorable	Unfavorable
Attend a "Happening"		
Rarely	31.3 (83)	4.5(201)
Occasionally	51.9 (54)	11.8 (84)
Frequently	73.5 (34)	25.6 (19)
"It's all right to get around the law, if you don't actually break it"		
Disagree	37.3 (75)	4.7(191)
Undecided	42.2 (45)	14.3 (61)
Agree	60.4 (48)	14.6 (55)
"Anti-establishment"		
No	39.8(103)	6.6(260)
Yes	54.9 (71)	19.3 (47)

among those students who have both a favorable attitude toward the use of marijuana and an adherence to the "hang-loose" ethic. In general, an unfavorable attitude toward the use of marijuana will be equated with the absence of marijuana smoking. However, even among those with an unfavorable attitude, use will be higher with adherence to the "hang-loose" ethic. Similarly, given a favorable attitude toward use of marijuana, actual use is much more likely to take place among those students displaying "hang-loose" attitudes, behavior, and personality.

On the basis of these interrelationships of demographic characteristics, attitudes, behavior, and personality to drug use, the following sequence or chain of events appears quite probable (although it would require a prospective study to test it); adherence to the "hang-loose" ethic is more likely to occur among certain predisposed personality types (i.e. rebellious, cynical) and in certain social subgroups (i.e. males, nonreligious); such adherence is likely to lead to a favorable attitude toward smoking marijuana both for its "high" effects and its symbolism of rebellion against authority; this favorable attitude will be supported by other students who also embrace the "hang-loose" ethic and engage in similar overt and covert expressions of rejection of the established order. Finally, given this climate of opinion and behavior, the smoking of marijuana becomes almost a "natural" act for many students far removed from the public's current efforts to define it either as a legal or a health problem.

SUMMARY AND DISCUSSION

The data presented in this report strongly support the major hypothesis that the more the student embraces the "hang-loose" ethic, the more frequently will he make use of marijuana. Also supported is the further hypothesis that certain social subgroups such as males will more frequently both smoke marijuana and adhere to the "hang-loose" ethic, but that regardless of group membership, the "hang-loose" ethic will be related to marijuana use. In regard to attitudes toward use, we find, as hypothesized, that the more the student subscribes to the "hang-loose" ethic, the more favorable will he be toward marijuana use; and the more favorable he is, the more will he actually use marijuana. These attitudes toward use and the "hang-loose" ethic become independent factors in marijuana smoking, reinforcing each other with the greatest use occurring among those students with a favorable attitude who also believe in the "hang-loose" ethic. Finally, the student's use of marijuana is strongly supported when his friends also smoke marijuana.

These findings have significance for both sociological theory and social action. From a theoretical point of view, they support the interpretation of drug use as part of a subcultural group way of life. Among students, this subculture is strongly characterized by a "hang-loose" ethic which attempts to cut itself loose from the traditional "establishment" and to develop freedom from conformity and the search for new experiences. This culture becomes expressed in such behaviors as attending "happenings," reading underground newspapers, participating in mass protests, avoiding the draft, engaging in sexual intercourse and, very much to the point of this report, smoking marijuana. Such use of marijuana constitutes an important means both of attaining "freedom" from the pressures of society and of expressing antagonism toward the "unfair" laws and restrictions of that society. For such students, marijuana serves much the same function as "social drinking" does for their parents, and their "law breaking" has the same social sanctions as drinking did during Prohibition. And just as "social drinking" is a far cry from "alcoholism," so is smoking marijuana far removed from "narcotics addiction."

The relationship of both social drinking to alcoholism and smoking marijuana to narcotics addiction illustrates a significant interaction between social problems, health problems, and legal problems (12, pp. 58–64). A social act (e.g. one carried out by members of a group as part of the subcultural norm of that group) will be labeled a social problem when it conflicts with the accepted norms of the larger society. In this sense, marijuana smoking among students has become a social problem, whereas drinking alcohol has not. The type of corrective action "legitimatized" by the larger society to meet this problem will then determine whether it is viewed as a health or a legal problem. The more the social problem threatens the "value system" of the society, the more likely is it to be labeled a legal as opposed to a health problem and to be assigned to the police rather than the doctor. Restriction and punishment become the means for handling the problem rather than understanding and treatment.

In the absence of any clear-act evidence that (1) marijuana smoking is physiologically addictive or has serious health effects, and (2) use of marijuana leads to crime and delinquency or use of other drugs, it seems premature to view it as either a health or a legal problem (13). Our data would strongly suggest that use of marijuana is predominantly a social act favored by a subgroup in our society which happens to be disenchanted with the established order and for whom such use has become simply a normal preference for their own particular recreational drug (14). To crack down on these youth with all of the powerful forces of law and order and to justify such a restriction of freedom in the name of preventing crime or disease seems more an uncontrolled expression of adult moral indignation and righteousness than of human concern or social justice—and, sadly, an ineffective and destructive expression at that (15). While there can be little question that the "hang-loose" ethic is contrary to the Protestant ethic and the spirit of capitalism, and may be socially disapproved for that and other reasons, the issue, it seems to us, should be openly faced and debated as one of conflicting social values and not of crime or health. As formulated by Simmons (14, p. 11), "It [the marijuana issue] seems to be the pivot around which far deeper conflicts and confrontations are raging—oldsters versus youngsters, hippies versus straight society, administered morality versus personal freedom."

Surely, it should be possible to express one's disapproval of marijuana and to seek its control without making its use a crime against society.

REFERENCES

1. GOLDSEN, ROSE K., et al. *What College Students Think.* Princeton, N.J.: D. Van Nostrand, 1960.

2. JACOB, PHILLIP E. *Changing Values in College.* New York: Harper and Brothers, 1957.

3. STRAUS, ROBERT and BACON, SELDEN D. *Drinking in College.* New Haven, Conn.: Yale University Press, 1953.

4. SIMMONS, JERRY and WINOGRAD, BARRY. *It's Happening: A Portrait of the Youth Scene Today.* Santa Barbara, Calif.: Marc-Laird Publications, 1966.

5. SUCHMAN, E. The addictive disease as socio-environmental health problems. In Freeman, H., et al. (eds.): *Handbook of Medical Sociology.* Englewood Cliffs, N.J.: Prentice-Hall, 1963, pp. 123–43.

6. PLAUT, THOMAS F. *Alcohol Problems: A Report of the Nation.* New York: Oxford University Press, 1967.

7. McGLOTHLIN, W. H. Toward a rational view of marijuana. In Simmons, Jerry (ed.): *Marijuana: Myths and Realities.* North Hollywood, Calif.: Brandon House, 1967, pp. 163–214.

8. *Time,* May 19, 1967.

9. *Reader's Digest,* November 1967.

10. BECKER, H. S. Becoming a marijuana user. *Amer. J. Sociol.,* 59:235–42, November 1953.

11. BLALOCK, HUBERT M. *Social Statistics.* New York: McGraw-Hill, 1960.

12. SUCHMAN, EDWARD A. *Sociology and the Field of Public Health.* New York: Russell Sage Foundation, 1963.

13. Mayor's Committee on Marijuana: The marijuana problem in the City of New York [1944]. In Solomon, David (ed.). *The Marijuana Papers.* Indianapolis: Bobbs-Merrill, 1966, pp. 233–360. For an excellent analysis of this report see Arnold, David: The meaning of the LaGuardia report. In Simmons, Jerry (ed.): *Marijuana: Myths and Realities.* North Hollywood, Calif.: Brandon House, 1967, pp. 111–35.

14. SIMMONS, JERRY (ed.). *Marijuana: Myths and Realities.* North Hollywood, Calif.: Brandon House, 1967.

15. LINDESMITH, ALFRED R. *The Addict and the Law.* Bloomington, Ind.: Indiana University Press, 1965.

24

Review of homosexuality research (1960-1966) and some implications for treatment*

PETER M. MILLER, JOHN B. BRADLEY,
RICHARD S. GROSS, and GENE WOOD

This paper reviews the psychological literature dealing with the dynamics and treatment of homosexuals. The review encompasses the past seven years and is limited to experimental findings.

Before dealing with dynamics and therapy we must consider the problem of clinical definition. The controversy in the recent literature revolves around whether or not homosexuality is necessarily a pathological syndrome always associated with neurotic patterns. Several experts (1, 2)[1] see homosexuality as a choice of symptoms by a primarily neurotic individual. Attempting to lend some empirical support to this argument, Cattell (3) reported that 16 PF profiles of homosexuals are similar to those of neurotics.

Evelyn Hooker (4) reports data to refute this position. She reported that three psychologists who examined the Rorschach protocols of 30 homosexuals and 30 heterosexuals agreed that two-thirds of the homosexuals were average to superior in adjustment. She concluded that some homosexuals may not be characterized by any demonstrable pathology.

* Reprinted with permission of the University of Chicago from *Psychotherapy: Theory, Research and Practice*, 5(1):3–6, Winter 1968.
[1] References at end of reading.

Armon (5) reported similar results with females. Miller and Hannum (6) found no differences between a group of homosexually involved and a group of nonhomosexually involved prisoners. (MMPI mean T scores.)

Thus, there exists evidence to support both sides of this controversy. There does seem to be more objective evidence for the fact that homosexuals do not exhibit any more pathology than nonhomosexuals. To some, this controversy may appear merely academic, although some implications for the formulation of therapeutic goals are evident. One proposition would necessarily assume that the homosexuality must be eliminated for an individual to be reasonably well adjusted. The other would imply that since homosexuality is not an outgrowth of neurotic patterns a legitimate therapeutic goal could be the elimination of current discomforting symptomatology without the necessary elimination of the homosexual behavior. From the above-mentioned studies the evidence would tend to support the latter position as a legitimate goal.

DYNAMICS

The studies dealing with the dynamics of homosexuality revolve around four general areas: (1) paranoia hypothesis, (2) genetic hypothesis, (3) role-conflict hypothesis, and (4) family patterns. The psychoanalysts, being the most prolific writers in the area of homosexuality, have provided most of the current material for hypothesis formulation and testing. The psychoanalytic paranoia hypothesis has elicited numerous investigations. Klaf (7) found that out of 100 homosexuals, paranoid ideation was prominent in 24.4 percent of the males and 18.2 percent of the females. In the author's view these data suggest an association between homosexuality and paranoid ideation. Moore and Selzer (8) corroborated these results while Watson (9) found no evidence for this proposition. Generally, the studies relating to the paranoid hypothesis of homosexuality present inconsistent results due to the lack of adequately designed studies. The majority of experiments include no control groups, no statistical analysis of results, and no controls against the investigators' biases. Thus, the validity of this proposition has not as yet been demonstrated.

In an attempt to test the genetic hypothesis of homosexuality, Pritchard (10) examined the chromosomes of a number of male homosexuals and found the normal male complement of one X and one Y chromosome in all his subjects. The hypothesis that intersexuality between the male and the female is the basis of homosexuality was therefore rejected.

Brenda Dickey (11) reported a failure to substantiate the role-conflict hypothesis. She found that subjectively adequate homosexual males were those who tended to identify with the masculine norms of the dominant culture. Contrary to a role-conflict hypothesis her results indicated that feelings of adequacy are associated with job satisfaction, preference for leisure time with heterosexuals, idealization of the role of the typical heterosexual male, and identification with the typical heterosexual male.

The experimental evidence dealing with particular family patterns among homosexuals is by far the most consistent of the areas yet reviewed. Chang and Block (12) reported supporting evidence for the Freudian notion that homosexuality in males is based on an overidentification with the mother figure and an underidentification with the father figure. West (13) investigated the backgrounds of 50 homosexuals and 50 controls and found that the homosexual family patterns were more significantly characterized by an overintense mother and an unsatisfactory relationship with the father. Ullman (14) found similar results in a study of 636 inmates of a California prison. On the basis of subject ratings he found that the typical homosexual family pattern included: (1) mothers who participated too much in training activities (bossing, criticism, discipline), and (2) fathers who participated too little in maintenance activities (attention, praise, love). McCord, McCord, and Verden (1962) and Bene (15) reported similar family patterns. Taken as a whole these studies indicate a characteristic family pattern associated with homosexuals which includes an overintense, overcritical mother and an unloving, critical, physically or psychologically absent father.

TREATMENT

The experimental studies to date concern (1) psychoanalysis, (2) group therapy, (3) behavior therapy.

In their recent book, *Homosexuality—a Psychoanalytic Study,* Bieber, Gershman, Ovesey, and Weiss (16) reported that of 106 homosexuals or bisexuals who undertook psychoanalysis, 29 (27 percent) became exclusively heterosexual. The amount of time in analysis varied from 150 to 350 hours or more. Bieber reported that the following factors appeared as favorable prognostic indicators:

(1) Patient was bisexual at the beginning of analysis.
(2) Began analysis before age 35.
(3) Continued analysis for at least 150 hours.
(4) Was motivated to become heterosexual.
(5) Had at least an ambivalent father.
(6) Patient's father respected and/or admired the patient, was affectionate, and was closer to the patient than with other male siblings.
(7) Patient idolizes women.
(8) Patient had erotic heterosexual activity in the manifest content of his dreams.

A comprehensive analysis of these results is somewhat hindered by the fact that Bieber remained quite vague as to certain of his procedural methodology. The absence of a control group also opens the question of whether or not 27 percent may become heterosexual without therapy. Even with this limitation, however, Bieber's general approach appears promising.

Very recent data dealing with group therapy with homosexuals are noteworthy. Mintz (17) reported that out of 10 homosexual men who voluntarily entered treatment and remained in combined individual and group therapy for two or more years all report improved general adjustment. Three reported satisfactory heterosexual adjustment. According to Mintz the advantages of combined therapy include: dissolution of rationalizations about homosexuality, development of a stronger sense of personal identity through contact with women and heterosexual men, corrective emotional experiences often resulting in enhanced self-esteem. Hadden (18) also reported that private, weekly sessions of one to one and one-half hours were held with groups of four to eight members. These were open ended groups some of which continued for ten years. Of 32 subjects, 12 have shown marked heterosexual adjustment and decrease in neurotic traits.

Stone (19) reported that homosexual patients in mixed groups benefit more than those in other therapeutic situations.

On behavior therapy, Rashman (20) describes Freud's treatment which consists of the administration of an emetic mixture by subcutaneous injection. While the noxious effects of the injection were being experienced, the patient was shown slides of dressed and undressed men. In the second phase of treatment, the patient was shown films of nude and semi-nude females approximately seven hours after the administration of testosterone. After analysis of results with three to five year follow up studies, it was concluded that 25.5 percent of 47 patients were permanently improved. Rashman indicated, however, that these results are no better than treatment by the more classic psychotherapies although much less time was involved. He also indicated that Freud's design could be improved somewhat with the use of a control group and the use of positive rewards for the heterosexual pictures.

Feldman and McCulloch (21) have recently initiated a research program on twelve subjects based on an anticipatory avoidance paradigm. Their procedure consisted of projecting photographic slides of males which were previously arranged by the subjects in a hierarchical order of attraction. The subject continues to look or remove these photos by use of an electric switch. In eight seconds, electric shock is presented if a particular picture is not removed. Almost always the subject learns to anticipate the coming shock by removing the picture before eight seconds. The procedure begins with pictures of males at the bottom of the hierarchy and when this photo is removed a photo of the most attractive female (chosen previously) is presented. Thus, the male stimulus is a signal that something unpleasant is about to happen and the female stimulus is associated with anxiety reduction. Since this research was presented in a preliminary report only one of the twelve subjects has thus far been evaluated. After a nine month follow-up he has dropped homosexual activity, and increased heterosexual activity. Solyom and Miller (22) treated six male homosexuals by associating electric shock with nude male photos and the termination of shock with pictures of nude females. Using GSR responses as their measure the investigators found no change in autonomic response to male pictures but there was an apparent increase in responsiveness to the female pictures. Stephenson and Wolpe (1960) reported the successful treatment of homosexuals by the use of assertion training, desensitization and environmental manipulations. The authors believe that these nonspecific procedures which do not deal directly with the homosexual behavior offer a promising outlook for the future.

CONCLUSIONS

These experiments representing the past seven years of research on homosexuality have both practical value for the clinician and theoretical value for future researchers. The implications of this research for therapy must be considered in the light of the therapeutic goal. If the homosexual behavior *per se* is to be changed the following considerations are important:

(1) Preliminary investigations indicate that the successful elimination of homosexual behavior by psychoanalytic procedures is associated with certain variables—motivation for change, presence of some heterosexual behavior, a relatively young patient, and a nondetached and at least ambivalent father. The clinician could use these indicators in formulating both therapeutic goals and prognostic evaluations.

(2) Mixed group therapy appears to eliminate rationalizations about homosexuality and encourage a desire to change. Thus, this treatment may be useful as an initial procedure devised to elevate the homosexual's motivation to become heterosexual and thus increase the probability for such a change.

(3) Behavior therapy, either the direct avoidance conditioning methods or Wolpe's indirect assertion training, seems quite promising.

Since this review has indicated that homosexuality is not necessarily the outgrowth of neurosis, an alternative therapeutic goal might be to eliminate current anxiety and discomfort without eliminating the homosexuality per se. With regard to this goal, the research has indicated that the most well adjusted homosexuals are those who identify with the typical heterosexual male. Thus, helping the homosexual to idealize and identify with the heterosexual male would be a useful approach related to this goal.

It is evident that more objective, controlled research involving more than a mere superficial treatment of a subject area is needed. Fruitful areas in need of experimentation include: the effects of the various methods of therapy, prognostic indicators associated with change to heterosexuality, the different characteristics of well-adjusted and poorly-adjusted homosexuals.

REFERENCES

1. BIEBER, I., GERSHMAN, H., OVESEY, L., and WEISS, F. The meaning of homosexual trends in therapy: a round table discussion. *Amer. J. Psychoanal.,* 24(1):60–76, 1964.

2. FREY, E. C. Dreams of male homosexuals and the attitude of society. *J. Individ. Psychol.,* 18:26–34, 1962.

3. CATTELL, RAYMOND B., and MORONY, JOHN H. The use of the 16 PF in distinguishing homosexuals, normals, and general criminals. *J. Consult. Psychol.,* 26(6):531–40, 1962.

4. HOOKER, E. Symposium on current aspects of the problems of validity: What is a criterion? *J. Project. Tech.,* 23:278-86, 1959.

5. ARMON, VIRGINIA. Some personality variables in overt female homosexuality. *J. Project. Tech.,* 24:292–309, 1960.

6. MILLER, W. G., and HANNUM, T. Characteristics of homosexuality involved in incarcerated females. *J. Consult. Psychol.,* 27(3):277, 1963.

7. KLAF, F. S. Female homosexuality and paranoid schizophrenia: A survey of seventy-five cases and controls. *Arch. Gen. Psychiat.,* 4:84–6, 1961.

8. MOORE, R. A., and SELZER, M. J. Male homosexuality, paranoia, and the schizophrenias. *Amer. J. Psychiat.,* 119:734–47, 1963.

9. WATSON, C. G. A test of the relationship between repressed homosexuality and paranoid mechanisms. *J. Clin. Psychol.,* 21(4):380–84, 1965.

10. PRITCHARD, M. Homosexuality and genetic sex. *J. Ment. Sciences, 108:*616–23, 1962.

11. DICKEY, B. Attitudes toward sex roles and feelings of adequacy in homosexual males. *J. Consult. Psychol.,* 25:116–22, 1961.

12. CHANG, JUDY, and BLOCK, J. A Study of identification in male homosexuals. *J. Consult. Psychol.,* 24:307–10, 1960.

13. WEST, D. J. Parental figures in the genesis of male homosexuality. *Int. J. Soc. Psychiat.,* 5:85–97, 1959.

14. ULLMAN, P. S. Parental participation in child rearing as evaluated by male social deviates. *Pacif. Soc. Rev.,* 3:89–95, 1960.

15. BENE, EVA. On the genesis of male homosexuality: An attempt at clarifying the role of the parents. *Brit. J. Psychiat.,* 111:803–13, 1965.

16. BIEBER, IRVING. *Homosexuality: A Psychoanalytic Study.* New York, Basic Books, 1962.

17. MINTZ, E. Overt male homosexuality in combined group and individual treatment. *J. Consult. Psychol.,* 30(3):193–98, 1966.

18. HADDEN, S. Treatment of male homosexuals in groups. *J. Group Psychother.,* 16(1):13–22, 1966.

19. STONE, M. B., SCHENGHER, J., and SEIFRIED, F. Treatment of a homosexual woman in a mixed group. *Int. J. Psychiat.*, *16*:425–32, 1966.

20. RASHMAN, S. Sexual disorders and behavior therapy. *Amer. J. Psychiat.*, *118*:235–40, 1961.

21. FELDMAN, M. P., and McCULLOCH, M. J. A systematic approach to treatment of homosexuality by conditioned aversion: Preliminary report. *Amer. J. Psychiat.*, *121*:167–71, 1964.

22. SOLYOM, L., and MILLER, S. A differential conditioning procedure as the initial phase of behavior therapy of homosexuality. *Behav. Res. Ther.*, *3*(3):147–60, 1965.

23. KLAF, F. S., and DAVIS, C. A. Homosexuality and paranoid schizophrenia: A survey of 150 cases and controls. *Amer. J. Psychiat.*, *116*:1070–75, 1960.

25

Abortion law reform and repeal: Legislative and judicial developments*

RUTH ROEMER, J.D.

In the three years from 1967 to 1970, a revolution has occurred in the abortion laws and practices in the United States. That revolution is still in process. Our once highly restrictive antiabortion laws have been reformed in 13 states and virtually repealed in four states. No other country has a statute which explicitly makes abortion a matter for decision by the woman and her physician. Although other countries permit abortion on request of the woman under certain circumstances, the four American states have pioneered in treating abortion, as a matter of law, like any other medical procedure.

As a result of recent developments, the United States has become a laboratory in which three different types of legal regulation of abortion can be compared and evaluated. We can also profit from the longer experience of other countries with abortion statutes of varying liberality, although account must be taken of differing family planning programs and systems of delivering health services.

* Reprinted from *Clinical Obstetrics and Gynecology*, Vol. 14, No. 4, December 1971. Earlier version appeared in *American Journal of Public Health*, Vol. 61, No. 3, March 1971. Copyright by the American Public Health Association, Inc., 1740 Broadway, New York, N.Y. 10019. [Reprinted by permission from *American Journal of Public Health*, Vol. 61, No. 3 (March 1971), pp. 500–509.]

Legislative developments in the United States

Three kinds of modernized abortion laws have been enacted in the United States since 1967: (1) Twelve states have enacted all or part of the Model Penal Code first proposed in 1957 by the American Law Institute (ALI), under which abortion is not a crime when performed by a licensed physician because of substantial risk that continuance of the pregnancy would gravely impair the physical or mental health of the woman or that the child would be born with grave physical or mental defect, or in cases of pregnancy resulting from rape or incest.[1] (2) One state, Oregon, has expanded the American Law Institute grounds to include a sociomedical ground proposed originally by the American College of Obstetricians and Gynecologists[2] and patterned after a provision of the British Abortion Act of 1967,[3] i.e., that in determining whether or not there is substantial risk to the woman's physical or mental health, account may be taken of her total environment, actual or reasonably foreseeable.[4] (3) Four states— Alaska,[5] Hawaii,[6] New York[7] and the State of Washington (by referendum in November 1970)—have repealed all criminal penalties for abortion, provided only that the abortion is done early in pregnancy and by a licensed physician (Alaska, Hawaii, and Washington also stipulate that the operation must take place in a licensed hospital or other approved facility).

---

[1] American Law Institute, Model Penal Code, sec. 230.3(2) (Proposed Official Draft, 1962). On Aug. 4, 1970, the Commissioners on Uniform State Laws issued a Second Tentative Draft of a Uniform Abortion Act, which authorizes abortions within 24 weeks after commencement of the pregnancy without specific grounds or after 24 weeks on the grounds set forth in the code. The 12 statutes incorporating all or part of the Model Penal Code are: Ark. Stat. Ann., secs. 41-301 to 41-310 (Supp. 1969); Cal. Health & Safety Code Ann., secs. 25950-54 (Supp. 1970); Colo. Rev. Stat. Ann., secs. 40-2-50 to 40-2-53 (Supp. 1967); Del. Code Ann., tit. 11, sec. 301 (1953) and Laws 1969; Ga. Code Ann., secs. 26-9920a to 26-9925a (1969); Kan. Stat. Ann., sec. 21-3407 (Supp. 1969) and Laws 1969; Md. Ann. Code, art. 43, secs. 149E to 149G (Supp. 1969); Miss. Code Ann., sec. 2223 (Supp. 1968); N. M. Stat. Ann., secs. 40A-5-1 to 40A-5-3 (Supp. 1969); N. C. Gen. Stat., secs. 14-44 to 14-45.1 (1969 Replacement Vol. 1B); S. C. Code, secs. 16-82 to 86 (1962) and Laws 1970; Va. Code Ann., secs. 18.1-62 to 18.1-62.3 (Supp. 1970). For discussion of these laws, see Lucas, Roy, "Laws of the United States" in *Abortion in a Changing World* (Robert E. Hall, Ed.), vol. I, p. 127, Columbia Univ. Press, 1970.

[2] The American College of Obstetricians and Gynecologists has recently liberalized its position further to approve abortion on the decision of the patient and her physician without additional medical consultation. AMA News, Sept. 28, 1970.

[3] Elizabeth II, Ch. 87 (1967) permitting termination of pregnancy on the opinion of two registered medical practitioners that continuance of the pregnancy would involve risk to the life of the pregnant woman or injury to the physical or mental health of any existing children of her family greater than if the pregnancy were terminated.

[4] S.B. 193, amending Ore. Rev. Stat., secs. 465.110, 677.188, and 677.190 and repealing sec. 163.060 (Laws 1969).

[5] S.B. No. 527 repealing and re-enacting Alaska Stat., sec. 11.15.060 (Laws 1970).

[6] Public Law No. 1 amending Hawaii Rev. Stat., ch. 768 (Laws 1970).

[7] N. Y. Penal Law, sec. 125.05(3) (McKinney Supp. 1970-71).

Thirty-three states, however, still have laws making abortion a crime except when performed to save the life (or, in a few instances, the health) of the woman. None of these states even requires that the abortion be performed by a licensed physician.

The details of the new laws vary in their provision.* The key developments relate to six general aspects:

1. All 17 states require that the abortion be performed by a licensed physician.

2. All the states with new laws, except Mississippi and New York, require that the abortion be performed in hospitals, with Kansas also permitting another place designated by law.[8] New York City has recently added the requirement that abortions be performed in hospitals or clinics, and not in doctors' offices.

3. All 17 states allow abortion to save the life of the woman, and also in pregnancies resulting from sex crimes.

   All these 17 states (except Mississippi, which authorizes abortion only for rape or to save life) allow abortion to preserve the health or the physical or mental health of the woman. The sociomedical standard of the Oregon law mentioned above is a broader standard than the medical standard of the ALI-style laws.

   Seven states set age limits on abortions for statutory rape. These limits may be lower than the age of consent. Thus, in California sexual intercourse with an unmarried girl below the age of 18 constitutes statutory rape; but if pregnancy results, it can be terminated only if the girl is below the age of 15.

   All 17 states, except California and Mississippi, allow abortion for fetal abormality.

4. The maximum time limits within which abortions may be performed vary from 16 weeks in Colorado, New Mexico, and Washington to 26 weeks in Maryland. In Oregon the time limit is 150 days; in Alaska and Hawaii, the fetus must be nonviable; and in New York the time limit is 24 weeks.

5. Medical approval by consultants, boards, or hospital therapeutic abortion committees is required in all states (except Mississippi) with ALI-

---

* The provisions of all the abortion laws in the United States are summarized in a table, "Current Status of Abortion Laws—August 1, 1970," available upon request from the National Center for Family Planning Services, Health Services and Mental Health Administration, U. S. Department of Health, Education, and Welfare, Rockville, Maryland 20852.

[8] Many states require that the hospital be not only licensed but accredited. For discussion of the unreasonableness and probable unconstitutionality of a requirement restricting performance of abortions to hospitals accredited by the Joint Commission on Accreditation of Hospitals, see Brief *Amici Curiae*, Ass'n for the Study of Abortion, Inc., Planned Parenthood Ass'n, et al., in *Vuitch* v. *Maryland,* Court of Special Appeals of Maryland, Sept. Term, 1970, No. 32, argued Sept. 28, 1970.

style laws, although the Model Penal Code did not propose such procedures. In Oregon, two physicians must certify the circumstances justifying an abortion; in Alaska, Hawaii, and New York, only one physician is required.

6. New York and the following ALI-style states have no residency requirement: California, Colorado, Kansas, Maryland, Mississippi, and New Mexico. South Carolina, Hawaii, and the State of Washington have a 90-day residency requirement, and Arkansas, Delaware, North Carolina, and Virginia require four months' residency. Oregon requires that the patient be a resident, and Alaska requires 30 days' residency.

Actual practice, of course, may differ from the provisions of the statutes. In some places, doctors will not perform abortions as late as the statute allows. Nonresidents may not be welcomed even though the state has no residency requirement. Consents, consultations, and committee approvals may be required that are not specified in the statutes. It is also possible that residency requirements may not be strictly enforced and procedures may be more simple than those provided in the statute.

On the federal level, a bill introduced in Congress by Senator Packwood to legalize abortion throughout the nation made no progress. A recent policy enunciated for U.S. military hospitals, however, permits abortions and sterilizations for military personnel, active or retired, and their families, regardless of state or local laws.[9] In October 1970, a White House task force on the mentally handicapped recommended that, in the interest of both maternal and child mental health, no woman should be forced to bear an unwanted child.

Judicial developments in the United States

Legislative developments have been accompanied by an emerging body of court decisions on the constitutionality of antiabortion laws. The picture changes almost from day to day. As of autumn, 1970, five cases were on the U.S. Supreme Court docket, more than 20 cases were before three-judge federal courts; and, excluding the 20 states with federal cases, many of which also had state cases, another 11 states had cases pending in local courts.[10] The following important cases may be noted.

1. In September 1969, the Supreme Court of California, in the first decision on the constitutionality of any antiabortion statute, invalidated the pre-1967 antiabortion law of California. In a four to three decision in *People* v. *Belous*,[11] the court held the statute unconstitutional on two principal

---

9 International Herald Tribune, p. 3, Aug. 19, 1970.

10 Personal communication from Roy Lucas, President and Associate Counsel, The James Madison Constitutional Law Institute, N. Y., Oct. 22, 1970.

11 71 Cal. 2d 954, 458 P. 2d 194, 80 Cal. Rptr, 354 (1969), cert. denied, 397 U. S. 915 (1970).

Sexual development and behavior

grounds: (1) that the phrase, "necessary to preserve life," was so vague as to be violative of the due process requirements for a criminal law, and (2) that the law was in violation of a woman's fundamental rights to life and to choose whether to bear children. The latter follows from the U.S. Supreme Court's acknowledgment of a right of privacy or liberty in matters related to marriage, family, and sex.[12]

The critical issue defined by the California Supreme Court was whether the state had any legitimate interest in the regulation of abortion which would justify so deep an infringement of the fundamental rights of women. The court held that the state had no such compelling interest. The court said that it would not speak to the constitutionality of the current California Therapeutic Abortion Act, since Dr. Belous was charged under the old law. But one might well infer from the decision that the current law may be declared unconstitutional on similar grounds. The court did express the view, however, that the decision to terminate pregnancy under the 1967 Therapeutic Abortion Act was solely a medical one, and so long as the physician follows the procedural requirements of the act his judgment may not later be challenged by a jury or prosecutor in a criminal case.

2. Following the landmark decision of the California Supreme Court, the first decision of a federal court invalidating an antiabortion statute was handed down. In *U.S. v. Vuitch*,[13] the U.S. District Court for the District of Columbia held unconstitutional the District of Columbia statute which made abortion a felony unless performed by a licensed physician for the preservation of the mother's life or health. The court held this phrase so uncertain and ambiguous as to invalidate the statute for want of due process, and it recommended appeal to the U.S. Supreme Court. The opinion of Judge Gerhard A. Gesell in *Vuitch* emphasized, as the *Belous* decision had done, the woman's liberty and right of privacy in matters related to family, marriage, and sex and the necessity for demonstrating affirmatively the interest of the state in infringing on such rights. The opinion pointed out the discriminatory application of the statute with respect to women who are poor. This case is now on appeal to the U.S. Supreme Court, which has raised certain jurisdictional questions concerning the propriety of direct appeal to the Supreme Court without first proceeding to the U.S. Court of Appeals for the District of Columbia.

3. In addition to these two decisions which broke new legal ground, a

---

12 Id. at 963, 458 P. 2d at 199.

13 305 F. Supp. 1032 (D.D.C. 1969), ques. of juris. postponed to merits, 397 U.S. 1061, further juris. questions propounded, 399 U.S. 923 (1970) (No. 84, Oct. 1970 Term). On the practical availability of abortion under D.C. law, see court order requiring the D.C. General Hospital to give abortions to women meeting the standards for admission to the hospital. *Doe v. Gen'l Hosp. of D.C.*, 313 F. Supp. 1170 (D.D.C. 1970), on motions to hold hospital officials in contempt, — F. 2d —, No. 24,011 (D.C. Cir. Mar. 20 and May 15, 1970).

number of other courts have invalidated pre-ALI-style antiabortion laws. These cases have arisen in both federal and state courts.

Three-judge panels of federal district courts have held the pre-ALI-style laws of Texas[14] and Wisconsin[15] unconstitutional because of overbreadth. One court also held the statute void for vagueness, and both courts found the statutes an unconstitutional invasion of private rights and not justified by a compelling interest of the state. Contrary is one federal court which, in a two to one decision, upheld the antiabortion statute of Louisiana.[16]

Similar suits have been brought in federal courts involving the Arizona,[17] Illinois,[18] and New Jersey laws.[19] Suits challenging the Kentucky[20] and Minnesota[21] laws were dismissed on jurisdictional grounds, and the New York case was dismissed as moot on repeal of New York's antiabortion statute.[22]

State courts have also struck down pre-ALI-style laws. In Illinois, a judge of the criminal court held the abortion statute unconstitutional on grounds of vagueness and infringement on the woman's right to control her body.[23] In Pennsylvania, a county court judge found that that state's statute impinges on constitutionally protected areas and is so broad, unlimited, and indiscriminate that it fails to meet present-day tests for constitutionality.[24] In South Dakota, a circuit court condemned the statute because it interferes with private conduct without serving any vital interest of society.[25] In Michigan, the statute was found defective as infringing on the right of privacy in the physician-patient relationship and as possibly

---

[14] *Roe* v. *Wade*, 314 F. Supp. 1217 (N.D. Tex. 1970) (per curiam), appeal docketed, 39 U.S.L.W. 3151 (U.S. Oct. 7, 1970) (No. 808, Oct. 1970 Term).

[15] *McCann* v. *Babbitz*, 306 F. Supp. 400 (E. D. Wis. 1969) (three-judge court convened), 310 F. Supp. 293 (1970) (per curiam) (on the merits), appeal dismissed, 400 U.S. —, 39 U.S.L.W. 3132 (Oct. 13, 1970) (per curiam), perm. injunc. issued, — F. Supp. — (E.D. Wis. Nov. 18, 1970) (per curiam).

[16] *Rosen* v. *La. State Bd. Med. Examiners,* 318 F. Supp. 1217 (1970) (Cassibry, J., dissenting).

[17] *Planned Parenthood Ass'n of Phoenix* v. *Nelson,* Civ. No. 70-334 PHX (D. Ariz. Aug. 24, 1970) (per curiam).

[18] *Doe* v. *Scott,* — F. Supp. — (N.D. Ill. 1971) (Illinois statute held unconstitutional as impermissibly vague and unduly infringing on the woman's right of privacy in restricting abortion during the first trimester of pregnancy.

[19] *YWCA* v. *Kugler,* Civ. No. 264-70 (D.N.J., filed Mar. 5, 1970).

[20] *Crossen* v. *Breckenridge,* Civ. No. 2143 (E.D. Ky.), dismissed June 15, 1970 by U. S. Judge Swinford, Lexington (Ky.) Herald, June 16, 1970. On appeal.

[21] *Doe* v. *Randall,* 314 F. Supp. 32 (D. Minn. 1970), rehearing denied, 314 F. Supp. 32 (D. Minn. July 1, 1970) (per curiam), appeal docketed *sub nom. Hodgson* v. *Randall,* 39 U.S.L.W. 3115 (Sept. 21, 1970) (No. 728, Oct. 1970 Term).

[22] *Hall* v. *Lefkowitz,* 305 F. Supp. 1030 (S.D.N.Y. 1969), dismissed as moot, Op. No. 36936 (S.D.N.Y. July 1, 1970) (per curiam).

[23] *People* v. *Anast,* No. 69-3429 (Ill. Cir. Ct., Cook County, 1970) (Dolezal, J.).

[24] *Commonwealth* v. *Page, Centre County Leg. J.* at 285 (Pa. Ct. Comm. Pl., Centre County July 23, 1970).

[25] *State* v. *Munson* (S.D. 7th Jud. Cir., Pennington County Apr. 6, 1970) (Clarence P. Cooper, J.).

violative of the patient's right to safe and adequate medical treatment.[26] Contra, however, is the Massachusetts Supreme Judicial Court, which upheld the constitutionality of the state's statute prohibiting "unlawful" abortion against a charge of vagueness in a case sustaining revocation of a medical license.[27] Suits challenging other pre-ALI-style laws are still pending elsewhere.[28]

4. Attempts are currently being made to obtain an adjudication of the constitutionality of reformed ALI-style laws.[29] Thus far, only one reformed ALI-style law has been invalidated by a federal court—Georgia's 1968 abortion law. The U.S. District Court in Atlanta held unconstitutional those parts of the 1968 Georgia law that limited the woman's right to abortion to the three ALI grounds.[30] The basis of the court's decision was violation of the woman's right of privacy. Retained as a proper exercise of state power, however, were the requirements for medical consultation, hospital committee approval, hospital accreditation and exemption provisions, and the residency requirement.

On the state level, the California Therapeutic Abortion Act has been challenged in three cases. Two cases involving Doctors Robb and Gwynne are still pending, but preliminary decisions involving these doctors have held the California statute unconstitutional.[31] In *People v. Barksdale,* a municipal court in Alameda County held the current California law unconstitutional as violative of the equal protection clause of the 14th Amendment, as a vague and improper delegation of legislative authority to the Joint Commission on Accreditation of Hospitals, as discriminatory between the rich and the poor, as lacking the certainty required for a criminal statute with respect to the definition of mental illness, and as violative of

---

[26] *State* v. *Ketchum* (Mich. Dist. Ct. Mar. 30, 1970) (Reid, J.).

[27] *Kudish* v. *Bd. of Registration in Med.,* 355 Mass. —, 248 N.E. 2d 264 (1969). Similar decisions have upheld the Iowa and Vermont statutes as not unconstitutionally vague.

[28] See, for example, *Arnold* v. *Sendak,* No. IP 70-C-217 (S.D. Ind., filed Mar. 29, 1970); *Rodgers* v. *Danforth,* Civ. No. 18360-2 (W.D. Mo., filed May 15, 1970); *Steinberg* v. *Brown,* No. C-70-289 (N.D. Ohio); *Doe* v. *Rampton,* Civ. No. 234-70 (D. Utah, Sept. 14, 1970). (Temporary restraining order against enforcement of Utah statute issued).

[29] *Corkey* v. *Edwards,* Civ. No. 2665 (W.D.N.C., filed May 12, 1970); *Gwynne* v. *Hicks,* Civ. No. 70-1088-CC (C.D. Calif., filed May 18, 1970); *Doe* v. *Dunbar,* Civ. No. C-2402 (D. Colo., filed July 2, 1970), juris. granted — F. Supp. — (D. Colo. Dec. 22, 1970). (One of the attorneys in the Colorado suit challenging the first ALI-style law enacted is Richard D. Lamm, sponsor of the reformed legislation in the Colorado Legislature.)

[30] *Doe* v. *Bolton,* — F. Supp. —, Civ. No. 13676 (N.D. Ga. July 31, 1970) (per curiam), appeal docketed, 39 U.S.L.W. 3227 (U.S. Nov. 17, 1970) (Nos. 971, 973, Oct. Term 1970).

[31] *People* v. *Robb,* Nos. 149005 & 159061 (Calif. Mun. Ct., Orange County, Jan. 9, 1970) (Mast, J.); *People* v. *Gwynne,* No. 173309 (Calif. Mun. Ct., Orange County, June 16, 1970) (Thomson, J.); *People* v. *Gwynne,* No. 176601 (Calif. Mun. Ct., Orange County, Aug. 13, 1970 (Schwab, J.).

the fundamental right of the woman to make a free choice whether or not to bear children.[32] In rejecting the argument that the state has a compelling interest in protecting the embryo, Judge T. L. Foley added the following poignant words:

> I might say that I belong to the religion that was just referred to, and I dislike to render this opinion. I must follow the law under my oath as a Judge. I am a Catholic which makes it very, very difficult—but my oath of office calls for me to follow the law as stated and set out by the Appellate Courts of this State.[33]

The judicial picture is in constant flux as new cases are filed in federal and state courts; as the defense of unconstitutionality is raised in criminal prosecutions of doctors; as issues are raised concerning jurisdiction of courts and standing of plaintiffs to sue; and as decisions come down and appeals are taken.

On at least eight occasions, the United States Supreme Court has declined to review state court decisions that involved restrictive antiabortion laws.[34] One of these cases was the landmark decision of the California Supreme Court in *Belous*. On October 13, 1970, the court dismissed an appeal from the decision of a three-judge federal court holding the Wisconsin antiabortion statute unconstitutional.[35] Action by the court on the merits of abortion cases will be decisive, but it is possible that some of the cases will go off on questions of jurisdiction or on grounds other than the basic constitutional issues.

Although the final outcome cannot be predicted, three eventualities seem fairly certain. First, more and more states will change their laws in accordance with one or another of the three patterns now prevailing in the United States. Second, as in other nations of the world, moderately reformed laws will be amended to expand the grounds and to simplify the

---

[32] *People* v. *Barksdale*, No. 33237C (Calif. Mun. Ct., Alameda County, Mar. 24, 1970) (Foley, J.).

[33] Ibid.

[34] The Jurisdictional Statement filed in the U.S. Supreme Court on Oct. 7, 1970 by *Roy Lucas et al. in Roe* v. *Wade*, 314 F. Supp. 1217 (N.D. Tex. 1970) (per curiam), No. 808, Oct. 1970 Term cites the following cases at p. 18, n. 30: *Muncie* v. *Missouri*, 398 U.S. 938 (June 1, 1970), denying cert. to 448 S.W. 2d 879 (Mo. 1970); *California* v. *Belous*, 397 U.S. 915 (Feb. 24, 1970), denying cert. to 71 Cal. 2d 954, 458 P. 2d 194, 80 Cal. Rptr. 354 (1969); *Molinaro* v. *New Jersey*, 396 U.S. 365 (Jan. 19, 1970) (per curiam), dismissing appeal from 54 N.J. 246, 254 A. 2d 792 (1969); *Knight* v. *Louisiana Bd. of Medical Examiners*, 395 U.S. 933 (June 2, 1969), denying cert. to 252 La. 889, 214 So. 2d 716 (1968) (per curiam); *Morin* v. *Garra*, 395 U.S. 935 (June 2, 1969), denying cert. to 53 N.J. 82 (1968) (per curiam); *Moretti* v. *New Jersey*, 393 U.S. 952 (Nov. 18, 1968), denying cert. to 52 N.J. 182, 244 A. 2d 499 (1968); *Fulton* v. *Illinois*, 390 U.S. 953 (Mar. 4, 1968), denying cert. to 84 Ill. App. 2d 280, 228 N.E. 2d 203 (1967); *Carter* v. *Florida*, 376 U.S. 648 (Mar. 30, 1964), dismissing appeal from 150 So. 2d 787 (Fla. 1963).

[35] *McCann* v. *Babbitz*, 310 F. Supp. 293 (E.D. Wis. 1970), appeal dismissed, 400 U.S. —, 39 U.S.L.W. 3132 (Oct. 13, 1970) (per curiam), supra note 15.

procedures; alternatively, antiabortion laws will be repealed. Third, in every state pressure will mount for making abortion available *de facto* as well as *de jure* to women, rich and poor, faced with the despair and desperation occasioned by unwanted pregnancy.

Recent developments in other countries

The abortion laws of the world have been described on a five-stage continuum, ranging from the most permissive to the most restrictive.[36] Recent legislative changes show that more and more countries are liberalizing their laws all along this continuum.

1. *Abortion on the Insistence of the Woman*—No new jurisdictions have joined this category, except the four states in the United States discussed previously. The tightening of the Bulgarian law in 1968[37] in order to encourage population growth has been eased by a 1970 interpretation that allows abortion virtually on request for unmarried women and women having at least one child.[38] The hope is that this interpretation will reduce the number of illegal abortions. In these cases, the Bulgarian law resembles once again the most liberal laws of the USSR and Hungary. Now that the German Democratic Republic has liberalized its policy on abortion, as mentioned below, the only restrictive abortion statutes remaining in eastern Europe are those of Romania and Albania.

2. *Abortion on Social Grounds*—Two Scandinavian countries, Finland and Denmark, have liberalized their statutes further to include social grounds. The 1970 law in Finland specifies, in addition to medical and humanitarian reasons and the age of the mother (under 17 or over 40 or already the mother of four children), the following social ground:

. . . when the delivery and care of the child would constitute, by reason of the conditions of existence of the woman and her family, as well as other circumstances, a change for her.[39]

A unique provision, relevant for all countries faced with expanding demand for abortions, requires the Finnish Department of Health to assure a sufficient number of qualified physicians and abortion hospitals and also impartial and uniform conduct from physicians.

The Danish law of 1970 permits abortion without authorization of a committee for reasons of life or health or in cases where the woman is

---

[36] R. Roemer, Abortion Law: The Approaches of Different Nations. A.J.P.H. 57,11:1906 (Nov.), 1967; R. Roemer, "Abortion Laws of the World: Recent Trends and Policy Issues" in *Abortion in a Changing World*, supra note 1 at p. 119.

[37] Bulgaria. Law of 16 Feb. 1968, Int. Dig. Health Leg., vol. 19, pp. 589–602, 1968.

[38] Henry P. David, *Family Planning and Abortion in the Socialist Countries of Central and Eastern Europe, A Compendium of Observations and Readings*, p. 69, The Population Council, New York, 1970.

[39] Finland. Law No. 239 of 24 Mar. 1970 on the interruption of pregnancy, Int. Dig. Health Leg., vol. 21, no. 4, 1970.

over 38 or has four children under age 18 who reside with her.[40] Authorization of a committee is required if the abortion is sought for sociomedical reasons, danger of fetal abnormality, or pregnancy resulting from a sex crime.

Sweden has not yet announced changes in its abortion law which have been under consideration for three years. Various alternatives are bruited about; that abortion may be permitted on the free choice of the woman provided she consults fully with an abortion service or, possibly, that the decision-making process may be decentralized in order to reduce the current delay which drives many women to illegal abortion.

3. *Abortion on Sociomedical Grounds*—Singapore has enacted sociomedical grounds for abortion along the lines of the British Abortion Act of 1967 but with approval required by a Termination of Pregnancy Authorisation Board, except when abortion is to preserve life or health.[41] This is the first Asian country, after Japan, to enact a liberalized abortion law.

The state of South Australia has also enacted an abortion law modeled after the new British law.[42] Similar legislation is under discussion in New South Wales. A poll of general practitioners in Sydney, N.S.W., found that 957 women approached 92 general practitioners with requests for help in obtaining an abortion in a single year.[43] The fact that each general practitioner is confronted with a major dilemma of this kind ten times a year explains the high proportion of general practitioners in Sydney (76 percent) who favor liberalization of the law.

Since 1965, the German Democratic Republic has liberalized interpretation of its law, so that abortion is now authorized on sociomedical grounds.[44]

Legislation is still pending in India, which in the form proposed would allow abortion on sociomedical grounds and in cases of contraceptive failure.[45]

Experience in England, Wales, and Scotland during the first 18 months of the operation of the 1967 British abortion law reveals a shift from illegal to legal abortion, a shift from the private sector to the National Health Service, a slowing down of the illegitimacy rate (47 percent of all abortions in the first 18 months were for single women), and a narrowing of regional discrepancies in the operation of the law.[46] With the aid of voluntary preg-

40 Denmark. Law of 18 Mar. 1970, Int. Dig. Health Leg., vol. 21, no. 3, 1970.

41 The Abortion Act of Singapore, 1969, Republic of Singapore, passed 29 Dec. 1969 and assented to by the President 31 Dec. 1969, Int. Dig. Health Leg., vol. 21, no. 4, 1970.

42 South Australia. An Act to amend the Criminal Consolidation Act, 1935–1966, No. 109 of 1969, assented to 8 Jan. 1970.

43 William Sussman and Anthony I. Adams, General Practitioners' Views on Pregnancy Termination. M. J. Australia, pp. 169–73, July 25, 1970.

44 Supra note 38 at p. 233.

45 India. The Medical Termination of Pregnancy Bill, 1969 (Bill No. XXII of 1969).

46 Peter Diggory and Malcolm Potts. Preliminary Assessment of the 1967 Abortion Act in Practice. Lancet, pp. 287–91. Feb. 7, 1970.

nancy advisory services, abortion is being made available to women in all geographic areas and income groups.[47] Attitudes of gynecologists are becoming more sympathetic to applicants for abortion, as reflected by "the granting of National Health Service abortions on an increasing scale and by bodies such as the Royal College of Obstetricians and Gynaecologists taking a sincere, if belated, interest in contraception and sterilization."[48] The most serious problem appears to be the universal need for improving contraceptive services and practices.

4. *Abortion on Medical Grounds*—Canada[49] and Peru[50] have broadened their abortion laws to permit abortion on the grounds of danger to the life or health of the woman.

5. *Abortion Only to Save the Life of the Woman*—This category has lost adherents. It will continue to do so as current law reform activities in many countries, e.g., France, increase in tempo.

Insights from abroad

As the United States moves into the problems associated with providing medical care under its new abortion laws, several lessons from the experience of other nations seem relevant.

1. A liberal abortion law will transfer a number of illegal abortions to safe, clinical practice; but as long as restrictions in grounds or procedures remain, some illegal abortion will persist.[51] Initial experience under the California Therapeutic Abortion Act confirms this finding.[52] Therefore, experience in the four states that have removed virtually all restrictions will be extremely important.

2. The earlier in pregnancy that abortion is provided, the less tendency there is to resort to illegal abortion. In eastern Europe, where abortion is generally done early in pregnancy, illegal abortion has been almost elimi-

---

[47] Id. at p. 290.
[48] Ibid.
[49] Stats. of Canada, C. 38, sec. 18 (1968–69).
[50] Peru. Decree-Law No. 17505 of 18 Mar. 1969, Ch. 11, sec. 19, Int. Dig. Health Leg., vol. 21, p. 137 at 140, 1970.
[51] D. Malcolm Potts, "Induced Abortion—the Experience of Other Nations" in *Population Control, Implications, Trends, and Prospects*, Proceedings of the Pakistan International Family Planning Conference at Dacca, Jan. 28–Feb. 4, 1969, p. 241, Sweden Pakistan Family Welfare Project, Lahore, West Pakistan, March 1969.
[52] See California State Department of Public Health, *A Report to the 1970 Legislature, Third Annual Report on the Implementation of the California Therapeutic Abortion Act*, p. 5, estimating that 81,600 abortions were done on California women in 1968, of which 76,600 were illegal. Even substantially increased numbers of therapeutic abortions—which have occurred since 1968—will not eliminate an illegal abortion problem of this magnitude. The source of the estimated number of illegal abortions was a carefully controlled study in North Carolina. James R. Abernathy; Bernard G. Greenberg; and Daniel G. Horvitz, "Estimates of Induced Abortion in Urban North Carolina." Demography, vol. 7, no. 1, p. 19, Feb., 1970.

nated. The reverse is true in Sweden, where administrative procedures delay authorization for legal abortion. The U.S. laws specify time periods within which the abortion must be performed, but, in addition, women should be educated to seek abortions early and procedures should be simplified to achieve this objective.

3. On the basis of experience from eastern Europe, mortality from legal abortion can be anticipated to be low, particularly if performed early in pregnancy.[53] Complications in eastern Europe affect less than three percent of patients.[54] England, as yet, has insufficient data on morbidity. One British authority has suggested that the requirement of a medical report within seven days after the abortion is too short a time to provide accurate information on complications.[55] Accurate records and reporting are essential.

4. As the British experience indicates, the climbing rate of illegitimacy in the United States may be slowed by increased availability of abortion. With nearly 10 percent of all U.S. births in 1967 illegitimate, the option of abortion will need to be made widely known and accessible if the risks to health and the social disabilities of births to unmarried mothers are to be lessened.[56]

5. Uneven application of the law by reason of varying attitudes on the part of physicians can be anticipated from the experience in England and Norway. California's experience is similar. Continuing education programs for the medical profession and reforms in medical education are urgent.

6. Shortages of medical and auxiliary personnel may impede full implementation of new laws. In England, however, it was found that, if evenly distributed among all gynecologists, the increased number of abortions would not constitute an excessive workload.[57] It has been suggested that in the United States the load might be distributed among a larger group of physicians than those specialized in gynecology, if the social policy expressed by the new laws is to be implemented. Residents and interns on all services might be expected to perform abortions. Nurse-midwives might also be trained and utilized to perform early abortions. Such a decision would require amendment of the licensure laws in the three states that now license nurse-midwives and enactment of such licensure laws in other states.

7. England's experience shows the bottleneck that may result from

---

[53] See Christopher Tietze. "Abortion Laws and Practices in Europe," *Excerpta Medica International Congress,* Series No. 207, April, 1969; and Christopher Tietze, "Mortality with Contraception and Induced Abortion," *Studies in Family Planning,* vol. 45, p. 6, Sept. 1969.

[54] Supra note 38 at p. 253.

[55] Supra note 46 at p. 290.

[56] On the higher risks of the unmarried mother and her child, see *Health Aspects of Family Planning,* Report of a WHO Scientific Group, World Health Organization Tech. Rep. Series, No. 442, p. 10, Geneva, 1970.

[57] Supra note 46 at p. 288.

shortage of facilities. Ambulatory care, as provided in other countries and as now demonstrated in the United States, is a promising solution for early abortions. Moreover, ambulatory treatment reduces the cost of abortions.

8. Evidence from Chile, South Korea, and Taiwan indicates that, in a country with a high or increasing abortion rate, the conditions are favorable for effective family planning programs.[58] A possible hazard is that the easy solution of abortion may generate a lack of responsibility in using contraceptives. Zeal to meet a long-neglected human need should be accompanied by efforts to use abortion as a means of encouraging effective contraception. A number of European statutes prohibit abortion if an abortion has been performed in the preceding six-month period. A more effective deterrent to repeated abortion would consist in aiding every woman who has an abortion to obtain and use effective methods of contraception.

The dynamic legislative and judicial developments in the laws governing abortion in the United States have generated a ground swell of change. The action of the U.S. Supreme Court is crucial to the rate of progress, but, regardless of the outcome of cases pending before the court, the clock can never be turned back. Safe, legal abortion is now recognized as a fundamental right of women, a protection of maternal health and family welfare, and an assurance that every child is a loved and wanted child. Abortion, however, should be only one service in an array of services that should also include effective contraception, education for responsible sexual relationships, and health protection for mothers and children.

Acknowledgments. For helpful information on recent legal cases, grateful acknowledgment is made to four authorities on abortion law: Roy Lucas, Norma Zarky, Alan Charles, and Zad Leavy. Any errors are, of course, the responsibility of the author.

ADDENDUM

Since this paper was written, the U.S. Supreme Court has upheld the legality of the District of Columbia statute permitting abortion only if "necessary for the preservation of the mother's life or health." *U.S.* vs. *Vuitch*, 402 U.S. 62 (1971). Although the Court found the statute not unconstitutionally vague, it emphasized the medical character of abortion by explicitly interpreting the word *health* to include mental health. Perhaps more importantly, it changed the rule on burden of proof. In a criminal action involving alleged violation of the abortion statute, the burden is now on the prosecution to plead and prove that the abortion was not necessary for the preservation of the woman's life or health rather than on the physician to prove that the abortion was necessary for these reasons.

---

[58] Lars Erik Engstrom. "Abortion as a Method of Population Control," in *Population Control, Implications, Trends, and Prospects,* supra note 51 at p. 340.

Two other cases, one involving the constitutionality of the Texas old-style antiabortion law and the other of the 1968 American Law Institute style law of Georgia, are before the U.S. Supreme Court at its October 1971 term. These cases raise squarely the constitutional issue of the right of privacy not decided by *Vuitch* and what Norma Zarky calls the woman's right of reproductive autonomy.

In California, on November 18, 1971, more than 250 medical school deans, professors and physicians filed an amicus curiae brief in two cases on appeal to the California Supreme Court urging the court to find the California Therapeutic Abortion Act unconstitutional as an invasion of the fundamental right of physicians to practice medicine and of the fundamental right of women to personal privacy. (*People* v. *Pettegrew* and *People* v. *Barksdale,* Crim. Nos. 15841 and 15866, California Supreme Court.)

26

The V.D. control problem*

COMMITTEE ON THE JOINT STATEMENT
AMERICAN PUBLIC HEALTH ASSOCIATION
AMERICAN SOCIAL HEALTH ASSOCIATION
AMERICAN VENEREAL DISEASE ASSOCIATION

The Joint Statement last year (1970) predicted an imminent increase in the incidence of infectious syphilis in many parts of the United States. This prediction has unfortunately been fulfilled: reported cases of infectious syphilis have risen at the alarming rate of 8.1 percent throughout the nation in fiscal year 1970.[1] In some of the larger cities the increase has been in excess of 50 percent. The annual decline in reported infectious syphilis which began in 1965 has ended.[2]

The situation is not only alarming for its impact during the year under report, but can also be expected to lead to an increasing number of un-diagnosed cases escaping detection during the primary and secondary stages of the disease. According to the U.S. Public Health Service, it is estimated that more than 500,000 Americans are unaware that they are suffering from syphilis and are in urgent need of skilled medical attention. The present increase in new cases will enlarge this national reservoir of undetected syphilis. Some of these undiscovered cases will progress to insanity, paralysis, blindness, cardio-vascular disease and other serious pathology.

---

* Reprinted by permission of the American Social Health Association. Condensed from *To-day's VD Control Problem—1971*.

[1] Fiscal Year 1970 is the year July 1, 1969 through June 30, 1970.

[2] Figures from the 1972 Joint Statement show a rise during fiscal 1971 of 15.6 percent for syphilis and 8.9 percent for gonorrhea.

Institutional care of the syphilitic insane alone is already costing over $40 million per year.

The U.S. for some years has had a high rate of congenital syphilis compared with other western nations. With the increase this year of infectious syphilis, the number of syphilitic still-births and infants born with the disease from infected mothers will undoubtedly increase in the future.

Cases of congenital syphilis actually occurring must be much higher than the number reported, since only one in six reported cases is diagnosed in the first year of life.

Reported cases of gonorrhea have increased by an additional 16 percent during fiscal 1970. It is estimated that more than 2,000,000 cases were treated during the year, thus making gonorrhea by far the most common reportable communicable disease in the nation.

An unknown number of cases escape detection and contribute to the *silent reservoir of infection in females*, a phenomenon of the present pandemic. In the 20–24 age group, as many as one in 20 sexually active females may be suffering from gonorrhea and unaware of her infection.

It is apparent that gonorrhea is undergoing rapid epidemiological as well as clinical change. The gonococcus is increasing its resistance to penicillin and to some other antibiotics. When penicillin was first introduced as the therapeutic agent of choice for the treatment of gonorrhea, comparatively small dosage resulted in a high percentage of "cures." A much larger dosage of penicillin is now required for "cure."

The practical upper dosage limit of penicillin required to produce the blood level which is needed to kill the gonococcus is rapidly being approached. Resistant strains are also being found to the second drug of choice, tetracycline. This resilient organism, which has been with us since time immemorial, will probably adapt itself successfully to the antibiotic era. Intensified research for an ideal therapeutic agent for gonorrhea which does not produce resistant strains is now essential.

Penicillin resistance is more apparent in the western part of the United States than in the eastern. A systematic national program to define the degree of resistance in various parts of the country has now become necessary. While the Center for Disease Control of the Public Health Service has re-established a surveillance program, major laboratories throughout the country must also become involved in such a program.

Treatment schedules for gonorrhea must keep pace with the increasing resistance of the organism. It is evident that clinical practice is not resilient enough to adjust to the ever changing situation. The therapeutic schedule which was effective last year may now produce a significant percentage of case failures in a specific locality. Frequent local evaluation of treatment schedules is a necessity.

Serious clinical complications of gonorrhea, especially in females, are being encountered with increasing frequency. There is reason to suspect that 10–12 percent of gonorrhea in females proceeds to inflammation of the fallopian tubes (salpingitis) which can result in sterility and may ultimately lead to abdominal surgery.

There are reports that cases of gonococcal arthritis in increasing numbers are being diagnosed when sought. Gonococcal ophthalmia neonatorum outbreaks have been reported in institutions where the routine of prophylactic drops applied to infants' eyes was relaxed. An awareness of the need for further clinical research into the complications of gonorrhea must be promoted.

Until recently many public health authorities had come to regard gonorrhea as low in the scale of priorities for organized community action. The significant changes in the disease pattern which have occurred recently call for a reassessment of these priorities.

Perhaps because of their special mode of transmission, and the traditional stigma associated with venereal diseases, federal, state and community action has fallen far short of requirements. Syphilis is again increasing, and gonorrhea is clearly out of control.

A satisfactory vaccine against syphilis is still in the theoretical stage and, at the present rate of progress, will not be available for some years.

Approaches towards producing a satisfactory immunizing or other preventive agent against gonorrhea have not been formulated.

Asymptomatic gonorrhea in females is a phenomenon of the present outbreak. To a lesser extent, asymptomatic gonorrhea also occurs in the male. A mass screening blood test for detection of active gonorrhea would facilitate early diagnosis. Some progress has been made at the Center for Disease Control, Atlanta, Georgia, toward developing such a laboratory test. The test, when further refined, will be available for screening large numbers of females in high incidence groups.

Today we have no foolproof chemical or mechanical prophylactic against contracting venereal disease. The present state of research into mechanical, chemical and antibiotic protective agents is far from conclusive. No recommendations can be made at this time on methods of prophylaxis against the venereal diseases.

In order to learn more about the type of sex partners involved in the transmission of venereal disease, the respondents to a Joint Statement questionnaire were asked to classify sex contacts to a venereal disease by type of exposure: single exposure; multiple (two or more) exposures; and marital partner exposure.

Of special epidemiological significance is the fact that three out of four contacts named were either marital or multiple exposures . . . a group of contacts that should be fairly easy to identify and locate through proper application of the interview technique and utilization of the infected patient's knowledge about his or her contacts. Also, about one out of every four contacts named were classified as single exposures; i.e. casual encounters, perhaps pick-ups or prostitutes . . . a group of contacts posing problems of location since the infected patient's knowledge about such contacts is sometimes limited. Good epidemiologic procedures—including reinterview of the patient, cross correlation of data from other interviews and other investigations, along with effective investigative techniques—are needed to bring such contacts to medical examination.

Exposure to a person of the same sex occurred in less than 15 percent of the named contacts. Although the data is limited, exposure to the same sex occurred relatively much more often among contacts to infectious syphilis (occurring in almost 19 percent of the named contacts) than for gonorrhea (occurring in less than 6 percent of the named contacts).

It is noted that relatively more than twice as many contacts to gonorrhea were classed as "single exposure of opposite sex" compared to contacts to primary and secondary syphilis. Generally somewhat less complete information is available on "single exposure" contacts. Special interview-investigative techniques may be needed to assure that such contacts are brought to medical examination, for a large number of contacts "not examined" would certainly contribute to further spread of the disease and make control a difficult, if not impossible, task.

Infants born with syphilitic infection contracted in utero from the mother are all too common in the United States today. They become infected through the placenta during the last five months of pregnancy. Antepartum therapy for syphilis can assure the birth of an uninfected child.

As shown in Table 1 there were 1,903 cases of congenital syphilis reported in fiscal 1970, of which only 300, or 15.8 percent, were diagnosed in the first year of life. These reported cases of congenital syphilis indicate a breakdown in the application of services which exist for control of congenital syphilis.

TABLE 1. Congenital syphilis, United States, fiscal years 1962–1970 (number of cases reported).

Fiscal year	Total	Under one year of age	
		Number	Percent
1962	4,085	330	8.1
1963	4,140	410	9.9
1964	3,737	374	10.0
1965	3,505	373	10.6
1966	3,464	370	10.7
1967	3,050	398	13.0
1968	2,596	327	12.6
1969	2,224	277	12.5
1970	1,903	300	15.8
1971*	2,047	400	19.5

Source: Department of Health, Education, and Welfare; Health Services and Mental Health Administration; Center for Disease Control; Atlanta, Georgia 30333.
* Figures from the 1972 Joint Statement have been added.

In 44 states and the District of Columbia, physicians are required to see that all pregnant women have a serologic test for syphilis performed. Serologic tests in both first and third trimesters are recommended in order to discover those women who become infected during their pregnancies. As shown in Table 2 below, only 23 cities replied that 90 percent or more of

TABLE 2. Percentage of pregnant women in 154 cities that had STS during both first and third trimesters of pregnancy (fiscal year 1970).

Percentage range	Number of health depts.
0	6
1-4	6
5-9	11
10-19	9
20-29	11
30-49	6
50-89	25
90 and up	23
Sub total	97
No Data	57
Total	154

Source: Joint Statement questionnaire

the pregnant women in their jurisdiction received STS during both first and third trimesters of pregnancy. Some 49 cities indicated that less than 50 percent (six cities said None) of the pregnant women received an STS during the first and third trimesters of pregnancy.

In an attempt to determine why congenital syphilis cases continue to occur, states and cities were asked: "How many mothers of congenital syphilis infants had prenatal care?" Replies from 25 cities stated that 47 percent of mothers of congenital syphilis cases received prenatal care. Twenty-seven cities reporting one or more cases of congenital syphilis under one year of age indicated that information on prenatal care of the mothers was not available.

To the question, "Do you routinely follow-up on some or all children born to women who have had a positive STS during or soon after pregnancy?" a total of 152 cities replied as follows: 130 Yes; 32 No.

Last year the Joint Statement recommended that a federal program be initiated to conduct retrospective studies of congenital syphilis cases in order to determine where prevention failed. The need for such studies is confirmed by replies to the Joint Statement this year, which show that health services do not at present assure the right of each child to be born undamaged by syphilitic infection.

Undoubtedly we can anticipate further increases in congenital syphilis among infants under one year of age as a result of the noted rise in infectious syphilis.

Routine serologic tests on all pregnant women should be required by law in every state. Already existing laws must be rigorously enforced. Such a basic public health procedure costs the community far less than medical care of congenital syphilitic patients, many of whom require institutional care. Few preventive procedures are as effective or as inexpensive as the routine prevention of congenital syphilis.

Venereal disease rates by age groups

While reported incidence of venereal disease is increasing throughout the sexually active segments of the population, the greatest increase continues to take place in the 20–24 year age group.

Review of calendar year 1969 figures (Table 4, page 339)* shows that the rate of primary and secondary syphilis per 100,000 is highest in the 20–24 age group, next highest in the 25–29 age group, followed by the 15–19 age group. The same applies to gonorrhea, although the 15–19 age group has a relatively higher rate. In gonorrhea, the 10–14 age group has a significantly high rate.

Primary and secondary syphilis rates are about equal in the age groups below and above 25. It is interesting to note that gonorrhea rates for persons under age 25 are more than double those for persons over age 25.

Although the rate of infection is much higher in the 20–24 age group, teenagers represent a relatively "captive audience" for preventive education about the venereal diseases. If they were fully informed about the dangers of VD and ways to prevent it, they might retain the information when they join the next age group, where the highest percentage of venereal disease is now found.

It must be emphasized that any analysis of the age-specific distribution of cases is of reported cases only. It is estimated that they represent only one-fourth of cases actually occurring. Most unreported cases are treated by doctors in private practice who would perhaps be inclined to report young single persons and not report older married persons. We are convinced that the present increase of venereal disease crosses all age and socioeconomic groups. Sex is an active part of the economic infrastructure purveying to an affluent middle class, middle aged population, rather than to the young. The venereal disease reservoir of infection is widespread, and offers an increasing chance of infection to all age groups involved in sexual risk taking behavior.

---

* Figures for the calendar year 1970, reproduced from the 1972 Joint Statement, appear in Table 5, page 340.

Treatment of minors

The number of states having laws permitting minors to give their own consent for venereal disease treatment has increased from 14 in 1968 to 30 (including the District of Columbia) in 1970. See Table 3, below. Of the

TABLE 3. States with laws permitting minors to give their own consent for VD treatment (as of June 30, 1970).

Alaska	Illinois	Massachusetts	Pennsylvania
Arkansas	Indiana	Michigan	Rhode Island
California	Iowa	Montana	Tennessee
Colorado	Kansas	Nebraska	Texas
Connecticut	Kentucky	Nevada	Washington
Delaware	Louisiana	New Jersey	District of
Florida	Maine	New York	Columbia
Hawaii	Maryland	Oregon	

Source: Joint Statement questionnaire

22 states (including Puerto Rico) remaining without such laws, the following indicated in replies to the Joint Statement that enactment was being sought: Arizona, Georgia, Minnesota, Missouri, New Mexico, South Carolina, South Dakota, Utah, Wyoming, Puerto Rico.

The following eight states have attorney general's opinions which allow treatment of minors for venereal disease without parental consent: Idaho, New Hampshire, North Carolina, Oklahoma, South Carolina, South Dakota, Vermont, Virginia.

Last year's Joint Statement recommended that new techniques of health education be developed to reach teenagers and young adults, who are now the source of more than one half of reported venereal disease. Although little systematic action was taken in this direction, there are indications that young people themselves are responding to a felt need and requesting more factual information on the sexually transmitted diseases. Discussion groups organized by high school and college students seem to be increasing. Some dissident groups with high venereal disease rates have organized their own free clinics. These developments indicate a distrust by the young of traditional organized community action. The tendency for the older generation to be "uptight" on the VD question and to talk down to their children is understandable. But they forget that their generation, during and following World War II, was responsible for a higher syphilis rate than today's, and an approximately equivalent gonorrhea rate.

The present outbreak is by no means confined to younger age groups or lower socioeconomic groups; some local pillars of society, just returning from conventions and business trips, present themselves in increasing numbers each year in doctors' offices. Their harried and secretive attitude re-

TABLE 4. VD infection by age groups.

Population block — columns: **Population** / **Pct. of total**

	1956 Population	Pct. of total	1966 Population	Pct. of total	1967 Population	Pct. of total	1968 Population	Pct. of total	1969 Population	Pct. of total
0–9 years	36,751,000	22.2	40,657,000	21.0	40,101,000	20.5	39,439,000	20.0	38,787,000	19.4
10–14 years	13,720,000	8.3	19,402,000	10.0	19,885,000	10.2	20,231,000	10.2	20,518,000	10.3
15–19 years	10,855,000	6.6	17,434,000	9.0	17,210,000	8.8	17,753,000	9.0	18,114,000	9.1
20–24 years	9,543,000	6.8	12,705,000	6.6	13,672,000	7.0	13,947,000	7.1	14,674,000	7.3
25–29 years	11,181,000	6.8	11,152,000	5.8	11,700,000	6.0	12,383,000	6.3	12,877,000	6.4
0–24 years	70,872,000	42.9	90,198,000	46.6	90,869,000	46.4	91,370,000	46.2	92,093,000	46.1
25 years up	94,470,000	57.1	103,503,000	53.4	104,836,000	53.6	106,201,000	53.8	107,592,000	53.9
Total	165,341,000	100.0	193,701,000	100.0	195,702,000	100.0	197,571,000	100.0	199,685,000	100.0

P & S syphilis — columns: **Number of cases** / **Rate per 100,000**

	1956 No. of cases	Rate per 100,000	1966 No. of cases	Rate per 100,000	1967 No. of cases	Rate per 100,000	1968 No. of cases	Rate per 100,000	1969 No. of cases	Rate per 100,000
0–9 years	11	.0	27	.1	31	.1	34	.1	35	.1
10–14 years	67	.5	215	1.1	208	1.0	215	1.1	223	1.1
15–19 years	1,163	10.7	3,846	22.1	3,806	22.1	3,423	19.3	3,423	18.9
20–24 years	1,758	18.4	6,033	47.5	6,152	45.0	5,405	38.8	5,295	36.1
25–29 years	1,263	11.3	4,339	38.9	4,181	35.7	3,733	30.1	3,758	29.2
0–24 years	2,999	4.2	10,121	11.2	10,197	11.2	9,077	9.9	8,976	9.7
25 years up	3,396	3.6	11,293	10.9	10,856	10.4	9,942	9.4	10,154	9.4
Total	6,395	3.9	21,414	11.1	21,053	10.8	19,019	9.6	19,130	9.6

Gonorrhea — columns: **Number of cases** / **Rate per 100,000**

	1956 No. of cases	Rate per 100,000	1966 No. of cases	Rate per 100,000	1967 No. of cases	Rate per 100,000	1968 No. of cases	Rate per 100,000	1969 No. of cases	Rate per 100,000
0–9 years	1,202	3.3	1,471	3.6	1,625	4.1	1,631	4.1	1,928	5.0
10–14 years	2,398	17.5	2,775	14.3	3,170	15.9	4,173	20.6	4,325	21.1
15–19 years	45,161	415.7	76,032	436.1	91,390	531.0	108,405	610.6	129,071	712.5
20–24 years	74,693	781.8	126,339	994.4	148,877	1,088.9	174,485	1,251.1	207,221	1,412.2
25–29 years	48,624	434.2	70,263	630.0	80,953	691.9	90,312	729.3	102,257	794.1
0–25 years	123,454	174.0	206,617	229.1	245,062	269.7	288,694	316.0	342,545	372.0
25 years up	101,229	106.9	145,121	140.2	159,774	152.4	175,849	165.6	192,327	178.8
Total	224,683	135.7	351,738	181.6	404,836	206.9	464,543	235.1	534,872	267.9

Source: Department of Health, Education, and Welfare; Health Services and Mental Health Administration; Center for Disease Control; Atlanta, Georgia 30333. Reported Cases Only.

TABLE 5. Primary and secondary syphilis and gonorrhea (morbidity and age-specific rates per 100,000 population by age groups of reported cases—United States, calendar year 1970).

| Age group | Primary and secondary syphilis | | Gonorrhea | |
	Number of reported cases	Rate per 100,000 population	Number of reported cases	Rate per 100,000 population
0–9	29	0.1	2,226	5.7
10–14	225	1.1	5,289	25.5
15–19	3,651	20.1	147,952	808.6
20–24	6,213	41.9	239,466	1,615.5
25–29	4,424	34.0	110,001	845.6
30–39	4,808	21.7	69,517	313.6
40–49	1,866	7.7	19,267	79.1
50+	766	1.6	6,354	12.9
Total	21,982	10.9	600,072	297.5

Source: Department of Health, Education, and Welfare, Health Services and Mental Health Administration, Center for Disease Control, Atlanta, Georgia 30333.

veals their problem. The visit ends with a "never again" promise—until the next trip.

The present increase in venereal disease is worldwide in scope, being highest in those areas experiencing civil unrest, social change and population mobility. The World Health Organization has upgraded the priority to be given to these diseases in its program of supporting national health administrations.

Where do we stand at the moment in the U.S.A. regarding this alarming increase in infectious syphilis and the pandemic of gonorrhea? Following outbreaks of such diseases as diptheria there is an immediate response leading to rapid action by the public, the government and the medical profession. Because of the traditional stigma surrounding the venereal diseases, the lag period between public concern and organized action is much longer. The United States is now in that extended lag period. The public has not yet realized the full significance of the present epidemic situation and so has not forced governmental and professional action.

However, the year 1970 has seen increased awareness, thanks partly to the activities of such voluntary agencies as the American Social Health Association, which has channeled the facts of the situation to the mass media. There is much work still to be done to stimulate public demand for additional appropriations for venereal disease control programs. Much will depend on how effective the proposed National Commission on Venereal Disease will be in further defining the problem, formulating a national technical strategy and outlining a control program—involving all sections of public and private medicine as well as the social sciences.

The rates of infection will continue to increase for some years to come and the venereal diseases will only be brought under control by rigorous and well planned, coordinated action. Federal leadership, including additional appropriations for research and grants, will be necessary. State and local health departments will have to invest much more in venereal disease control than they are doing at present. Voluntary groups at local levels must stimulate programs to correct the social aspects of the problem and work to influence patterns of individual behavior. Above all, the medical profession must become more involved.

27
Swinging in wedlock*

CHARLES and REBECCA PALSON

Since the later 1960s, an increasing number of middle-class couples have turned to mate swapping or "swinging" as an alternative to strictly monogamous marriage. That is, married couples (or unmarried couples with an apparently stable relationship) willingly and knowingly relinquish sexual rights to their own mates so that others may temporarily enjoy these rights. This phenomenon, which is fairly recent in its openness and proportions, provides an opportunity of testing, on a large scale, the traditional theories about the consequences of extramarital sexual activity. It has often been assumed that sexual infidelity, where all the concerned parties know of it, results to some degree in jealousy. The intensity of jealousy is thought to increase in proportion to the amount of real or imagined emotional involvement on the part of the unfaithful member of the couple. Conversely, the more "purely physical" the infidelity, the less likely that there will be any jealousy. Thus it is often hypothesized that where marital stability coexists with infidelity, the character of the extramarital involvement is relatively depersonalized.

In the film *Bob and Carol and Ted and Alice*, Bob finds Carol, his wife, entertaining another man in their bedroom. Although he had previously told her that he was having an affair, and they had agreed in principle that she too could have affairs, he is obviously shaken by the reality. Nervously trying to reassure himself, he asks, "Well, it's just *sex*, isn't it? I mean, you don't *love* him?" In other words, Bob attempts to avoid feelings of jealousy by believing that Carol's affair involves only depersonalized sex in contrast to their own relationship of love.

In his book, *Group Sex*, Gilbert Bartell offers the same hypothesis about those people he calls "organization swingers":

They are terrified of the idea that involvement might take place. They take comfort from the fact that if they swing with a couple only once or at most twice, the chances of running into a marriage-threatening involvement are small.

These swingers, who can be described as organizational only in the sense that they tend to use swinger magazines or special swinging nightclubs to make their contacts, are mostly beginners who *may* act in ways that approximate Bartell's description. Near the end of the book, however, he mentions some couples he interviewed whom he calls dropouts. These people either had never desired depersonalized swinging or had passed through a depersonalized stage but now preferred some degree of emotional involvement and long-term friendship from their swinging relationships. Bartell does not explain how these couples continue to keep stable relationships and can remain free of jealousy, but the fact that such couples exist indicates that depersonalization is not the only way to jealousy-free swinging.

Our involvement with the subject has been partly a personal one, and this requires some introductory explanation. In September 1969, we read an article about swinging and became fascinated by the questions it raised about sex and the American family. Did this practice signal the beginning of the breakup of the family? Or was it a way to inject new life into marriage as the authors of the article suggested? How do people go about swinging and why? We contemplated these and many other questions but, not knowing any swingers, we could arrive at only very limited answers. It seemed to us that the only way to find out what we wanted to know was to participate ourselves. In one way this seemed natural because anthropologists have traditionally lived with the people they have studied. But our curiosity about swinging at that time was more personal than professional, and we knew that ultimately our participation would have personal consequences, although we had no idea what their nature might be. We had to decide whether exploration of this particular unknown was worth the risk of changing the perfectly sound and gratifying relationship which we had built during the previous three-and-a-half years. Finally, our misgivings gave way to curiosity and we wrote off to some couples who advertised in a national swinger's magazine.

Although, like most beginners, we were excited about swinging, we were nervous too. We didn't know what swinging in reality was like or what "rules" there were, if any. In general, however, we found those first experiences not only enjoyable from a personal point of view, but stimulating intellectually. It was then that we decided to study swinging as anthropologists. But, like many anthropologists who use participant observation as a method of study, we could never completely divorce ourselves from the personal aspects of our subject.

The method of participant observation is sometimes criticized as being too subjective. In an area such as sex, where experiences are highly individual and personal, we feel that participant observation can yield results even more thorough and disciplined than the more so-called objective methods. Most of our important insights into the nature of swinging could only have been found by actually experiencing some of the same things that our informants did. Had we not participated, we would not have known how to question them about many central aspects of their experience.

This article presents the results of our 18-month, participant observation study of 136 swingers. We made our contacts in three ways. First, we reached couples through swinger magazines. These are magazines devoted almost exclusively to ads placed by swingers for the purpose of contacting other interested couples and/or singles. Many, although not all, of the couples we contacted in this way seemed to be beginners who had not yet found people with whom they were interested in forming long-term relationships. Second, we were introduced to couples through personal networks. Couples whom we knew would pass our name on to others, sometimes explicitly because they wanted our study to be a success. Third, some couples contacted us as a result of lectures or papers we presented, to volunteer themselves as informants. It should be noted that we did not investigate the swingers' bars, although second-hand reports from couples we met who had used them for making contacts seem to indicate that these couples did not significantly differ from those who do not use the bars. Our informants came from Pennsylvania, New Jersey, New York, Massachusetts, Louisiana, California, Florida and Illinois. They were mostly middle class, although ten could be classified as working class.

Usually we interviewed couples in very informal settings, and these interviews were often indistinguishable from ordinary conversation that swingers might have about themselves and their activities. After each session we would return home, discuss the conversation and write notes on our observations. Later several couples volunteered to tape interviews, enabling us to check the accuracy of the field notes we had taken previously.

In spite of our efforts to find informants from as many different sources as possible, we can in no way guarantee the representativeness of our sample. It should be emphasized that statistics are practically useless in the study of swingers because of insurmountable sampling problems. We therefore avoided the statistical approach and instead focused the investigation on problems of a nonstatistical nature. The information we obtained enabled us to understand and describe the kinds of cultural symbols—a "symbolic calculus," if you will—that swingers must use to effectively navigate social situations with other swingers. This symbolic calculus organizes widely varying experiences into a coherent whole, enabling swingers to understand and evaluate each social situation in which they find themselves. They can thereby define the choices available to them and the desirability of each. Our research goal, then, was to describe the symbols that infuse meaning into the experiences of all the swingers that we contacted.

Unlike Bartell, we had no difficulty finding couples who either wanted to have or had succeeded in having some degree of emotional involvement and long-term friendship within a swinging context. In fact, many of them explained to us that depersonalization simply brought them no satisfaction. In observing such couples with their friends it was evident that they had formed close and enduring relationships. They host each other's children on weekends, celebrate birthdays together, take vacations together and, in general, do what close friends usually do. It should be noted that there is no way of ascertaining the numbers of couples who have actually succeeded in finding close friends through swinging. In fact, they may be under-represented because they tend to retreat into their own small circle of friends and dislike using swinger magazines to find other couples. Thus they are more difficult to contact.

In order to see how swingers are able to form such relationships it is necessary to understand not how they avoid jealousy, but how they deal with its causes. Insecurity and fear of being replaced are the major ingredients in any experience with jealousy. An effective defense against jealousy, then, would include a way to guarantee one's irreplaceability as a mate. If, for example, a wife knows that she is unlike any other woman her husband has ever met or ever will meet, and if they have a satisfying relationship in which they have invested much time and emotion, she can rest assured that no other relationship her husband has can threaten her. If, on the other hand, a woman feels that the continuance of her marital relationship depends on how well she cooks, cleans and makes love, jealousy is more likely to occur, because she realizes that any number of women could fill the same role, perhaps better than she.

Similarly, a man who feels that the continuance of his wife's loyalty depends on how well he provides financial security will be apt to feel more jealousy because many men could perform the same function. To one degree or another, many swingers naturally develop towards a more secure kind of marital relationship, a tendency we call *individuation*. Among the couples we contacted, individuation was achieved for the most part at a level that precluded jealousy. And we found that, to the extent that couples did not individuate, either jealousy occurred or swinging had to take other, less flexible forms in order to prevent it.

We found evidence of individuation in two areas. First, we found that patterns of behavior at gatherings of swingers who had passed the beginning stages were thoroughly pervaded by individuation. Second, we found that by following changes in a couple's attitudes toward themselves, both as individuals and as a couple and toward other swingers, a trend of increasing individuation could be observed.

INDIVIDUATING BEHAVIOR AT GATHERINGS

When we first entered the swinging scene, we hypothesized that swinging must be characterized by a set of implicit and explicit rules or patterns of behavior. But every time we thought we had discovered a pattern, another encounter quickly invalidated it. We finally had to conclude that any particular swinging gathering is characterized by any one of a number of forms, whatever best suits the individuals involved. The ideal, as in nonswinging situations, is for the initiation of sexual interaction to appear to develop naturally—preferably in a nonverbal way. But with four or more people involved and all the signaling and cross-signaling of intentions that must take place, this ideal can only be approached in most cases. The initiation may begin with little or no socializing, much socializing with sex later on as a natural outgrowth of the good feelings thus created, or some mixture in-between. Socializing is of the variety found at many types of nonswinging gatherings. The sexual interaction itself may be "open" where couples participate in the same room or "closet" where couples pair off in separate rooms. In open swinging, a "pretzel," "flesh pile" or "scene" may take place, all terms which signify groups of more than two people having sex with each other. Like Bartell, we found that females are much more likely to participate in homosexuality—probably near 100 percent—while very few men participate in homosexuality. Younger people tend to be much more accepting about the latter.

All of this flexibility can be summed up by saying that swingers consider an ideal gathering one in which everyone can express themselves as individuals *and* appreciate others for doing the same. If even one person fails to have an enjoyable experience in these terms, the gathering is that much less enjoyable for everyone.

An important consequence of this "do your own thing" ethic is that sexual experiences are talked about as a primarily personal matter. Conversely they are not evaluated according to a general standard. Thus one hears about "bad experiences" rather than "bad swingers." This is not to say that swingers are not aware of general sexual competence, but only that it is largely irrelevant to their appreciation of other people. As one informant said:

Technique is not that much. If she's all right, I don't care if she's technically terrible—if I think she's a beautiful person, she can't be that bad.

Beginners may make certain mistakes if they do not individuate. They may, for example, take on the "social director" role. This kind of person insists that a party become the materialization of his own fantasies without regard for anyone else's wishes. This can make the situation very uncomfortable for everyone else unless someone can get him to stop. Or, a nervous beginner may feel compelled to look around to find out what to do and, as a result, will imitate someone else. This imitation can be disturbing to others for two reasons. First, the imitator may not be enjoying himself. Second, he may be competing with someone else by comparing the effects of the same activity on their different partners. In either case, he is not involved with perceiving and satisfying the individual needs of his own partner. This would also be true in the case of the person who regularly imitates his or her own previous behavior, making an unchanging formula for interaction, no matter who he is with. Swingers generally consider such behavior insensitive and/or insincere.

MODIFICATION OF ATTITUDES

Beginners tend to approximate the popular stereotype of sex-starved deviates. A 50-year-old woman described one of her beginning experiences this way:

It was one after another, and really, after a point it didn't make any difference *who* it was. It was just one great big prick after another. And I *never* experienced anything like that in my whole life. I have never had an experience like that with quite so many. I think in the course of three hours I must have had 11 or 12 men, and one greater than the next. It just kept on getting better every time. It snowballed.

The manner in which she describes her experience exemplifies the attitudes of both male and female beginners. They are not likely to develop a long lasting friendship with one or a small number of couples, and they focus much more on sex than the personalities involved. Frequently, they will be more interested in larger parties where individual personality differences are blurred by the number of people.

Simple curiosity seems to be the reason for this attitude. As one beginner told us, "Sometimes, we get titillated with them as people, knowing in the long run that it won't work out." It seems that because the beginner has been prevented so often from satisfying his curiosity through sexual liaisons in "straight" life, an important goal of early swinging is to satisfy this curiosity about people in general. This goal is apt to take precedence over any other for quite some time. Thus, even if a couple sincerely hopes to find long-lasting friendships, their desire to "move on" is apt to win out at first.

Bartell has asserted that both personality shallowness and jealousy are always responsible for this focus on sex and the search for new faces. For the most part, neither of these factors is necessarily responsible. First, the very same couples who appear shallow in fact may develop friendships later on. Second, as we shall see below, some couples who focus almost exclusively on sex nevertheless experience jealousy and must take certain precautions. On the other hand, some swingers *do* couple-hop because of jealousy. The Races, for example, dislike swinging with a couple more than once or twice because of the jealousy that arises each time. Very often only one member is jealous of the other's involvement but the jealousy will be hidden. Pride may prevent each from admitting jealousy for quite some time. Each partner may feel that to admit jealousy would be to admit a weakness and instead will feign disinterest in a particular couple to avoid another meeting.

This stage of swinging eventually stops in almost all cases we know of, probably because the superficial curiosity about people in general is satisfied. Women are usually responsible for the change, probably because they have been raised to reject superficial sexual relationships. Sometimes this is precipitated by a bad experience when, for example, a man is particularly rough or inconsiderate in some way. Sometimes a man will be the first to suggest a change because of erection problems which seem to be caused in some cases by a general lack of interest in superficial sexual contacts. In other words, once his general curiosity is satisfied, he can no longer sustain enough interest to be aroused.

The termination of the curiosity stage and the beginning of a stage of relative selectivity is characterized by increasing individuation of self and others. Among men this change manifests itself in the nature of fantasies that give interest to the sexual experience. The statement of one male informant exemplifies the change:

Now, I don't fantasize much. There's too much reality to fantasize, too much sex and sex realities we've experienced. So there is not too much that I *can* fantasize with. I just remember the good times we've actually had.

Instead of fantasies being what one would wish to happen, they are instead a kind of reliving of pleasant past experiences with particular people. Also, some informants have noticed that where their previous fantasies had been impersonal, they eventually became tied to specific people with whom pleasant sexual experiences had been shared.

Increasing individuation is also noticeable in beginners' changing perceptions of certain problems that arise in swinging situations. Many male swingers have difficulty with erections at one time or another. Initially, this can be quite ego shattering. The reason for this trauma is not difficult to understand. Most Americans believe that the mere sight of a nude, sexually available woman should arouse a man almost instantly. A male who fails to be aroused may interpret this as a sign of his hitherto unknown impotency. But if he is not too discouraged by this first experience he may eventually find the real reasons. He may realize that he does not find some women attractive mentally and/or physically even though they are sexually available. He learns to recognize when he is being deliberately though subtly discouraged by a woman. He may discover that he dislikes certain situational factors. For example, he may find that he likes only open or only closet swinging or that he cannot relax sufficiently to perform after a hard day's work. Once a swinger realizes that his physical responses may very well be due to elements that inhere to the individual relationship rather than to an innate sexual inadequacy, he has arrived at a very different conception of sexual relationships. He is better able to see women as human beings to whom he may be attracted as personalities rather than as objects to be exploited for their sexual potential. In our terms, he can now more successfully individuate his relationships with women.

Women must cope with problems of a slightly different nature when they begin to swing. Their difficulties develop mostly because of their tendency to place decorum above the expression of their own individual desires in social situations. This tendency manifests itself from the time the husband suggests swinging. Many women seem to swing merely because their husbands want to rather than because of their own positive feelings on the matter. This should not be interpreted to mean that wives participate against their will, but only that as in most recreational activity, the male provides the initial impetus that she can then choose to go along with or reject. Her lack of positive initiative may express itself in the quality of her interaction. She is apt to swing with a man not because he manifests particular attributes that she appreciates, but because he lacks any traits that she finds outright objectionable. One woman describes one of her first experiences this way:

As I recall, I did not find him particularly appealing, but he was nice, and that was OK. He actually embarrassed me a bit because he was so shy and such a kind of nonperson.

This is not to say that women do not enjoy their experiences once they begin participating. The same woman remarks about her first experience in this way:

Somehow, it was the situation that made the demand. I got turned on, although I hadn't anticipated a thing up to that point. In fact, I still have a hard time accounting for my excitement that first time and the good time which I did actually have.

In fact, it sometimes happens at this stage that women become more enthusiastic about swinging than men, much to the latter's embarrassment.

Their enjoyment, however, seems to result from the same kind of psychology that is likely to propel them into swinging in the first place, the desire to please men. Hence, like her nonswinging counterparts, a woman in swinging will judge herself in terms of her desirability and her attractiveness to men much more than thinking about her own individuality in relation to others.

After swinging for awhile, however, her wish to be desired and to satisfy can no longer be as generalized because it becomes apparent that she is indeed desired by many men, and thus she has no need to prove it to herself. In order to make the experience meaningful, she arrives at a point where she feels that she must begin to actually refuse the advances of many men. This means that she must learn to define her own preferences more clearly and to learn to act on these preferences, an experience that many women rarely have because they have learned to rely on their husbands to make these kinds of decisions in social situations. In short, a woman learns to individuate both herself and others in the second stage of swinging.

Another change that swingers mention concerns their feelings towards their mates. They say that since they started swinging they communicate better than they did before. Such couples, who previously had a stable but uninteresting or stale marriage ("like brother and sister without the blood"), say that swinging has recreated the romantic feelings they once had for each other. These feelings seem to find concrete expression in an increasing satisfaction with the sexual aspects of the marital relationship, if not in an actual increase in sexual intercourse. This is almost always experienced by older couples in terms of feeling younger.

An explanation for this change, again, involves the individuation process. Marriage can grow stale if a couple loses a sense of appreciation of each other's individuality. A husband may look too much like an ordinary husband, a wife like an ordinary wife. This can happen easily especially when a couple's circumstances (job, children and so forth) necessitate a great deal of routinization of their life together. Such couples find in swinging the rare opportunity to escape from the routine roles that must be assumed in everyday life. In this setting individual differences receive attention and appreciation and, because of this, married couples can again see and appreciate their own distinct individuality, thus reactivating their romantic feelings for each other.

It is interesting to note that, those couples who do not answer in this way almost always experience jealousy, not romanticization, as a result of swinging. This is the case with one couple we interviewed, each of whom insists that the other is "better than anyone else," although it was clear by their jealousy of each other that neither was entirely confident of this.

Individuation, then, pervades the swinging scene and plays an important role in minimizing jealousy. But it alone cannot guarantee the control of jealousy—because there is always the possibility that a person will appreciate and be equally attracted to two unique individuals. Clearly, individuation must be complemented with something more if the marriage is to be effectively distinguished from other extramarital relationships.

This "something else" is compatibility. Two individuals who perceive and appreciate each other's individuality may nevertheless make poor living mates unless they are compatible. Compatibility is a kind of super-individuation. It requires not only the perception and appreciation of uniqueness, but the inclusion of this in the solutions to any problems that confront the relationship. Each partner must have the willingness and the ability to consider his or her mate's needs, desires and attitudes, when making the basic decisions that affect them both. This is viewed as something that people must work to achieve, as indicated by the phrase, "He failed in his marriage."

Unlike swinging, then, marriage requires a great deal of day-to-day giving and taking, and an emotional investment that increases with the years. Because such an investment is not given up easily, it provides another important safeguard against jealousy.

The dimension of marital compatibility often shows itself in swinging situations. If and when serious problems are encountered by one marriage partner, it is expected that the other partner will take primary responsibility for doing what is necessary. One couple, for example, was at a gathering, each sitting with their swinging partners. It was the first time they had ever tried pot, and the wife suddenly became hysterical. The man she was with quickly relinquished his place to her husband, who was expected to take primary responsibility for comforting his wife, although everyone was concerned about her. Another example can occur when a man has erection problems. If he is obviously miserable, it is considered wrong for his wife to ignore his condition, although we have heard of a few cases where this has happened. His wife may go to his side and they will decide to go home or she may simply act worried and less than completely enthusiastic, thus evincing some minimal concern for her husband. In other words, the married couple is still distinguished as the most compatible partners and remains therefore the primary problem-solving unit.

The importance of compatibility also shows up in certain situations where a couple decides that they must stop swinging. In several cases reported to us, couples who had been married two years or less found that swinging tended to disrupt their marital relationship. We ourselves encountered three couples who had been married for under one year and had not lived together before marriage. All three had difficulties as a result of swinging, and one is now divorced. These couples evidently had not had the time to build up the emotional investment so necessary to a compatible marriage.

It is clear, then, that to the degree that couples individuate and are compatible, jealousy presents no major problems. Conversely, when these conditions are not satisfied, disruptive jealousy can result.

There are, however, some interesting exceptions. For a few couples who seem to place little emphasis on individuation, marital compatibility is an issue which remains chronically unresolved. Compatibility for them is a quality to be constantly demonstrated rather than a fact of life to be more or less taken for granted. Hence, every give-and-take becomes an issue.

These couples focus on the mechanics of sexual competence rather than on personal relationships. These are the people who will talk about "good swingers" and "bad swingers" rather than good and bad experiences. One of these husbands once commented:

Some people say there's no such thing as a good lay and a bad lay. But in my experience that just isn't true. I remember this one woman I went with for a long time. She was just a bad lay. No matter what I did, she was just lousy!

In other words, his bad lay is everyone's bad lay. One of his friends expressed it differently. He didn't understand why some swingers were so concerned with compatibility; he felt it was the sex that was important—and simply "having a good time."

Because they do not consider individuation important, these couples tend to approximate most closely the popular stereotypes of swingers as desiring only "pure sex." Swinging for these couples is primarily a matter of sexual interaction. Consequently, they are chiefly interested in seeing how sexually competent a couple is before they decide whether or not to develop a friendship. Competence may be defined in any or all of a number of ways. Endurance, size of penis, foreplay competence—all may be used to assess competence during the actual sexual interaction whether it be a large open party or a smaller gathering.

It is clear, then, that such couples perceive sex in a way that individuators find uncongenial or even repugnant. When we first observed and interviewed them, we interpreted their behavior as the beginning stage of promiscuity that new couples may go through. But when we asked, we would find that they had been swinging frequently for a period of two years, much too long to be considered inexperienced. How, we asked ourselves, could such couples avoid jealousy, if they regularly evaluated sexual partners against a common standard? It seemed to us that a husband or wife in such a situation could conceivably be replaced some day by a "better lay," especially if the issue of marital compatibility remained somewhat unresolved. Yet these couples did not appear to experience any disruptive jealousy as a result of swinging. We found that they are able to accomplish this by instituting special, somewhat less flexible arrangements for swinging. First, they are invariably exclusive open swingers. That is, sexual interaction must take place in the same room. This tends to reduce any emotional involvement in one interaction. They think that closet swinging (swinging in separate rooms) is "no better than cheating." They clearly worry about the possibility of emotional infidelity more than individuators. An insistence on open swinging reduces the possibility of emotional involvement, and with it, the reason for jealousy. Second, they try to control the swinging situation as much as possible. So, for example, they are much more likely to insist on being hosts. And they also desire to state their sexual preferences ahead of time, thereby insuring that nothing very spontaneous and unpredictable can happen. Third, the women are more likely to desire female homosexuality and more aggressively so. This often results in the women experiencing more emotional involvement with each other than with the men, which is more acceptable because it does not threaten the marital relationship.

. . . . .

CONCLUSION: THE SOCIAL SIGNIFICANCE OF SWINGING[1]

A full explanation of the reasons for the rise in popularity of swinging cannot be made adequately within the space of this article. But we would like to sketch briefly some of our findings in order to apply a corrective to the rather optimistic view which swingers have of swinging, the view which we have presented in this article.

A glance at the recent history of Western civilization reveals the locus of an adequate explanation. In the United States during this century, an increase in sexual freedom has always been followed by periods of relatively greater sexual repression. The flappers of the 1920s were followed by the more conservative women of the 1930s, and the freer female role of World War II was superceded by a wave of conservatism that sent women flocking back to the home. And, finally, in the 1960s, Americans have witnessed unprecedented heights of sexual freedom in this country. In its level of intensity, this last period is most analogous to what occurred in Germany during the 1920s and early 1930s. The interesting thing about these ebbs and flows in sexual freedom is that they correlate quite closely with certain kinds of economic developments. In these cases, where sexual freedom appears as a general trend in the population, it is clearly a function of factors which are beyond the immediate control of individuals. Such factors as investment flows, limited resources, fluctuations in world markets, and so forth, all events that seem isolated from the arena of intimacy which people carve for themselves are in fact very much a part of their most personal relationships.

Three questions present themselves here. First, what exactly is the nature of the social conditions which surround swinging? Second, what is the relationship between those conditions and the consciousness of individual swingers? And finally, why should the two have anything to do with each other?

Taking last things first, for a moment, it is important to consider swinging as a social event which seems appropriate to the participants. By "appropriate" we mean that it makes sense to them in terms of how they see

---

[1] This conclusion is the author's substitution for the original Trans-action conclusion. (August 1972.)

their relationships to other people, in terms of their conceptions of social reality, and in terms of their notions about value. These ideas appear rational only insofar as they seem to address themselves to the objective realities which people face in their day-to-day existence.

An interesting example of the relationship between objective reality and morality is the effect which Germany's great inflation during the 1920s had on the morality of the middle class in Berlin. Otto Freidrich in his book *Before the Deluge* interviews a woman who vividly describes the effect that this development had.

Yes, the inflation was by far the most important event of this period. The inflation wiped out the savings of the entire middle class, but those are just words. You have to realize what that *meant*. There was not a single girl in the entire German middle class who could get married without her father paying a dowry. Even the maids—they never spent a penny of their wages. They saved and saved so that they could get married. When money became worthless, it destroyed the whole system for getting married, and so it destroyed the whole idea of remaining chaste until marriage.

The rich had never lived up to their own standards, of course, and the poor had different standards anyway, but the middle class, by and large, obeyed the rules. Not every girl was a virgin when she was married, but it was generally accepted that one *should* be. But what happened from the inflation was that the girls learned that virginity didn't matter any more. The women were liberated.

It may seem odd to think of a person confronting his system of values and suddenly finding it obsolete, but that is exactly what happened to many of the swingers we talked to. This was not only reflected in their comments to us, but in their approach to swinging as beginners. Couples who seemed otherwise very cautious and conservative would often persist through one, two, or as many as six perfectly horrendous initial experiences, absolutely determined to find a compatible couple. Such tenacity is remarkable in that these couples like many middle-class Americans, were prone to form strong opinions on the basis of their own personal experience. In addition to persistence, another important indicator of swingers' need to modify their system of values is their stated satisfaction with swinging as a new life style. Generally, these couples feel that swinging benefits them not only as a form of entertainment, but as an activity which increases their self confidence, their understanding of others, and which helps them shed their "hypocritical" attitudes.

The fact that swingers say they feel better about themselves as a result of swinging indicates that swinging and the ideology that goes along with it are more appropriate to the present conditions of their existence than were the values which these couples held previous to swinging. The question is, what were these new "facts of life" which the middle class had to deal with in the middle 1960s?

Two interconnected developments occurring during the middle 1960s which affected practically every member of this society were rising inflation and increased speculation. By speculation we refer to the massive shift in investments away from increasingly productive capacity into such areas as land speculation, conglomerate building, defense production, insurance, and various other "service industries."

Where inflation did not result in outright cuts in the real disposable income of the middle class, it at least generated considerable anxiety. Many women were forced into the job market in order to maintain the standard of living of their families—to meet the unexpectedly high cost of owning a home, of college education, or of paying taxes. Many young couples began to restrict the size of their families, simply because they feared that they would not be able to provide adequately for their children. These couples felt that under such circumstances childrearing would prove a singularly unrewarding experience, both for themselves and their children.

This movement away from traditional forms of adulthood, which included marriage and a family was exacerbated by the speculative trend in the economy which made it necessary. That is, far from causing anxiety, the new life styles were often viewed as desirable. This is because they expressed the kind of human relationships inherent in a society where the economy runs on speculation and nonproductive enterprise. In this atmosphere, the social forms associated with production began to seem less and less appropriate.

Swinging as an ideology addresses itself to the new conditions which the middle class faces as a result of economic stagnation. Before swinging, the nature of relations between husband and wife had more or less reflected the role of the family in its relation to production as an important biological and social reproductive unit of society. That is, the ideal of monogamous sexual relationships, realized even in the institution of cheating, reflected the notion that the family unit was not only for rearing children, but for the maintenance of these divisions of labor. Both the husband and wife formed an interdependent productive whole that was absolutely crucial to the continuance of the society. Swinging, however, breaks with the past in that it does not reflect any productive relation to society whatsoever. Sex within the context of swinging at its best merely symbolizes a loosely defined friendship. As one swinger told us, "Its all a lot of fun, but it sure is irrelevant to anything." This notion of "sex for fun," as many have called it, does not confine itself to swinging, however. The trend towards a revivification of marriage through romance essentially returns fun and adventure to the marriage to replace or de-emphasize the old productive functions.

In essence swinging helps a couple change their self-conceptions to be more in tune with the conditions that surround them—those generated by social breakdown and decay. As a successful adaptation, however, it can in no way address itself to solving those problems.

28
Changes in the modern family: Their impact on sex roles*

JANET ZOLLINGER GIELE

We have just passed through an era, lasting roughly from 1920 to 1960, in which women were extraordinarily satisfied with and optimistic about their status. There was, in some circles, a derisive attitude toward the feminists of an earlier era who had been aggressive in the cause of winning equal political rights for themselves. During that recent period it took an intellectual effort to remember that female suffragists had to *fight* against considerable *opposition* to accomplish their goal.

In 1971 the mood has changed. College students who five years ago showed no interest in the status of women (although they were very much interested in the problems of blacks) are today demanding and getting courses on the history, sociology, psychology, and literature of women Betty Friedan's (6)[1] *The Feminine Mystique* commands more attention now than when it first appeared in 1963. The women's movement is a topic of interest even to the mass media. And since *Sexual Politics* (13) appeared, more women are wary of "patriarchal" domination by men. Furthermore, some people are now broadening the question of sex roles to take

* From Vol. 41, No. 5, October 1971, pp. 757–66, *The American Journal of Orthopsychiatry*, with permission from Janet Zollinger Giele. Copyright ©, the American Orthopsychiatric Association, Inc. Reproduced by permission.
[1] References at end of reading.

issue with the whole structure of the nuclear family, particularly with the division of labor that makes the husband the sole provider and keeps the wife at home in charge of the children.

THE PROBLEM

The question I wish to pose is this: Why do we find this new *consciousness* emerging, critical of women's status and the relationship between the sexes?

The easy answer is that women have been converted to the feminist cause. Such an explanation assumes that the ideology of a Kate Millet, once it has been developed and propagated, is irresistible. But this is hardly satisfying, for it fails to account for the relative lack of response to Simone de Beauvoir's (3) powerful statement, *The Second Sex,* which appeared in America in 1952.

A more satisfying approach looks to deeper changes in process in the society, which have laid a foundation for a change of consciousness in those born since 1930. It is in these generations that we see budding interest in the new feminism and in possible new forms of family life.

SOME ALTERNATIVE THEORIES

Previous explanations of the relation between the sexes have generally been of three sorts, ascribing the main cause of change or stability to technology, ideology, or the division of labor. Each provides elements of an explanatory theory, but any one, taken alone, cannot satisfactorily account for the current burst of consciousness.

The technological theory of change, long associated with the name of W. F. Ogburn (16) in sociology, points to labor-saving devices, improved contraception, better health and longer life span as some of the important factors that have freed women from the family and contributed to the rise in their labor force participation. Such a theory explains a gradual increase in percent of women working, but it explains neither the quiescence of the 1950s nor the angry outburst of the late 1960s.

The ideological theory of change represented by Friedan or Millet points to subtle attitudes that allow men to dominate women. But taken alone, it cannot account for the emergence of a new consciousness which rejects patriarchy and the feminine mystique.

Parsons and Bales (17) have developed a more complete theoretical position that could encompass both technology and values by focusing on the division of labor. According to their theory, American men and women together value equality of opportunity and achievement, but their roles are different: Men achieve in work outside the home; women cultivate the opportunity of the child to realize his full potential by staying inside the home. Though this theory provided an adequate interpretation for the 1950s, it did not foresee the turmoil we now observe.

CONSCIOUSNESS AND THE UNIVERSALIZATION OF SEX ROLES

The fault of Parsons and Bales' analysis was that it froze men's and women's roles at one point in time, while in fact those roles were changing with the increasing complexity of the surrounding social structure.[2]

When a society becomes more complex, roles become more specialized, or differentiated. That is, a job is broken down into several different operations, some of which may be performed by the person who originally did the whole job, some of which may be taken over by experts who perform only newly specialized functions.

When a job is broken up like this (*i.e.*, differentiated), two other things happen at the same time. First, parts of the job can now be performed by persons who under the old rule were not qualified. Second, the very fact of breaking up the job into component parts has an effect on the consciousness of all the people involved: They become aware that certain qualifications they once thought intrinsically necessary to the performance of the job are not in fact so, at least not for certain parts of the operation. As a result the original role, which was seen to be segmentally related to others around it, is now seen as an *integral* made up of several components, a number of which are like the components in other units. Thus is built the possibility of a *shared consciousness*—a sense of commonality or of universal qualities in persons and roles that were initially felt to be totally different from each other.[3] It was a similar process that Marx and Engels described when they observed the relation between the introduction of the factory system and the emergence of class consciousness.

If the change in men's and women's roles is a process of differentiation with its greater potential for recognizing human qualities that are shared across the sexes, then it should be possible to identify forces in the larger society that have served to split up traditional sex roles into several component parts, allowing some previously performed by only one sex to be carried out by persons with requisite qualifications without regard to sex.

It is my thesis that such a process of differentiation has been going on in men's and women's roles. Women's work such as cooking or washing has been routinized and rationalized to a point that a man can put a load of laundry in the dryer or a frozen dinner in the oven as well as any woman. Similarly, men's work is less and less tied to physical strength in which

---

[2] Had they applied the theory of their Chapter VII to the evolution of adult sex roles, they would have avoided this difficulty.

[3] My analysis of the differentiation process owes much to a theoretical formulation by Talcott Parsons in *Societies* (Prentice-Hall, 1965), pp. 21–24.

presumably males excel, and women are therefore able to do many of the manual, clerical, or intellectual operations that men do. The upshot is that a cross-over is possible in many aspects of role performance that were formerly linked to sex. Consequently, a shared consciousness is possible in which men and women can perceive more clearly each other's problems and satisfactions, and as a result identify with each other.

INSTITUTIONAL CHANGES

Such an outcome is not due to changed technology alone. If it were, we would be hard pressed to explain why sex roles received so little attention only a few years ago, when admittedly technology had already made great strides. Important changes have also been occurring in more subtle aspects of the sexual division of labor such as child care and the nature of family life. I shall argue that, roughly since the 1930s, relevant changes have occurred in four major institutional areas of the society that have had a formative influence on the generations born since then and have laid the foundations for a revolution of consciousness about sex roles that is just beginning to emerge.

These changes occurred in (1) the relation of the individual to the accepted moral code; (2) the relation of the individual to the family; (3) the relation of family to government; and (4) the relation of the family to the economy.

In each of these areas, I shall describe two phases of functional differentiation that have set the stage for change in attitudes about sex roles. The first phase is a process of *specialization* in which one primary concern is selected. The second phase is a process of *inclusion* in which other necessary functions are also identified as worthy of attention. As a result of both these processes *universalization of consciousness* becomes possible.

CHANGES IN THE MORAL CODE

The first important institutional change was based on discovery of a new basis for morality, initially apparent in sexual conduct, later in other moral issues. Moral changes were significant for family and sex roles because they could transform general assumptions about the boundaries between behavior appropriate to youth and adults, to single and married people, and to men and women.

Specialization of the sexual function as expression of individuality. The central theme of the sexual revolution has been a change in standards of premarital chastity. As Reiss (18) has pointed out, the rates of non-virginity at marriage have changed little since the 1920s. What has changed is the acceptance of premarital intercourse if it occurs within the context of affection (32).

Sexual mores changed because sexuality came to be regarded as *the* means of individual self-expression and gratification if it occurred in the context of a continuing relationship. As such, sexual intercourse gained legitimacy outside marriage and apart from its reproductive aspect. It was available to youth as well as to adults. Its exercise was regulated not by traditional authority but by consideration for the feelings of the individuals involved.[4]

Inclusion of self-expression and the New Morality in moral transformation. Once the sexual function had been differentiated from the total married adult state, it became apparent that performance of other aspects of adult life might also be subjected to redefinition. In the 1960s, young people began to experiment with other than sexual forms of expression—drugs and the hippie style. Youth also gave expression to a new kind of moral concern for war, peace, and responsible exercise of authority in universities, industry, and the military. SNCC, the Peace Corps, and Vista all voiced a moral purpose in areas once thought the sole province of adults.

Universalization of sexual and moral consciousness. The consequence of moral transformation was the emergence of youth as a distinct stage in the life cycle, a period when boys and girls could, as Keniston (11) has said, "acknowledge both self and society, personality and social process, without denying the claims of either." By such a standard, sexuality could occur outside marriage; responsible moral positions could be argued by persons who are not yet adults.

Significantly, at each stage of the moral revolution, *both men and women have been involved.* Women have been allowed to become as sexually expressive as men had earlier been. Young men have become as morally concerned with peace and community well-being as were women of Jane Addams's era. The result has been new consciousness of universal qualities shared between the sexes.

PSYCHOLOGY AND FAMILY LIFE

While the sexual revolution and the emergence of youth clarified the nature of responsible moral and sexual behavior *outside* the family, new attitudes about child-rearing clarified the central activities occurring *within* the family. Later still came concern with the development of adult personality. The outcome of these changes was a new sensitivity to the question of whether the family as it is presently constituted can serve the needs of individual men and women.

Specialization of the family in childcare. Following as they did the loss of important productive functions from the home, the decades of the

---

[4] Of course technical improvements in contraception facilitated this change, but they alone do not account for it.

1920s and 1930s saw a concentration on the child-rearing functions of the family. The goal was to bring up children able to live in a peaceful and democratic world, capable of cooperation and self-direction, and not merely obedient to authority. To this end the whole child development movement was oriented (5). By the end of the depression, nursery schools, permeated by these ideas and linked to efforts at parent education, had spread across the country. The new ideas were followed most closely by the middle classes, but by the late 1950s there was evidence that even working class parents had felt the effects (1).

Initially the mother was seen as the expert in child-rearing. She was more open to the new ideas, while the father might revert to being "heavy-handed." Gradually, however, the importance of the father's role was also recognized. In 1939, L. K. Frank (4) wrote,

While the mother is largely responsible for the child's patterns of intimacy, the father is primarily responsible for the child's ideals of social conduct and his major aspirations and ambitions toward the social world.

Thus eventually *both* mother and father were seen as important in child-rearing.

Inclusion of concern for development of adults. While at first the special function of the family was seen as child-rearing, in recent years the marital role has been singled out for increased attention (7). Perhaps it is because child-rearing is bunched in the early years of marriage that more attention is given the needs of adults who continue in the family. Perhaps, also, husband and wife now need to find greater satisfaction in each other because their high mobility has uprooted them from single sex social networks that supported them in the past.

Whatever the dynamics of this development, its consequences have been more striking for women than for men. Women are now demanding that the home serve their individual needs for self-realization as much as it appears to serve the husband (by letting him do his work in peace and providing rest and recreation at the end). They protest the "shitwork" that constantly serves others' needs and not their own (31). In their demand is the belief that the home should be a place that facilitates women's personal growth rather than a prison of stagnation.

Universalization of parental and marital roles. If child-rearing and stabilization of adult personality are identified as the special functions of the family, the structure of the family has to become more flexible. During the early years of married life child-rearing will predominate and sex roles may diverge sharply. Later a couple may devote themselves to common interests such as travel or life in a retirement village in which their roles become more similar. Such flexibility is not unknown to us now. It may eventually result in more widespread questioning of traditional family patterns. Today among the avant garde, alternative forms of child care (day care, etc.) and marriage (serial or communal) are already being considered and tried out.

GOVERNMENT POLICY TOWARD THE FAMILY

Simultaneous with the evolution of a new sexual ethic and deepening awareness of the psychological significance of the family, there has been a gradual and at times painful effort to formulate government policy toward the family. Initially, in the 1930s, the concern of government was to ensure support of children under conditions of depression and unemployment. During the 1960s, however, government concern broadened to consider the problem of maintaining incentive for work, and proposals for a negative income tax and family allowances were put forward. Despite considerable resistance to these proposals, I believe we are on the threshold of an era when the family's crucial contribution to the formation and maintenance of responsible citizens in a free society will be publicly recognized.

Specialization of family support to aid dependent children. The crisis of the depression created a distinction in the public mind between adults' economic roles and their family responsibilities. It was recognized that persons might be unemployed through no fault of their own and yet have families whose lives depended on their work. A patchwork of insurance, pension, and Social Security programs developed to provide for the young, the old, and the infirm (27). Of these the most relevant to family change was AFDC, Aid to Families with Dependent Children, established under Title IV of the Social Security Act.

During the 1930s, governmental support of the family identified the child-rearing function as being of special importance. And again, as in the child psychology of the era, the mother was seen as the specialist who could carry on this activity more or less alone if she and her children were provided with support.

Inclusion of the incentive problem in family support. In the 1960s, however, with the discovery of poverty in the midst of an affluent society, and the recognition that a disproportionate number of draft rejects were children who had received AFDC, there was a new willingness to recognize the hazards of father absence and the self-perpetuating cycle of dependence. The Moynihan Report and ensuing proposals for a negative income tax and family allowances pointed to the necessity of assuring fathers jobs (or compensation commensurate with their family responsibilities) so that they would not desert and would instead maintain incentive to support their families and fulfill the important paternal role (14).

In 1968, Moynihan (14) wrote, "Men are paid for the work they perform on the job, not for the role they occupy in the family." But his point was that they should be paid for that too. He had earlier argued that it would save the government money to ensure fathers jobs and foster stable family life, rather than later have to rehabilitate disadvantaged children by expensive government programs (14).

Universalization of family consciousness across sex and class lines. It is easy to see conditions for one kind of universalization of consciousness emerging that recognizes that *both* men and women are important to family life and that children can suffer from *pa*ternal deprivation as well as *ma*ternal deprivation.

But the storm that the Moynihan report raised suggests that another kind of universalization is also occurring—albeit haltingly and painfully. This is a sharing of consciousness across class, ethnic, and racial groups. Blacks bitterly protested the Moynihan report because they thought it was saying that one kind of family, the white, middle-class, "intact" family was best. Actually their protest may point to an enlarged consciousness of the future that will assert that it is not important which person (mother, father, or other family member) performs the provider role, or performs the parental function. What may instead be the crucial question in the future is simply, are these functions being performed adequately?

THE FAMILY IN AN AFFLUENT ECONOMY

Government policy toward the family is gradually moving away from an implicitly anti-natalist policy that gives only minimal support to the poor, to a policy of universal family allowances that would be neither pro-natalist nor anti-natalist but would give compensation for performance of parental functions. This still leaves open the question of population control. In the 1950s, women chose to have a third or fourth child to fill the time left free by diminishing household tasks. In the 1960s there is growing awareness that women may better use their leisure by taking a job outside the home, thereby making not only a productive contribution to the economy but also a step toward control of population.

Specialization of the household in consumption. The striking achievement of the affluent society has been elimination of toil within the household. Seeley (19) and Whyte (30) in their accounts of suburbs in the 1950s both note the acquisition of new household appliances and the kind of "managerial" role the housewife performed as she coordinated the purchase and serving of packaged foods, the care of household and clothing, and the scheduling of her own and her family's activities. Gone is the 19th century pattern of hours spent sewing, cleaning, baking or gardening (21). These activities are now done by *choice*, for ready-made articles are easily bought. The modern household's specific function is to consume rather than to produce. And it is the woman who is seen as the expert in home management.

Her life is not always satisfying, however. Seeley found that "many a

Crestwood mother, while 'accepting' the culturally approved maternal role, reveals an underlying resentment." One "creative" solution was to have more children (19). Another was to invest more time in their care. Van Bortel (29) found in 1953 that homemakers used about as many hours in cooking and housework as they had in the late 1920s. But they spent nearly twice as many hours in "caring for the family."

Inclusion of occupation in the choice of alternatives. By the beginning of the 1960s, however, there were indications that the baby boom would not last forever and that the choice of outside employment was an increasingly accepted alternative. In an affluent society where the ideal is to do work that is interesting and satisfying, not tiring or boring, (7) it is understandable that women would frequently choose the satisfactions of employment over the sometimes less satisfying routines of housework. But, in addition, women's work might bring extra money into households, not as in the past to cover the bare necessities, but to further new and higher goals of consumption.

Universalization of family planning and commitment to occupation. As the household conveniences of the affluent society have grown, women have had more choice in how they will spend their time, and they have come into more control of consumer decisions than they have ever had before. Among all such decisions, perhaps the most far-reaching has to do with family size. The number and spacing of children determines the time and resources that will be available for other uses. Women liberationists currently emphasize the right of women to control their own bodies and their right to easy contraception and abortion. But generally, I believe, our emerging desire for population control implies that not just the woman but each couple will engage in rational planning about family size and that the outcome will be the result of a *joint decision.* Thus the issue of family planning is universalized to touch the consciousness of both men and women.

As more women enter paid employment, the possibility arises for another kind of exchange of consciousness between men and women. On the one hand, women may learn to share with men the frustrations and demands, as well as the stimulations, of occupation. On the other hand, women may be able to teach men how better to integrate work and family by arguing for parttime work, more flexible hours, parent leaves—all of which can relieve some of the strain on the working man as well as on the working woman.

DEMOGRAPHIC TRENDS

Recent changes in rates of marriage, child-bearing, and employment of women all suggest that parental and marital roles have been differentiated so that they are no longer seen as coterminous with women's lives. Since the 1940s, more women are free to combine activities that were once thought to be mutually exclusive. Like men, they are free to do several things at once: marry, have children, *and* work.

A key factor in this change has been the shortening of the child-bearing period. Beginning with the 1920s the average number of children per family dropped to 3.5 (25). This factor, combined with earlier marriage, resulted in the average woman bearing her last child by the age of 26. Clearly a great deal of her time was set free for other activities.

A second key development has been the drop in number of people who remain single. The change was most striking during the 1940s among highly educated women for whom the rate of change was twice that of the general population (8). Given that a higher proportion of college-educated women work than those with less education, the combined effect of these trends was to bring more married women into the labor force.[5]

A third significant shift was in the employment rate of mothers with young children, which more than doubled in the years between 1948 and 1967 (23). That such an increase could occur during a period of general affluence suggests a remarkable reorganization of marital and parental roles. Women had time, energy, and motivation to fulfill several kinds of obligations at once, perhaps because housework, child-rearing, marriage, and occupation were all specific and limited enough in their demands to permit such integration.

CONCLUSIONS

Change in the family, demographic trends, and new consciousness about sex roles are linked. Institutional change impinging on the family facilitated women's entry into the labor force. At the same time, actual changes in men's and women's behavior undoubtedly influenced the mores of family life. But this two-way relationship does not in itself explain the *sudden* rise of consciousness about sex roles in the late 1960s.

The fact that the great majority of women in the current liberation movement were born since 1930 is suggestive here. Perhaps it was only when these generations had come of age that a concerted assault on traditional family roles could take place. These younger people had been steeped in the new morality, the new psychology, the experience of mechanization and the interchangeability of personnel. It took only a small step to extend these principles to sex roles.

Change will require a much larger step from older generations and people unfamiliar or unsympathetic with these trends. The elements of a stereotyped sex role ideology are still very much with us. Nevertheless, it

---

[5] However, it was probably this same increase in marriage rate that also accounted for the drop in percent of women receiving advanced degrees after 1940 (25).

is not amiss to suggest that there may be a more rapid acceptance of sex equality *in principle* (as distinguished from all aspects of behavior) than is presently supposed. For it is after all not only the generation under forty that has experienced post-depression changes, but the whole society. If people can be shown that liberation of men and women is not a wild idea but an extension of reasonable principles they have already accepted, and in fact *lived,* then it is only a matter of time until we shall see further change of remarkable proportions.

REFERENCES

1. BRONFENBRENNER, U. "Socialization and social class through time and space." In *Readings in Social Psychology,* 3d ed., E. Maccoby, T. Newcomb, and E. Hartley, eds. New York: Holt, 1958.

2. CLAUSEN, J. "A historical and comparative view of socialization theory and research." In *Socialization and Society,* J. Clausen, ed. Boston: Little, Brown, 1968.

3. DE BEAUVOIR, S. *The Second Sex.* New York: Modern Library, 1952.

4. FRANK, L. "The father's role in child nurture." *Child Study* 16 (March 1939), pp. 135–36.

5. FRANK, L. "The beginnings of child development and family life education in the twentieth century." Merrill-Palmer Quart. 8 (July 1962), pp. 207–27.

6. FRIEDAN, B. *The Feminine Mystique.* New York: Norton.

7. GALBRAITH, J. *The Affluent Society.* Boston: Houghton Mifflin, 1958.

8. GLICK, P. *American Families.* New York: Wiley, 1957.

9. HILL, R. and ALDOUS, J. "Socialization for marriage and parenthood." In *Handbook for Socialization Theory and Research,* D. Goslin, ed. Chicago: Rand McNally, 1969.

10. HOFFMAN, L. and WYATT, F. "Social change and motivations for having larger families: some theoretical considerations." Merrill-Palmer Quart. 6 (July 1960), pp. 235–44.

11. KENISTON, K. *Young Radicals.* New York: Harcourt Brace, 1968.

12. LIFTON, R. *The Woman in America.* Boston: Beacon Press, 1964.

13. MILLET, K. *Sexual Politics.* Garden City, N.Y.: Doubleday, 1970.

14. MOYNIHAN, D. "A family policy for the nation." In *The Moynihan Report and the Politics of Controversy,* L. Rainwater and W. Yancy, eds. Cambridge, Mass.: M.I.T. Press, 1967.

15. NYE, I. and HOFFMAN, L. *The Employed Mother in America.* Chicago: Rand McNally, 1963.

16. OGBURN, W. and NIMKOFF, M. *Technology and the Changing Family.* Boston: Houghton Mifflin, 1953.

17. PARSONS, T. and BALES R. *Family, Socialization and Interaction Process.* Glencoe, Ill.: The Free Press, 1955.

18. REISS, I. "Premarital sexual standards." In *The Individual, Sex and Society,* C. Broderick and J. Bernard, eds. Baltimore: Johns Hopkins Press, 1969.

19. SEELEY, J., SIM, R. and LOOSLEY, E. *Crestwood Heights.* New York: Wiley (Science Editions), 1956.

20. SIMON, K. and GRANT, W. *Digest of Educational Statistics.* U.S. Department of Health, Education and Welfare. Washington, D.C.: U.S. Government Printing Office, 1969.

21. SMUTS, R. *Women and Work in America.* New York: Columbia University Press, 1959.

22. THOMASSON, R. "Why has American fertility been so high?" In *Kinship and Family Organization.* B. Farber, ed. New York: Wiley, 1966.

23. U.S. DEPARTMENT OF LABOR, BUREAU OF LABOR STATISTICS. *Handbook of Labor Statistics,* Bulletin No. 1630, 1969.

24. U.S. WOMEN'S BUREAU. *Handbook of Women Workers,* Bulletin 294, 1969.

25. U.S. WOMEN'S BUREAU. *Trends in Educational Attainment,* 1969.

26. U.S. WOMEN'S BUREAU. *Women's Occupations through Seven Decades,* Bulletin 218, 1947.

27. VADKIN, J. *Family Allowances: An Analysis of Their Development and Implications.* Miami, Fla.: University of Miami Press, 1958.

28. VADKIN, J. *Children, Poverty, and Family Allowances.* New York: Basic Books, 1968.

29. VAN BORTEL, D. *Homemaking: Concepts, Practices and Attitudes in Two Social Class Groups.* Unpublished Ph.D. dissertation, University of Chicago, 1954.

30. WHYTE, W. *The Organization Man.* New York: Simon and Schuster, 1956.

31. WOMEN: A JOURNAL OF LIBERATION, INC. "How We Live and with Whom." 3028 Greenmount Avenue, Baltimore, Md., Winter 1971.

32. WOOD, F. *Sex and the New Morality.* New York: Association Press, 1968.

Index

Index

371

Sex object preference, 56, 64–68
    homosexual; *see* Homosexuality
    nongenital, 105–6
    role of imprinting in, 2
"Sex play," definition, 39
Sex roles
    adoption, 59–61, 66
    age of demands for appropriate be-
        havior, 50–51
    and biological structure, 273
    and changes in family, 356–67
    component in sexual development, 59–
        64
    concepts, and double standard, 272–73
    conflict, and homosexuality, 312–13
    deviation from biological composition,
        61–64
    differences, child's realization of, 9
    dual, 62–63, 67
    of hermaphrodites, 7, 56, 60–61, 66
    through history, 193–204
    identification, 2, 46–54, 56, 59–60
    international sample of attitudes to,
        151–53, 163–64
    inversion, 62–64, 67
    learning, 30, 37, 46–54, 56
    parental training in, 6–7
    preferences, development, 52–54, 59
    relationship to body scheme, 11
    splitting of, 358–59
Sexual behavior
    attitudes as prediction of, 243–44
    attitudes toward, changes in, 94, 95,
        98–99, 109–10, 139–48, 154–57,
        165, 182–88, 190–204, 205–13,
        215–16, 232–49, 250–53, 258–62,
        264–67, 359–60
    biological core of, 99–101
    changes in, 189–90, 192–204
    in childhood, 2, 20–35, 272
    of college students, 94, 139–67, 214–63,
        268–69, 304, 305–6, 308
    compared with sexual attitudes, 141,
        149–67, 239–44
    and cultural background, 93, 108–25
    in dating, international sample, 157–63,
        165–66
    decisions concerning, research on, 274–
        75
    definitions, 21, 39
    discrepant with attitudes, 215, 242–43,
        247–48
    double standard for; *see* Double
        standard
    and drug use, 289–90, 304, 305–6, 308
    in early Christian era, 98
    and economic conditions, 353–55
    effect of guilt on, 141–42
    effect of hormones on, 15, 101

Sexual behavior—*Cont.*
    factors influencing, 93–95
    healthy and unhealthy, 107
    and independence for women, 174–76
    and mass media, 258
    in middle life, 69–79
    need for value framework, 210–12
    "normal" and "deviant," 97–107
    in old age, 2–3, 69–70, 80–91
    in permissive primitive societies, 23
    "polymorphous perverse," 102, 103, 106
    possible future trends, 289–93
    preadolescent, 24–29, 38–44
    and quality of relationship, 264–78
    relationship to physical attractiveness,
        217, 218–19, 223–24, 229
    in Scandinavia, 94–95, 152–66, 168–77,
        191, 235–47
    and social class, 38–41, 110, 126–38
    in Soviet Union, 95, 186–88
    standards, who should set, 153
    swinging, 342–55
    and violence, 113, 114
Sexual development, 1–3, 55–68
    biological-constitutional component,
        56–59
    childhood, 20–45
    emotional aspects of, 5–19
    Freud's theory of, 20–21, 22, 29–30,
        33, 36, 102–3
    in infants, 2, 5–7
    normal, primary conditions for, 31–33
    sex object preference in, 56, 64–68
    sex-role component, 59–64
Sexual deviation
    definition of, 105–6
    psychodynamics of, 106
Sexual differences, 8–9, 37
Sexual experience, effect of psychotherapy
    on, 270
Sexual knowledge, 8–9
    of Appalachian youth, 119
    of preadolescents, 38, 41–45
    of Puerto Rican youth, 122
    and social class, 41–45
    sources of, 42–45
    of Washington Negro youth, 116–17
Sexual responsiveness
    of children, 21–33
    factors in, 100
"Sexual revolution," 139, 189, 205–13,
    232–34, 264
Sexuality; *see* Sexual behavior *and* Sexual
    development
Social class
    differences, and race differences, 140
    and marijuana use, 301
    and sexual behavior, 38–41, 110, 126–
        38